Real Estate Finance

Real Estate Finance

First Edition, Second Printing

SHERRY SHINDLER PRICE

ASHLEY CROWN SYSTEMS, INC.

This publication is designed to provide accurate and current information regarding the subject matter covered. The principles and conclusions presented are subject to local, state and federal laws and regulations, court cases and revisions of the same. If legal advice or other expert assistance is required, the reader is urged to consult with a competent professional in that field.

Director of Publishing & Course Development
Lars Jentsch

Real Estate Publisher
Leigh Conway

Senior Technical Writer
Judy Moyer

Writer
Sue Carlson

Technical Writer
Ben Hernandez

Copy Editor
Emily Rehkopf

Administrative Assistant
Stephanie Pratap

Creative Editor/ Production Coordinator
Judy Hobbs

Graphic Design
Susan Mackessy

Published by
Ashley Crown Systems, Inc.
22952 Alcalde Drive
Laguna Hills, California 92653

Printed in the United States of America

ISBN #0-934772-18-5

Table of Contents

Preface xv

Introduction xix

CHAPTER 1 **History of Finance and Lending** 1

Introduction 1

How Did It All Start? 2

Early Lending Practices 2

What Kept It Going? 9

A Growing Economy 10

Federal Participation in Real Estate Finance 10

Laws Impacting Mortgage Lending 11

The 20th Century—The Last 20 Years 16

The 1980s 16
The 1990s 17

Market Trends 19

Chapter Quiz 21

Answers 23

CHAPTER 2 **Real Property** 24

Introduction 24

Bundle of Rights 24

Types of Estates in Real Property 25

Freehold Estates 25
Less-Than-Freehold Estates 27

Real Property vs. Personal Property 27

Real Property 28

Land 28
Anything Permanently Attached to the Land 29
Anything Appurtenant to the Land 29
Anything Immovable by Law 30

Fixtures 30

Five Tests of a Fixture 31

Trade Fixtures 32

Land Descriptions 32

    U.S. Government Section and Township Survey 33

    Recorded Lot, Block and Tract System 40

    Metes and Bounds 40

Chapter Quiz 41

Answers 43

CHAPTER 3   **Land Titles and Estates**   **44**

Introduction 44

Background of Land Title 44

Adopting a Recording System 46

Recording Specifics 46

    The Effect: Public Notice 47

    Priorities in Recording 47

Ownership of Real Property 48

    Separate Ownership 48

    Concurrent Ownership 48

Limitations on Real Property: Encumbrances 56

    Money Encumbrances (Liens) 57

    Non-Money Encumbrances 60

Homestead Exemption 64

    Obligations Unaffected by the Declaration 66

    Contents of the Declaration of Homestead 66

    Effect of Recording—How Terminated 66

    Federal Homestead Act of 1862 67

Assuring Marketability of Title 68

Title Insurance 68

Chapter Quiz 70

Answers 72

CHAPTER 4   **Instruments of Finance**   **73**

Introduction 73

How Does It Work? 74

Promissory Note 75

    Negotiable Instrument 79

    Types of Promissory Notes 79

    Holder in Due Course 85

    Conflict in Terms of Note and Trust Deed 86

Transfer of Property by the Borrower 87

    Loan Assumption 88

    "Subject To" 88

Special Clauses in Financing Instruments 89

    Acceleration Clause 89

    Alienation Clause 89

    Assumption Clause 89

    "Subject To" Clause 89

    Subordination Clause 89

    Prepayment Clause 89

    "Or More" Clause 90

Junior Trust Deeds 90

    Outside Financing 90

    Seller Financing 91

    Balloon Payment Loans 95

    Other Types of Loans Secured by Trust Deeds or Mortgages 95

Unsecured Loan 103

Alternative Financing 104

    Pledged Savings Account Mortgage 104

    Graduated Payment Mortgage 104

    Shared Appreciation Mortgage 105

    Rollover Mortgage 105

    Reverse Annuity Mortgage 105

    Contract of Sale 106

Chapter Quiz 107

Answers 109

CHAPTER 5 **Trust Deeds and Mortgages** 110

Introduction 110

Trust Deeds (Deeds of Trust) 111

Characteristics of Trust Deeds 122

    Parties 122

    Title 123

    Statute of Limitations 124

    Remedy for Default 124

    Reinstatement 124

    Redemption 124

    Deficiency Judgment 124

    Reconveyance 124

Foreclosure 125

    Trustee's Sale—Non-Judicial Foreclosure Process 126

    Judicial Foreclosure 132

Benefits of a Trust Deed 133

Mortgages 134

Characteristics of a Mortgage 136

    Parties 136

    Title 136

Statute of Limitations   136
Remedy   136
Reinstatement   136
Redemption   140
Deficiency Judgment   140
Satisfaction   140

Foreclosure Under a Mortgage   140
Nonjudicial Foreclosure   141
Judicial Foreclosure   142

Chapter Quiz   148

Answers   150

CHAPTER 6   Mortgage Lenders   151

Introduction   151

Institutional Lenders   153
Commercial Banks   153
Thrifts   153
Insurance Companies   165

Non-Institutional Lenders   165
Mortgage Bankers and Brokers   168
Investment Companies   169
Private Individuals   171
Non-Financial Institutions   171

Chapter Quiz   171

Answers   173

CHAPTER 7   The Mortgage Market   174

Introduction   174

The National Economy   176
Real Estate's Four Major Roles in the U.S. Economy   176

The Federal Reserve Bank System (The Fed)   178
Basic Tools of the Federal Reserve System   178
History of the Federal Reserve System   179
Structure   184
Providing Financial Services   187

The Mortgage Market   190
Primary Mortgage Market   190
Secondary Mortgage Market   191
Ancillary Services   199

Real Property Loan Law   200

Personal Property Secured Transactions   202

Chapter Quiz   203

Answers   205

CHAPTER 8   **Mortgage Insurance and Government Participation in Finance 206**

Introduction 206

Types of Mortgage Default Insurance 206

Government Insurance 208
- Federal Housing Administration (FHA) 208
- Veterans Administration (VA) 210
- California Veteran Loans (Cal-Vet) 213

Private Mortgage Insurance (PMI) 217
- Benefits of PMI 217
- New PMI Requirements 217
- Why a Change in PMI Requirements? 217
- The Homeowner's Protection Act (HPA) of 1998 217
- How Does a Borrower Cancel or Terminate PMI? 218
- What Disclosures Does the Homeowners Protection Act (HPA) Require? 219
- What if the Value of the Home Has Increased? 220

Chapter Quiz 221

Answers 222

CHAPTER 9   **Real Estate as an Investment 223**

Introduction 223

Why Invest in Real Estate 224
- Types of Return on Investment (ROI) 225

Investment Process 230
- Preparation and Planning 231
- Gathering Resources 238
- Targeting the Right Property 244
- Negotiating Terms 250
- Closing the Purchase and Taking Over 253

Real Estate Investment Analysis Tools 257
- Operating Expenses 258
- Carrying Costs 259
- Net Operating Income 261
- Debt Service Ratio 265
- Return On Investment 266
- Development Market's Cycle 269

Real Estate Investment Tactics 271
- Collateral 272
- Income Stream 274
- Value Appreciation 280
- Subdivision 281
- Development 282
- Purchase Options 283
- Master Lease 284
- Tax Shelters 284
- Tax-Deferred Exchanges 287

Chapter Quiz   288

Answers   289

CHAPTER 10   **Choosing a Lender**   **290**

Introduction   290

How Consumers Choose a Lender   291

How Loans Are Originated   293
Retail Loan Origination   293
Wholesale Loan Origination   295

Chapter Quiz   299

Answers   301

CHAPTER 11   **Appraisal**   **302**

Introduction   302

Definition of Appraisal   303

Fair Market Value   304

Price, Cost and Value   304
Four Elements of Value   305

Forces Influencing Value   306

Other Factors Influencing Value   307

Principles of Valuation   308
Principle of Conformity   308
Principle of Change   308
Principle of Substitution   308
Principle of Supply and Demand   308
Principle of Highest and Best Use   308
Principle of Progression   308
Principle of Regression   308
Principle of Contribution   308
Principle of Anticipation   309
Principle of Competition   309
Principle of Balance   309
Principle of Three-Stage Life Cycle   309

The Appraisal Process   310
State the Problem   310
Gather the Data   311
Site Analysis   312
Buildings and Other Permanent Structures   314

Three Methods of Appraising Property   321
Sales (or Market) Comparison Approach   321
Cost Approach   323
Income Capitalization (or Income) Approach   328

Reconcile or Correlate   332

The Appraisal Report   332

Appraisal Licensing Standards   337

Types of Appraisal Licenses   337

Professional Appraisal Organizations   337

Chapter Quiz   338

Answers   339

CHAPTER 12 **Processing the Loan   340**

Introduction   340

Overview of the Loan Process   341

The Procedure   342

Debt-to-Income Ratios   343

Loan Application Package   344

Steps Involved in Getting a Real Estate Loan   346

Application   346

Required Disclosures Upon Application for a Loan (RESPA)   353

Required Disclosures Upon Application for a Loan—Truth in Lending Act   361

Processing   365

FICO Scores   368

Chapter Quiz   374

Answers   376

CHAPTER 13 **Underwriting and Closing the Loan   377**

Introduction   377

Risk Analysis   377

Underwriting Guidelines   378

Loan-to-Value Ratios   379

Loan Amount   379

Down Payment   379

Income Ratios   379

Employment   380

Credit History   381

Appraisal   381

Federal and State Disclosures and Notice of Rights   382

Disclosures at Settlement/Closing   382

Disclosures after Settlement   385

Closing   386

Chapter Quiz   386

Answers   388

CHAPTER 14   Loan Servicing   389

Introduction   389

What are the Responsibilities of a Mortgage Servicer?   390

What Does the Housing Act Require Lenders or Servicers to Do?   390

Provide a Disclosure Statement   390
Give Proper Notification When the Loan Servicing is Going to Be Sold   391
Grant a Grace Period During the Transfer of the Loan Servicing   392
Respond Promptly to Written Inquiries   392

What Can a Borrower Do if there is a Complaint?   394

What Can a Borrower Do About Problems With a Loan Servicer?   394

What Does Transfer of Servicing Mean?   395

How Does Transfer of Service Affect a Loan?   396
When Will the Borrower Be Notified?   396
An Important Consumer Safeguard   396
Where Does the Borrower Pay the Next Payment?   396
What Happens to the Borrower's Escrow Account?   397
What About Insurance Policies and Taxes?   398
Who Sends the Borrower the End of the Year Tax Statement?   398

Consumer Checklist   398

Chapter Quiz   399

Answers   402

CHAPTER 15   Consumer Protection   403

Introduction   403

What Creditors Look For   404

Information the Creditor Can't Use   405
Special Rules   405
Application Denied   409
Building a Good Record   409
Maintaining Complete and Accurate Credit Records   410
Negative Information   410
Old Information   411
Filing a Complaint with Federal Enforcement Agencies   411

Federal Consumer Protection Laws   412

Equal Credit Opportunity Act (ECOA)   413
Real Estate Settlement Procedures Act (RESPA)   419
Truth in Lending Act—Regulation Z   423
Rights to Financial Privacy Act   433
Expedited Funds Availability Act   433
Fair Debt Collection Practices Act   433
The Federal Trade Commission Act   433
Home Equity Loan Consumer Protection Act   434
Home Mortgage Disclosure Act (HMDA)   434
Home Mortgage Disclosure Act Aggregation Project   434
National Flood Insurance Act   435
Credit Practices Rule   435

Electronic Fund Transfer Act   435
The Interstate Land Sales Full Disclosure Act   435
Fair Credit Reporting Act (FCRA)   435
The Community Reinvestment Act   437

The Fair Housing Laws   437
1866 Civil Rights Act   438
Civil Rights Act of 1968 and 1988 Amendments   438
Fair Housing Act   438
Age Discrimination Act of 1975   442
The Age Discrimination in Employment Act of 1967 (ADEA)   442
Title II of The Americans with Disabilities Act of 1990 (ADA)   442
The Architectural Barriers Act of 1968   442

State Laws   443
Complaint Filing Process   443
Complaints   446

Chapter Quiz   448

Answers   450

GLOSSARY   451

INDEX   471

Preface

HOW IMPORTANT IS REAL ESTATE FINANCE TO YOU?

Real estate agents help people buy and sell real property. They make money by working hard, conforming to the accepted procedures of real estate practice, observing real estate law and following the golden rule. Anyone who holds a real estate license is expected to have some knowledge about finance in order to pass a state licensing exam.

The *average* real estate agent, however, does not need to possess an abundance of information about finance, personally, to practice real estate. All he or she needs to do is request the help of the loan broker who is likely to be on call 24/7 for any licensee who needs assistance arranging financing for a sale. The capable and efficient loan agent will meet with buyers to help them decide what kind of financing they need. The real estate agent will close the sale and collect a commission because the loan agent possessed the necessary financing information to put the transaction together.

That's the *average* real estate agent. But what if the buyers never get to the point of making an offer because their real estate agent couldn't overcome the buyer's objection or obstacle to the sale because it was about financing? What if the listing agent didn't know enough about finance to counsel the seller and explain the offer when it is made on the listed property? The *average* real estate agent will never get close to closing those sales. The *average* agent is someone who avoids getting smart about real estate finance and will miss out on earning those extra commissions because of it.

Peter and Barbara Jones owned a fourplex, but wanted to sell it and buy another investment property. They had already found a duplex they liked, but needed to sell the fourplex before they could buy the duplex. When they finally got an offer, they were disappointed because the buyer wanted them to carry a note as part of the down payment and they thought they needed the cash to buy the duplex. This is what the offer looked like.

Peter and Barbara's Offer

$500,000	Purchase price
−400,000	Buyer to obtain new loan
$100,000	Peter and Barbara's equity

Buyer's down payment:

$50,000	Cash
+$50,000	Note and trust deed in favor of Peter and Barbara
$100,000	

Peter and Barbara's agent, Jerry, was a smart agent, however. He asked them if they were sure the seller of the duplex needed the whole $100,000 they were getting out of the apartment building in cash. They weren't sure, so Jerry recommended they accept the offer on their apartment building with the contingency that they would be able to get their offer on the duplex accepted. The Joneses then made the following offer on the duplex.

The Jones' Offer on the Duplex

$500,000	Purchase price
−$400,000	New loan
$100,000	Down payment required

Down payment:

$50,000	Cash
+$50,000	Note and trust deed from sale of the fourplex
$100,000	

The seller of the duplex did not need all cash and accepted the offer with the assignment of the trust deed from the sale of the apartment building as part of the down payment.

If the real estate agent, Jerry, had not been capable and imaginative about finance, thinking in terms of solutions, Peter and Barbara would not have sold one property and bought another and Jerry would not have made two commissions. His satisfied client will also be a loyal customer for future business.

If you are reading this book as a consumer, seeking knowledge about real estate finance for your own accounts, you will find that it contains the information you will need to understand almost any basic real estate transaction. Use it as a ready reference manual for your own real estate purchases and sales, as well as general information about real estate finance.

Introduction

Imagine buying a house and being required to pay the total price in cash. The sweet pleasure of home ownership probably would occur decades from now for most of us. With the average price of single-family homes being so extreme, buying a home would be unthinkable without the practical benefit of financing.

By allowing a homebuyer to obtain a loan for the difference between the sales price and the down payment, real estate lenders have provided the solution to the problem of how property can be bought and sold without the requirement of an all-cash sale.

What started out as a simple loan by a local bank—with an agreement that the borrower pay it all back in a timely manner—is now a complex process. Buyers and sellers need to rely on experts to explain all the choices there are on financing the purchase or sale of property. A real estate licensee is one of the experts to whom they will turn.

Now that you know real estate finance is nothing more than lenders loaning money so people can buy real property, let's start with an examination of how it all got started.

History of Finance and Lending

INTRODUCTION

At the center of nearly all real estate transactions is some kind of financing. Without an understanding of how the transfer of real property is financed, the developer, the contractor, the real estate broker and the property manager would find themselves out of a job. Most sellers would not be able to sell, because most buyers would be financially unable to pay cash, or unwilling to purchase unless a large part of the purchase price could be borrowed.

Proven sources of funds include lending institutions such as thrifts, commercial banks and insurance companies. Other reliable sources are non-institutional lenders, such as mortgage bankers, mortgage brokers, private individuals, pension funds, mortgage trusts and investment trusts. The real estate licensee and the consumer must stay alert to the changing credit sources, mortgage sources and mortgage methods to be competitive in the real estate market.

Throughout the past century, lending institutions were under great pressure to adapt to the changing needs of consumers. As the economy shifted and stalled, mortgage lenders had to become responsive to the public's needs if they were going to survive. As a result of the changing economy and special demands put upon the banking industry, adjustments were made in lending practices. Drift and deadlock were replaced with renewal and reform as the 20th Century came to a close.

Events that Put Pressure on the Real Estate and Lending Industry in the 20th Century

The Great Depression
Pent-up need for housing after World War II
World War II
Energy crises
Technological growth
Worldwide economic stress
Capital shortages
Growing inflation with unreliable drift in interest rates
Tight money and credit for the private sector
Soaring deficit spending and borrowing by the government
High unemployment
OPEC
Social spending
Depressed major industries
Savings and loan scandals

HOW DID IT ALL START?

Mortgage lending was complex from the start. Problems with lenders and borrowers that existed hundreds of years ago have persisted in one form or another today. An understanding of the history of borrowing and lending will help us to become aware of the rich legacy we have inherited and will allow us to understand how mortgage lending works today.

Early Lending Practices

In the beginning—as it is now—it was the land that indicated wealth. Early societies flourished and grew from cultivation and development of the land. As individual wealth became apparent with the expansion of private ownership of land in ancient societies, laws regulating the ownership of real property and rights of landowners were soon needed.

Indeed, in some places, the longing to obtain land, how it was to be used, and the need to develop conforming laws to legitimize its transfer were basic reasons for the growth of governments and laws. Since most early cultures were based on agriculture, land was of great value and began to be used as security for debts. Indications of early mortgage borrowing transactions have been found in the Middle East (Iraq), Egypt as well as ancient Greece.

Roman Mortgage Lending

Owners of real property during the time of the Roman Empire (753 B.C. to 476 A.D.) were allowed to participate in a highly developed system of mortgage lending. During this time, when a landowner borrowed money, the property was transferred to the lender, with the understanding that when the borrower repaid the debt, the property would be reconveyed. Just as it does today, however, the law grew more defined and useful to the citizens as time went by. The practice that eventually became part of the law was not unlike our present day system. The lender had the right to "foreclose" or take ownership of the property being used for security if the borrower did not repay the debt, but the borrower kept title and possession during the term of the loan.

After Rome fell (476 A.D.), the system of lending that depended on a strong government enforcing effective laws lost its appeal. Lenders could not be sure that the weakened central authority would charge unwilling borrowers with repayment of their debts. This repayment anxiety tended to cause mortgage lending to lose some of its attraction and popularity. The sophisticated system of lending that had profited from the growth of the great Roman Empire had lost the benefit of a working legal system.

German Mortgage Lending

With the authority of Rome in decline, German customs became the ruling influence in Europe. German law accepted the concept of a *gage*, or a deposit made in promise of the fulfillment of an agreement. A borrower could provide, as a "live" *gage*, an item of personal property as collateral for a loan. If the borrower defaulted on the loan, the lender kept the item. When the security for a loan was real property, known as a "dead" *gage*, the borrower stayed in possession of the property unless he or she defaulted, at which time the lender could take ownership.

English Mortgage Lending

After 1066 when William the Conqueror invaded England, the French spread the use of the *gage* system in England. When real property was used as collateral for a loan, or as a "dead" *gage*, the French called it a mort (the French word for dead) gage, or mortgage, the word we use today.

Meanwhile, in England and Europe in general, as time went by, mortgage lending came to a halt for a time because of the feudal nature of society. Because the king controlled all property, with the right of possession given to a citizen in return for loyalty and military service to the king, real property could not be used as security for a debt as we think of it today. The property, however, was used to secure the military obligation demanded by the king. If that duty was not performed, the reluctant warrior was separated from his land and it was given to someone else more loyal to the monarch.

During the time common law was growing and changing the medieval society in England, mortgage lending was not common. One reason was, until the serial husband Henry VIII changed the country's religion in the mid-16th Century, the Catholic Church decreed that the charging of interest for money loaned was sinful, and therefore illegal. The basis of this prohibition of interest was thought to be "natural law," or those events in society or nature which seemed to be "natural." Agriculture was thought to be "natural" in order to produce food for the population; animals "naturally" reproduced. It was not "natural" for money to reproduce and so the practice of charging interest, or usury, was thought to be unnatural and sinful. With no profit to be made, would-be lenders kept their money in their purses.

The law did specify, however, that charging interest could be defended where the lender suffered harm because of making the loan. The definition of harm was stretched to mean lost opportunity, therefore allowing medieval lenders to make loans, not for interest, but with the right to possess and acquire the benefit of ownership in case of default.

When a citizen did need to borrow money, however, the procedure was for the lender to take title and possession of a specific part of the borrower's land and thus be entitled to all rents and profits until the debt was repaid. If the outstanding debt was not repaid, the lender kept title and possession permanently, with the borrower still owing the money.

During the reign of Elizabeth I, in the last part of the 16th Century in England, common law grew to protect the rights of citizens whose entire estates were seized by lenders upon default of a small debt for which the real property had been used as security. The courts ruled that taking the entire property when its value was far greater than the debt was unfair, and allowed the borrowers to redeem their property upon payment of the amount owed to the lender. This right of the borrower to regain ownership after default was known as *equitable right of redemption*.

In all states in the U.S. today, we have retained the concept of that medieval custom of *equity of redemption* by allowing a borrower in default to reinstate a loan by making up all delinquent payments, taxes and other fees up until the time of the sale. In some states, depending on individual state laws, the borrower has a predetermined time period during which he or she can pay off all delinquent amounts and regain ownership of the property even after the foreclosure sale.

As the law began to lean toward the borrower, allowing the debtor to repay the loan and redeem the property even after the debt had become delinquent or payable in full, the practice of mortgage lending almost stopped entirely. That meant the lender never knew when a borrower might pay off the debt and reclaim the property, which the lender was now used to owning. Lenders, however, could ask the court to give the borrower a certain time limit in which to redeem the property or forever lose the right to do so.

United States Mortgage Lending

In 1690, when bold immigrants created a new society, known as the Massachusetts Bay Colony, out of the wilderness that would later become the United States, they needed to create a system that would support economic order and growth. Until then, money consisted of gold and silver coins from England, Spain and other countries. Most economic exchange was done on a cash or barter basis. Very little, if any, financing of real estate was done during this period. Indeed, the citizens of the new country did not need mortgage loans because most of the population lived on small farms they had inherited through their families.

During the Revolutionary War, in 1781, the Continental Congress chartered the Bank of North America in Philadelphia to lend support to the war as the nation's first commercial bank. Soon the Congress adopted the dollar as the unit for national currency.

After the Revolutionary War was over, leaders of the new nation had the overwhelming job of building a national government that would invite economic growth as well as provide the political and social framework desperately needed by the nation. Congress established the First Bank of the United States in 1789, approving the issuance of money, or paper bank notes as they were called. The First Bank of the United States also acted as the U.S. Treasury's fiscal agent, performing the first central bank functions in the United States.

During the next quarter century, American banking was an authentic mess with state-chartered banks all printing their own money of different sizes, shapes and designs. With no federal oversight, notes of the same denomination had different values depending on what backed the currency and what state it was in. Indifferent and reckless federal and state banking laws allowed almost anyone—states, private banks, railroads, stores and individuals—to issue paper money. A dollar issued by one city wasn't necessarily worth as much as a dollar printed by another. Mortgage lending occurred rarely during this time except for those loans that were made by individuals, not financial institutions.

Until people had enough cash to deposit as savings in institutions, the mortgage lending business could not become an important part of the economy. Then, as now, the business relied on using customer's savings to make real estate loans. During the first half of the 19th Century, most people still lived on farms, did not have much of a cash flow or need of one. Even in cities, people were not in the habit of saving if they did have disposable income.

After 1864, as the population moved West, people were still involved mainly in farming, but did need to borrow to finance new farms as they settled in remote areas of the country. A farm mortgage business developed as a result of this need.

During this time, mortgage companies making real estate loans to farmers sold the loans immediately to wealthy investors or institutions such as life insurance companies. Since buyers for these loans originating in the farm belt were located on the East Coast, they needed local lenders to originate the loans for them to purchase, thus furnishing the cash to Midwest lenders to make more loans to local farmers.

Commonly, during this time, lenders in the Midwest financed farms with a loan-to-value ratio of 40 to 50%. That meant the lender would only loan 40 or 50% of the value of the property. So if the farm was worth $10,000, a lender would loan no more than $4,000 to $5,000. Typically, semiannual payments were made on the interest, with the principal or original amount borrowed, due in five years or less. This kind of a loan was known as a *non-amortizing loan*, where none of the principal is included in the payments. The huge number of loans made during this time by mortgage companies was just the beginning of a business that would lead America's economy into the 21st Century.

By 1900, a few owners of single-family homes were able to obtain loans from mortgage companies. These types of loans were a small part of business for lending institutions at first, but as more people moved to the cities and were able to earn money to purchase homes, the volume of residential lending grew.

The way lenders look at the reality of making a loan, risks are diminished when loans are made to creditworthy borrowers based on a certain acceptable ratio of the loan to the value of the property. In addition, the lender must be able to gain possession of the property used as collateral in a timely manner in order to minimize loss of investment.

Mortgage lenders had no idea of what constituted a risk for them or their investors at the beginning. There was no history to give them a clue, so they kept the loan-to-value ratio at no more than 50%. In other words, if the home was worth $10,000, they would make a loan of $5,000. The payments were usually interest only, payable twice yearly, with the original amount borrowed all due in three to five years. The lender originating the loan would charge anywhere from one to three points of the amount borrowed (one point is 1%) as a fee. Since it was a rare borrower who could save enough to pay off the loan when it was due, the amount could be renewed by paying a 1% renewal fee.

Many lending institutions expanded their lending capabilities and developed new lending markets throughout the 20th Century. Thrift institutions such as savings banks, and savings and loan companies became common as they spread across the country, following the westward direction of the population.

The 1920s were a decade of unrestrained enthusiasm and wild expectation that the "good times" were here to stay. Growth and abundance were seen as a sign that the economic direction of the country was in an upward spiral that would never end. Optimists of the time may be forgiven because they had no history to guide them in making loans on properties that had appreciated 25 to 50% per year. There was no one to tell the mortgage bankers not to loosen their underwriting or loan approval standards and not to over-appraise properties based on their rapid appreciation and inflation. The belief was that prices would keep going up and protect any dubious loan.

Those lenders of the '20s would be the first in a long line of optimists to be left holding loans on properties worth less than the amount loaned against them when the boom comes to an end and property values nose-dive. This is a familiar mantra to those of us who remember the booms that ended in busts throughout the 20th Century as history repeated itself.

Just as happens today, the real estate market was the first to notice that something was wrong with the economy. Property values began to drop radically by 1927, and by 1929 not only was the real estate business in trouble but the entire country was in a fast economic spiral downward that led to the Great Depression. The failure of the stock market and the loss of financial vigor plunged the United States into one of the blackest economic declines the country had ever experienced.

Mortgage lenders were faced with several dilemmas. They were not getting their quarterly or semiannual interest payments from borrowers on their mortgages because of the epidemic unemployment. Because it took so long for the lenders to realize that default was a possibility, 3 to 6 months would go by before they knew the mortgages were in trouble. By that time, lenders would have serious cash flow problems because no one was paying on their loans. The only solution for the institutional lenders was to sell their real estate and mortgage holdings under very unpromising circumstances, which meant taking huge losses.

Homeowners who could not make the required payments, nor refinance when their 5-year loans became due, lost their homes to foreclosure. Lenders were not just being mean by foreclosing on borrowers. It was a matter of survival for the lenders just as it was for the homeowners. Either the loan had to be repaid or the property given to the bank to sell so they could get the cash. Because cash-poor mortgage lenders were forced to sell their real estate holdings at a loss to get money, and the inevitable mortgage defaults occurred at breakneck speed, the decline in the real estate market was in free-fall by 1935.

All types of financial institutions began to fail as customers showed their lack of faith in the banks by withdrawing their money. This *disintermediation*, along with the epidemic foreclosures, worsened the cash flow problem for mortgage lenders, causing some of them to abandon what customers they had remaining and close the doors for good.

The greatest number of people to lose their homes or farms to foreclosure was in the Midwest where dry prairies and weather combined to worsen the economic blow to families living there. As the number of defaults increased, the necessity of a moratorium on foreclosures became evident. Some lenders did offer *forebearance* by allowing borrowers to stop making mortgage payments for as long as two years. By 1933, more than 26 states had passed legislation declaring a moratorium on most foreclosures.

These moratoria gave families needed relief from home loss anxiety while the federal government tried to find a new direction for the dismal economy.

WHAT KEPT IT GOING?

By the time the economic downturn had become the Great Depression in the early 1930s, the federal government determined that legislation was needed to help strengthen and stabilize the real estate market. By creating conforming and central lending programs the federal government hoped to reverse the negative cycle of loan and default and at the same time defeat the lethargic economy.

The hope was that by getting involved in the healing of the real estate market, the government could expect the general economy to recover on its coattails. In retrospect, that is exactly what happened then and proceeded to happen every time there was a recession throughout the 20th Century.

The first institutions to benefit from federal interest in lending were the commercial banks. The Reconstruction Finance Corporation (RFC) was created in 1932, giving commercial banks liquidity and putting them back in business making loans once again.

A second program initiated by the federal government was the Federal Home Loan Bank (FHLB) which established a central credit authority for home financing, serving primarily savings and loan institutions.

Next came the Home Owners Loan Act (HOLA) in 1933. Savings and loans were given federal charters and the Home Owners Loan Corporation (HOLC) was created to give emergency relief to families by refinancing or purchasing their defaulted mortgages.

In 1934 the now familiar Federal Housing Authority (FHA) was created to develop the framework for a national mortgage market. The FHA is acknowledged for insuring the first long-term, fully amortized mortgages. During this time the Federal Savings and Loan Insurance Corporation

(FSLIC) and the Federal Deposit Insurance Corporation (FDIC) were established to encourage savers to return to their former habit of making regular deposits in banks.

A Growing Economy

During the Great Depression and until the end of World War II individuals built their own homes, inherited them or rented a home. There was no large scale availability of homes for families until after 5 million soldiers returned from the war, requiring housing. To meet that need, the federal government passed the Servicemen's Readjustment Act (1944) which allowed former servicemen and women to buy homes with no down payment and provided a government guaranty for the financing of the loan amount.

A huge need for housing grew from 1945 to 1955, creating the biggest increase in home building in the history of the United States. The new availability of long-term loans, the reality of government housing plans, the built-up demand for housing and the repaired cash flow of mortgage lenders all conspired to create an environment that was more than kind to mortgage lending. A national promise was made by legislators to do everything in their power to enable every American to own a home. Developers built large numbers of homes, and families were able to buy them easily for the first time in the history of our economy.

FEDERAL PARTICIPATION IN REAL ESTATE FINANCE

In 1965, several federal housing authorities were combined to form one agency, the Department of Housing and Urban Development (HUD). One of the many important jobs of HUD was in regulating real estate and mortgage lending. During the years to follow, the regulation of mortgage lending and new legislation reflected the growing awareness of the federal government that the good health of the country depended on the good health of the real estate and lending business.

By passing the Housing and Urban Development Act (1968), the federal government was taking important beginner steps to regulate the real estate and mortgage market. The capacity or the right of the federal government to subsidize interest rates was a new concept causing some uneasiness about the fiscal and political impact of such a commitment.

The two federal agencies that were created to participate in real estate financing were the Federal Housing Administration (FHA) and the Veterans Administration (VA). Together, the agencies made it possible for people to buy homes they would never be able to purchase without government involvement. Economic growth, along with government participation in finance programs, inspired builders and developers to continue to be optimistic; and building starts were the highest they had ever been.

Because the promise of equality and fairness is given to all citizens by our constitution, and because citizens demand protection, the federal government has been particularly attentive to the interests of consumers regarding real estate financing. The Consumer Protection Act of 1968 was the first of several laws that fixed new guidelines for residential lending. Since then, legislation has been passed requiring specific disclosures at critical stages of a loan to guard the consumer against both ignorance and fraud.

The actions of the federal government, through legislation, have contributed to the ability of most citizens to purchase a home. Because of the availability of mortgage funding and credit, the average family can now imagine themselves being homeowners. The following is a list of federal laws that have influenced residential mortgage lending throughout the 20th Century.

Laws Impacting Mortgage Lending

1913—Federal Reserve Act
Established the Federal Reserve System and authorized federally chartered commercial banks to make real estate loans.

1916—Federal Farm Loan Act
Provided for the formation of Federal Land Bank Associations as units of the Federal Land Bank System, which was given authority to generate funds for loans to farmers by the sale of bonds.

1932—Reconstruction Finance Act
Created the Reconstruction Finance Corporation, which was designed, among other things, to provide liquidity to commercial banks.

1932—Federal Home Loan Bank Act
Established the Federal Home Loan Bank Board and 12 regional banks to provide central credit facilities for home finance institutions that were members of the FHLB.

1932—Home Owners Loan Act
This act produced two results: (1) created the Home Owners Loan Corporation with authority to purchase defaulted home mortgages and to refinance as many as prudently feasible; (2) provided the basic lending authority for federally chartered savings and loan associations.

1934—National Housing Act

Authorized the creation of the Federal Housing Administration and Federal Savings and Loan Insurance Corporation.

1938—National Mortgage Association of Washington

This governmental agency, soon renamed the Federal National Mortgage Association, was authorized to provide secondary mortgage market support for FHA mortgages.

1944—Servicemen's Readjustment Act

Established within the Veterans Administration as a mortgage guarantee program for qualified veterans.

1949—Housing Act

Stated that the national housing goal was to provide "a decent home and suitable living environment for every American family." Consolidated past lending programs of the Farmers Home Administration.

1961—Consolidated Farmers Home Administration

Extended authority for the agency to make mortgage loans to nonfarmers in rural areas.

1965—Housing and Urban Development Act

Consolidated many federal housing agencies into a new Department of Housing and Urban Development with expanded authority.

1966—Interest Rate Adjustment Act

Authorized the setting of maximum savings rates and the creation of a differential between the savings rates of commercial banks and thrift institutions.

1968—Fair Housing Act

Prohibited discrimination in real estate sales and mortgage lending based on race, color, national origin and religion.

1968—Interstate Land Sales Full Disclosure Act

Required complete and full disclosure of all facts regarding interstate sale of real estate.

1968—Consumer Credit Protection Act

Title I, better known as Truth In Lending, which authorized the Federal Reserve Board to formulate regulations (Reg Z) requiring advanced disclosure of the amount and type of finance charge and a calculation of the annual percentage rate.

Title VI, better known as the Fair Credit Reporting Act, established disclosure requirements regarding the nature of credit information used in determining whether to grant a loan.

1968—Housing and Urban Development Act

This act put the existing Federal National Mortgage Association (FNMA) in private hands and authorized it to continue secondary mortgage market support. The act created a new government agency, the Government National Mortgage Association (GNMA), and authorized it to continue the FNMA special assistance function and guaranteed mortgage-backed securities.

1969—National Environmental Policy Act

Required the preparation of an Environmental Impact Statement for the Council on Environmental Quality in order to determine the environmental impact of real estate development.

1970—Emergency Home Finance Act

Created a new secondary mortgage market participant, the Federal Home Loan Mortgage Corporation (FHLMC), which had as its stated objective providing secondary mortgage support for conventional mortgages originated by thrift institutions. The act also gave FNMA authority to purchase conventional mortgages in addition to FHA/VA.

1974—Flood Disaster Protection Act

Effective in 1975, mortgage loans could not be made in a flood hazard area unless flood insurance had been purchased.

1974—Real Estate Settlement Procedures Act

This act and its amendments required mortgage lenders to provide mortgage borrowers with an advance disclosure of loan settlement costs and charges. It also prohibited kickbacks to any person for referring business. The 1976 amendment required lenders to provide applicants with a Good Faith Estimate of Settlement Costs and a HUD booklet. A Uniform Settlement Statement (HUD-l) must be furnished to the borrower before or at the settlement. The 1992 amendment extended RESPA to subordinate financing, effective 1993.

1974—Equal Credit Opportunity Act (ECOA)

This act and its amendments prohibited discrimination in lending on the basis of sex, marital status, age, race, color, national origin, religion, good faith reliance on consumer protection laws, or the fact that a borrower receives public assistance. In addition, if an application is rejected, the borrower must be notified within 30 days of the reason for rejection.

1975—Home Mortgage Disclosure Act (HMDA)

This act and its amendments required disclosure by most mortgage lenders of geographic distribution of loans in metropolitan statistical area. The purpose was to establish lending patterns of lenders.

1978—Fair Lending Practices Regulations

These FHLB regulations required members to develop written underwriting standards, keep a loan registry, not deny loans because of age of dwelling or condition of neighborhood, and direct advertising to all segments of the community.

1978—Community Reinvestment Act

This act required FSLIC-insured institutions to adopt a community reinvestment statement, which delineate the community in which they will invest; maintain a public comment file; and post a CRA notice.

1979—Housing and Community Development Amendments

This legislation exempted FHA-insured mortgages from state and local usury ceilings. (Other concurrent legislation exempted VA and conventional mortgages).

1980—Depository Institutions Deregulation and Monetary Control Act

Congress extended the savings interest rate control and thrift institution's one quarter of 1% differential for six years. The act also extended the federal override of state usury ceilings on certain mortgages. Other changes included simplified truth-in-lending standards and eased lending restrictions, including geographical limitations, loan-to-value ratios, and treatment of one-family loans exceeding specified dollar amounts.

1980—Omnibus Reconciliation Act

Limited the issuance of tax-exempt housing mortgage revenue bonds.

1982—Garn-St. Germain Depository Institutions Act

Preempted state due-on-sale loan restrictions; mandated phase-out of

interest rate differential by January l, 1984; provided FSLIC and FDIC assistance for institutions with deficient net worth; and allowed savings and
loans to make consumer, commercial and agricultural loans.

1984—Deficit Reduction Act

Extended the tax exemption for qualified mortgage subsidy bonds; created
new reporting procedures for mortgage interest.

1986—Tax Reform Act

Reduced top corporate tax rate from 46% to 34%; reduced taxable income
bad debt deduction from 40% to 8%; provided for 3-year carrybacks and
15-year carryforwards for savings institution net operating losses.

1987—Competitive Equality Banking Act

Set the FSLIC $10.8 billion recapitalization in motion, kept intact savings
Bank Life Insurance, and gave thrifts flexibility to form different types of
holding companies.

1987—Housing and Community Development Act

Notice of availability of counseling must be given with 45 days of delinquency on single-family primary residence.

1989—Financial Institutions Reform, Recovery and Enforcement Act (FIRREA)

Restructured the regulatory framework by eliminating FHLBB and FSLIC;
created the Office of Thrift Supervision (OTS) under the Treasury Department; enhanced FDIC to supervise safety and soundness of financial institutions, the Savings Institutions Insurance Fund, and the Bank Insurance
Fund; created the Resolution Trust Corporation (RTC) to dispose of failed
savings and loans; established new capital standards for thrifts.

1992—RESPA amendment

Coverage of RESPA is extended to subordinate financing.

1992—HMDA amendment

Mortgage companies and other non-depository institutions required to
comply with HMDA.

During the last 30 years of the 20th Century, real estate construction and
financing benefited more people than it had in the history of the country.

THE 20th CENTURY—THE LAST 20 YEARS

During the 1980s the country was on an economic roller coaster. The economy was undisciplined, with double-digit inflation, a major recession, and a stock market crash far worse than that at the end of the 1920s. The scandal plagued savings and loan industry disgraced itself and ended up losing billions of dollars before being bailed out by taxpayers. On the positive side for the decade, the Dow-Jones average hit a record high, the use of mortgage-backed securities was growing, alternative mortgage instruments were becoming common and more sources of needed mortgage money were available. As a result of all of the above, the economy went through difficult but much needed changes. Because of these changes, the residential mortgage lending market and mortgage lenders became more responsive to the needs of borrowers.

The 1980s

By 1980, the country's economy was in chaos. The Federal Reserve had been managing and regulating interest rates and the money supply to control inflation. By 1979, the Fed stopped regulating short-term interest rates and tried to check out-of-control growth in the money supply that had led to inflation.

The thinking was that by limiting the amount of money in circulation, inflation could be chased downward, decreasing the obligation of interest rates to go up. When the Fed raised interest rates, money became more expensive to borrow, which led people to borrow less. By borrowing less, there was less money to spend, therefore interrupting the downward spiral of too much money chasing too few goods. Because of inflation it took more money to buy less.

Interest rates did eventually go down, after rising abruptly as a result of the Fed's change in policy. In 1981, the prime rate (the short-term rate charged to a bank's most creditworthy customers) rose to 21½%, causing gridlock in banking and particularly the mortgage lending business. Because borrowers could not qualify for home loans whose interest rates had reached 17½%, very few people applied for loans or attempted to purchase homes. Tight money, strict credit underwriting and high interest rates made mortgage money scarce and expensive. That led the real estate industry and building industry into a decline that deepened into a recession for the entire country, with unemployment at more than 10%.

Finally, by the middle of the decade, inflation was under control, interest rates were going down and the country was optimistic about the economy once again. Developers were building homes and families were able to buy them.

In 1987, however, the stock market soared to previously unseen heights before its fundamentally flawed over-valuation of stocks caused a catastrophic collapse that surprised and shocked the investor world. The combination of a massive federal deficit in the last years of the decade and the falling stock market was more than the recovering economy could endure and by the early 1990s the shadow of wintry recession was once more threatening the ability of families to buy homes.

Failure of Savings and Loans

For many years the savings and loans institutions had been operating behind a veil of supposed integrity and virtue, hoping to conceal their deceptive business dealings. Speculative lending, negative earning, low capital and poor management led to the failure of many savings and loan associations and the bankruptcy of the Federal Savings and Loan Insurance Corporation (FSLIC)—the deposit insurance fund for savings and loan associations.

Because of dubious business practices, the savings and loan associations had allowed the vital nourishment of their industry, the savings of individuals, to be used at best, unwisely, at worst, unscrupulously. The failure of the FSLIC was a danger to the entire economy because of the many other businesses that were involved in the complex betrayal, not just individuals who had lost their money as well as their faith in the banking system.

After the closing of hundreds of savings and loans, the federal government stepped in and pledged to save the ailing banks by selling bonds to finance the bailout. The 1989 legislation that gave authority to the bailout by the federal government was the Financial Institutions Reform, Recovery and Enforcement Act (FIRREA).

The 1990s

The economic picture of the 1990s was dominated by profits made through initial public offerings (IPO's) to produce unimagined wealth for those lucky enough to buy and sell decisively. Individuals prospered through the spectacular rise in mutual funds, stock options or other dazzling investments.

With the benefit of time, we can now make a more realistic evaluation of the inclusive business cycle of the 1990s: the listless recovery that started early in the decade; the astonishing boom; the technology bust leading to the downturn of 2001. The decade was more, however, than the characteristic beliefs that we hold about the star status of upper management of large corporations and the profits-will-never-end mentality of those corporations and newly rich stockholders.

Something unexpected and unnoticed was happening beyond the corporate world of acquisitions, take-overs and book-cooking. An almost overlooked trend during the decade was the considerably higher rise in productivity compared to the 1980s or previous years. Surprisingly, in the end, it was the workers, not the investors, who gained the most from the extra production. It was the hard-working individual whose diligence and talent prevailed long after the blaze-out of the stunning but brief period that made temporary millionaires out of lucky investors.

A majority of American workers benefited from the dramatic wage growth during the 1990s, particularly in the lower paying, less-skilled occupations. Because unemployment was so low, many individuals had jobs with boosted salaries in every industry. From top executives to the lowest paid workers, the 1990s brought the greatest period of wage growth at all levels in the last 30 years.

The question asked most often about why consumer spending and the real estate market stayed strong during the 2001 recession could be answered, in part, by those workers with discretionary income and good jobs who had benefited from the increased production and pay in the 1990s. Consumers who had the advantage of enjoying the growth in earnings during the 1990s could use those dependably larger paychecks to buy goods and services, including new homes, into the next century.

Individuals were getting better jobs and being paid more for several reasons. Greater educational opportunities allowed people to qualify for the new jobs in technology, wages were higher because of the falling unemployment, and new jobs were created by the impetus of investors eager to provide financing for equipment and training that would boost productivity.

As the decade came to a close, labor costs were blamed for taking up a huge percentage of the earnings of corporations. Even though profits were growing steadily, workers had become accustomed to prosperity and were demanding their fair—but still enormous—piece of the pie.

At the beginning of the decade, it looked like corporations, not workers, were going to prevail in the productivity-labor costs struggle. While profits grew wildly, wages crept along slowly behind corporate gains. Characteristically, however, increases in salaries have tagged along behind productivity gains by a few years, and as the decade wore on, compensation per hour, including benefits, rose to levels unheard of since the 1950s.

Worker's paychecks quickly made up for the slow growth in the early 1990s. As a matter of fact, individuals with jobs requiring less skill in a diverse range of occupations particularly prospered in the worker-centric economy as the 20th Century ended and a new era began.

For many families home ownership had always been an elusive fantasy that couldn't come true. Because of the newly found financial independence and prosperity of workers during the last part of the decade, the real estate industry, in particular, experienced an unexpected and welcome bonus. Individual dreams became reality as more people than ever in the history of the country were able to own their own homes.

MARKET TRENDS

As we have seen, the state of the national economy is of vital importance to the mortgage and real estate markets. An unhealthy national economy leads to few, if any, economically healthy markets. The mortgage and real estate markets are driven by changes in the business climate and in the economy. The changes occur as trends, cycles, or short-term fluctuations. **Trends** are changes in the market in a consistent direction that occur over a long-term period. **Cycles** are periodic, irregular up-and-down movements in economic activity that take place over a period of two to six years. **Short-term fluctuations** are changes in business and economic activity that occur within the year. These changes in the economy affect mortgage and real estate markets.

Real Estate Cycles

The real estate industry contributes to the wealth in the economy, generates significant banking activity, and strongly affects the job market. Real estate markets are cyclical due to the relationship between demand and supply for a particular property type.

There are national real estate cycles, city and neighborhood market cycles, and cycles for individual property types within a city. Real estate cycles exist in both the residential and commercial property markets and their submarkets. In addition, each market and submarket is impacted by different economic, financial, and demographic factors.

Real Estate Agents need to know where the real estate market is heading, which submarket is hot, which submarket is losing market share, and where new supply will show up over the next few years. They also must be aware of the involvement of the Federal government in the current economic climate and be informed of any new laws that pass regarding mortgage lending practices.

Analysis of a Real Estate Cycle

As with the business cycle, the real estate cycle has four phases: (1) recovery, (2) expansion, (3) peak, and (4) contraction.

In the **recovery phase**, which is the bottom of the real estate cycle, the marketplace is in a state of oversupply caused by negative demand. In the **expansion phase**, demand continues to increase. This creates a need for more properties. Expansion continues as long as demand growth rates are higher than supply growth rates. It peaks when demand and supply grow at the same rate. The **peak phase** occurs when supply growth is higher than demand growth. New construction that was started in the expansion phase must now compete for fewer buyers in the marketplace. As more homes are delivered to the market with less demand, the market **contracts** and sales growth slows. Eventually, market participants realize that the market has turned down, which causes commitments for new construction to slow down or completely stop.

In time the cycle begins anew as construction ceases, or as demand growth turns up and begins to grow at rates higher than that of new supply in the marketplace.

CHAPTER QUIZ

1. In early societies, which of the following indicated wealth?

   a. gender
   b. land
   c. job
   d. social status

2. In Germany, after the fall of the Roman Empire, what was a "live" gage?

   a. an item of personal property used as collateral for a loan
   b. a person whose life was pledged as security for a loan
   c. an item of real property used as collateral for a loan
   d. a mortgage loan

3. What was the right of the borrower to regain ownership after default called, starting in Elizabethan England?

   a. mortgage insurance
   b. equitable right of redemption
   c. deficiency judgment
   d. statute of limitations

4. What caused the development of the farm mortgage business in the United States in the nineteenth century?

   a. the Civil War
   b. the need to invest disposable income after the Revolutionary War
   c. the need to borrow to finance new farms as families moved into remote areas of the country
   d. low interest rates

5. During the 19th Century, mortgage lenders in the Midwest financed farms with a loan-to-value ratio of:

   a. 10-20%
   b. 30-40%
   c. 50-60%
   d. 40-50%

6. What is a nonamortizing loan?

    a. a loan where none of the principal is included in the payments

    b. a loan whose payments include principal and interest

    c. a loan with no payments, principal and interest due at the end of the term

    d. a loan with irregular payments

7. What section of the business world is usually the first to notice a change, either up or down in the health of the economy?

    a. the movie business

    b. politicians

    c. stock market

    d. real estate market

8. What is disintermediation?

    a. depositing money in savings accounts

    b. withdrawing from savings accounts

    c. charging interest on loans

    d. reviewing depositor's savings histories

9. The 1989 legislation that gave authority to the bailout of the savings and loan industry by the federal government was:

    a. Financial Institutions Reform, Recovery and Enforcement Act (FIRREA)

    b. Federal Savings and Loan Insurance Corporation (FSLIC)

    c. Depository Institutions Deregulation and Monetary Control Act

    d. Garn-St. Germain Depository Institutions Act

10. What was the best period of wage growth at all levels of employment in the last 30 years?

    a. 1970s

    b. 1980s

    c. 1990s

    d. 2000

ANSWERS

1. *b*
2. *a*
3. *b*
4. *c*
5. *d*
6. *a*
7. *d*
8. *b*
9. *a*
10. *c*

2

chapter two

Real Property

INTRODUCTION

Ownership is the basic element in the whole subject of real estate. That precious, desirable, seemingly out-of-reach dream most of us share is considered a basic right in our culture. It has not always been that way. Our laws of property ownership had their beginnings in English common law. Originally, all property was owned by the monarch at the time, or an appointed noble. As time went by, people became annoyed by their lack of rights regarding property ownership.

Their discontent set powerful forces of change in motion, so that eventually each owner of real property—or real estate, as it is now called—acquired certain rights along with property ownership.

BUNDLE OF RIGHTS

Known collectively as the *bundle of rights*, this very important package includes: the right to own, possess, use, enjoy, borrow against and dispose of real property.

Bundle of Rights

Possession
- The right to live on the property and the right to keep others out

Use
- The right to use property, within the law, in any way, or for any purpose

Enjoyment
- The right to peace and quiet without being bothered by others

Encumber
- The right to borrow money and use property as security for the loan

Transfer
- The right to sell property, give it as a gift or dispose of it in any way permitted by law

TYPES OF ESTATES IN REAL PROPERTY

An *estate* is the ownership interest or claim a person has in real property. There are two types of estates that may be owned: *freehold* and *less-than-freehold*. The type of estate determines how much of a claim exists. Each type of estate is described in terms of its duration and the rights that accompany it.

Freehold Estates

The word freehold comes from feudal England. When the land owner was not subject to demands of the overlord and held the land freely, he held a freehold estate. This type of estate continues for an indefinite period of time and may be the estate of a homeowner or a landlord. It includes the bundle of rights.

Today, when we think of a freehold estate, we must consider the two types: *estates in fee* and *life estates*.

Estates in Fee

Sometimes known as a fee simple estate or a fee, this is the most complete form of ownership. Since an owner of an estate in fee may dispose of it in his or her lifetime or after death by will, it is also known as an estate of inheritance.

This is commonly the kind of estate that is transferred in a normal real estate transaction. If the property is transferred or sold with no conditions or limitations on its use, it is known as an estate in fee simple absolute.

If a seller imposes qualifications or conditions, the buyer then holds *a fee simple qualified* or *fee simple defeasible estate*. For example, a seller may require the property to be used for a specified purpose such as a church or a rehabilitation center. The owner sells the property with the condition that this requirement be met. If the buyer breaches this *condition subsequent* after the sale, the seller may take possession of the property and regain title. In another example of a condition subsequent, the seller may place special limitations on the use of the property after the sale. A buyer may be denied the right to sell alcoholic beverages on the property or allow a board-and-care use. If either of those events occurs, ownership of the property reverts to the seller or his or her heirs.

The parties to a contract may also impose a restriction known as a *condition precedent*. In this case, something must occur before a transaction becomes absolute and final. For example, a sale may be contingent on the buyer obtaining financing or qualifying for a VA or FHA loan.

Life Estates

A life estate is one that is limited in duration to the life of some designated person.

- Amy grants to Bill a life estate with the provision that upon Bill's death, the property reverts to Amy. Bill is then the life tenant, or the designated party on whom the life estate is based. Amy holds an estate in reversion.

- Greg grants to Linda a life estate, with the provision that upon Linda's death, the property goes to a third party, Charles. The interest that Charles holds is known as an estate in remainder.

- Lee grants to Heather a life estate for the life of Elizabeth, with the provision that it goes to Laura when Elizabeth dies. Heather may enjoy the benefits of the life estate as long as Elizabeth is alive. Upon Elizabeth's death, the estate goes to Laura or her heirs. That is called reserving a life estate.

Since a life estate is a type of freehold, or fee estate, the holder of a life estate has all the rights that go with fee ownership except disposing of the estate by will. Remember, the life estate is tied to a designated life, and when that party dies, the estate goes either to the person in reversion or the person in remainder, or their heirs.

Life estate holders must pay the taxes and maintain the property. They may collect all rents and keep all profits for the duration of the life estate. They may encumber the property or dispose of it in any way except by will. Any interest the life estate holders may create in the property —extending beyond the life of the person used to measure the estate—will become invalid when that designated person dies.

A Life Estate Holder

• Must pay the taxes and maintain the property
• May collect all rents and keep all profits for the duration of the life estate
• May encumber the property or dispose of it in any way except by will

---

Less-Than-Freehold Estates

We have just discussed estates in real property. A freehold estate, as we have seen, is the most complete form of ownership, the one that includes the most rights. The less-than-freehold estate is sometimes known as a *leasehold estate* or a *lease*. Renters or tenants hold this kind of an estate.

Leasehold estates are personal property or *chattel real*, and include the right to use property for a fixed period of time. Renters, or lessees, have the right of possession and quiet enjoyment. That means they have the right to the exclusive use of the rented property and the right to live quietly without privacy invasion. Those rights are as legally secure as the rights of a landlord or lessor.

REAL PROPERTY VS. PERSONAL PROPERTY

Something that may be owned is known as property. It can be real or personal. Anything that is not real property is personal property. Personal property includes money, movable goods and evidences of debt—such as a promissory note. Real property is immovable and is usually transferred or sold by a deed.

When real property is sold, anything that has become attached to it goes to the *buyer* as part of the sale unless other arrangements have been made. Personal property, sometimes known as chattel, is movable and transferred or sold using a *bill of sale*. When real property is sold, items of personal property go with the seller unless other arrangements have been made. Real and personal property can change from one to the other. A tree is real property until it is cut as timber; then it becomes the personal property of whoever cut it. If that timber is milled into lumber, sold and used to build a house, it becomes real property. As the house ages and deteriorates, is torn down and hauled away as scrap lumber, it becomes personal property once again.

REAL PROPERTY

Real property may be described as land, anything permanently attached to the land, anything appurtenant (we'll define that word shortly) to the land or anything immovable by law.

Land

Let's look at the land we walk on. This is the soil and the rocks that extend to the center of the earth. Included in the definition of land as real property is *airspace, mineral rights* and *water rights*.

Land As Real Property

- Airspace
- Mineral rights
- Water rights

Airspace is considered real property to a reasonable height. A good example of the efficient use of airspace is the building of high rise condominiums, sometimes known as vertical subdivisions. An owner/developer may sell this airspace as real property.

Minerals are owned as real property unless they are non-solid, migratory minerals such as oil or gas. These may not be owned until taken from the ground, at which time they become the personal property of whoever removed them.

Certain *water rights* go with the land and are considered real property. Because of the many disputes over the use of underground (percolating) water and surface water, the law is very clear about the rights of owners. Water cannot be owned, nor can it be channeled or dammed for the benefit of one landowner. Under the *doctrine of correlative user*, an owner may take only a reasonable share of underground waters. The owner of property bordering on a stream or river has what is known as riparian rights (a riparian owner).

Owners may use the water to their benefit in a reasonable amount not to exclude adjoining owners. Owners of land bordering a lake (littoral owners) generally own to the average low water mark or the edge of the lake. The boundary line of land touching the ocean is the ordinary high-tide mark.

When there is a need for the government to divert water for public use, its *right of appropriation* is applied.

Anything Permanently Attached to the Land

Those items that are permanently attached to the land are also considere real property and belong to the owner. Houses, garages, fences, swimming pools or anything resting on the land to become permanent are owned as a part of the property. Anything permanently attached to the building, such as a fixture, is owned as real property, as is anything attached by roots, such as trees, shrubs and flowers.

The exception to this is crops that are growing and are cultivated annually for sale—such as peaches in a commercial orchard or avocados in a commercial grove. These are known as *emblements* and are personal property. Emblements may be owned by tenants as well as fee owners. Remember, the crops are the personal property, not the trees or plants they grow on.

Anything Appurtenant to the Land

Anything used with the land for its benefit is known as an *appurtenance*. Easements and stock rights in a mutual water company are the two most common appurtenances to real property. An easement is a right-of-way across a parcel of land, and is transferred automatically with the property whenever it is sold. The easement is appurtenant to the property.

Stock in a mutual water company is owned by water users who have organized to form a water company for their mutual benefit. The shares in this water company are appurtenant to the land and go with the sale of the property.

Anything Immovable by Law

Established crops and trees are considered immovable by law and must be sold with the property. A seller may not sell the property and exclude the orange grove from the sale. The seller may have sold the crop resulting from the trees as personal property, but the trees remain real property and may not be excluded from the sale.

Real Property

- Land
- Anything attached to land
- Anything appurtenant to land
- Anything immovable by law

FIXTURES

A *fixture* is an item of real property that used to be personal property. It has become a fixture because it is permanently attached to real property.

Now that you know what real property is—and is not— let's examine what that means to the consumer. Imagine that you are a prospective buyer. You walk into a house and fall in love with the chandelier hanging from the ceiling in the dining room. You make an offer to buy the house, it is accepted and the escrow goes through smoothly. The sellers get their money and you get the deed to the house.

When you arrive with your moving van, your anticipation turns to hostility when you discover a lonely light bulb hanging where the elegant chandelier had been. The former owners wonder why you are annoyed when you call to arrange the return of your chandelier. They tell you it is not your chandelier; it has been in the family for generations. They never intended it to go with the house.

If you didn't know the difference between real and personal property, you might think the sellers had a right to the chandelier.

Part of a real estate agent's job is to make sure all parties involved in a sale know what goes and what stays. In the above case, the listing agent should have asked the sellers if they wanted to keep the chandelier, and notified prospective buyers that it did not go with the house.

Since it was not excluded from the listing, it was reasonable for the buyer to assume it was real property. It had become a fixture and therefore should have gone with the sale.

When a buyer makes an offer on a property, there is a section in the offer-to-purchase contract where he or she may request any item of real or personal property such as the chandelier, washer/dryer, a refrigerator or a bedspread that matches the custom drapes. The buyer should always put an intention in writing to make sure the seller is informed and agrees.

Disputes about real and personal property have caused the courts to adopt a set of five tests to help them decide who is in the right when two parties disagree about what are fixtures: method of attachment, adaptation, relationship of the parties, intent of the parties and agreement of the parties.

Five Tests of a Fixture

Method of Attachment

How is the disputed item attached to the property? If it's permanently attached, it's real property. In the case of the chandelier, it had been wired into the electrical system, which made it a fixture, or real property. It would be included in the sale of the house as something attached or affixed to the land unless the sellers specifically mentioned they wanted to take it with them.

Adaptation

Has the item been made especially for the property? For example, have the drapes been custom-made for the windows? Has the carpet been cut especially to fit the rooms? Is the stove built into the counter? If so, each has become a fixture and has lost its status as personal property.

Relationship of the Parties

In a dispute about fixtures, when there is no convincing evidence of the right of one party, courts will look at whether the parties are landlord-tenant, lender-borrower, or buyer-seller. The court then makes a decision based on the relationship of the parties in the case.

Intent of the Parties

If apparent, either in writing or by the actions of either party involved, this is considered to be the *most* important test of a fixture. Let's look at the tenant who wired special cosmetic lights into the bathroom wall, telling the landlord he intended the lights to remain his personal property. He said he would repair the wall when he moved and would take the lights with him. This was a clear case of a tenant's intention to keep the lights as his personal property. A fixture may remain personal property if all parties are informed. Intention should always be put in writing, however.

Agreement of the Parties

When there has been a clear agreement between the parties in a dispute about fixtures, the courts will apply this test to determine who is in the right.

TRADE FIXTURES

Items of personal property—such as shelves, cash registers, room partitions or wall mirrors—are known as *trade fixtures* when used to conduct a business. Tenants retain ownership of the items as personal property when they vacate the premises, but are responsible for repairing any damage that results from placing the trade fixtures.

LAND DESCRIPTIONS

Exploring new land captured the imagination of the hardy individuals and families who opened up the U.S. frontier. As they moved west and improved the land on which they settled, these pioneers created a need for systematic property description.

A street address was adequate for social contacts and for delivering mail, but it was not precise enough to identify a particular property.

Today, a legal description is required before a deed may be recorded to transfer title to a new owner. There are three common ways to describe property.

Three Ways to Identify Property

- U.S. Government Section and Township Survey
- Recorded Lot, Block and Tract System
- Metes and Bounds

U.S. Government Section and Township Survey

By the late 19th Century, the U.S. government had established a system of land description for new territories, states and other public lands. The rectangular survey system, also known as the U.S. Government Section and Township Survey, uses imaginary lines to form a grid to locate land. North-south longitude lines, called meridians, and east-west latitude lines called base lines, intersect to form an imaginary starting point from which distances are measured.

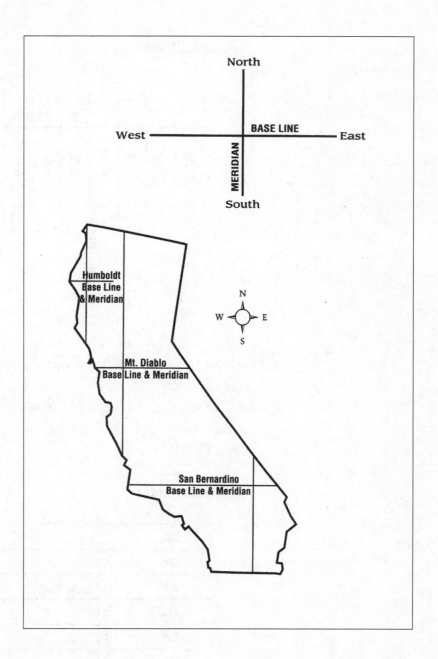

In California there are three such starting points: the *Humboldt Base Line and Meridian* (northwestern California), *the Mt. Diablo Base Line and Meridian* (northeastern and central California) and the *San Bernardino Base Line and Meridian* (Southern California).

After establishing a starting point at the intersection of a chosen principal meridian and base line, the government surveyors drew imaginary lines called range lines every 6 miles east and west of the meridian to form columns called ranges. Each range was numbered either east or west of the principal meridian. For example, the first range east of the meridian was called Range 1 East (R1E), and the first range west of the meridian was called Range 1 West (R1W).

Range Lines

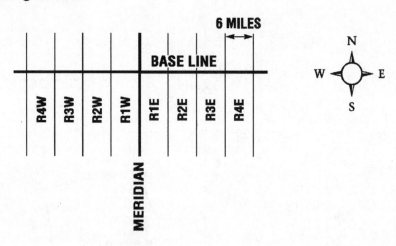

Imaginary township lines were drawn every 6 miles north and south of the base line to form a row or tier of townships. Then these rows were numbered according to their distance from the base line. For example, the first row of townships north of the base line was called Township 1 North (T1N) and the first row of townships south of the base line was called Township 1 South (T1S).

Township Lines

T3N	↕ 6 MILES
T2N	
T1N	BASE LINE
T1S	
T2S	
T3S	

Thus, a grid of squares, called townships—each 6 miles by 6 miles (36 square miles)—appears.

Townships

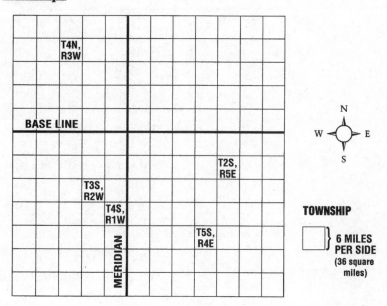

Each township is described by its location, relative to the intersection of the base line and meridian we have just discussed. A particular township in the fourth tier north of the base line and in the third range west of the meridian—with "T" for township and "R" for range—would be described as follows: T4N,R3W, San Bernardino Base Line and Meridian.

Township and Range

- Range Lines – every 6 miles east and west of meridian
- Township Lines – every 6 miles north and south of base line

The way to locate T4N,R3W is to start at the intersection of the base line and meridian and count up—or north—four rows and then count to the left—or west—three rows. Following is an exercise to test your understanding.

Exercise 1: Locating Townships and Ranges

1. Locate the following areas on the "Townships" diagram.

   T2S,R5E
   T3S,R2W
   T5S,R4E
   T4S,R1W

2. How far in miles is the west side of T4N,R3W from the principal meridian?

3. How far in miles is the east side of T2S,R5E from the principal meridian?

4. How many miles from the base line is the south side of T5S, R4E?

5. How many miles from the base line is the north side of T4S, R1W?

Answers

1. See "Townships" diagram, pg. 35
2. 18 miles
3. 30 miles
4. 30 miles
5. 18 miles

As you see from the section diagram below, each section is 1 mile by 1 mile and contains 640 acres.

Section

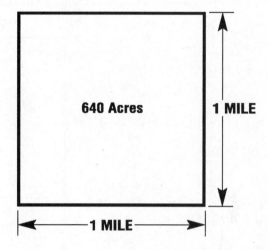

A section may then be divided further into quarter sections containing 160 acres each, and then divided into smaller and smaller parcels. These parcels are identified by their compass direction (NE, SE, NW, SW).

Quarter Sections

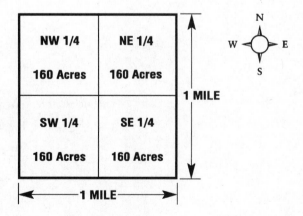

Armed with this knowledge, a student may locate any size parcel, no matter how large or small, by simply dividing the section. Another important number for you to know is 5,280, the number of linear feet in a mile. Linear refers to length rather than area.

The next illustration shows how a section may be divided and each parcel described. It is followed by an exercise that tests your ability to locate sections and determine acreage.

Section Divisions

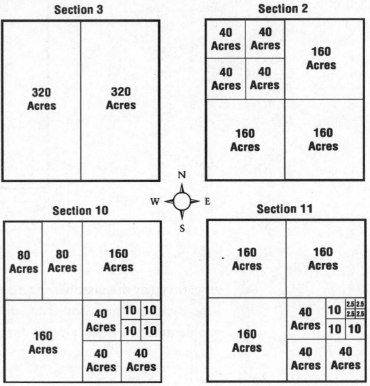

Exercise 3: Figuring Acreage

(Use section divisions diagram above.)

1. Locate the E 1/2 of Section 3. How many acres?

2. Locate the SE 1/4 of Section 2. How many acres?

3. Locate the E 1/2 of the NW 1/4 of Section 10. How many acres?

4. Locate the NW 1/4 of the SE 1/4 of Section 11. How many acres?

5. How many feet are there around 1/4 section?

6. **Bonus question: Can you find the SW 1/4 of the NE 1/4 of the SE 1/4 of Section 11? How many acres?**

(continued on next page)

(continued)

(Hint: Always read the description backwards to locate a particular parcel, starting with the last and largest part, proceeding to the first and smallest part of the description. Then you will have located the property in question.)

Answers

1. 320 acres
2. 160 acres
3. 80 acres
4. 40 acres
5. 10,560 feet
6. **Bonus answer: 10 acres**

Here is a summary of the basic facts about U.S. Government Section and Township Survey. Use it as a reference to calculate land measurement.

Three Base Lines and Meridians in California

Humboldt Base Line and Meridian
Mt. Diablo Base Line and Meridian
San Bernardino Base Line and Meridian

System for Locating Land

- *Meridians* run north and south
- *Base Lines* run east and west
- *Range Lines* run north and south, parallel to the principal meridian, every 6 miles
- *Township Lines* run east and west, parallel to the base line, every 6 miles
- *Townships* are 6 miles by 6 miles, 36 square miles
- *Sections* are 1 mile by 1 mile, 36 in each township and contain 640 acres
- 5,280 feet=1 mile
- 43,560 square feet=1 acre
- 640 acres=1 square mile
- 4 miles=distance around a section/square mile

Recorded Lot, Block and Tract System

Another land description method is the recorded lot, block and tract system. When developers divide parcels of land into lots, they are required by the California Subdivision Map Act to prepare and record a plat map.

This shows the location and boundaries of each separate new lot in the subdivision, and must be recorded in the county recorder's office. It is the most convenient and easily understood method of land description.

After the subdivision map has been filed or recorded, it is public knowledge and is available to anyone. Each lot in a subdivision is identified by number, as is the block in which it is located; each lot and block is in a referenced tract. Recorded map descriptions of land are most likely to be found in cities where developers have planned communities and commercial growth areas.

Metes and Bounds

A *metes and bounds* description of land delineates boundaries and measures distances between landmarks (or monuments) to identify property. This is a method of land description in which the dimensions of the property are measured by distance and direction. Land that is irregular in shape or cannot be described using either of the two other methods may have a metes and bounds description.

Think of measuring when you think of metes, and boundaries when you think of bounds. Generally, you will only need to recognize this type of description when you see it. A surveyor will measure the distances and establish the legal description.

A metes and bounds description starts at a well-marked point of beginning, and—following the boundaries of the land—measures the distances between landmarks, then returns to the beginning.

Here is a description of an uneven, hilly parcel of land with an avocado grove in Vista, California.

> *Beginning at the intersection of the east line of Buena Creek Road and the south line of Cleveland Trail; thence east along the south line of Cleveland Trail 300 feet; thence south 657.5 feet to the center line of Buena Creek; thence northwesterly along the center line of Buena Creek to its intersection with the east line of Buena Creek Road; thence north 325 feet along the east line of Buena Creek road to the place of beginning.*

A metes and bounds description of city property might begin as follows.

Beginning at a point on the southerly side of Del Cerro Street, 200 feet easterly from the intersection of the southerly side of Del Cerro Street and the easterly side of Vista Las Lomas; thence...

A metes and bounds description of land in section and township areas might begin as follows.

That part of lots 20, 21, 22 in the Harbor Lights Subdivision in the NW1/4 of the SE1/4 of Section 35, Township 24 north, Range 22 east of the San Bernardino Base Line and Meridian described as follows, beginning...

CHAPTER QUIZ

1. The rights that go along with ownership of real property are called:

   a. Bill of Rights
   b. Bundle of Rights
   c. Cradle of Rights
   d. Deeded Rights

2. Which kind of estate may be willed?

   a. less-than-freehold
   b. leasehold
   c. freehold
   d. life estate

3. The ownership interest or claim a person has in real property is known as:

   a. an estate in real property
   b. an encumbrance
   c. a lien
   d. an encroachment

4. Sheila deeded a house she owned to her mother, Janet, with the condition that title to the house return to Sheila upon the death of her mother. What kind of estate does Janet hold?

   a. less-than-freehold
   b. estate of inheritance
   c. fee simple defeasible
   d. life estate

5. Another name for a leasehold estate is:

    a. fee simple absolute
    b. fee simple qualified
    c. less-than-freehold
    d. freehold

6. Personal property is:

    a. immovable
    b. a house
    c. a built-in Jacuzzi
    d. movable

7. Chattel is:

    a. real property
    b. personal property
    c. neither real nor personal
    d. both real and personal

8. When real property is sold, anything that has become attached to it:

    a. goes to the buyer
    b. goes with the seller
    c. is divided between buyer and seller
    d. goes to the broker

9. Under the doctrine of correlative user:

    a. a riparian owner may take all
       the water he or she needs
    b. a riparian owner does not have
       access to underground water
    c. a riparian owner must negotiate with
       non-riparian owners for water rights
    d. an owner may take only his or her
       share of underground water

10. The method of land description most likely to be used in a city is:

    a. U.S. government section and
       township survey
    b. recorded lot, block and tract system
    c. metes and bounds
    d. common address

ANSWERS

1. *b*
2. *c*
3. *a*
4. *d*
5. *c*
6. *d*
7. *b*
8. *a*
9. *d*
10. *b*

3

chapter
three

Land Titles and Estates

INTRODUCTION

Historically, the question has been, "Who owns this property, and what is their interest in it?" Consumers still want to know how property may be owned, what kind of ownership may be taken, how it is measured, what the duration of that ownership is, and how much is owned.

This chapter answers basic questions on titles and estates. This knowledge will be useful every time the reader is involved in the transfer of real property, whether it's from the point of view of borrower, lender or seller. So let's start with who owned the land in the first place.

BACKGROUND OF LAND TITLE

As we have seen in earlier chapters, the growth of land ownership developed as a result of the importance of land to agrarian societies. At some point, early wandering tribes stopped following game and drifting without purpose through the seasons. Visionaries, who could see the benefit of residing permanently on the land rather than enduring the uncertainties of a nomadic life, began growing their food in permanent locations and domesticating animals, creating a desire for the exclusive right to the use of that land.

As permanent cultures grew and people became attached to their personal production potential, each family group was given the right to use a portion of the tribal land in return for loyalty in defense of the collectively owned property in particular, and the entire area claimed by the tribe in general.

With the continuing growth of societies, significant ownership traditions became law as the societies became political states. Eventually, a king or tribal leader emerged to claim ownership of all real property in the realm. In return for the loyalty of certain individuals, the king granted the right (called a feud) to the possession and use of particular parcels of his land to those who were willing to serve and defend him. These citizens, called lords, did not own the property, but usually remained tenants for life, as long as they served the king. The result of this early form of land ownership was known as feudalism.

The lord then gave ordinary citizens the right to use certain parcels of his land in return for a share of the crops and their loyalty in protecting his estate. These citizens, or vassals, were tenants of the lord, with no rights to sell or will the land they possessed. The feudal system of land ownership was replaced by the *allodial system*, under which people were allowed more rights than they had ever possessed, regarding real property. Finally, those citizens who possessed the land were permitted to convey their tenancy rights to others and eventually pass their interest to their heirs. In England, the feudal system was over by 1650, and the French Revolution, in 1789, ended the lord's feudal rights over his subject's land in France. At first, the lords became owners of the king's land, with the ordinary citizens becoming tenants. Later, the peasants were allowed to purchase their land or it was given as a gift by the lord. The centuries-long dream of personal land ownership had finally become a reality for some ordinary citizens.

The first settlers in America who came from England were given ownership of the land they claimed as their own, with title to unclaimed lands still in the name of the king. The American Revolution ended any plans the king of England had for keeping the colonies under his rule, and the newly formed nation of immigrants, under the allodial system of private ownership, began its slow but reliable encounter with economic prosperity.

ADOPTING A RECORDING SYSTEM

As Americans began to occupy the vast acreage of the new nation and develop the frontier and limitless plains into vigorous towns and then cities, agriculture was the primary occupation of citizens. Just as in the development of ancient cultures, because of the importance of land to the survival of each family, the owning of land became a symbol of wealth. In the pursuit of prosperity and affluence and to assure the permanence of acquired wealth, citizens needed some method to notify others of their ownership of real property. Property owners desired a method whereby public notice was given of their claim or right to a particular parcel of land.

In a move that was strictly an American device for safeguarding the ownership of land, states adopted a system of recording evidence of title or interest. This system meant records could be collected in a convenient and safe public place, so that those purchasing land would be more fully informed about the ownership and condition of the title. Citizens were protected against secret conveyances and liens, and title to real property was freely transferable.

Today, all states have laws that provide for the recording of documents that describe ownership interests in land, as well as its conveyances and encumbrances. In each county, a public recorder's office is charged with recording documents that deal with real property in that county. After a document has been recorded, the public is considered notified regarding all aspects of ownership of the property.

RECORDING SPECIFICS

Recording acts of the individual states provide that, after acknowledgment or being signed before a notary or certain public officials, any instrument or judgment affecting the title to—or possession of—real property may be recorded. Recording permits, rather than requires, the filing of documents that affect title to real property.

The process consists of copying the instrument to be recorded in the proper index, and filing it in alphabetical order, under the names of the parties, without delay. The document must be recorded by the county recorder in the county within which the property is located to be valid there.

When the recorder receives a document to be filed, he or she notes the time and date of filing and at whose request it was filed. After the contents of the document are copied into the record, the original document is marked "filed for record," stamped with the proper time and date of recording, and returned to the person who requested the recording.

The Effect: Public Notice

Public notice may be given in two ways. The process, also known as *constructive notice*, may be given by recording a document in the public records at the county recorder's office. Public notice may also be given by occupying or using the property in such a way as to notify anyone interested that the party in possession is, indeed, the legal owner. Priority wise, whoever records the deed or moves onto the property first holds legal title.

The process of recording gives public, or constructive, notice of the content of any instrument recorded to anyone who cares to look into the records. Recording is considered to be public notice of the information filed there. Possession is also considered constructive notice. A buyer should always check to be sure there is no one living on the property who might have a prior claim to ownership. It is the buyer's duty to conduct proper inquiry before purchasing any property. Failure to do so does not relieve the buyer of that responsibility.

Priorities in Recording

As we have seen, recording laws are meant to protect citizens against fraud and to give others notification of property ownership. Other information that might influence ownership can be recorded also, such as liens and other encumbrances. To obtain priority through recording, a buyer must be a good faith purchaser, for a valuable consideration, and record the deed first.

Priority means the order in which deeds are recorded. Whether or not it is a grant deed, trust deed or some other evidence of a lien or encumbrance, the priority is determined by the date stamped in the upper right-hand corner of the document by the county recorder.

If there are several grant deeds recorded against the property, the one recorded first is valid. In a case where there are several trust deeds recorded against a property, no mention will be made about which one is the first trust deed, which is the second, and so forth.

A person inquiring about the priority of the deeds should look at the time and date the deed was recorded for that information. You will see, as we proceed in our study, the importance of the date and time of recording.

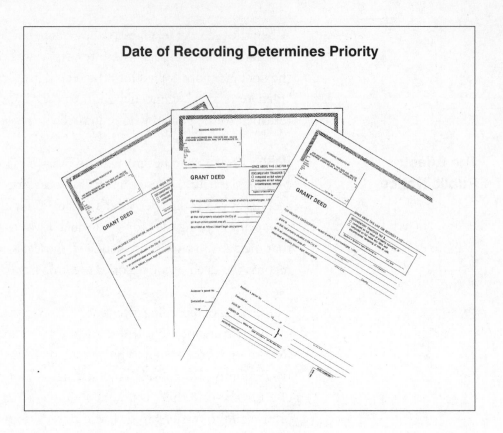

There are certain instruments that are not affected by the priority of recording rule, however. Certain liens, such as tax liens, and mechanic's liens take priority even though they are recorded after a deed. We will discuss liens and encumbrances later in detail, but it is helpful to note here the impact of the recording laws on this subject.

OWNERSHIP OF REAL PROPERTY

All property has an owner, either the government or a private institution or an individual. Title is the evidence that the owner of land is in lawful possession. It is the proof of ownership. Separate ownership and concurrent ownership are the two ways real estate may be owned.

Separate Ownership

Property owned by one person or entity is known as sole and separate, or ownership in severalty. A corporation is known to hold title in severalty, because it is a sole entity.

Concurrent Ownership

When property is owned by two or more persons or entities at the same time, it is known as concurrent ownership, or co-ownership. Concurrent ownership comes in several forms such as *joint tenancy, tenancy in common, community property, tenancy in the entirety* and *tenancy in partnership.*

Five Types of Concurrent Ownership

- Joint tenancy
- Tenancy in common
- Community property
- Tenancy in the entirety
- Tenancy in partnership

Joint Tenancy

When two or more parties own real property as co-owners, with the right of survivorship, it is called joint tenancy. The right of survivorship means that if one of the joint tenants dies, the surviving joint tenant automatically becomes sole owner of the property. The deceased's share does not go to his or her estate or heirs, but becomes the property of the co-tenant without becoming involved in probate. Also, the surviving joint tenant is not liable to creditors of the deceased who hold liens on the joint tenancy property.

In order to have a joint tenancy, there are four unities that must be in existence: *time, title, interest and possession.*

The Four Unities of Joint Tenancy

Time
- All parties must become joint tenants at the same time.

Title
- All parties must take title on the same deed.

Interest
- All parties have an equal undivided interest in the property.

Possession
- All parties have equal right of possession, or an undivided interest.

All four items must occur to have a joint tenancy. If any one of the unities is broken or not present, the joint tenancy is dissolved.

Joint tenants may sell their interest, give it away or borrow money against it, without consent of the other co-owners. Because of the right of survivorship, a joint tenant may not will his or her share, unless there are no other surviving joint tenants.

> *Lisa, Bob, Carol and David are joint tenants. David dies and his interest automatically goes to Lisa, Bob and Carol as joint tenants with equal one-third interests.*
>
> *Kelly and Roger own a house as joint tenants. Roger dies and Kelly now owns the house as her sole and separate property, without probate. Roger's heirs are not entitled to his share because of the right of survivorship.*
>
> *Janet, Caara and Connie own an apartment building together as joint tenants. Connie sells her share to Maria, who becomes a tenant in common with Janet and Caara, with no right of survivorship for Maria. If Maria dies, her heirs will inherit her share, but if Janet or Connie dies, the surviving joint tenant will inherit her share.*

Tenancy in Common

When two or more persons, whose interests are not necessarily equal, are owners of undivided interests in a single estate, a tenancy in common exists. Whenever some other form of ownership or vesting is not mentioned specifically, and there are co-owners, title is assumed to be a tenancy in common.

The only requirement of unity for tenants in common is the equal right of possession or undivided interest—as it is called. That means each owner has a certain equitable interest in the property (such as one-half interest, or one-fourth interest), but has the right to use the whole property. None of the owners may exclude any co-owner from the property, nor claim any portion of the property for exclusive use.

The Four Characteristics of Tenants in Common

- Tenants in common may take title at different times.
- Tenants in common may take title on separate deeds.
- Tenants in common may have unequal interests.
- Tenants in common have an undivided interest or equal right of possession.

Any tenant in common may sell, encumber or will his or her interest, with heirs simply becoming a tenant in common among the others. A tenant in common must pay a proportionate share of any expenses incurred on the property, including money spent for repairs, taxes, loan payments and insurance.

When tenants in common do not agree on matters pertaining to the property, any of the co-owners may file a partition action which asks the court to decide the fate of the investment.

> *Stacey, Craig, Catherine and Dan are joint tenants. Dan sells his interest to Eve. The joint tenancy has been broken regarding the interest Dan had in the property. The new vesting, after the sale of Dan's interest, is Stacey, Craig and Catherine as joint tenants with equal interests, and the right of survivorship, with Eve as a tenant in common.*

> *Stacey, Craig, Catherine and Eve, in the above property, want to restore a joint tenancy with each of the four having the right of survivorship. Eve holds a tenancy in common, so she will have to be added to the joint tenancy. Since all joint tenants must take title at the same time, on the same document, Stacey, Craig, Catherine and Eve must sign a new deed that lists Stacey, Craig and Catherine as joint tenants and Eve as a tenant in common. Then the property can be deeded to all four parties as joint tenants. All requirements for a joint tenancy—time, title, interest and possession—will then be fulfilled.*

Community Property

All property acquired by a husband and wife during a valid marriage—except for certain separate property—is called community property.

Separate Property Includes:

- All property owned before marriage
- All property acquired by either of the parties during marriage by gift or inheritance
- All income derived from separate property

If spouses want to maintain the status of their separate property, they must be very careful not to commingle it with their community property. Separate property (such as an apartment building with a negative cash flow) may not be supported with community property funds, nor can the income of either spouse be used in any way to maintain separate property. Any income, including wages from either spouse, is considered community property.

Community property cannot be sold or encumbered by only one of the partners. Either spouse may *buy* real or personal property without the consent of the other; both are bound by the contract made by either one, unless the new property is bought specifically as separate property, with funds from a separate property account.

However, a married couple in California has three choices when it comes to how they may take title. The first is *joint tenancy*, which includes the right of survivorship if one of the spouses dies but also may include a tax liability for the surviving spouse. The second is *community property*, which does include the right of survivorship, but also includes probate after a spouse dies and all the costs involved in that process. The third type of vesting is *community property with the right of survivorship*, which includes the better of the first two types of vesting. There is no particular tax liability because of the death of a spouse and there is also no probate with its seemingly endless costs.

When title is taken simply as community property, either party may will one-half of the community property. When vesting is community property, if there is no will, the surviving spouse inherits all community property. This is important to know, particularly with multiple marriages, for estate planning. Property may be owned with the intention that it go to one's children, only to learn after the parent's death that children of the first marriage are no longer natural heirs. If there is a subsequent husband or wife and no will has been made, the new spouse will become the natural heir to any property owned or community property.

Regarding separate property, if there is no will, the surviving spouse gets one-half and one child gets one-half. If there is more than one child, the surviving spouse gets one-third and the children get two-thirds.

Do All States Recognize Community Property Law? Nine states—Arizona, California, Idaho, Louisiana, Nevada, New Mexico, Texas, Washington and Wisconsin—use the community property system to determine the interest of a husband and wife in property acquired during marriage. If you now live or previously lived in one of these states, you should be aware that some special rules apply to community property. Any property you may have acquired while living in one of these nine states is probably community property even today.

Tenancy by the Entirety

The foundation for this legal concept is the idea that a husband and wife are an undividable legal entity. The two most important attributes of this form of concurrent ownership are: the surviving spouse becomes the sole owner of the property upon the death of the other, and, secondly, neither spouse has a disposable interest in the property during the lifetime of the other. In other words, it takes two signatures to convey title to another party while both spouses are alive and married to each other. Tenancy by the entirety is much like joint tenancy, with the right of survivorship, except joint tenants can convey title to another party without approval of the other joint tenant. Both husband and wife must sign any conveyance of the property when title is vested in tenancy in the entirety.

The Five Unities of Tenancy by the Entirety

Time
- All parties must become joint tenants at the same time.

Title
- All parties must take title on the same deed.

Interest
- All parties must have an equal undivided interest in the property.

Possession
- All parties have equal right of possession, or an undivided interest.

Unity of person
- A husband and wife are unity of person, requiring agreement from both parties before conveying the property to another person.

Tenancy in Partnership

Ownership by two or more persons who form a partnership for business purposes is known as tenancy in partnership. Each partner has an equal right of possession for the partnership, with the property held in the name of the partnership.

Concurrent Co-Ownership Interests

	Tenancy in Common	Joint Tenancy	Community Property	Partnership Interest
Parties	Two or more persons or entities (can be husband and wife)	Two or more persons (can be husband and wife) provided the tenancy is properly created	Only husband and wife	Only partners (more than one)
Division	Ownership can be divided into any number of interests equal or unequal	Joint tenants have one and the same interest	Ownership interests equal	Ownership interest is in relation to interest in partnership
Title	Each co-owner has a separate title to his/her undivided interest	There is only one title to the whole property	Title is in the "community." Each interest is separate	Title is in the "partnership"
Possession	Equal right of possession	Equal right of possession	Both co-owners have equal possession	Equal right of possession but only for partnership purposes
Conveyance	Each co-owner's interest may be conveyed separately by its owner	All joint tenants must join in any conveyance document. Conveyance by the owner without the others breaks his/her joint tenancy	Real property requires written consent of other spouse, and separate interest cannot be conveyed except upon death	Conveyance of partnership property is generally defined in the partnership agreement. No partner may sell his individual interest in the partnership without the consent of the co-partners

(continued on next page)

Concurrent Co-Ownership Interests   *(continued)*

Death	On co-owner's death his/her interest passes by will to his/her devisees or his/her heirs subject to administration by the local Superior Court. No survivorship right	On co-owner's death the entire tenancy remains to the survivor. The right of survivorship is the primary incident of joint tenancy	On co-owner's death belongs to survivor in severalty, goes by will to decedent's devisee's subject to administration by the local Superior Court	On partner's death his/her partnership interest passes to the surviving partner pending liquidation of the partnership. Share of deceased partner then goes to his estate
Successor's Status	Devisees of heirs become tenancy in common	Last survivor owns property in severalty	If passing by will, tenancy in common between devisee and survivor results	Heir's or devisee's have rights in partnership interest but not in specific property
Creditor's Rights	Co-owner's interest may be sold on execution sale to satisfy his/her creditor. Creditor becomes a tenant in common	Co-owner's interest may be sold on execution sale to satisfy creditor. Joint tenancy is broken, creditor becomes a tenant in common	Property of community is liable for contracts of either spouse, which are made after marriage and prior to or after January 1, 1975. Co-owner's interest can't be sold separately, whole property may be sold on execution to satisfy creditor	Partner's interest cannot be seized or sold separately by his personal creditor but a personal creditor may obtain his share of profits. Whole property may be sold on execution sale to satisfy partnership creditor

CONCURRENT OWNERSHIP BY STATES

	Tenancy in Common	Joint Tenancy	Tenancy by the Entirety	Community Property		Tenancy in Common	Joint Tenancy	Tenancy by the Entirety	Community Property
Alabama	X	X			Missouri	X	X	X	
Alaska	X	X	X		Montana	X	X		
Arizona	X	X		X	Nebraska	X	X		
Arkansas	X	X	X		Nevada	X	X		X
California	X	X		X	New Hampshire	X	X		
Colorado	X	X			New Jersey	X	X	X	
Connecticut	X	X			New Mexico	X	X		X
Delaware	X	X	X		New York	X	X	X	
District of Columbia	X	X	X		North Carolina	X	X	X	
Florida	X	X	X		North Dakota	X	X		
Georgia	X	X			Ohio	X		X	
Hawaii	X	X	X		Oklahoma	X	X	X	
Idaho	X	X		X	Oregon	X		X	
Illinois	X	X			Pennsylvania	X	X	X	
Indiana	X	X	X		Rhode Island	X	X	X	
Iowa	X	X			South Carolina	X	X		
Kansas	X	X			South Dakota	X	X		
Kentucky	X	X	X		Tennesee	X	X	X	
Louisiana				X	Texas	X	X		X
Maine	X	X			Utah	X	X	X	
Maryland	X	X	X		Vermont	X	X	X	
Massachusetts	X	X	X		Virginia	X	X	X	
Michigan	X	X	X		Washington	X	X		X
Minnesota	X	X			West Virginia	X	X	X	
Mississippi	X	X	X		Wisconsin	X	X		
					Wyoming	X	X	X	

LIMITATIONS ON REAL PROPERTY: ENCUMBRANCES

An encumbrance is an interest in real property that is held by someone who is not the owner. Anything that affects the title or the use of the property is an encumbrance. A property is encumbered when it is burdened with legal obligations against the title.

Encumbrances fall into two categories: those that affect the title, known as money encumbrances, and those that affect the use of the property, known as non-money encumbrances. The encumbrances that create a legal obligation to pay are known as liens. A lien uses real property as security for the payment of a debt.

Common types of liens are trust deeds and mortgages; mechanic's liens; tax liens; and special assessments, judgments and attachments . Those types of encumbrances that affect the physical use of the property are easements, building restrictions, and zoning requirements and encroachments.

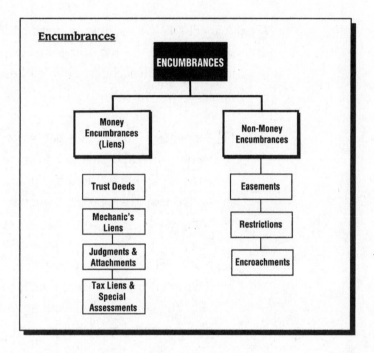

Money Encumbrances (Liens)

A lien is an obligation to pay a money encumbrance that may be voluntary or involuntary. An owner may choose to borrow money, using the property as security for the loan, creating a voluntary lien.

On the other hand, if the owner doesn't pay property taxes or a debt owed, a lien may be placed against his or her property without permission.

A lien may be specific or general. A specific lien is one that is placed against a certain property, while a general lien affects all property of the owner.

Trust Deeds and Mortgages

Trust deeds and mortgages are both instruments used in real estate financing to create voluntary, specific liens against real property. They will be discussed in detail in a later chapter.

Mechanic's Liens

A mechanic's lien may be placed against a property by anyone who has supplied labor or material used to improve real property who does not get paid. A contractor, a subcontractor, a laborer on a job, or any person who furnishes materials such as lumber, plumbing or roofing is eligible to file a mechanic's lien.

A mechanic's lien must be verified and recorded. The law is very time specific about the recording, however. The statutory procedure must be followed exactly if the mechanic's lien is to be valid. Here are the required procedures to be taken.

(1) *Preliminary Notice:* This is a written notice that must be given to the owner within 20 days of first furnishing labor or materials for a job by anyone eligible to file a mechanic's lien. This document gives owners notice that their property may be liened if they do not pay for work completed.

(2) *Notice of Completion:* If the owner files a notice of completion within 10 days after finishing the project, the original contractors have 60 days after the notice is filed, and all others have 30 days after the notice is filed, to record a mechanic's lien.

(3) *No Notice of Completion:* If the owner does not file a notice of completion, all claimants have 90 days from the day work was finished to record a mechanic's lien.

(4) *Foreclosure Action:* After a mechanic's lien is recorded, the claimant has 90 days to bring foreclosure action to enforce the lien. If he or she does not bring action, the lien will be terminated and the claimant loses the right to foreclose.

If an owner discovers unauthorized work on the property, he or she must file a *notice of non-responsibility.* This is a notice that must be recorded and posted on the property to be valid, stating the owner is not responsible for work being done. This notice releases the owner from liability for work done without permission. The owner must file this notice within 10 days after discovering the unauthorized work. The notice normally is posted with a commercial lease at the beginning of a job, if a tenant is ordering the job.

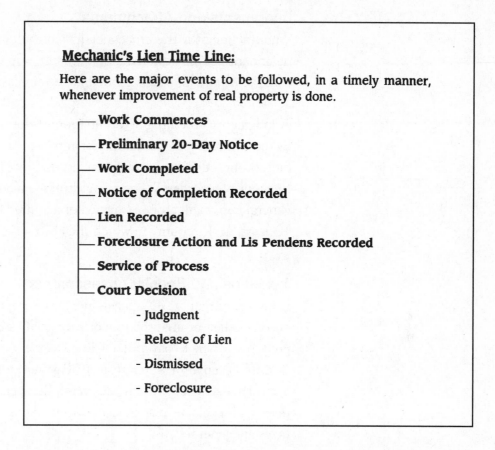

Mechanic's Lien Time Line:

Here are the major events to be followed, in a timely manner, whenever improvement of real property is done.

- Work Commences
- Preliminary 20-Day Notice
- Work Completed
- Notice of Completion Recorded
- Lien Recorded
- Foreclosure Action and Lis Pendens Recorded
- Service of Process
- Court Decision
    - Judgment
    - Release of Lien
    - Dismissed
    - Foreclosure

Determining the starting time for a mechanic's lien is *very* important. A mechanic's lien has priority over any other liens filed *after* the commencement of labor or delivery of materials. That means if there is a foreclosure action, the mechanic's lien would be paid before any other liens that were recorded after work started on the job.

That includes trust deeds or mortgages recorded prior to the filing of the mechanic's lien, but after the start of the work. Lenders will make a physical inspection of the property to determine that no materials have been delivered and no work has been done before recording a construction loan to assure the priority of their trust deed or mortgage.

In the following example, note the mechanic's lien has the priority.

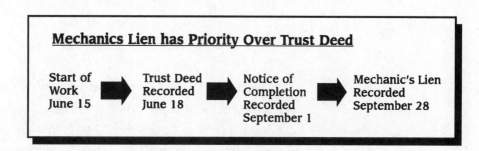

Mechanics Lien has Priority Over Trust Deed

Start of Work June 15 → Trust Deed Recorded June 18 → Notice of Completion Recorded September 1 → Mechanic's Lien Recorded September 28

Judgments and Attachments

An attachment is the process by which the court holds the property of a defendant pending outcome of a lawsuit. An attachment lien is valid for three years and may be extended in certain cases.

A judgment is the final determination of the rights of parties in a lawsuit by the court. A judgment does not automatically create a lien. A summary of the court decision, known as an abstract of judgment, must be filed with the county recorder. When the abstract is filed, the judgment becomes a general lien on all property owned or acquired by the judgment debtor for 10 years, in the county in which the abstract is filed.

Tax Liens and Special Assessments

If any government taxes, such as income or property taxes, are not paid, they become a lien against the property. Special assessments are levied against property owners to pay for local improvements, such as underground utilities, street repair or water projects. Payment for the projects is secured by a special assessment which becomes a lien against real property. Property taxes and special assessments are specific liens, whereas other government taxes are general liens.

Lis Pendens

A lis pendens is a recorded notice that indicates pending litigation affecting the title on a property. It clouds the title, preventing the sale or transfer of the property until removed.

Non-Money Encumbrances

A non-money encumbrance is one that affects the use of property such as an easement, a building restriction or an encroachment.

Easements

An easement is the right to use another's land for a specified purpose, sometimes known as a right-of-way. An interest in an easement is non-possessory. That means the holder of an easement can use it only for the purpose intended and may not exclude anyone else from using it. The right to enter onto a property using an easement is called *ingress*. Exit from a property using an easement is called *egress*.

The party giving the easement is known as the servient tenement. The servient tenement is the one encumbered by the easement. The party receiving the benefit of the easement is known as the dominant tenement. An easement is appurtenant to the dominant tenement.

As you recall, the definition of real property included anything appurtenant to the land. Anything used for the benefit of the land is appurtenant to it. An easement appurtenant automatically goes with the sale of the dominant tenement.

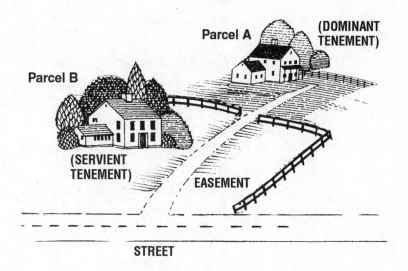

It is possible to have an easement that is not appurtenant to any particular land. Thus, Jacob—who owns no land—may have an easement over Salvadore's land for the purpose of getting to the stream where he regularly fishes. Or a commercial camping enterprise may use an easement over private property to take clients to remote sites, which might be inaccessible otherwise.

Public utilities also have easements that are not appurtenant to any one parcel. These easements are known as easements in gross. Make sure you understand the difference between an easement in gross and a license. An easement may not be terminated arbitrarily, as you will see in the following section. However, a license to use may be revoked at any time.

Easements are created in various ways—commonly by express grant or reservation in a grant deed or by a written agreement between owners of adjoining land. An easement always should be recorded to assure its continued existence. It is recorded by the party benefiting from the easement as the dominant tenement.

There are five ways to create an easement.

(1) *Express Grant:* The servient tenement, or the giver of the easement, grants the easement by deed or express agreement.

(2) *Express Reservation:* The seller of a parcel who owns adjoining land reserves an easement or right-of-way over the former property. It is created at the time of the sale with a deed or express agreement.

(3) *Implied Grant or Reservation:* The existence of an easement is obvious and necessary at the time a property is conveyed, even though no mention is made of it in the deed.

(4) *Necessity:* An easement created when a parcel is completely land locked and has no access. It is automatically terminated when another way to enter and leave the property becomes available.

(5) *Prescription:* An easement by prescription may be created by continuous and uninterrupted use, by a single party, for a period of five years. The use must be against the owner's wishes and be open and notorious. The party wishing to obtain the prescriptive easement must have some reasonable claim to the use of the property.

Easements may be terminated or extinguished in the following ways.

- *Express Release:* The only one who can release an easement is the dominant tenement.

- *Legal Proceedings:* Quiet title action to terminate the easement brought by the servient tenement against the dominant tenement.

- *Merger:* This joins the dominant tenement and the servient tenement.

- *Non-Use:* When applied to a prescriptive easement for a period of 5 years, this terminates the easement.

- *Abandonment:* Obvious and intentional surrender of the easement.

- *Destruction of the Servient Tenement:* If the government takes the servient tenement for its use, as in eminent domain, the easement is terminated.

- *Adverse Possessions:* The owner of the servient tenement may, by his or her own use, prevent the dominant tenement from using the easement for a period of 5 years, thus terminating the easement.

Restrictions

Another type of encumbrance is a restriction. This is a limitation placed on the use of property and may be placed by a private owner, a developer or the government. It is usually placed on property to assure that land use is consistent and uniform within a certain area.

Restrictions are created in the deed at the time of sale by the grantor, or in the general plan of a subdivision by the developer. For example, a developer may use a height restriction to ensure views from each parcel in a subdivision.

When there is a conflict between local minimum building requirements and subdivision regulations, the developer must comply with whichever is the most restrictive.

Private restrictions are placed by a present or past owner and affect only a specific property or development, while zoning is an example of government restrictions that benefit the general public.

Restrictions are commonly known as CC&Rs, or Covenants, Conditions and Restrictions. A covenant is a promise to do or not do certain things. The penalty for a breach of a covenant is usually money damages. An example of a covenant might be that the tenant agrees to make some repairs, or that a property may be used only for a specific purpose.

A condition is much the same as a covenant, a promise to do or not do something (usually a limitation on the use of the property), except the penalty for breaking a condition is return of the property to the grantor.

A *condition subsequent* is a restriction, placed in a deed at the time of conveyance, upon future use of the property. Upon breach of the condition subsequent, the grantor may take back the property. A *condition precedent* requires that a certain event, or condition, occur before title can pass to the new owner.

Encroachments

The placement of permanent improvements on adjacent property owned by another is known as an encroachment. Fences, walls or buildings can encroach on adjoining land and limit its use. An owner has 3 years to remove an unauthorized encroachment.

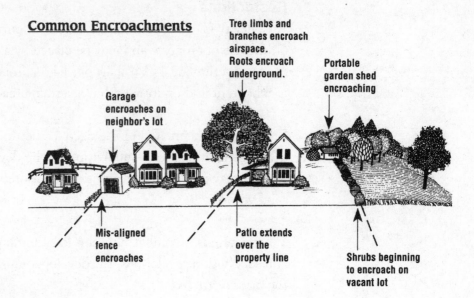

Common Encroachments

Garage encroaches on neighbor's lot

Tree limbs and branches encroach airspace. Roots encroach underground.

Portable garden shed encroaching

Mis-aligned fence encroaches

Patio extends over the property line

Shrubs beginning to encroach on vacant lot

HOMESTEAD EXEMPTION

One of the greatest advantages of a home investment is that, in many states, personal residences are legally protected from the claims of many creditors due to the benefit of a *homestead exemption*.

The purpose of a homestead exemption is to limit the amount of liability for certain debts against which a home can be used to satisfy a judgment. Even though a *declared homestead* will protect a home against creditors of certain types whose claims might be enforced through judgment liens, few areas of real property law are more misunderstood by consumers.

Declared homestead exemption laws may be different in each state. Kansas, Florida, Iowa, South Dakota and Texas provide an unlimited dollar value homestead exemption. Florida and Texas, in fact , are well known as debtor-friendly states because of their homestead exemptions. The Florida homestead exemption is especially valuable because a U.S. Court of Appeals has held that the exemption applies even when the owner acquires or enlarges it with the intent of defrauding creditors.

States with no dollar cap on their homestead exemption do limit the exemption to a certain area of land, which is much larger in rural areas. For example, in Florida the exemption is limited to half an acre in the city and 160 contiguous acres elsewhere. In practice, this limitation will only rarely be a factor.

In contrast, Delaware, the District of Columbia, Maryland, New Jersey, Pennsylvania and Rhode Island provide no specific homestead exemption.

Most states offer exemptions between these extremes. Even here, however, the exemption can be anywhere along the spectrum. For example, the exemption is $25,000 in Ohio, $80,000 in North Dakota and $550,000 in Nevada.

Under the federal bankruptcy provisions, the homestead exemption is $150,000. Where a state's homestead exemption is lower than $150,000, a consumer contemplating a bankruptcy filing should consider using the federal exemption (if the state law permits it), all other things being equal.

The homestead exemption is considered such a basic and important right in some states, including Florida and Texas, that it is mandated by the states' constitutions. This prevents the state's legislature from modifying or repealing the exemption by statute.

Generally, consensual liens, such as mortgages, cannot be eliminated inside or outside of bankruptcy, even when they are attached to property subject to an exemption. Thus, the homestead exemption can actually be worth nothing if the home is very heavily mortgaged.

Some states require individuals to record their homestead exemption at the county recording office, or wherever legal documents are normally recorded in the state. If the exemption is not recorded, a homeowner may not be able to use it. In some of these states, recording must take place before bankruptcy filing, while in others, recording must occur before a forced sale of the home. In some states, recording is optional, and may give no greater rights than if the homeowner hadn't filed the papers. It isn't necessary to sort out all the differences. If recording is allowed or required, the homeowner should simply record the homestead exemption.

The following states allow, or require, the recording of the homestead exemption.

Recordation of the Homestead Exemption		
Alabama	Massachusetts	Texas
Arkansas	Michigan	Utah
California	Montana	Virginia
Florida	Nebraska	Washington
Idaho	Nevada	
Iowa	South Dakota	

Obligations Unaffected by the Declaration

Over the years the homestead exemption amount has been increased from time to time. The validity of a homestead, however, depends not only upon the recordation of the homestead declaration but on certain off-record matters as well, such as actual residency in the declared homestead dwelling at the time the declaration is recorded and an actual interest in the dwelling.

Homestead Declaration Protection

The homestead declaration does not protect the homestead from all forced sales. The home may be subject to forced sale if a judgment is obtained:

- Prior to the recording of the homestead declaration
- On debts secured by the encumbrances on the property executed by the owner before the declaration was filed for record
- On obligations secured by mechanic's liens on the property

Contents of the Declaration of Homestead

A recorded homestead declaration will contain all of the following.

- The name of the declared homestead owner. A husband and wife both may be named as declared homestead owners in the same homestead declaration if each owns an interest in the dwelling selected as the declared homestead.

- A description of the declared homestead.

- A statement that the declared homestead is the principal dwelling of the declared homestead owner or such person's spouse, and that the declared homestead owner or such person's spouse resides in the declared homestead on the date the homestead declaration is recorded.

Effect of Recording— How Terminated

When a valid declaration of homestead has been filed in the office of the county recorder where the property is located, containing all of the statements and information required by law, the property becomes a homestead protected from execution and forced sale, except as otherwise provided by the statute, and it remains so until terminated by conveyance, abandoned by a recorded instrument of abandonment, or sold at execution sale. A homestead declaration does not restrict or limit any right to convey or encumber the declared homestead.

```
┌──────────────────────────────────────────────┐
│  RECORDING REQUESTED BY                        │
│                                                │
│  AND WHEN RECORDED MAIL TO                     │
│  NAME                                          │
│  STREET                                        │
│  ADDRESS                                       │
│  CITY                                          │
│  STATE                                         │
│  ZIP                                           │
└──────────────────────────────────────────────┘
```

(SPACE ABOVE THIS LINE FOR RECORDER'S USE)

HOMESTEAD DECLARATION

I, _____
(Full Name of Declarant)

do hereby certify and declare as follows:

(1) I hereby claim as a declared homestead the premises located in the City of _____.

County of _____, State of _____ commonly known as

_____
(Street Address)

and more particularly described as follows: [Give complete legal description]

(2) I am the declared homestead owner of the above declared homestead.

(3) I own the following interest in the above declared homestead:

(4) The above declared homestead is [strike inapplicable clause] my principal dwelling, the principal dwelling of my spouse, and [strike inapplicable clause] I am / my spouse is currently residing on that declared homestead.

(5) The facts stated in this Declaration are true as of my personal knowledge.

Dated: _____, 19___   _____
(Signature of Declarant)

STATE OF _____ }
COUNTY OF _____ } ss.

On _____ before me, _____
(Name, title of officer-i.e., "Jane Doe, Notary Public")

personally appeared _____

personally known to me (or proved to me on the basis of satisfactory evidence) to be the person(s) whose name(s) is/are subscribed to the within instrument and acknowledged to me that he/she/they executed the same in his/her/their authorized capacity(ies), and that by his/her/their signature(s) on the instrument the person(s), or the entity upon behalf of which the person(s) acted, executed the instrument.

WITNESS my hand and official seal.

_____
Signature

(Seal)

WOLCOTTS FORM 756—HOMESTEAD DECLARATION —Rev. 1-93
(price class 3)   ©1993 WOLCOTTS FORMS, INC.

This standard form is intended for the typical situations encountered in the field indicated. However, before you sign, read it, fill in all blanks, and make whatever changes are appropriate and necessary to your particular transaction. Consult a lawyer if you doubt the form's fitness for your purpose and use.

Federal Homestead Act of 1862

The declared homestead discussed above has nothing to do with the term "homesteading" as applied to filings on federal lands whereby a person acquired title to acreage by establishing residence or making improvements upon the land.

The purpose of the Federal Homestead Act of 1862 was to encourage settlement of the nation. Except for Alaska, homesteading was discontinued on public lands in 1976 when, because all the good agricultural land had already been homesteaded/deeded, Congress recognized that the Homestead Act had outlived its usefulness and passed the Federal Land Policy and Management Act of 1976, which immediately repealed the old law as it applied to all states except Alaska.

ASSURING MARKETABILITY OF TITLE

A marketable title does not mean a perfect title. It means that the title is one a reasonable person would accept as clear and free from likely challenge. The documentary record of ownership, or the *chain of title* in the recorder's office in the county where the property is located, becomes very important in determining who actually owns what.

Before reliable histories of properties came into existence, abstractors investigated the status of title to property. They searched available records and pertinent documents, and prepared a summary called an *abstract of title*. This listed all the conveyances and any other facts relating to the property for a prospective buyer or lender to inspect. This chain of title, along with an attorney's opinion, was the original basis for establishing marketable title.

In time, these records—kept in a title plant—were used to supply interested parties with a certificate of title. This stated that the property was found to be properly vested in the present owner, subject to noted encumbrances. The next step was the *guarantee of title* under which the title insurance company provided written assurances about the title to real property, insuring against loss.

TITLE INSURANCE

Finally, title insurance companies, responding to the public need, began issuing policies of title insurance. The main benefit: Title insurance extends protection against matters of record and many non-recorded types of risks, depending on the type of policy purchased.

A standard policy of title insurance, in addition to matters of record, protects against:

- Off-record hazards such as forgery, impersonation, or failure of a party to be legally competent to make a contract

- The possibility that a deed of record was not in fact delivered with intent to convey title

- The loss which might arise from the lien of federal estate taxes, which is effective without notice upon death

- The expense incurred in defending the title

A standard policy does *not* protect against:

- Defects in the title known to the holder to exist at the date of the policy, but not previously disclosed to the title insurance company

- Easements and liens which are not shown by the public records

- Rights or claims of persons in physical possession of the land, but whose claims are not shown by the public records

- Rights or claims not shown by public records, yet which could be discovered by physical inspection of the land

- Mining claims

- Reservations in patents or water rights

- Zoning ordinances

Most of these risks are covered by a policy that may be purchased at added cost called an extended policy. The American Land Title Association offers an owner's extended coverage policy known as A.L.T.A. that includes the same coverage as a standard policy, with the following additions.

- Protection against claims of parties in physical possession of the property, but no recorded interest

- Reservations in patents

- Unmarketability of title

Lenders may also purchase an A.L.T.A. policy, with the same extended coverage, to protect against loss of their investment in the property because of a defective title.

Policies of title insurance are now commonly used throughout California, usually in the standardized forms prepared by the California Land Title Association, which is the trade organization of the title companies in the state.

Every title insurer must adopt and make available to the public a schedule of fees and charges for title policies. In addition, each title insurance company must have on deposit with the Insurance Commissioner a guarantee fund for the protection of title insurance policy holders.

CHAPTER QUIZ

1. Which of the following is benefited by an easement appurtenant?

    a. dominant tenement
    b. servient tenement
    c. the easement
    d. the owner of the servient tenement

2. Vesting refers to:

    a. co-ownership
    b. how property is owned
    c. something to wear
    d. syndication

3. Debby and Jeff, brother and sister, want to buy a property together. Which of the following vestings would not be considered?

    a. joint tenants
    b. tenants in common
    c. community property
    d. tenancy in partnership

4. How does a corporation take title to real property?

    a. joint tenancy
    b. community property
    c. tenancy in common
    d. severalty

5. If the interest each person has in a tenancy in common is not stated in the deed:

    a. it is presumed to be a joint tenancy
    b. it is understood that each owner has an equal interest
    c. it is voidable
    d. it is invalid

6. All of the following are liens against real property except:

    a. a judgment
    b. a trust deed
    c. property taxes
    d. encroachments

7. Agreements affecting the use of real property are known as:

    a. covenants, conditions and restrictions
    b. trust deeds
    c. lis pendens
    d. liens

8. Deed restrictions are imposed on a property by:

    a. the legislature
    b. the developer
    c. Board of Equalization
    d. city council

9. Which of the following is a legal, non-exclusive use of someone else's property?

    a. adverse possession
    b. trespassing
    c. an easement
    d. condemnation

10. A claimant has how many days to bring foreclosure action after a mechanic's lien is recorded?

    a. 40
    b. 50
    c. 90
    d. 120

ANSWERS

1. *a*
2. *b*
3. *c*
4. *d*
5. *b*
6. *d*
7. *a*
8. *b*
9. *c*
10. *c*

Instruments of Finance

INTRODUCTION

Imagine buying a house and being required to pay the total price in cash. The sweet pleasure of home ownership probably would belong somewhere in the next century for most of us. With the average price of a single family home being so high, buying a home would be unthinkable without the practical benefit of financing.

By allowing a home buyer to obtain a loan for the difference between the sales price and the down payment, real estate lenders have provided the solution to the problem of how property can be bought and sold without the requirement of an all-cash sale.

What started out as a simple loan by a local bank—with an agreement that the borrower pay it all back in a timely manner—is now a complex subject. Buyers and sellers need to rely on experts to explain all the choices there are on financing the purchase or sale of property.

HOW DOES IT WORK?

When a loan is made, the borrower signs a promissory note, or note—as it is called, which states that a certain amount of money has been borrowed. The note, then, is the evidence of the debt.

When money is loaned for the purpose of financing real property, some kind of *collateral*, or security, is usually required as well as the promise to pay the money back. That means the lender wants some concrete assurance of getting the money back beyond the borrower's written promise to pay. The property being bought or borrowed against is typically used as security, or collateral, for the debt. In other words, the lender feels more secure about making the loan if assured of the property ownership in case of default, or nonpayment, of the loan. Then the lender can sell it to get the loan money back.

Depending on which state the property being financed is in, the note is secured by either a trust deed or mortgage. After signing the promissory note, the borrower is required to execute a *trust deed* or *mortgage* at the same time, which is the security guaranteeing loan repayment. This is known as *hypothecation*, a process that allows a borrower to remain in possession of the property while using it to secure the loan. If the borrower does not make payments per the agreement, he or she then loses the rights of possession and ownership.

The lender holds the trust deed, along with the note, until the loan is repaid.

About the Note and Trust Deed or Mortgage

The promissory note is the evidence of the debt, or the money borrowed, and the trust deed or mortgage is the security for the debt.

The trust deed allows the lender, in case of loan default, to order the trustee to sell the property described in the deed. A mortgage allows the lender, itself, to foreclose on the property. Both trust deed and mortgage will be explained in detail in later chapters.

When a buyer obtains a loan to purchase property, he or she is using the lender's money to finance the sale. This is known as *leverage*. The use of borrowed capital to buy real estate is a process that permits the buyer to use little of one's own money and large amounts of someone else's.

There are several reasons leverage is appealing to both the home buyer and the investor. The principal advantage to the home buyer is not having to amass the entire purchase price to become a home owner. The investor can use leverage to control several investments, rather than just one, each purchased with a small amount of personal funds, and a large amount of a lender's money. The investor can then earn a return on each property, therefore increasing the amount of yield on investment dollars.

PROMISSORY NOTE

A *promissory note* is a written promise to pay back a certain sum of money at specified terms at an agreed upon time. Sometimes it is simply called the note. Informally, it could be called an I.O.U. The *maker* is the person borrowing the money, or making the note. It is a personal obligation of the borrower and a complete contract in itself, between the borrower and lender. The *holder* is loaning the money, or the one holding the note.

According to the Uniform Commercial Code, to be valid or enforceable, a promissory note must meet certain requirements.

A Promissory Note Is:

- An unconditional written promise to pay a certain sum of money
- Made by one person to another, both able to legally enter into a contract
- Signed by the maker, or borrower
- Payable on demand or at a definite time
- Paid to bearer or to order
- Voluntarily delivered by the borrower and accepted by the lender

NOTE

November 15, 20XX

Property Address

1. BORROWER'S PROMISE TO PAY

In return for a loan that I have received, I promise to pay **Three Hundred Forty Nine Thousand Three Hundred and 00/100** Dollars (U.S. **$349,300.00**) (this amount will be called "Principal"), plus Interest, to the order of the Note Holder. The Principal may include points, origination fees and other amounts permitted by applicable law. The Note Holder is **Wonderful Bank of Anywhere, National Association**, a national banking association organized and existing under the laws of the United States of America. I understand that the Note Holder may transfer this Note. The Note Holder or anyone who takes this Note and who is entitled to receive payments under this Note will be called the "Note Holder."

2. INTEREST

I will pay Interest at an annual rate of **6.23%** ("Interest"). Interest will be charged on the unpaid Principal and will continue until the full amount of Principal has been paid. Interest shall continue to accrue at this rate after the maturity or default of this loan. Each payment I make on this Note will be applied first to scheduled Interest, next to unpaid Principal, and then other charges, if any, until the entire indebtedness, evidenced by this Note, is fully paid.

3. PAYMENTS

I will pay Principal plus Interest by making payments each month ("monthly payments"). My monthly payment will be the sum of U.S. **$2,146.16**.

[X] If checked, I will make **360** monthly payments on the **1st** day of each month beginning on **January 01, 2003**. If on, **December 01, 2032**, any sum still remains unpaid, I will pay what I owe in full on that date.

[ ] **If checked, this loan contains a Balloon Payment feature.** I will make _____ monthly payments on the _____ day of each month beginning on _____. These payments are based upon a _____ month amortization. I understand that these payments will not completely amortize the outstanding Principal, Interest and other charges, and that there will be an outstanding balance remaining on my loan at maturity. I agree to pay the Note Holder in full the remaining outstanding Principal balance plus Interest and any other charges which are due under the terms of this Note in a single balloon payment which shall be due and payable on _____.

I will make my monthly payments payable to GoodEq Servicing Corporation and mailed to P. O. Box 55555, Anywhere, CA 00000-0000, or at a different address if required by the Note Holder.

I agree that if, during the term of this Note, if in the Note Holder's sole discretion, the Note Holder permits me to modify or defer my obligation to the Note Holder, or request other services related to servicing or administering my loan for which the Note Holder has a scheduled charge, I will pay the Note Holder the then-current fee for such services or request if the Note Holder agrees to perform such service or request.

4. BORROWER'S FAILURE TO PAY AS REQUIRED

(A) **Late Charge for Overdue Payments:** If the Note Holder has not received the full amount of any of my monthly payments by the end of fifteen (15) calendar days after the date it is due, I will promptly pay a late charge to the Note Holder. The amount of the charge will be four (4%) of the full monthly payment. I will pay this late charge only once on any late monthly payment.

(B) **Default:** I will be in default under this Note if any of the following things happen:
   (1) if I fail to make any payment or comply with any of the terms of this Note or any other note with the Note Holder now or in the future; or
   (2) if I make any false, incorrect or misleading representation or warranty at any time during the application process; or
   (3) if I die or become involved in any bankruptcy or insolvency proceeding; or
   (4) if I fail to abide by the term(s) of any Security Instrument which secures payment of this Note; or
   (5) if I fail to furnish financial statements or other financial information reasonably requested by the Note Holder.
   I understand that the loan is subject to repayment in full upon demand of the Note Holder in the event the real estate securing this debt is sold, conveyed or otherwise transferred.

(C) **Notice of Default:** If I am in default, then the entire Principal balance, accrued Interest fees, and collection costs, permitted to be collected under applicable law will be immediately due and payable. At its option or if required by law, the Note Holder may send me a written notice informing me of said default and acceleration. If I make any payment after the Note Holder has demanded payment of the entire balance due, my payment will be applied to the Unpaid Balance due under the Note. The Unpaid Balance consists of the Principal Amount remaining due, plus accrued finance charges, unpaid late charges, collection costs, and all other amounts due to the Note Holder under this Note. The Note Holder shall also have other rights and remedies provided by law. If the net proceeds of collateral sold do not pay my indebtedness in full, I will pay the Note Holder the difference, plus Interest at the Note Interest Rate until the Unpaid Balance is paid in full. Any default of this Note will also constitute an event of default of any separate Mortgage, Deed of Trust or Security Deed securing this Note ("Security Instrument"). Upon default, Note Holder may proceed to enforce the terms of the Note or enforce any rights that it may have under the Security Instrument.

(D) **No Waiver by Note Holder:** Even if, at a time when I am in default, the Note Holder does not require me to pay immediately in full as described above, the Note Holder will still have the right to do so if I am in default at a later time.

(E) **Payment of Note Holder's Costs and Expenses:** If the Note Holder has required me to pay immediately in full as described above, the Note Holder will have the right to be paid back for all of its costs and expenses to the extent not prohibited by applicable law. Those expenses include, for example, reasonable attorneys' fees for an attorney who is not the Note Holders salaried employee, foreclosure fees and court costs.

(F) **Check Collection Charges:** If I present the Note Holder with a check, negotiable order of withdrawal, share draft or other instrument in payment that is returned or dishonored for any reason, I will pay a check collection charge to the Note Holder for each time such instrument is returned. The amount of the charge will not be greater than U.S $25.00.

5. THIS NOTE SECURED BY A SECURITY INSTRUMENT

In addition to the protections given to the Note Holder under this Note, the Security Instrument, on real property (the "Property") described in the Security Instrument and dated the same date as this Note, protects the Note Holder from possible losses which might result if I do not keep the promises which I make in this Note. The Security Instrument describes how and under what conditions I may also be required to make immediate payment in full of all amounts I owe under this Note. I agree to these conditions. I acknowledge that I may obtain property insurance and/or credit life insurance from any insured.

6. BORROWER'S PAYMENTS BEFORE THEY ARE DUE

Subject to the order of application of payments described in Section 2, I have the right to make payments of Principal at any time before they are due. A prepayment of all of the unpaid Principal is known as a "full prepayment." A prepayment of only part of the unpaid Principal is known as a "partial prepayment."

If I make a partial prepayment, my next due date will not be advanced. I must still make each subsequent payment as it becomes due and in the same amount.

[ ] If checked, I may make a full or partial prepayment at any time without penalty.

[X] If checked, I may make a full or partial prepayment at any time, however, if within the first 24 months from the date of this loan I make any full prepayment of the Principal amount of this loan, I will pay a prepayment charge equal to 2% of the outstanding Principal balance.

7. BORROWER'S WAIVERS

I waive my rights to require the Note Holder to do certain things. Those things are (a) to demand payment of amounts due (known as "presentment"); (b) to give notice that amounts due have not been paid (known as "notice of dishonor"); and (c) to obtain an official certification of nonpayment (known as "protest"). Anyone else who agrees to keep the promises made in this Note, or who agrees to make payments to the Note Holder if I fail to keep my promises under this Note, or who signs this Note to transfer it to someone else, also waives these rights. These persons are known as "guarantors," "sureties" and "endorsers."

8. GIVING OF NOTICES

Unless applicable law requires a different method, any notice that must be given to me under this Note will be given by delivering it or by mailing it by first class mail addressed to me at the Property Address described herein. A notice will be delivered or mailed to me at a different address if I give the Note Holder a notice of my different address.

Any notice that must be given to the Note Holder under this Note will be given by mailing it by first class mail to the Note Holder at the address stated in Section 3. A notice will be mailed to the Note Holder at a different address if I am given a notice of that different address.

9. PAYMENT IN FULL

I AGREE THAT THE NOTE HOLDER MAY ACCEPT PAYMENTS MARKED "PAID IN FULL" WITHOUT ANY LOSS OF THE NOTE HOLDERS RIGHTS UNDER THIS NOTE UNLESS I SEND THEM FOR SPECIAL HANDLING TO GOODEQ SERVICING CORPORATION, 4837 BETTY AVENUE, SUITE 000 , SOUTH YOURTOWN, CA 00000, ATTN: PAYOFF PROCESSING – M05334.

10. RESPONSIBILITY OF PERSONS UNDER THIS NOTE

If more than one person signs this Note, each of us is fully and personally obligated to pay the full amount owed and to keep all of the promises made in this Note. Any guarantor, surety, or endorser of this Note (as described in Section 7 above) is also obligated to do these things. The Note Holder may enforce its rights under this Note against each of us individually or against all of us together. This means that any one of us may be required to pay all of the amounts owed under this Note. Any person who takes over my rights or obligations under this Note will have all of my rights and must keep all of my promises made in this Note. Any person who takes over the rights or obligations of a guarantor, surety, or endorser of this Note (as described in Section 7 above) is also obligated to keep all of the promises made in this Note. This Note is intended by Note Holder and me as a complete and exclusive statement of its terms, there being no conditions to the enforceability of this Note. This Note may not be supplemented or modified except in writing signed by me and the Note Holder. This Note benefits Note Holder, its successors and assigns, and binds me and my heirs, personal representatives and assigns.

11. APPLICABLE LAW

This Note shall be governed by the laws of the State of Anywhere and applicable federal law. If a law which applies to this loan and sets maximum loan charges is finally interpreted so that the Interest and other charges collected or to be collected in connection with this loan exceed the permitted limits, then: (A) any such Interest or other charge shall be reduced by the amount necessary to reduce the Interest or other charge to the permitted limit; and (B) any sums already collected from me which exceeded permitted limits will be refunded to me. The

Note Holder may choose to make this refund by reducing the Principal I owe under this Note or by making a direct payment to me. If a refund reduces Principal, the reduction will be treated as a partial payment.

12. EXTENSIONS AND MODIFICATIONS

All endorsers, sureties and guarantors and I further consent to any and all extensions of time, renewals, waivers or modifications which may be granted or consented to by the Note Holder as to the time of payment or any other provision of this Note. If an extension, renewal or modification is made to this Note, I agree to pay a charge, as additional Interest, of the greater of $50.00 or one-quarter (1/4) of one percent (1%) of the loan balance then outstanding. All makers, sureties, guarantors, and endorsers hereby waive presentment, notice of dishonor, and protest hereof. This Note is the joint and several obligation of each maker and shall be binding upon them and their heirs, successors and assigns.

NOTICE TO BORROWER:

1. **CAUTION – IT IS IMPORTANT THAT YOU READ ALL PAGES OF THIS NOTE BEFORE YOU SIGN IT.**
2. **DO NOT SIGN THIS NOTE IF IT CONTAINS ANY BLANK SPACES.**
3. **You are entitled to a copy of this Note.**
4. **You acknowledge receipt of a completed copy of this Note.**
5. **This Note provides for the payment of a penalty if you wish to repay the loan prior to the date provided for repayment in this Note.**

By signing and sealing this Note, I agree under seal to the terms set forth above.

_____[SEAL]

_____[SEAL]

(Sign Original Only)

Negotiable Instrument

A *negotiable instrument* is a written unconditional promise or order to pay a certain amount of money at a definite time or on demand.

A promissory note is a negotiable instrument. It is a written promise or order to pay money. The most common type of negotiable instrument is an ordinary bank check. A check is an order to the bank to pay money to the person named. A promissory note is the same thing. It can be transferred by endorsement (signature), just like a check. If correctly prepared, it is considered the same as cash.

In order to be considered a negotiable instrument, however, the document must be consistent with statutory definition and all of the following elements must be present.

A Negotiable Promissory Note Must Be:

- Signed by the maker or drawer
- An unconditional promise or order to pay a certain amount in money
- Payable on demand or at a definite time
- Payable to order or bearer

Types of Promissory Notes

Commonly, a promissory note is referred to as "the note" and we shall do the same here as we study the basic types of notes in use as evidence of a debt. A promissory note may stand alone as an unsecured loan or note, or may be secured by either a trust deed or mortgage. The promissory note, however, is the prime instrument, and if there are conflicts in the terms of the note and trust deed or mortgage, generally the terms of the note are controlling.

There are several types of promissory notes, each with a different kind of obligation made clear by the terms of the note. Some promissory notes have a fixed interest rate, where the interest rate and term do not change over the life of the loan. Others may include a movable interest rate as well as changes in the payment over the life of the loan.

Fully Amortized Note

A *fully amortized note* is the most common type of loan with institutional lenders. Interest is charged on the outstanding principal balance (original loan amount plus any loan costs that the borrower wants to add instead of paying them at the time of funding the loan) at the rate and term agreed upon by the lender and borrower. After the interest is calculated for the term of the loan and added to the principal to obtain the amount to be *amortized*, payments are determined by dividing that amount (principal plus interest) by the number of payments in the term of the loan. Regular, periodic payments of both interest and principal are made, which pay off the debt completely by the end of the term.

A common type of fully amortized note is a fixed-rate loan. These types of loans are available for 30 years, 20 years, 15 years and even 10 years. There are also bi-weekly mortgages, which shorten the loan by calling for half the monthly payment every two weeks. (Since there are 52 weeks in a year, the borrower makes 26 payments, or 13 months worth, every year.)

Fixed rate, fully amortizing loans have two distinct features. First, the interest rate remains fixed for the life of the loan. Secondly, the payments remain level for the life of the loan and are structured to repay the loan by the end of the loan term. The most common fixed rate loans are 15-year and 30-year loans.

During the early amortization period, a large percentage of the monthly payment is used for paying the interest. As the loan is paid down, more of the monthly payment is applied to principal. A typical 30-year, fixed rate mortgage takes 22.5 years of level payments to pay half of the original loan amount.

Monthly Average Rate for 30 Year Fixed Rate Mortgages

	2007		2006		2005		2004		2003	
	Rate	Pts	Rate	Pts	Rate	Pts	Rate	Pts	Rate	Pts
January	6.22	0.4	6.15	0.5	5.71	0.7	5.71	0.7	5.92	0.6
February	6.29	0.4	6.25	0.6	5.63	0.7	5.64	0.7	5.84	0.6
March	6.16	0.4	6.32	0.6	5.93	0.7	5.45	0.7	5.75	0.6
April	6.18	0.5	6.51	0.6	5.86	0.6	5.83	0.7	5.81	0.6
May	6.26	0.4	6.60	0.5	5.72	0.6	6.27	0.7	5.48	0.6
June	6.66	0.4	6.68	0.5	5.58	0.6	6.29	0.6	5.23	0.6
July	6.70	0.4	6.76	0.5	5.70	0.5	6.06	0.6	5.63	0.5
August	6.57	0.4	6.52	0.4	5.82	0.5	5.87	0.7	6.26	0.7
September	6.38	0.5	6.40	0.5	5.77	0.6	5.75	0.7	6.15	0.6
October	6.38	0.5	6.36	0.4	6.07	0.5	5.72	0.7	5.95	0.6
November	6.21	0.4	6.24	0.5	6.33	0.6	5.73	0.6	5.93	0.6
December	6.10	0.5	6.14	0.4	6.27	0.5	5.75	0.6	5.88	0.7
Annual Average	**6.34**	**0.4**	**6.41**	**0.5**	**5.87**	**0.6**	**5.84**	**0.7**	**5.83**	**0.6**

Source: Freddie Mac - http://www.freddiemac.com

Partially Amortized Installment Note

A *partially amortized installment note* calls for regular, periodic payments on the principal, or amount loaned. Interest accrues during the term of the loan, to be paid at the end, along with any surplus principal that has not been paid. This type of note is most likely to be used by private lenders.

Straight Note

A *straight note* calls for payment of interest only, or no payments, during the term of the note, with all *accrued* money (either principal only, or principal and interest if no payments have been made) due and payable on a certain date. This type of note is not common with an institutional lender, but may be used between a buyer and seller or other private lenders.

Adjustable Rate Mortgage (ARM)

An adjustable note, or ARM—*adjustable rate mortgage*, is one whose interest rate is tied to a movable economic index. The interest rate in the note varies upward or downward over the term of the loan, depending on the money market conditions and an agreed upon index.

This type of loan was first offered as a result of the major recession and banking crisis in the early 1980s. Currently, these ARMs come in all flavors. The basic adjustable loan, however, is one whose interest rate is tied to a certain government economic index.

A lender may offer several choices of interest rate, term, payments, or adjustment periods to a borrower with an ARM. The initial interest rate is determined by the current rate of the chosen index. Then, a *margin*, which might be anywhere from one to three percentage points, is added to the initial interest rate to determine the actual beginning rate the borrower will pay. The margin is maintained for the life of the loan and does not change. The interest rate may change, however, as the chosen index changes, depending on economic conditions that lead it.

The borrower's payment will stay the same for a specified time period, which might be six months or a year, depending on the agreement with the lender. At the agreed upon time, the lender re-evaluates the loan to determine if the index has changed, either up or down, and calculates a new payment based on the changed interest rate plus the same margin. That will then be the borrower's payment until the next 6 months or year pass and the loan will be reviewed again.

There is usually a limit on how much the interest rate can change on an annual basis, as well as a lifetime cap, or limit, on changes in interest rate. The annual maximum increase is usually 1 to 2% while the lifetime cap is usually not allowed to go five or six points above the starting rate.

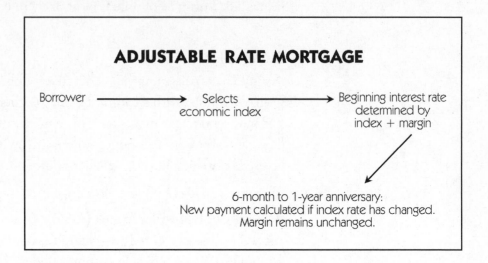

ADJUSTABLE RATE MORTGAGE

Borrower → Selects economic index → Beginning interest rate determined by index + margin

6-month to 1-year anniversary:
New payment calculated if index rate has changed.
Margin remains unchanged.

ARM Characteristics: Not all ARMs are the same, but they are similar enough to share the following characteristics.

Introductory Rate—Many adjustable rate loans (ARMs) have a low introductory rate or start rate, sometimes as much as 5.0% below the current market rate of a fixed loan. This start rate is usually good from 1 month to as long as 10 years. As a rule the lower the start rate, the shorter the time before the loan makes its first adjustment.

Index—The index of an ARM is the financial instrument that the loan is tied to, or adjusted to. The most common indices, or indexes, are the 1-Year Treasury Security, LIBOR (London Interbank Offered Rate), Prime, 6-Month Certificate of Deposit (CD) and the 11th District Cost of Funds (COFI). Each of these indices move up or down based on conditions of the financial markets.

Margin—The margin is one of the most important aspects of ARMs because it is added to the index to determine the interest rate that a borrower pays. The margin added to the index is known as the fully indexed rate. As an example, if the current index value is 5.50% and the loan has a margin of 2.5%, the fully indexed rate is 8.00%. Margins on loans range from 1.75% to 3.5% depending on the index and the amount financed in relation to the property value.

Interim Caps—All adjustable rate loans carry interim caps. Many ARMs have interest rate caps of 6 months or 1 year. There are loans that have

interest rate caps of 3 years. Interest rate caps are beneficial in rising interest rate markets, but can also keep the interest rate higher than the fully
indexed rate if rates are falling rapidly.

Payment Caps—Some loans have payment caps instead of interest rate
caps. These loans reduce payment shock in a rising interest rate market,
but can also lead to deferred interest or *negative amortization*. These loans
generally cap the annual payment increases to 7.5% of the previous payment.

Lifetime Caps—Almost all ARMs have a maximum interest rate or lifetime
interest rate cap. The lifetime cap varies from company to company and
loan to loan. Loans with low lifetime caps usually have higher margins,
and the reverse is also true. Those loans that carry low margins often have
higher lifetime caps.

ARM Index: Several index options are available to fit individual needs
and risk tolerance with the various market instruments. ARMs with different indexes are available for both purchases and refinances. Choosing
an ARM with an index that reacts quickly lets a borrower take full advantage of falling interest rates. An index that lags behind the market lets a
borrower take advantage of lower rates after market rates have started to
adjust upward.

Standard ARM Indexes and Programs

6-Month Certificate of Deposit (CD) ARM
Has a maximum interest rate adjustment of 1% every 6 months.
The 6-month Certificate of Deposit (CD) index is generally considered
to react quickly to changes in the market.

1-Year Treasury Spot ARM
Has a maximum interest rate adjustment of 2% every 12 months.
The 1-Year Treasury Spot index generally reacts more slowly than the
CD index, but more quickly than the Treasury Average index.

6-Month Treasury Average ARM
Has a maximum interest rate adjustment of 1% every 6 months.
The Treasury Average index generally reacts more slowly in fluctuating
markets so adjustments in the ARM interest rate will lag behind some
other market indicators.

(continued on next page)

Standard ARM Indexes and Programs *(continued)*

12-Month Treasury Average ARM

Has a maximum interest rate adjustment of 2% every 12 months. The treasury Average index generally reacts more slowly in fluctuating markets so adjustments in the ARM interest rate will lag behind some other market indicators.

LIBOR—London Interbank Offered Rate

LIBOR is the rate on dollar-denominated deposits, also know as Eurodollars, traded between banks in London. The index is quoted for 1 month, 3 months, 6 months as well as 1-year periods.

LIBOR is the base interest rate paid on deposits between banks in the Eurodollar market. A Eurodollar is a dollar deposited in a bank in a country where the currency is not the dollar. The Eurodollar market has been around for over 40 years and is a major component of the International financial market. London is the center of the Euromarket in terms of volume.

The LIBOR rate quoted in the Wall Street Journal is an average of rate quotes from five major banks. Bank of America, Barclays, Bank of Tokyo, Deutsche Bank and Swiss Bank.

COFI—Cost of Funds Index

The 11th District Cost of Funds is more prevalent in the West and the 1-Year Treasury Security is more prevalent in the East. Buyers prefer the slowly moving 11th District Cost of Funds and investors prefer the 1-Year Treasury Security.

The monthly weighted average 11th District has been published by the Federal Home Loan Bank of San Francisco since August 1981. Currently more than one-half of the savings institutions loans made in California are tied to the 11th District Cost of Funds (COF) index.

The Federal Home Loan Bank's 11th District is comprised of saving institutions in Arizona, California and Nevada.

Hybrid Note

While many consumers prefer the more familiar types of loans, a new loan called a *hybrid mortgage* may be suitable for some borrowers. The interest rate is fixed for an initial period of 3, 5, 7 or 10 years; after that the interest rate is tied to an economic index and adjusts every year. It's called a hybrid mortgage because it combines the features of a fixed-rate loan with those of the adjustable-rate loan.

A hybrid note may be desirable for borrowers who plan on selling their homes or paying off their loan within a few years because the initial interest rates on these loans are typically lower than a fixed rate loan, but allow the security, as least for the first years of fixed payments, of a fixed rate loan.

The borrower can then decide to either sell the property or refinance the loan when it turns into an adjustable loan, especially if prevailing interest rates at the time are higher, requiring a higher monthly payment. The borrower takes a gamble with a hybrid loan, hoping that interest rates will be low when the interest rate adjusts.

Holder in Due Course

As we have seen, notes are negotiable instruments, easily transferable from one person to another. However, the transferee or buyer of a note must have confidence in getting the money when the note is paid.

A holder in due course is someone who obtains (buys) an existing promissory note (negotiable instrument) for value, in good faith, and without notice that it is overdue or has been dishonored or claimed by another person.

Holder in Due Course Takes a Negotiable Instrument which is:

- Complete and regular in appearance and form
- Without notice that it is overdue, or has been dishonored or has any claim on it by any person
- Taken in good faith for valuable consideration

A holder in due course has a favored position with respect to the instrument because the maker (borrower) cannot raise certain "personal defenses" in refusing to pay. Personal defenses include lack of consideration, setoff and fraud.

The favored position that the holder in due course enjoys is a greater claim to the note's payment than the original holder. If a court action is necessary to bring payment on the note, the maker cannot use any of the following defenses to refuse payment to a holder in due course, even though they could be used against the original lender.

Defenses Not Allowed by the Maker of a Note:

- The maker cannot claim non-receipt of what the payee promised in exchange for the note.

- The maker cannot claim the debt was already paid. Even if it was, with no proof (as in marking the note "paid"), and the original payee transfers the note to a holder in due course, the original maker might still be required to pay.

- The maker cannot use fraud (in the original making of the note) as a defense.

- The maker cannot claim a setoff. For example, if the amount owed is $10,000, but the payee owes $15,000 to the holder, the difference cannot be used as a defense against paying the note.

All the above defenses may be used against the original payee, or lender, but are not good against a holder in due course.

Indeed, some real defenses are good against any person, a payee or holder in due course.

Defenses Allowed Against Anyone:

- Forgery, if the maker didn't really sign the note
- Secret material changes in the note
- Incapacity, if the maker is a minor or an incompetent
- Illegal object, if the note is connected to an illegal act or if the interest rate is usurious

Because of this preferred treatment or "safety net" for a holder in due course, people are more willing to accept such instruments without needing to check the credit of the borrower or even knowing the borrower.

Conflict in Terms of Note and Trust Deed

As you recall, a note is the evidence of a debt. A trust deed or mortgage, even though it is the security for the debt, is still only an incident of the debt. A trust deed or mortgage must have a note to secure, but a note does not need a trust deed or mortgage to stand alone. If there is a conflict in the terms of a note and the trust deed or mortgage used to secure it, the provisions of the note will control. If a note is unenforceable, the presence of a trust deed will not make it valid. However, if a note contains an acceleration clause (due on sale), the trust deed must mention it as well for the clause to be enforceable.

About Notes, Trust Deeds and Mortgages

- A trust deed or mortgage must have a note to secure, but a note does not need a trust deed to stand alone.

- If the conditions of a note and trust deed or mortgage are in conflict, the terms of the note have the authority.

The term that describes the interest of a creditor (lender) in the property of a debtor (borrower) is *security interest*. The security interest allows certain assets of a borrower to be set aside so that a creditor can sell them if the borrower defaults on the loan.

Proceeds from the sale of that property can be taken to pay off the debt. The rights and duties of lenders and borrowers are described in a document called a security instrument. In some states, trust deeds are the principal instruments used to secure loans on real property and in other states, mortgages are used.

Mortgages accomplish the same thing as trust deeds, and are used as security for real property loans. You will hear the term mortgage used loosely in California and some other trust deed states, as in mortgage company, mortgage broker and mortgage payment—but the mortgage reference here really is a trust deed.

TRANSFER OF PROPERTY BY THE BORROWER

Under certain circumstances, a property owner may transfer responsibility for the loan to the buyer when he or she sells the property to another party. A buyer may *assume* an existing loan, or may buy a property *subject to* an existing loan.

Loan Assumption

When a property is sold, a buyer may assume the existing loan. Usually with the approval of the lender, the buyer takes over primary liability for the loan, with the original borrower secondarily liable if there is a default. What that means is that even though the original borrower is secondarily responsible, according to the loan assumption agreement, no actual repayment of the loan may be required of that person. As long as a *deficiency judgment* is not allowed under the laws of the particular state, the original borrower's credit will be affected by the foreclosure, but he or she will not be required to pay off the loan. If the new owner defaults, the property is foreclosed by the lender, the current owner loses the property and the former owner gets a ding on his or her credit for the foreclosure.

The original borrower (seller) can avoid any responsibility for the loan, however, by asking the lender for a substitution of liability, known as a *novation,* relieving the seller of all liability for repayment of the loan.

In most cases, a buyer assumes an existing loan with the approval of the underlying lender. An *alienation* clause, sometimes known as a *due-on-sale* clause, however, in the note would prevent a buyer from assuming the loan.

"Subject To"

A buyer may also purchase a property *"subject to"* the existing loan. The original borrower remains responsible for the loan, even though the buyer takes title and makes the payments. In this case, also, the property remains the security for the loan. In the case of default, it is sold and the proceeds go to the lender, with no recourse to the original borrower. Again, the default would show up as a ding against the original borrower's credit. In some states, the lender can get a deficiency judgment against the original borrower, holding him or her personally responsible for the loan, to make up for any loss suffered by the lender in the case where the property sold for less than the loan amount.

When a buyer takes a property "subject to" the existing loan, the underlying lender may not always be informed. The buyer simply starts making the payments and the seller hopes he or she is diligent and does not default.

The occurrence of "subject to" sales is relative to economic and market conditions. In a real estate market where there are more buyers than sellers (a seller's market), a homeowner does not need to sell "subject to" his loan. When money is tight and interest rates high, and sellers are wondering where all the buyers are, a "subject to" sale might be more attractive to a seller.

SPECIAL CLAUSES IN FINANCING INSTRUMENTS

When a borrower signs a note promising to repay a sum, the lender usually will include some specific requirements in the note regarding repayment. These are special clauses meant to protect the lender and the lender's interests.

Acceleration Clause

An *acceleration clause* allows a lender to call the entire note due, on occurrence of a specific event such as default in payment, taxes or insurance, or sale of the property.

Alienation Clause

Another clause, known as an *alienation or due-on-sale clause*, is a kind of acceleration clause. A lender may call the entire note due if there is a transfer in property ownership from the original borrower to someone else. This clause protects the lender from an unqualified, unapproved buyer taking over a loan. Justifiably, the lender fears possible default, with no control over who is making the payments.

Assumption Clause

An *assumption clause* allows a buyer to assume responsibility for the full payment of the loan with the lender's knowledge and consent.

"Subject To" Clause

A *"subject to" clause* allows a buyer to take over a loan, making the payments without the knowledge or approval of the lender. The original borrower remains responsible for the loan.

Subordination Clause

A *subordination clause* is used to change the priority of a financial instrument. Remember, the priority of a trust deed is fixed by the date it is recorded: the earlier the date, the greater the advantage. When a note and trust deed includes a subordination clause, a new, later loan may be recorded, and because of the subordination clause, assume a higher priority. This clause is used mainly when land is purchased for future purposes of construction that will require financing. The lender on the new financing would want to be in first position to secure his or her interest, so the trust deed on the land would become subordinate to a new loan on the structure when the new loan was funded and recorded.

Prepayment Clause

Occasionally, a trust deed will include a *prepayment clause* in case a borrower pays off a loan early. When lenders make loans, they calculate their return, over the term of the loan. If a loan is paid off before that time, the lender gets less interest than planned, thus the return on investment is threatened.

So the borrower has to make it up by paying a penalty. It may not make a lot of sense to us as consumers, but that's the banking business.

For residential property, the prepayment penalty cannot exceed six month's interest. A borrower may prepay up to 20% of the loan amount in any 12 month period without a penalty. A prepayment penalty can then be charged only on the amount in excess of 20% of the original loan amount. Other rules apply for non-residential property.

"Or More" Clause

An *"or more" clause* allows a borrower to pay off a loan early, or make higher payments without penalty.

JUNIOR TRUST DEEDS

Another way to finance a property, either at the time of a sale, or afterward, is by using a *junior trust deed*, which is any loan recorded after the first trust deed, secured by a second, third or subsequent trust deed. Many times in a sale, where the first trust deed loan plus the buyer's down payment are not enough to meet the purchase price, additional money is needed.

Outside Financing

One way to get the needed financing is for the buyer to obtain a secondary loan through an outside source, such as a mortgage lender, or private investor. At the same time the buyer is applying for a loan secured by a first trust deed from a conventional lender, a second—or junior—loan is arranged to complete the financing.

As you recall, any loan made at the time of a sale, as part of that sale, is known as a purchase money loan. At the close of escrow, then, the loan from the first trust deed is funded and sent to the escrow holder to be given to the seller after all necessary loan documents have been signed by the buyer.

The same is true of the new purchase money loan secured by a second trust deed. That loan is also funded and the money sent to the escrow holder to be given to the seller after all loan documents have been signed by the buyer. At the same time, the escrow holder asks the buyer to bring in the down payment. The net proceeds after costs of sale from both the first and the second loan, plus the down payment, are then given to the seller at the close of escrow.

After several weeks of looking for the right home, Jose and Delia found one that was exactly what they wanted. They only had 10% of the purchase price as a down payment, but had excellent credit and felt sure they could qualify to obtain secondary financing.

The house was priced at $200,000. They made a full price offer, with the buyer to qualify for an 80% first trust deed, a 10% second trust deed and 10% as a down payment. Their offer was accepted and the seller was given all cash at the close of escrow.

Jose and Delia's Offer

New First Trust Deed	$160,000
New Second Trust Deed	20,000
Down Payment	+ 20,000
Sales Price	$200,000

Seller Financing

Another common source for secondary financing of a sale is the seller. If the seller is going to be the lender, he or she agrees to "carry back," or act as a banker, and make a loan to the buyer for the needed amount. That loan is secured by a trust deed, in favor of the seller, recorded after the first trust deed.

When a seller "carries the paper" on the sale of his or her home, it is also called a purchase money loan, just like the loan made by an outside lender. If a seller receives a substantial amount from the proceeds of a first loan, plus the buyer's down payment, it may be in the seller's interest to carry a second trust deed—possibly for income or to reduce tax liability by accepting installment payments.

Dominick made an offer on a house owned by Bruno, who accepted an offer of $275,000, with $27,500 as the down payment. The buyer qualified for a new first loan in the amount of $220,000, and asked Bruno to carry a second loan in the amount of $27,500 to complete the purchase price.

When the seller extends credit in the form of a loan secured by a second deed of trust, the note may be written as a straight note, with interest-only payments, or even no payments. Or it could be an installment note with a balloon payment at the end, or fully amortized note with equal payments until it is paid off. The term of the loan is decided by the buyer and seller. The instructions of the buyer and seller regarding the seller financing are usually carried out through escrow.

A trust deed held by the seller may be sold by the seller to an outside party, usually a mortgage broker. The note and trust deed will be discounted, or reduced in value by the mortgage broker, but it is one way a seller can get cash out of a trust deed that was carried back.

> *Ben and Jerry owned a house together as investors. After several years, they put the house on the market for $350,000 and hoped to get a full-price offer so they could go their separate ways with the profit from the house.*
>
> *After a short time, they did get a full price offer. The buyer offered to put $70,000 down, get a $240,000 new first loan and asked Ben and Jerry to carry $40,000 for five years, as a second trust deed. Ben and Jerry would have turned the offer down if their agent hadn't suggested they accept and sell the second trust deed after the close of escrow. Even though it would be discounted, it was one way they could get most of the cash out of their investment.*
>
> *If the second trust deed was sold at a discounted 20%, or $8,000, Ben and Jerry would end up with $40,000, less $8,000, or $32,000. In that way they would get the cash out of the sale, though they would be netting less than they originally planned because of the discount. They followed their agent's suggestion, and were satisfied with the result.*

Whenever there is seller financing in a real estate transaction, the law requires the buyer and seller to complete a Seller Financing Disclosure Statement. It gives both the seller and buyer all the information needed to make an informed decision about using seller financing to complete the sale.

The seller can see from the disclosure whether or not the buyer has the ability to pay off the loan by looking at the buyer's income, and whether or not the buyer has a good credit history. The buyer can see what the existing loans are, as well as such things as due date and payments on existing loans that would be senior to the loan in question.

SELLER FINANCING DISCLOSURE STATEMENT
(California Civil Code 2956-2967)
CALIFORNIA ASSOCIATION OF REALTORS® (CAR) STANDARD FORM

This two page disclosure statement from the Purchaser (Buyer) and Vendor (Seller) is prepared by an arranger of credit [defined in Civil Code 2957 (a)] and provided to **both** the Purchaser (Buyer) and Vendor (Seller) in a residential real estate transaction involving four or fewer units whenever the Seller has agreed to extend credit to the Buyer as part of the purchase price.

Buyer: _____
Seller: _____
Arranger of Credit: _____
Real Property: _____

A. Credit Documents: This extension of credit by the Seller is evidenced by ☐ note and deed of trust, ☐ all-inclusive note and deed of trust, ☐ installment land sale contract, ☐ lease/option (when parties intend transfer of equitable title), ☐ other (specify) _____

B. Credit Terms:
1. ☐ See attached copy of credit documents referred to in Section A above for description of credit terms; **or**
2. ☐ The terms of the credit documents referred to in Section A above are: Principal amount $_____ interest at _____% per annum payable at $_____ per _____ (month/year/etc.) with the entire unpaid principal and accrued interest of approximately $_____ due _____ 19_____ (maturity date).

Late Charge: If any payment is not made within _____ days after it is due, a late charge of $_____ or _____% of the installment due may be charged to the Buyer.

Prepayment: If all or part of this loan is paid early, the Buyer ☐ will, ☐ will not, have to pay a prepayment penalty as follows: _____

Due on Sale: If any interest in the property securing this obligation is sold or otherwise transferred, the Seller ☐ has, ☐ does not have, the option to require immediate payment of the entire unpaid balance and accrued interest.

Other Terms: _____

C. Available information on loans/encumbrances * that will be **senior** to the Seller's extension of credit:

	1st	2nd	3rd
1. Original Balance	$____	$____	$____
2. Current Balance	$____	$____	$____
3. Periodic Payment (e.g. $100/month)	$____ /	$____ /	$____ /
4. Amt. of Balloon Payment	$____	$____	$____
5. Date of Balloon Payment	____	____	____
6. Maturity Date	____	____	____
7. Due On Sale ('Yes' or 'No')	____	____	____
8. Interest Rate (per annum)	____%	____%	____%
9. Fixed or Variable Rate: If Variable Rate:	☐ a copy of note attached ☐ variable provisions are explained on attached separate sheet	☐ a copy of note attached ☐ variable provisions are explained on attached separate sheet	☐ a copy of note attached ☐ variable provisions are explained on attached separate sheet
10. Is Payment Current?			

☐ SEPARATE SHEET WITH INFORMATION REGARDING OTHER SENIOR LOANS/ENCUMBRANCES IS ATTACHED.
*IMPORTANT NOTE: Asterisk (*) denotes an estimate.

D. Caution: If any of the obligations secured by the property calls for a balloon payment, then Seller and Buyer are aware that refinancing of the balloon payment at maturity may be difficult or impossible depending on the conditions in the mortgage marketplace at that time. There are no assurances that new financing or a loan extension will be available when the balloon payment is due.

E. Deferred Interest:
"Deferred interest" results when the Buyer's periodic payments are less than the amount of interest earned on the obligation, or when the obligation does not require periodic payments. This accrued interest will have to be paid by the Buyer at a later time and may result in the Buyer owing more on the obligation than at origination.
☐ The credit being extended to the Buyer by the Seller does **not** provide for "deferred interest," **or**
☐ The credit being extended to the Buyer by the Seller does provide for "deferred interest."
The credit documents provide the following regarding deferred interest:
☐ All deferred interest shall be due and payable along with the principal at maturity (simple interest); **or**
☐ The deferred interest shall be added to the principal _____ (e.g., annually, monthly, etc.) and thereafter shall bear interest at the rate specified in the credit documents (compound interest); **or**
☐ Other (specify) _____

F. All-Inclusive Deed of Trust or Installment Land Sale Contract:
☐ This transaction does **not** involve the use of an all-inclusive (or wraparound) deed of trust or an installment land sale contract; **or**
☐ This transaction **does** involve the use of either an all-inclusive (or wraparound) deed of trust or an installment land sale contract which provides as follows:
1) In the event of an acceleration of any senior encumbrance, the responsibility for payment or for legal defense is:
☐ **Not** specified in the credit or security documents; **or**
☐ Specified in the credit or security documents as follows: _____

Buyer and Seller acknowledge receipt of copy of this page, which constitutes Page 1 of 2 Pages.
Buyer's Initials (_____) (_____) Seller's Initials (_____) (_____)

BUYER'S COPY

OFFICE USE ONLY
Reviewed by Broker or Designee _____
Date _____

(continued on next page)

☐

2) In the event of the prepayment of a senior encumbrance, the responsibilities and rights of Seller and Buyer regarding refinancing, prepayment penalties, and any prepayment discounts are:
☐ **Not** specified in the credit or security documents; **or**
☐ Specified in the credit or security documents as follows:

_____

_____

3) The financing provided that the Buyer will make periodic payments to _____
[e.g., a collection agent (such as a bank or savings and loan); Seller; etc.] and that _____
will be responsible for disbursing payments to the payee(s) on the senior encumbrance(s) and to the Seller.

CAUTION: The parties are advised to consider designating a neutral third party as the collection agent for receiving Buyer's payments and disbursing them to the payee(s) on the senior encumbrance(s) and to the Seller.

G. **Buyer's Creditworthiness:** Section 580(b) of the California Code of Civil Procedure generally limits a Seller's rights in the event of a default by the Buyer in the financing extended by the Seller, to a foreclosure of the property.
☐ No disclosure concerning the Buyer's creditworthiness has been made to the Seller; **or**
☐ The following representations concerning the Buyer's creditworthiness have been made by the Buyer(s) to the Seller:

1. Occupation: _____	1. Occupation: _____
2. Employer: _____	2. Employer: _____
3. Length of Employment: _____	3. Length of Employment: _____
4. Monthly Gross Income: _____	4. Monthly Gross Income: _____
5. Buyer ☐ has, ☐ has **not**, provided Seller a current credit report issued by: _____	5. Buyer ☐ has, ☐ has **not**, provided Seller a current credit report issued by: _____
6. Buyer ☐ has, ☐ has **not**, provided Seller a completed loan application.	6. Buyer ☐ has, ☐ has **not**, provided Seller a completed loan application.
7. Other (specify): _____	7. Other (specify): _____

H. **Insurance:**
☐ The parties' escrow holder or insurance carrier has been or will be directed to add a loss payee clause to the property insurance protecting the Seller; **or**
☐ No provision has been made for adding a loss payee clause to the property insurance protecting the Seller. Seller is advised to secure such clauses or acquire a separate insurance policy.

I. **Request for Notice:**
☐ A Request for Notice of Default under Section 2924(b) of the California Civil Code has been or will be recorded; **or**
☐ No provision for recording a Request for Notice of Default has been made. Seller is advised to consider recording a Request for Notice of Default.

J. **Title Insurance:**
☐ Title insurance coverage will be provided to **both** Seller and Buyer insuring their respective interests in the property; **or**
☐ No provision for title insurance coverage of **both** Seller and Buyer has been made. Seller and Buyer are advised to consider securing such title insurance coverage.

K. **Tax Service:**
☐ A tax service has been arranged to report to Seller whether property taxes have been paid on the property. _____ (e.g., Seller, Buyer, etc.) will be responsible for the continued retention and payment of such tax service; **or**
☐ No provision has been made for a tax service. Seller should consider retaining a tax service or otherwise determine that the property taxes are paid.

L. **Recording:**
☐ The security documents (e.g., deed of trust, installment land contract, etc.) will be recorded with the county recorder where the property is located; **or**
☐ The security documents will **not** be recorded with the county recorder. Seller and Buyer are advised that their respective interests in the property may be jeopardized by intervening liens, judgments or subsequent transfers which **are** recorded.

M. **Proceeds to Buyer:**
☐ Buyer will **NOT** receive any cash proceeds at the close of the sale transaction; **or**
☐ Buyer will receive approximately $_____ from _____ (indicate source from the sale transaction proceeds of such funds). Buyer represents that the purpose of such disbursement is as follows:_____

N. **Notice of Delinquency:**
☐ A Request for Notice of Delinquency under Section 2924(e) of the California Civil Code has been or will be made to the Senior lienholder(s); **or**
☐ No provision for making a Request for Notice of Delinquency has been made. Seller should consider making a Request for Notice of Delinquency.

The above information has been provided to: (a) the Buyer, by the arranger of credit and the Seller (with respect to information within the knowledge of the Seller); (b) the Seller, by the arranger of credit and the Buyer (with respect to information within the knowledge of the Buyer).

Arranger of Credit _____

Date _____, 20 _____   By _____

Buyer and Seller acknowledge that the information each has provided to the arranger of credit for inclusion in this disclosure form is accurate to the best of their knowledge.

Buyer and Seller hereby acknowledge receipt of a completed copy of this disclosure form.

Date _____, 20 _____   Date _____, 20 _____

Buyer _____   Seller _____

Buyer _____   Seller _____

OFFICE USE ONLY

BUYER'S COPY   Reviewed by Broker or Designee _____

Page 2 of _____ Pages.   Date _____

M-PM 2/93

Balloon Payment Loans

Often, when a hard money lender makes a first trust deed loan for $30,000 or more, or a junior trust deed loan for $20,000 or more, or when a seller takes back a junior purchase money note and trust deed, the monthly installment payments required do not amortize the loan over the term. The result is a large payment of principal and interest, called a *balloon payment*, due on the last payment. Loans with balloon payments are usually short term: 3 to 5 years.

In the interest of consumer welfare, the law requires the holder of a balloon note secured by an owner-occupied building of one-to-four units to give 90- to 150-days' warning of the balloon payment due date.

About Balloon Payment Loans

A final payment on a loan that is substantially larger than any other payment and repays the debt in full.

Regarding hard money junior loans negotiated by loan brokers (under $20,000), if payments are made in installments and the term is less than three years, the final payment may not be more than twice the amount of the smallest payment.

The law dealing with balloon payments is for loans other than purchase money loans extended by a seller to help a buyer finance a sale.

Hard Money Loan

A hard money loan is one made in exchange for cash, as opposed to a loan made to finance a certain property.

Other Types of Loans Secured by Trust Deeds or Mortgages

Home Equity Loan

Another way a junior loan can be created is by a *home equity loan*. Assuming there is enough equity, or the difference between the value of a home and the money that is owed against it, a homeowner can apply for a cash loan for any purpose.

A lender uses strict standards about the amount of equity required in a property before loaning money, and particularly for a junior loan. The reason is simple. All a lender wants is to get his or her money back in a timely manner, along with the calculated return on the investment. Care must be taken, in case of a decrease in the value of the subject property, to make sure there is enough of a margin between the total amount owed and the value of the property. If the lender has to sell the property at a foreclosure sale, he or she will be assured of getting the money back. By only loaning up to 75%-90% of the property value, the lender leaves some room for loss.

> *Michael's home was appraised at $100,000, with a $40,000 first trust deed recorded against it. Michael wants a $40,000 home equity loan. To determine whether or not to make the loan, the lender adds the amount owed to the amount desired in the loan to determine the percentage that would be encumbered by the existing first trust deed, and the desired second trust deed. If the lender would only loan up to 80% of the appraised value of the property, would Michael get his loan?*

The priority of the loan will depend on what other instruments are recorded ahead of it, but it will be known as a hard money loan (subject to state laws) and will be secured by a deed of trust or mortgage against the property. (*Of course Michael does get his loan because he has enough equity in the property to qualify.*)

Home Equity Line of Credit (HELOC)

More and more lenders are offering *home equity lines of credit*. By using the equity in their homes, borrowers may qualify for a sizable amount of credit, available for use when and how they please, at an interest rate that is relatively low. Furthermore, under the Tax Law—depending on each borrower's specific situation—he or she may be allowed to deduct the interest because the debt is secured by the home.

What is a home equity line of credit?   A home equity line of credit is a form of revolving credit in which a borrower's home serves as collateral. Because, in most cases, the home is likely to be a consumer's largest asset, many homeowners use their home equity credit lines only for major items such as education, home improvements, or medical bills and not for day-to-day expenses.

With a home equity line, a borrower will be approved for a specific amount of credit—the credit limit—meaning the maximum amount he or she can borrow at any one time.

Many lenders set the credit limit on a home equity line by taking a percentage (75%-90%) of the appraised value of the home and subtracting the balance owed on the existing mortgage. For example:

Formula for Setting Credit Limit

Appraisal of home	$100,000
Percentage of appraised value	×75%
	$75,000
Less balance owed on existing mortgage	−40,000
Potential credit line	$35,000

In determining the borrower's actual credit line, the lender also will consider his or her ability to repay, by looking at income, debts, and other financial obligations, as well as a borrower's credit history.

Home equity plans often set a fixed time during which a homeowner can borrow money, such as 10 years. When this period is up, the plan may allow the borrower to renew the credit line. But in a plan that does not allow renewals, a borrower will not be able to borrow additional money once the time has expired. Some plans may call for payment in full of any outstanding balance. Others may permit a borrower to repay over a fixed time, for example 10 years.

Once approved for the home equity plan, usually a borrower will be able to borrow up to the credit limit whenever he or she wants. Typically, a borrower will be able to draw on the line by using special checks.

Under some plans, borrowers can use a credit card or other means to borrow money and make purchases using the line. However, there may be limitations on how the borrower may use the line. Some plans may require the homeowner to borrow a minimum amount each time he or she draws on the line (for example, $300) and to keep a minimum amount outstanding. Some lenders also may require that the borrower take an initial advance when he or she first sets up the line.

Interest Rate Charges and Plan Features: Home equity plans typically involve variable interest rates rather than fixed rates. A variable rate must be based on a publicly available index (such as the prime rate published in some major daily newspapers or a U.S. Treasury bill rate); the interest rate will change, mirroring fluctuations in the index. To calculate the interest rate that the borrower will pay, most lenders add a margin of one or two percentage points, which represents the profit the lender will make, to the index value. Because the cost of borrowing is tied directly to the index rate, it is important to find out what index and margin each lender uses, how often the index changes, and how high it has risen in the past.

Sometimes lenders advertise a temporarily discounted rate for home equity lines—a rate that is unusually low and often lasts only for an introductory period, such as six months.

Variable rate plans secured by a dwelling must have a ceiling (or cap) on how high the interest rate can climb over the life of the plan. Some variable-rate plans limit how much the payment may increase, and also how low the interest rate may fall if interest rates drop.

Some lenders may permit a borrower to convert a variable rate to a fixed interest rate during the life of the plan, or to convert all or a portion of the line to a fixed-term installment loan.

Agreements generally will permit the lender to freeze or reduce a credit line under certain circumstances. For example, some variable-rate plans may not allow a borrower to get additional funds during any period the interest rate reaches the cap.

Costs to Obtain a Home Equity Line: Many of the costs in setting up a home equity line of credit are similar to those a borrower pays when he or she buys a home. For example:

- A fee for a property appraisal, which estimates the value of the home.

- An application fee, which may not be refundable if the borrower is turned down for credit.

- Up-front charges, such as one or more points (one point equals 1 percent of the credit limit).

• Other closing costs, which include fees for attorneys, title search, mortgage preparation and filing, property and title insurance, as well as taxes.

• Certain fees during the plan. For example, some plans impose yearly membership or maintenance fees.

• The borrower also may be charged a transaction fee every time he or she draws on the credit line.

How Will the Borrower Repay the Home Equity Plan?   Before entering into a plan, a borrower should consider how he or she will pay back any money that is borrowed. Some plans set minimum payments that cover a portion of the principal (the amount borrowed) plus accrued interest. But, unlike the typical installment loan, the portion that goes toward principal may not be enough to repay the debt by the end of the term. Other plans may allow payments of interest alone during the life of the plan, which means that the borrower pays nothing toward the principal. If the homeowner borrows $10,000, he or she will owe that entire sum when the plan ends.

Regardless of the minimum payment required, the borrower can pay more than the minimum and many lenders may give him or her a choice of payment options. Consumers often will choose to pay down the principal regularly as they do with other loans.

Whatever the payment arrangements during the life of the plan—whether the borrower pays some, a little, or none of the principal amount of the loan—when the plan ends the borrower may have to pay the entire balance owed, all at once. He or she must be prepared to make this balloon payment by refinancing it with the lender, by obtaining a loan from another lender, or by some other means.

Comparing a Line of Credit and a Traditional Second Mortgage Loan: If a homeowner is thinking about a home equity line of credit he or she also might want to consider a more traditional second mortgage loan. This type of loan provides a fixed amount of money repayable over a fixed period. Usually the payment schedule calls for equal payments that will pay off the entire loan within that time. A HELOC gives the borrower more flexibility and the traditional second mortgage is likely to give the borrower more security.

Disclosures from Lenders: The Truth in Lending Act requires lenders to disclose the important terms and costs of their home equity plans, including the APR, miscellaneous charges, the payment terms, and information about any variable-rate feature. And in general, neither the lender nor anyone else may charge a fee until after the borrower has received this information. The borrower usually gets these disclosures when he or she receives an application form, and will get additional disclosures before the plan is opened. If any term has changed before the plan is opened (other than a variable-rate feature), the lender must return all fees if the borrower decides not to enter into the plan because of the changed term.

Package Loan

A loan on real property that is secured by more than the land and structure is known as a *package loan*. It includes fixtures attached to the building (appliances, carpeting, drapes, air conditioning) and other personal property.

Blanket Loan

A trust deed or mortgage that covers more than one parcel of property may be secured by a *blanket loan*. It usually contains a release clause that provides for the release of any particular parcel upon the repayment of a specified part of the loan. Commonly, it is used in connection with housing tracts, or construction loans.

Open-End Loan

An additional amount of money may be loaned to a borrower in the future under the same trust deed. The effect is to preserve the original loan's priority claim against the property with this *open-end loan*.

Swing Loan

A *swing loan or bridge loan* is a temporary, short term loan made on a borrower's equity in his or her present home. It is used when the borrower has purchased another property, with the present home unsold, and needs the cash to close the sale of the new home. The new loan is secured by a trust deed or mortgage against the borrowers home. Usually there are no payments, with interest accruing during the term of the loan. When the borrower's home sells, the swing loan plus interest is repaid, through escrow, from the proceeds of the sale.

Wrap-Around Loan

Also known as an *All-Inclusive Trust Deed* (AITD), this type of loan wraps an existing loan with a new loan, and the borrower makes one payment for both. In other words, the new trust deed (the AITD) includes the present encumbrances, such as first, second, third, or more trust deeds, plus the amount to be financed by the seller.

Anyone desiring to use this type of financing to secure real property should make sure the existing loan can be legally combined (wrapped) by the new AITD. Many loans contain alienation (due-on-sale) clauses as part of the promissory note which prohibit the transfer of the property to a new owner without the approval of the underlying lender. Legal advice is recommend-ed to assure that all parties are aware of legal consequences of their actions.

The AITD is subordinate to existing encumbrances because the AITD is created at a later date. This means any existing encumbrances have priority over the AITD, even though they are included, or wrapped, by the new All-Inclusive Trust Deed. At the closing the buyer receives title to the property.

Typically an AITD is used in a transaction between buyer and seller to make the financing attractive to the buyer and beneficial to the seller as well. Instead of the buyer assuming an existing loan and the seller carrying back a second trust deed, the AITD can accomplish the same purpose with greater benefit to both parties.

Benefits of a Wrap-Around-Loan

Seller
- Usually gets full-price offer
- Increased percent on amount carried

Buyer
- Low down payment
- No qualifying for a loan or payment of loan fees

Buyer and sellers might use an AITD in times of credit shortages or tight money when it is difficult for many buyers to qualify for conventional loans or for sellers to refinance existing loans.

The AITD does not disturb the existing loan. The seller, as the new lender, keeps making the payments while giving a new increased loan at a higher rate of interest to the borrower. The amount of the AITD includes the unpaid principal balance of the existing (underlying) loan, plus the amount of the new loan being made by the seller. The borrower makes payment on the new larger loan to the seller, who in turn makes payment to the holder of the existing underlying loan. The new loan "wraps around" the existing loan.

A seller usually will carry back a wrap-around trust deed at a higher rate of interest than the underlying trust deed, thereby increasing the yield. The seller continues to pay off the original trust deed from the payments on the wrap-around, while keeping the difference. This type of financing works best when the underlying interest rate is low, and the seller can then charge a higher rate on the wrapped loan.

A wrap-around loan isn't for everyone. If a seller needs to cash out, it won't work. Also, most loans contain a due-on-sale clause, and cannot be wrapped without the lender's knowledge and approval. Depending on the buyer's and seller's motivation, sometimes an AITD will be created, with full knowledge of the risk. This is how the term "creative financing" came into being.

Generally, these payments are collected by the note department of a bank or a professional collection company and sent on to the appropriate parties. This assures the maker (borrower) of the AITD that all underlying payments are being forwarded and are kept current by a neutral party.

> *Arthur wanted to sell his house, and listed it for $100,000. The existing first trust deed was for $50,000 at 8%, payable at $377 monthly. He thought about carrying a second trust deed at 10%, counting on the income from the note. However, Bonnie, his listing agent, explained he could get a greater return from carrying an all-inclusive trust deed (AITD) instead of just a note and second trust deed from a buyer. She also told him any offer that included an AITD should be referred to an attorney. Arthur, with his attorney's approval, accepted the following offer soon after listing the house.*

Arthur's Offer

Sales price	$100,000
Cash by buyer (down payment)	– 20,000
AITD in favor of Arthur	$80,000

- Payments on new AITD of $80,000 at 10% to be $702 made monthly to Arthur

- Payments on existing first trust deed of $50,000 at 8%, in the amount of $377 monthly, to be paid by Arthur to original lender

AITD payment to Arthur	$702
Existing First Trust Deed payment	– 377
Monthly difference to Arthur	$325

Wrap-Around Loans (AITDs)

- Secured by a trust deed that "wraps," or includes existing financing plus the amount to be financed by the seller.

UNSECURED LOAN

The lender receives a promissory note from the borrower, without any security for payment of the debt, such as a trust deed or mortgage. The only recourse is a lengthy court action to force payment. This is truly the traditional I.O.U.

ALTERNATIVE FINANCING

Alternative financing is one way lenders and borrowers can respond to the realities of today's unsteady economy. Because there are different kinds of lenders and different kinds of borrowers who are in need of credit to buy homes, there is no single type of financing that fits everyone.

The changing needs of consumers have caused lenders to respond by offering various solutions to credit demands. In the past, the only way people could buy a home was to use the fixed-rate loan. Today, any number of adjustable-rate loans are available to serve consumers.

After the public began to see the benefits of these "alphabet soup" loans, they realized this was one solution to the uncertainty of a rapidly changing marketplace. It is the job of real estate and loan agents to help consumers understand these new types of loans and to select the one that best suits their needs.

Pledged Savings Account Mortgage

When a borrower has a large amount of money in a savings or thrift account, one way he or she can use that to an advantage is to maintain the account as security for a lender. The new lender will require a certain ratio of new loan amount to the balance in the account, and the borrower must keep that amount in the account for a specified length of time. The lender may release the *pledge account* when the property has acquired enough equity to qualify under normal loan-to-value ratios.

Graduated Payment Mortgage

The loan known as a *Graduated Payment Mortgage* (GPM) has partially deferred payments of principal at the start of the term, increasing as the loan matures. This loan is for the buyer who expects to be earning more after a few years and can make a higher payment at that time. It is also known as a flexible rate mortgage.

The GPM is another alternative to the conventional adjustable rate mortgage, and is making a comeback as borrowers and mortgage companies seek alternatives to assist in qualify for home financing.

Unlike an ARM, GPMs have a fixed note rate and payment schedule. With a GPM the payments are usually fixed for one year at a time. Each year for 5 years the payments graduate at 7.5%–12.5% of the previous years payment.

GPMs are available in 30-year and 15-year amortization, and for both conforming and jumbo loans. With the graduated payments and a fixed note rate, GPMs have scheduled negative amortization of approximately 10% - 12% of the loan amount depending on the note rate. The higher the note rate the larger degree of negative amortization. This compares to the possible negative amortization of a monthly adjusting ARM of 10% of the loan amount. Both loans give the consumer the ability to pay the additional principal and avoid the negative amortization. In contrast, the GPM has a fixed payment schedule so the additional principal payments reduce the term of the loan. The ARMs additional payments avoid the negative amortization and the payments decrease while the term of the loan remains constant.

The note rate of a GPM is traditionally .5% to .75% higher than the note rate of a straight fixed rate mortgage. The higher note rate and scheduled negative amortization of the GPM makes the cost of the mortgage more expensive to the borrower in the long run. In addition, the borrowers monthly payment can increase by as much as 50% by the final payment adjustment.

The lower qualifying rate of the GPM can help borrowers maximize their purchasing power, and can be useful in a market with rapid appreciation. In markets where appreciation is moderate, and a borrower needs to move during the scheduled negative amortization period, the property could, in the end, be encumbered for more than it is worth.

Shared Appreciation Mortgage

Under a *shared appreciation mortgage* (SAM), the lender and the borrower agree to share a certain percentage of the appreciation in the market value of the property which is security for the loan. In return for the shared equity, the borrower is offered beneficial loan terms.

Rollover Mortgage

The *rollover mortgage* (ROM) is a loan where the interest rate and monthly payment is renegotiated, typically every five years.

Reverse Annuity Mortgage

This type of loan—the *reverse annuity mortgage* (RAM)—is used by older homeowners who have owned their homes for a long time and have a large amount of equity but not much of a monthly income. This loan uses their built-up equity to pay the borrower a fixed annuity, based on a percentage of the property value.

The borrower is not required to repay the loan until a specified event such as death or sale of the property, at which time the loan is paid off. A retired couple can draw on their home equity by increasing their loan balance each month.

Contract of Sale

The *contract of sale* is the financing instrument with many names. It may be called an installment sales contract, a contract of sale, an agreement of sale, a conditional sales contract or a land sales contract.

RECORDING REQUESTED BY

AND WHEN RECORDED MAIL TO:

NAME

STREET
ADDRESS

CITY
STATE
ZIP

FORM 2   SPACE ABOVE THIS LINE FOR RECORDER'S USE

LONG FORM SECURITY (INSTALLMENT) LAND CONTRACT WITH POWER OF SALE

THIS AGREEMENT, made and entered into this _____ day of _____ , 20 _____ , by and between _____ (Vendor's name), whose address is _____ (hereinafter sometimes referred to as "Vendor"), and _____ (Vendee's name), whose address is _____ (hereinafter sometimes referred to as "Vendee"); and

CONTINENTAL LAND TITLE COMPANY (hereinafter sometimes referred to as "Trustee")

W I T N E S S E T H :

WHEREAS, Vendor is now the owner of certain real property situated in the County of _____ State of California, commonly known as _____ (Property street address), and described as follows:

WHEREAS, Vendor has agreed to sell, and Vendee has agreed to buy said real property on the terms and conditions hereinafter set forth;

Whereas, Vendor shall retain legal title as a security interest in said real property until the payment of the balance of the purchase price has been paid by Vendee to Vendor as set forth below.

NOW, THEREFORE, THE PARTIES HERETO DO HEREBY AGREE AS FOLLOWS:

PURCHASE PRICE

1. Vendor agrees to sell, and Vendee agrees to buy all of the aforedescribed real property for the sum of _____ (Total purchase price) (_____), lawful money of the United States, as hereinafter more fully set forth.

REQUEST FOR NOTICE OF DEFAULT

2. In accordance with Section 2924b, Civil Code, request is hereby made by the undersigned Vendor and Vendee that a copy of any Notice of Default and a copy of any Notice of Sale under Deed of Trust recorded _____ in Book _____ Page _____ , Official Records of _____ County, California, as affecting above described property, executed by _____ as Trustor in which _____ is named as beneficiary, and _____ as Trustee, be mailed to Vendor and Vendee at address in paragraph 3 below.

NOTICES AND REQUEST FOR NOTICE

3. Notices required or permitted under this agreement shall be binding if delivered personally to party sought to be served or if mailed by registered or certified mail, postage prepaid in the United States mail to the following:

Vendor: _____

Vendee: _____

Vendor and Vendee hereby request that notice of default and notice of sale hereunder be mailed to them at the above address

PAYMENT OF PURCHASE PRICE

4. Vendee shall pay the purchase price of $ _____ as follows:
    (a) Vendee shall pay to Vendor the sum of $ _____ (down payment) as and for a down payment.
    (b) The balance of purchase price of $ _____ shall be paid by Vendee to Vendor and shall bear interest at the rate of _____ percent per annum of any balance unpaid. Said sum shall be paid in installments of $ _____ on the _____ day of each and every month commencing _____ and continuing thereafter until paid in full; each payment first to be credited to interest with balance to principal. This agreement will require _____ years and _____ months to complete payment in accordance with its terms. Vendor shall make payment of any installments on existing first, second and/or third deeds of trust in accordance with paragraph (c) hereinbelow.

Title Order No. _____   Escrow or Loan No. _____

TT-281

In this type of agreement, the seller retains legal ownership of the property until the buyer has made the last payment, much like the buying of a car. This is a contract between a buyer and seller, and can be used during times when usual financing is difficult.

The buyer, or *vendee*, holds what is known as equitable title. The vendee may enjoy possession and use of the property even though legal title is held by the seller, or *vendor*. Like the holder of an AITD, the vendor pays off the original financing while receiving payments from the vendee on the contract of sale. Indeed, a contract of sale and an AITD are very similar. The most important distinction is that with the AITD—title passes to the buyer; under a contract of sale—title stays with the seller until the contract is paid off.

Difference Between AITD and Contract of Sale

- AITD: buyer gets title to property
- Contract of sale: seller keeps title until loan is paid off

CHAPTER QUIZ

1. When an owner uses a property as security for a loan, but does not give up possession, it is called:

    a. hypothecation
    b. pledge
    c. alienation
    d. amortization

2. A written promise to pay back a certain sum of money at specified terms at an agreed upon time is a:

    a. mortgage
    b. promissory note
    c. trust deed
    d. security agreement

3. Which of the following is the security for a debt?

    a. mortgage
    b. promissory note
    c. financing statement
    d. grant deed

4. An "or more" clause allows:

    a. a borrower to borrow as much as
       he or she wants
    b. a borrower to negotiate a new loan
       at the end of the term
    c. a borrower to pay off a loan early
       with no penalty
    d. a borrower to renegotiate his or
       her loan whenever the interest
       rate changes

5. Someone who buys an existing negotiable note is
   known as:

    a. the maker
    b. the holder
    c. the holder in due course
    d. the trustee

6. If there is a conflict in the terms of a note and the trust
   deed or mortgage used to secure it, which will control?

    a. the trust deed will control
    b. either one will control
    c. the provisions of the note will control
    d. neither can stand alone

7. What clause allows a lender to call the entire note due,
   on occurrence of a specific event such as default in
   payment, taxes or insurance, or sale of the property?

    a. partition clause
    b. "or more" clause
    c. acceleration clause
    d. assumption clause

8. Whenever there is seller financing in a real estate
   transaction, the law requires the buyer and seller to
   complete a:

    a. Seller Financing Disclosure Statement
    b. Transaction Disclosure Statement
    c. Mello-Roos Statement
    d. Statement of Financing

9. What type of note calls for payment of interest only, or no payments, during the term of the note, with all accrued money (either principal only, or principal and interest if no payments have been made) due and payable on a certain date?

   a. partially amortized note
   b. adjustable note
   c. fully amortized note
   d. straight note

10. Which of the following is inconsistent with the others?

   a. agreement of sale
   b. contract of sale
   c. all-inclusive trust deed (AITD)
   d. land contract

ANSWERS

1. *a*
2. *b*
3. *a*
4. *c*
5. *c*
6. *c*
7. *c*
8. *a*
9. *d*
10. *c*

5

chapter five

Trust Deeds and Mortgages

INTRODUCTION

When a consumer enters into an agreement to buy real property, he or she normally pays a small portion of the price as a down payment and borrows the rest of the money, usually from a mortgage lender. The borrower then executes a *promissory note* and either a *trust deed* or *mortgage* to secure the loan.

The interest of a *creditor* (lender) in the property of a *debtor* (borrower) is called the *security interest*, with the trust deed or mortgage as evidence of that security interest. The security interest allows the creditor to sell the identified property if the borrower defaults on the loan. Proceeds from the sale of that property can be taken to pay off the debt. The rights and duties of lenders and borrowers are described in a document called a *security instrument*. In California, and other states mentioned below, trust deeds are the principal instruments used to secure loans on real property.

Mortgages accomplish the same thing as trust deeds, and are used in some states as security for real property loans. You will hear the term mortgage used loosely in California and other trust deed states, as in mortgage company, mortgage broker and mortgage payment—but the mortgage reference really is a trust deed.

TRUST DEEDS (DEEDS OF TRUST)

A trust deed is used to secure a loan on real property, and the property is referred to as the *collateral* for the loan. When a promissory note is secured by a deed of trust, three parties are involved: the borrower (trustor), the lender (beneficiary) and neutral third party (trustee).

The actual trust deed includes the date of its *execution*, the borrower's name as trustor, the name of the lender as beneficiary and the name of the trustee. The trust deed identifies the promissory note following the trust deed and states that the purpose of the trust deed is to provide security for the note, as well as stating the loan amount being secured.

By agreeing, in the trust deed, to give the trustee limited title (*bare legal title*), the borrower may benefit from the use and enjoyment of the property as long as he or she maintains the good health of the loan, and the restricted title given the trustee lies inactive unless called on either to reconvey the title to the borrower or foreclose.

The address of the property used to secure the loan is included, as well as mention of giving the power of sale to the trustee and the right to collect rents to the lender in the event of foreclosure.

A Trust Deed Contains

- Date of signing
- Names of borrower as trustor, lender as beneficiary, trustee
- Reference to promissory note and amount of loan
- Description of property securing the loan
- Power of sale
- Assignment of rents
- Notarized signature of borrower

The lender makes the loan to the borrower, and the borrower signs a promissory note and a deed of trust. In the trust deed the borrower conveys bare legal title to the trustee, to be held in trust until the note is paid in full.

The deed of trust, signed by the borrower, is usually recorded in the county where the property is located, and then sent, along with the promissory note, to the lender to keep until the note is paid in full. Recording creates a lien against the property, giving public notice of the existence of a debt against the property.

The bare legal title held by the trustee allows the trustee to do only two things: *reconvey* the property back to the borrower upon final payment of the debt, or *foreclose*. The trustee holds the title in trust until the loan is paid off and then signs a reconveyance deed which is then recorded to give public notice that the lien has been paid in full. If the borrower defaults, the trustee is notified by the beneficiary to start foreclosure and proceeds with that event.

Even though the borrower has signed the trust deed giving the trustee bare legal title, the trustee's powers are limited to just the two jobs of reconveyance or foreclosure. The borrower is the legal owner of the property with all the usual rights that go with ownership, such as the right to possess, will, encumber and transfer.

In most cases, the trustee is not aware of the loan until notified to do one or the other of the two limited jobs required by the trust deed. In most states, a title or trust company, escrow holder or the trust department of a bank may perform the duties of a trustee.

Under a deed of trust, when the loan is being paid off, the lender sends the note and deed of trust to the trustee along with a request for a reconveyance. The trustee cancels the note and signs a reconveyance deed that gives title back to the borrower. The borrower should record the reconveyance deed to give public notice of the *discharge of the loan*, which would remove the lien from the property.

If the borrower *defaults*, the beneficiary (lender) sends the deed of trust to the trustee with directions to sell the property and pay the balance due on the note (foreclose). The trustee can start the sale without a court foreclosure order because the borrower has already given title to the trustee in the trust deed, and, secondly, given the trustee the authority to sell the property through the power of sale, also given in the trust deed.

(continued on page 121)

After Recording, Mail To:
Good Bank of Anywhere , National Association
P.O. Box 0000
Yourtown, CA 00000

Prepared By:
Good Bank of Anywhere , National Association
C/O Service Center
1111 West Street
Yourtown, CA 00000

Application Number:

DEED OF TRUST

THIS DEED OF TRUST is made this day of **November 15, 20XX,** among the Trustor,
and   HUSBAND AND WIFE, TRUSTEES OF THE   FAMILY TRUST
DATED MAY 10, 20XX, whose mailing address is the property address (herein "Borrower"), andFIRST
BANKER TITLE INSURANCE COMPANY whose mailing address is 1 FIRST BANKER   WAY, ,
YOURTOWN, CA 00000, (herein "Trustee"), and the Beneficiary, **Good Bank of Anywhere, National
Association**, a national banking association organized and existing under the laws of the United States
of America, whose address is   One George Circle, 000 Banker Street, Yourtown, CA 00000   (herein
"Lender").

WHEREAS, Borrower is indebted to Lender in the principal sum of U.S. **$349,300.00**, which indebtedness
is evidenced by Borrower's note dated **November 15, 20XX** and extensions, modifications and renewals
thereof (herein "Note"), providing for monthly installments of principal and interest, with the balance of
indebtedness, if not sooner paid, due and payable on **December 01, 20XX**;

TO SECURE to Lender the repayment of the indebtedness evidenced by the Note, with interest thereon;
the payment of all other sums, with interest thereon, advanced in accordance herewith to protect the
security of this Deed of Trust; and the performance of the covenants and agreements of Borrower herein
contained, Borrower does hereby grant and convey to Trustee in trust with power of sale the following
described property located in the County of **COUNTY**, State of **CALIFORNIA**:

SEE ATTACHED SCHEDULE A.

Parcel No. 000-00-000 which has the address of   (herein
"Property Address");

TOGETHER with all the improvements now or hereafter erected on the property, and all easements, rights, appurtenances and rents all of which shall be deemed to be and remain a part of the property covered by this Deed of Trust; and all of the foregoing, together with said property (or the leasehold estate if this Deed of Trust is on a leasehold) are hereinafter referred to as the "Property."

Any Rider ("Rider") attached hereto and executed of even date is incorporated herein and the covenant and agreements of the Rider shall amend and supplement the covenants and agreements of this Deed of Trust, as if the Rider were a part hereof.

Borrower covenants that Borrower is lawfully seized of the estate hereby conveyed and has the right to grant and convey the Property, and that the Property is unencumbered, except for encumbrances of record. Borrower covenants that Borrower warrants and will defend generally the title to the Property against all claims and demands, subject to encumbrances of record.

UNIFORM COVENANTS. Borrower and Lender covenant and agree as follows:

1. Payment of Principal and Interest. Borrower shall promptly pay when due the principal and interest indebtedness evidenced by the Note and late charges as provided in the Note. This Deed of Trust secures payment of said Note according to its terms, which are incorporated herein by reference.

2. Prior Mortgages and Deeds of Trust; Charges; Liens. Borrower shall perform all of Borrower's obligations, under any mortgage, deed of trust or other security agreement with a lien which has priority over this Deed of Trust, including Borrower's covenants to make payments when due. Borrower shall pay or cause to be paid all taxes, assessments and other charges, fines and impositions attributable to the Property which may attain a priority over this Deed of Trust, and leasehold payments or ground rents, if any.

3. Hazard Insurance. a) Borrower shall keep the improvements now existing or hereafter erected on the Property insured against loss by fire, hazards included within the term "extended coverage", and any other hazards, including floods or flood, for which Lender requires insurance. This insurance shall be maintained in the amounts and for the periods that Lender requires. The insurance carrier providingthe insurance shall be chosen by Borrower subject to Lender's approval which shall not be unreasonably withheld. If Borrower fails to maintain coverage described above, Lender may, at Lender's option, obtain coverage to protect Lender's rights in the Property in accordance with paragraph 5.

b) All insurance policies and renewals shall be acceptable to Lender and shall include a standard mortgagee clause. Lender shall have the right to hold the policies and renewals. If Lender requires, Borrower shall promptly give to Lender all receipts of paid premiums and renewal notices. In the event of loss, Borrower shall give prompt notice to the insurance carrier and Lender. Lender may make proof of loss if not made promptly to Borrower.

c) Unless Lender and Borrower otherwise agree in writing, insurance proceeds shall be applied to restoration or repair of the Property damaged, if the restoration or repair is economically feasible and Lender's security is not lessened. If the restoration or repair is not economically feasible or Lender's security would be lessened, the insurance proceeds shall be applied to the sums secured by this Security Instrument, whether or not then due, with any excess paid to Borrower. If Borrower abandons the Property or does not answer within 30 days a notice from Lender that the insurance carrier has offered to settle a claim, then Lender may collect the insurance proceeds. Lender may use the proceeds to repair or restore the Property or to pay sums secured by this Security Instrument, whether or not then due. The 30-day period will begin when the notice is given.

d) Except as provided in subparagraph 3(e) below, should partial or complete destruction or damage occur to the Property, Borrower hereby agrees that any and all instruments evidencing insurance proceeds received by Lender as a result of said damage or destruction, shall be placed in a non-interest

(continued)

bearing escrow account with Lender. At Lender's discretion, Lender may release some or all of the proceeds from escrow after Borrower presents Lender with a receipt(s), invoice(s), written estimates(s) or other document(s) acceptable to Lender which relates to the repair and/or improvements of the Property necessary as a result of said damage and/or destruction. Absent an agreement to the contrary, Lender shall not be required to pay Borrower any interest on the proceeds held in the escrow account. Any amounts remaining in the account after all repairs and/or improvements have been made to the Lender's satisfaction, shall be applied to the sums secured by this Deed of Trust, Deed to Secure Debt, or Mortgage. Borrower further agrees to cooperate with Lender by endorsing all, checks, drafts and/or other instruments evidencing insurance proceeds; and any necessary documents. Should Borrower fail to provide any required endorsement and/or execution within thirty (30) days after Lender sends borrower notice that Lender has received an instrument evidencing insurance proceeds, or document(s) requiring Borrower's signature, Borrower hereby authorizes Lender to endorse said instrument and/or document(s) on Borrowers behalf, and collect and apply said proceeds at Lender's option, either to restoration or repair of the Property or to sums secured by this Deed of Trust, Deed to Secure Debt, or Mortgage. It is not the intention of either party that this escrow provision, and/or Lender's endorsement or execution of an instrument(s) and/or document(s) on behalf of Borrower create a fiduciary or agency relationship between Lender and Borrower.

e) Unless Lender and Borrower otherwise agree in writing, any application of proceeds to principal shall not extend or postpone the due date of the monthly payments referred to in paragraph 1 or change the amount of the payments. If under paragraph 15 the Property is acquired by Lender, Borrower's right to any insurance policies and proceeds resulting from damage to the property prior to the acquisition shall pass to Lender to the extent of the sums secured by this Security Instrument.

4. Preservation and Maintenance of Property; Leaseholds; Condominiums; Planned Unit Developments. Borrower shall keep the Property in good repair and shall not commit waste or permit impairment or deterioration of the Property and shall comply with the provisions of any lease if this Deed of Trust is on a leasehold. If this Deed of Trust is on a unit in a condominium or a planned unit development, Borrower shall perform all of Borrower's obligations under the declaration or covenants creating or governing the condominium or planned unit development, the by-laws and regulations of the condominium or planned unit development, and constituent documents.

5. Protection of Lender's Security. If Borrower fails to perform the covenants and agreements contained in this Deed of Trust, or if any action or proceeding is commenced which materially affects Lender's interest in the Property, then Lender, at Lender's option, upon notice to Borrower, may make such appearances, disburse such sums, including reasonable attorneys' fees, and take such actions as is necessary to protect Lender's interest.

Any amounts disbursed by Lender pursuant to this paragraph 5, with interest thereon from the date of disbursal, at the Note rate, shall become additional indebtedness of Borrower secured by this Deed of Trust. Unless Borrower and Lender agree to other terms of payment, such amounts shall be payable upon notice from Lender to Borrower requesting payment thereof. Nothing contained in this paragraph 5 shall require Lender to incur any expense or take any action hereunder.

6. Inspection. Lender may make or cause to be made reasonable entries upon and inspections of the Property, provided that Lender shall give Borrower notice prior to any such inspection specifying reasonable cause therefore related to Lender's interest in the Property.

7. Condemnation. The proceeds of any award or claim for damages, direct or consequential, in connection with any condemnation or other taking of the Property, or part thereof, or for conveyance in lieu of condemnation, are hereby assigned and shall be paid to Lender subject to the terms of any mortgage, deed of trust or other security agreement with a lien which has priority over this Deed of Trust.

8. Borrower Not Released; ForbearanceBy Lender Not a Waiver. The Borrower shall remain liable for full payment of the principal and interest on the Note (or any advancement or obligation) secured hereby, notwithstanding any of the following: (a) the sale of all or a part of the premises, (b) the assumption by another party of the Borrower's obligations hereunder, (c) the forbearance or extension of time for payment or performance of any obligation hereunder, whether granted to Borrower or a subsequent owner of the property, and (d) the release of all or any part of the premises securing said obligations or the release of any party who assumes payment of the same. None of the foregoing shall in any way affect the full force and effect of the lien of this Deed of Trust or impair Lender's right to a deficiency judgment (in the event of foreclosure) against Borrower or any party assuming the obligations hereunder, to the extent permitted by applicable law.

Any forbearance by Lender in exercising any right or remedy hereunder, or otherwise afforded by applicable law, shall not be a waiver of or preclude the exercise of any such right or remedy.

9. Successors and Assigns Bound; Joint and Several Liability; Co-signers. Borrower covenants and agrees that Borrower's obligations and liability shall be joint and several. However, any Borrower who co-signs this Security Instrument but does not execute the Note (a "co-signer"): (a) is co-signing this Security Instrument only to mortgage, grant and convey the co-signer's interest in the Property under the terms of this Security Instrument; (b) is not personally obligated to pay the sums secured by this Security Instrument; and (c) agrees that Lender and any other Borrower can agree to extend, modify, forbear or make any accommodations with regard to the terms of this Security Instrument or the Note without the co-signer's consent.

Subject to the provisions of Section 14, any Successor in Interest of Borrower who assumes Borrower's obligations under this Security Instrument in writing, and is approved by Lender, shall obtain all of Borrower's rights and benefits under this Security Instrument. Borrower shall not be released from Borrower's obligations and liability under this Security Instrument unless Lender agrees to such release in writing. The covenants and agreements of this Security Instrument shall bind and benefit the successors and assigns of Lender.

10. Notice. Except for any notice required under applicable law to be given in another manner, (a) any notice to Borrower provided for in this Deed of Trust shall be given by delivering it or by mailing such notice by first class mail addressed to Borrower or the current owner at the Property Address or at such other address as Borrower may designate in writing by notice to Lender as provided herein, and any other person personally liable on this Note as these person's names and addresses appear in the Lender's records at the time of giving notice and (b) any notice to Lender shall be given by first class mail to Lender's address stated herein or to such other address as Lender may designate by notice to Borrower as provided herein. Any notice provided for in this Deed of Trustshall be deemed to have been given to Borrower or Lender when given in the manner designated herein.

11. Governing Law; Severability. The state and local laws applicable to this Deed of Trust shall be the laws of the jurisdiction in which the Property is located. The foregoing sentence shall not limit the applicability of Federal law to this Deed of Trust. In the event that any provision or clause of this Deed of Trust or the Note conflicts with applicable law, such conflicts shall not affect other provisions of this Deed of Trust or the Note which can be given effect without the conflicting provision, and to this end the provisions of this Deed of Trust and the Note are declared to be severable. As used herein "costs", "expenses" and "attorneys' fees" include all sums to the extent not prohibited by applicable law or limited herein.

12. Borrower's Copy. Borrower shall be furnished a conformed copy of the Note, this Deed of Trust and Rider(s) at the time of execution or after recordation hereof.

13. Rehabilitation Loan Agreement. Borrower shall fulfill all of Borrower's obligations under any home rehabilitation, improvement, repair or other loan agreement which Borrower enters into with Lender.

Lender, at Lender's option, may require Borrower to execute and deliver to Lender, in a form acceptable to Lender, an assignment of any rights, claims or defenses which Borrower may have against parties who supply labor, materials or services in connection with improvements made to the Property.

14. Transfer of the Property or a Beneficial Interest in Borrower, Assumption. As used in this Section 14, "Interest in the Property" means any legal or beneficial interest in the Property, including, but not limited to, those beneficial interests transferred in a bond for deed, contract for deed, installment sales contract or escrow agreement, the intent of which is the transfer of title by Borrower at a future date to a purchaser.

If all or any part of the Property or any Interest in the Property is sold or transferred (or if Borrower is not a natural person and a beneficial interest in Borrower is sold or transferred) without Lender's prior written consent, Lender may require immediate payment in full of all sums secured by this Security Instrument. However, this option shall not be exercised by Lender if such exercise is prohibited by federal law.

If Lender exercises this option, Lender shall give Borrower notice of acceleration. The notice shall provide a period of not less than 30 days from the date the notice is given in accordance with Section 10 within which Borrower must pay all sums secured by this Security Instrument. If Borrower fails to pay these sums prior to the expiration of this period, Lender may invoke any remedies by this Security Instrument without further notice or demand on Borrower.

15. Default Acceleration; Remedies. If any, monthly installment under the Note is not paid when due, of if Borrower should be in default under any provision of this Deed of Trust, or if Borrower is in default under any other Deed of Trust or other instrument secured by the Property, the entire principal amount outstanding under the Note and this Deed of Trust and accrued interest thereon shall at once become due and payable at the option of Lender without prior notice and regardless of any prior forbearance. In such event, Lender, at its option, may then or thereafter deliver to the Trustee a written declaration of default and demand for sale and shall cause to be filed of record a written notice of default and of election to cause to be sold the Property. Lender shall also deposit with the Trustee this Deed of Trust and any Notes and all documents evidencing expenditure secured thereby. After the lapse of such time as then may be required by law following recordation of such notice of default, and notice of sale having been given as then required by law following recordation of such notice of default, that notice of sale having been given as then required by law, the Trustee, without demand on Borrower, shall sell the Property at the time and place specified by such Trustee in such notice of sale, or at the time to which such noticed sale has been duly postponed, at public auction to the highest bidder for cash in lawful money of the United States, payable at time of sale, except that Lender may offset his bid to the extent of the total amount owing to him under the Note and this Deed of Trust, including the Trustee's fees and expenses. The Trustee may sell the Property as a whole or in separate parcels if there is more than one parcel, subject to such rights as Borrower may have by law to direct the manner or order of sale, or by such other manner of sale which is authorized by law. The Trustee may postpone the time of sale of all or any portion of the Property by public declaration made by the Trustee at the time and place last appointed for sale.

The Trustee shall deliver to such purchaser its deed conveying the Property so sold, but without any covenant or warranty, express or implied. The recital in such deed of any matters of fact shall be conclusive proof of the truthfulness thereof. Any person, including Borrower, the Trustee or Lender may purchase the Property at such sale. After deducting all costs, fees and expenses of the Trustee, and of this Deed of Trust, including costs of evidence of title in connection with such sale, the Trustee first shall apply the proceeds of sale to payment of all sums expended under the terms of this Deed of Trust, not then repaid, with accrued interest at the rate then payable under the Note or Notes secured thereby, and then to payment of all other sums secured thereby and, if thereafter there be any proceeds remaining, shall distribute then to the person or persons legally entitled thereto.

(continued)

16. Borrower's Right to Reinstate. Notwithstanding Lender's acceleration of the sums secured by this Deed of Trust, Borrower shall have the right to have any proceedings begun by Lender to enforce this Deed of Trust discontinued if: (a) Borrower pays Lender all sums which would be then due under this Deed of Trust, this Note and Notes securing Future Advances, if any, had no acceleration occurred; (b) Borrower cures all breaches of any other covenants or agreements of Borrower contained in this Deed of Trust; (c) Borrower pays all reasonable expenses incurred by Lender and Trustee in enforcing the covenants and agreements of Borrower contained in this Deed of Trust, and in enforcing Lender's and Trustee's remedies as provided in Paragraph 15 hereof, including, but not limited to, reasonable attorneys' fees; and (d) Borrower takes such action, as Lender may reasonably require to assure that the lien of this Deed of Trust, Lender's interest in the Property and Borrower's obligation to pay the sums secured by this Deed of Trust shall continue unimpaired. Upon such payment and cure by Borrower, this Deed of Trust and the obligations secured hereby shall remain in full force and effect as if no acceleration had occurred.

17. Assignment of Rents; Appointment of Receiver. As additional security hereunder, Borrower hereby assigns to Lender the rents of the Property, provided that so long as Borrower is not in default hereunder, Borrower shall have the right to collect and retain such rents as they become due and payable.

Upon Borrower's default or abandonment of the Property, Lender, in person or by agent, shall be entitled to collect all rents directly from the payors thereof, or have a receiver appointed by a court to enter upon, take possession of and manage the Property and to collect the rents of the Property including those past due. All rents collected by the receiver shall be applied first to payment of the costs of management of the Property and collection of rents, including, but not limited to receiver's fees, premiums on receiver's bonds and reasonable attorneys' fees, and then to the sums secured by this Deed of Trust. The receiver shall be liable to account only for those rents actually received.

18. Loan Charges. If the loan secured by this Deed of Trust is subject to a law which sets maximum loan charges, and that law is finally interpreted so that the interest or other loan charges collected or to be collected in connection with the loan exceed permitted limits, then: (1) any such loan charge shall be reduced by the amount necessary to reduce the charge to the permitted limit; and (2) any sums already collected from Borrower which exceeded permitted limits will be refunded to Borrower. Lender may choose to make this refund by reducing the principal owed under the Note or by making a direct payment to Borrower. If a refund reduces principal, the reduction will be treated as a partial prepayment under the Note.

19. Legislation. If, after the date hereof, enactment or expiration of applicable laws have the effect either of rendering the provisions of the Note, the Deed of Trust or any Rider, unenforceable according to their terms, or all or any part of the sums secured hereby uncollectible, as otherwise provided in this Deed of Trust or the Note, or of diminishing the value of Lender's security, then Lender, at Lender's option, may declare all sums secured by the Deed of Trust to be immediately due and payable.

20. Satisfaction. Upon payment of all sums secured by this Deed of Trust, this Deed of Trust shall become null and void and Lender or Trustee shall release this Deed of Trust. If Trustee is requested to release this Deed of Trust, all instruments evidencing satisfaction of the indebtedness secured by this Deed of Trust shall be surrendered to Trustee. Borrower shall pay all costs of recordation, if any. Lender, at Lender's option, may allow a partial release of the Property on terms acceptable to Lender and Lender may charge a release fee.

21. Substitute Trustee. Lender may from time to time at Lender's discretion and without cause or notice, remove Trustee and appoint a Successor Trustee to any Trustee appointed hereunder. Without conveyance of the Property, the Successor Trustee shall succeed to all the title, power and duties conferred upon the Trustee herein and by applicable law.

(continued)

22. Waiver of Homestead. Borrower hereby waives all rights of homestead exemption in the Property and relinquishes all marital property rights in the Property.

23. Hazardous Substances. Borrower shall not cause or permit the presence, use, disposal, storage, or release of any Hazardous Substances on or in the Property. Borrower shall not do, nor allow anyone else to do, anything affecting the Property that is in violation of any Environmental Law. The preceding two sentences shall not apply to the presence, use, or storage on the Property of small quantities of Hazardous Substances that are generally recognized to be appropriate to normal residential uses and to maintenance of the Property.

Borrower shall promptly give Lender written notice of any investigation, claim, demand, lawsuit, or other action by any governmental or regulatory agency or private party involving the Property and any Hazardous Substance or Environmental Law of which Borrower has actual knowledge. If Borrower learns, or is notified by any governmental or regulatory authority, that any removal, or other remediation of any Hazardous Substance affecting the Property is necessary, Borrower shall promptly take all necessary remedial actions in accordance with Environmental Law.

As used in this paragraph 23, "Hazardous Substances" are those substances defined as toxic or hazardous substances by Environmental Law and the following substances: gasoline, kerosene, other flammable or toxic petroleum products, toxic pesticides and herbicides, volatile solvents, materials containing asbestos or formaldehyde, and radioactive materials. As used in this paragraph 23, "Environmental law" means federal laws and laws of the jurisdiction where the Property is located that relate to health, safety, or environmental protection.

CA Deed of Trust   Page 7

(continued on next page)

(continued)

IN WITNESS WHEREOF, Borrower has executed this Deed of Trust.

_____**[SEAL]**
            TRUSTEE OF THE   FAMILY TRUST DATED MAY 10, 2001

_____**[SEAL]**

_____**[SEAL]**
                      TRUSTEE OF THE   FAMILY TRUST DATED MAY 10, 2001

_____**[SEAL]**

[Space Below This Line For Acknowledging]

STATE OF **CALIFORNIA**   )
) ss
COUNTY OF _____   )

On   (date)   _____, _____   before   me
_____, (name & title of the officer), personally appeared
                              , TRUSTEE OF THE   FAMILY TRUST DATED MAY 10,
2001 personally known to me (or proved to me on the basis of satisfactory evidence) to be the person(s)
whose name(s) is/are subscribed to the within instrument and acknowledged to me that he/she/they
executed the same in his/her/their authorized capacity(ies), and that by his/her/their signature(s) on the
instrument the person(s), or the entity upon behalf of which the person(s) acted, executed the instrument.

WITNESS my hand and official seal

Signature: _____ (SEAL)

My Commission Expires: _____

REQUEST FOR RECONVEYANCE

TO TRUSTEE:

The undersigned is the holder of the note or notes secured by this Deed of Trust. Said note or notes,
together with all other indebtedness secured by this Deed of Trust, have been paid in full. You are
hereby directed to cancel said note or notes and this Deed of Trust, which are delivered hereby, and to
reconvey, without warranty, all the estate now held by you under this Deed of Trust to the person or
persons legally entitled thereto.

Dated: _____   _____
                                                                                       Vice President

CA Deed of Trust   Page 8

(continued from page 112)

Some trust deeds contain an assignment of rents clause that gives the lender the right to take physical possession of the property and collect any rents or income produced by it during the foreclosure period. The rents would then be used to help offset the loss of payment on the loan.

Trust Deeds Include:

Power of Sale Clause

- Trustor gives trustee the right (by signing the trust deed) to foreclose, sell and convey ownership to a purchaser of the property if the borrower defaults on the loan

Assignment of Rents Clause

- Upon default by the borrower, the lender can take possession of the property and collect any rents being paid

The thing to remember about a trust deed is that it is the security for a loan. If the borrower fails to pay, the lender can use the proceeds from the sale of the property used as collateral (secured by the trust deed) for payment. Foreclosure is the procedure used by the lender who must exercise the right to collect what is owed if the borrower defaults on payments. Under a deed of trust, depending on the *statutory* time frame, it can be as short a time as four months. We will study foreclosure later in this chapter.

Once recorded, a trust deed becomes a *lien* on a certain described property to secure the repayment of a debt. The trust deed does not have to be recorded to be valid. It stills acts as the security for the loan, whether it is recorded or not. Recording, however, does establish priority for the trust deed in case of foreclosure, with trust deeds getting paid off in the order in which they were recorded.

Either a trust deed or mortgage may be used to secure a loan, depending on the locale of the property, or the state in which it is located. Some states use trust deeds and some use mortgages as security for a mortgage loan.

States Using Trust Deeds as the Basic Security Instrument

- Alaska
- Arizona
- California
- Colorado
- District of Columbia
- Idaho
- Maryland

- Mississippi
- North Carolina
- Oregon
- Tennessee
- Texas
- Virginia
- West Virginia

Other States Using Trust Deeds in Part

- Alabama
- Delaware
- Hawaii
- Illinois
- Montana

- Nevada
- New Mexico
- Utah
- Washington

CHARACTERISTICS OF TRUST DEEDS

Trust deeds differ from mortgages in several important ways as we shall see below.

Parties

There are three parties to a trust deed: the trustor (borrower), the trustee and the beneficiary (lender).

- Trustor, or borrower; holds *equitable title* while paying off the loan; conveys bare legal title to trustee by way of the trust deed.

- Trustee, or neutral third party; holds bare legal title until reconveyance or foreclosure occurs; normally is not involved with the property until asked to reconvey or foreclose.

- Beneficiary, or lender; holds the note and trust deed until reconveyance, or until the debt is paid off.

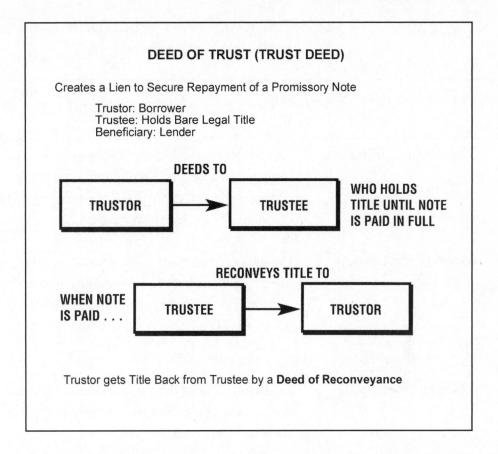

Title

The most distinguishing feature of a trust deed is the conveyance of *title* to a trustee by the borrower until the debt is paid off. When a trust deed is used to secure a loan, even though the borrower technically owns the property, bare legal title is transferred to the trustee by the deed of trust.

The trustee is only given the right to do what is necessary to carry out the terms of the trust. The trustee can foreclose or reconvey, but does not have any of the other ownership rights relating to the property. Commonly, the trustee is not even notified until either foreclosure (in case of loan default) or reconveyance (when the loan is paid in full), as required.

Think of the trustee as a neutral party, holding limited title for the borrower until the loan is paid off, or foreclosing for the lender if the borrower defaults. Upon payment of the debt in full, the trustee is notified by the beneficiary to sign the reconveyance deed, which states that clear legal title is now vested in the name of the actual property owner.

After being signed by the trustor (borrower), the trust deed—not the note—is recorded in the county where the property is located, then is sent to the lender to hold for the life of the loan. Recording of the trust deed gives public notice of the lien against the property for anyone interested in searching the title of the property.

The reconveyance deed is also recorded, after being signed by the trustee, to give public notice of the lien payment.

Statute of Limitations

The rights of the lender (beneficiary) under a deed of trust do not end when the *statute* has run out on the note. The trustee has the bare legal title with power of sale and can still sell the property to pay off the debt. The power of sale in a trust deed never expires.

Remedy for Default

Under a deed of trust, the lender has a choice of two types of foreclosure. He may choose between foreclosure under the *power of sale*, which is an auction type sale held by the trustee, with the property going to the highest bidder, or *judicial* foreclosure where the property is foreclosed through court action.

Reinstatement

When a trust deed debtor is in default on a loan, the loan may be *reinstated* if all delinquencies and fees are paid prior to five business days before the trustee's sale.

Redemption

Under a trust deed with a power of sale, there is no right of *redemption* after the trustee's sale. The sale is final.

Deficiency Judgment

A *deficiency judgment* is a *judgment* against a borrower for the difference between the unpaid amount of the loan, plus interest, costs and fees of the sale, and the amount of the actual proceeds of the foreclosure sale. This means if the property sells for less than what is owed to the lender, the borrower will be personally responsible for repayment after the deficiency judgment is filed.

When a loan is secured by a trust deed and the lender forecloses under a power of sale (trustee's sale), a deficiency judgment is not allowed in most cases. In states where trust deeds are used almost exclusively to secure loans, the only security for a beneficiary is the property itself. Any other personal or real assets of the borrower in default are protected from judgment under the trust deed.

Reconveyance

When payment in full is made, the trustee issues a *deed of reconveyance* upon request from the beneficiary.

RECORDING REQUESTED BY

WHEN RECORDED MAIL TO:

NAME

STREET
ADDRESS

CITY
STATE
ZIP

———— SPACE ABOVE THIS LINE FOR RECORDER'S USE ————

					ALL
					PTN

Title Order No. _____
Escrow or Loan No. _____

FULL RECONVEYANCE

Recon No. _____

_____ a Corporation, as Trustee under Deed of Trust,
dated _____ , 19 _____ , made by _____
_____

Trustor; and recorded as Instrument No. _____ on _____ , 19 _____ ,
in Book _____ , Page _____ , of Official Records in the office of the County Recorder of
_____ County, California, describing land therein as

having received from holder of the obligations thereunder a written request to reconvey, reciting that all
sums secured by said Deed of Trust have been fully paid, and said Deed of Trust and the note or notes
secured thereby having been surrendered to said Trustee for cancellation, does hereby RECONVEY without
warranty, to the person or persons legally entitled thereto, the estate now held by it thereunder.

IN WITNESS WHEREOF, _____ , as Trustee, has caused its
corporate name and seal to be hereto affixed by its duly authorized officer.

Dated _____

State of **CALIFORNIA** _____ } SS.

County of _____

On _____ before me,

Notary Public, personally appeared _____ ,

personally known to me (or proved to me on the basis of
satisfactory evidence) to be the person(s) whose name(s) is/are
subscribed to the within instrument and acknowledged to me
that he/she/they executed the same in his/her/their authorized
capacity(ies), and that by his/her/their signature(s) on the
instrument the person(s), or the entity upon behalf of which the
person(s) acted, executed the instrument.

WITNESS my hand and official seal.

Signature _____

Name (Typed or Printed)

as Trustee

By _____
Assistant Secretary

_____

_____

_____

(This area for official notarial seal)

FORECLOSURE UNDER A TRUST DEED

When a borrower defaults or stops making payments on a loan secured by a
trust deed, the lender can use the legal process of foreclosure. That process
terminates the rights and title of the borrower by selling the encumbered
property and using the proceeds to pay off the loan and other liens.

A trust deed containing a power of sale may be foreclosed either by a non-judicial foreclosure (trustee sale) or by judicial foreclosure.

**Trustee's Sale—
Non-Judicial
Foreclosure Process**

A trustee's sale may occur only when there is a power of sale included in the trust deed. The power of sale is given to the trustee by the buyer (borrower, trustor) in the trust deed he or she signs at the time of closing. This is generally a part of all trust deeds, and a trustee's sale is the most common way to foreclose in California and some other states. In a trustee's sale, as we have seen, normally no deficiency judgments are allowed. Nor does the debtor have any rights of redemption after the sale.

During the *statutory reinstatement period*, which runs until five days before the date of sale, the debtor or any other party with a *junior lien* may reinstate (bring current and restore) the loan in default. After the statutory reinstatement period, the debtor may still redeem the property and stop the foreclosure sale by paying off the entire debt, plus interest, costs and fees, prior to the date of the sale.

The Procedure

First, at the lender's request, the trustee files (records) a *notice of default*. This notice gives the legal description, the borrower's name, the lender's name and basically spells out the reason for the default. A typical default might state: "Non-payment of the installment of principal and interest which became due January 15, 1996, and all subsequent installments of principal and interest, plus late fees, plus delinquent real estate taxes, plus fees and costs." The notice will further state the amount of default. The trustor (borrower) has three months from the date of recording to *cure* the default by paying all the payments due, including the trustee's foreclosure charges and any unpaid real estate taxes. In some instances, the note's maturity date has passed and the entire principal is due in addition to accrued interest, late fees, foreclosure fees, etc.

If the trustor has not cured the default within three months, the trustee then records a second notice, a *notice of trustee's sale*. This notice sets forth the date for a public auction of the property. The terms of that sale (auction) are generally all cash. The sale is usually held 21-30 days after the filing of the notice of trustee's sale. The trustor retains the opportunity to cure the default up to five days before the actual trustee's sale. If the trustor were to attempt to cure the default a day or two prior to the sale, the beneficiary (lender) could demand the entire principal sum, as the curing period has passed.

As indicated before, the sale is a public auction and any interested bidders show up with cash or cashier's checks for 100% of the bid. The opening bid is generally the amount of money owed to the beneficiary, including all accrued interest, late fees, foreclosure fees, etc. In recent years, it has become common for the opening bid to be less than the amount owed. In the event that outside bidders are at the auction, the beneficiary (lender) will then join the bidding process until the amount owed has been realized or the lender is satisfied with an amount less than actually owed. At the sale, the trustee collects the winning bid price from the successful bidder and issues a *trustee's deed* to the successful bidder. If there are no outside bidders at the sale, the property reverts to the beneficiary. In this instance, the trustee issues a trustee's deed to the original beneficiary and the lender now owns the property. The foreclosure process eliminates any junior liens.

As an example, if a first trust deed goes to trustee's sale and there are no bidders at the sale, the first trust deed beneficiary would own the property and that sale would extinguish any second or third trust deeds on the property. Conversely, if a second trust deed goes to sale the new owner will acquire the property "subject to" the first trust deed of record.

A non-judicial foreclosure is a relatively uncomplicated process that does not involve attorneys or courts. The trustee's fees on a trust deed of $90,000 or less would be hundreds of dollars instead of thousands of dollars. The total length of the foreclosure process is approximately four months. The lender declaring the default will either be cured or paid off, or become the owner of the property within the four month process.

Notice of Default

The notice of default must be *executed* by the beneficiary or trustee and must be recorded in the office of the county recorder where the property is located at least three months before notice of sale is given. Within 10 days after recording the notice of default, a copy of the notice must be sent by certified or registered mail to all persons who have recorded a *request for notice*. A copy must also be sent within one month after recording to parties who have recorded interests in the property.

Notice of Default Must be Sent to:

- Successors in interest to the trustor
- Junior lienholders
- Vendee of any contract of sale
- State Controller if there is a tax lien against the property

Notice of Default and Election to Sell Under Deed of Trust
IMPORTANT NOTICE
IF YOUR PROPERTY IS IN FORECLOSURE BECAUSE YOU ARE BEHIND IN YOUR PAYMENTS, IT MAY BE SOLD WITHOUT ANY COURT ACTION, and you may have the legal right to bring your account in good standing by paying all of your past due payments plus permitted costs and expenses within the time permitted by law for reinstatement of your account, which is normally five business days prior to the date set for the sale of your property. No sale date may be set until three months from the date this notice of default may be recorded (which date of recordation appears on this notice). This amount is _____
as of _____, and will increase until your account becomes current.
          (Date)

You may not have to pay the entire unpaid portion of your account, even though full payment was demanded, but you must pay the amount stated above. However, you and your beneficiary or mortgagee may mutually agree in writing prior to the time the notice of sale is posted (which may not be earlier than the end of the three-month period stated above) to, among other things, (1) provide additional time in which to cure the default by transfer of the property or otherwise: (2) establish a schedule of payments in order to cure your default; or both (1) and (2).

Following the expiration of the time period referred to in the first paragraph of this notice, unless the obligation being foreclosed upon or a separate written agreement between you and your creditor permits a longer period, you have only the legal right to stop the sale of your property by paying the entire amount demanded by your creditor.

To find the amount you must pay, or to arrange for payment to stop the foreclosure, or if your property is in foreclosure for any other reason, contact:

_____
(Name of beneficiary or mortgagee)

_____
(Mailing address)

_____
(Telephone)

If you have any questions, you should contact a lawyer or the government agency which may have insured your loan.

Notwithstanding the fact that your property is in foreclosure, you may offer your property for sale, provided the sale is concluded prior to the conclusion of the foreclosure.

Remember, **YOU MAY LOSE LEGAL RIGHTS IF YOU DO NOT TAKE PROMPT ACTION.**

NOTICE IS HEREBY GIVEN, THAT   a corporation, is duly appointed Trustee under a Deed of Trust dated   executed by

                                        as Trustor, to secure certain obligations
in favor of   ‹

                                                          , as beneficiary,
recorded   , as instrument no.   , in book   , page   , of Official Records
                                                      in the Office of the
Recorder of   County, California, describing land
therein as:

                                                          said obligations

including   note   for the   sum of $

that the beneficial interest under such Deed of Trust and the obligations secured thereby are presently held by the undersigned; that a breach of, and default in, the obligations for which such Deed of Trust is security has occurred in that payment has not been made of:

that by reason thereof, the undersigned, present beneficiary under such Deed of Trust, has executed and delivered to said duly appointed Trustee, a written Declaration of Default and Demand for Sale, and has deposited with said duly appointed Trustee, such Deed of Trust and all documents evidencing obligations secured thereby, and has declared and does hereby declare all sums secured thereby immediately due and payable and has elected and does hereby elect to cause the trust property to be sold to satisfy the obligations secured thereby.

_____

Dated _____

Request for Notice

Anyone interested in a particular deed of trust may ensure being informed of a notice of default and notice of sale by recording a *request for notice* with the county recorder where the property is located. A request for notice is usually recorded at the time the trust deed is created. The party most interested in being notified of a default on a trust deed would be a seller who is carrying a second trust deed. If the borrower defaulted on the first trust deed, the holder of the second would want to be informed as soon as possible so he or she could start foreclosure on the second trust deed.

RECORDING REQUESTED BY

AND WHEN RECORDED MAIL TO:

NAME

STREET
ADDRESS

CITY
STATE
ZIP

_____ SPACE ABOVE THIS LINE FOR RECORDER'S USE _____

REQUEST FOR NOTICE

UNDER SECTION 2924b CIVIL CODE

				ALL
				PTN

Escrow or Loan No._____

Title Order No. _____

In accordance with section 2924b, Civil Code, request is hereby made that a copy of any Notice of Default and a copy of any Notice of Sale under the Deed of Trust recorded as Instrument No. _____ on _____ _____ , in book _____ , page _____ , Official Records of _____ County, California, and describing land therein as

Executed by _____ . as Trustor,
in which _____ is named as
Beneficiary, and _____ . as Trustee,
be mailed to _____
at _____
　　　　　Number and Street

　　　　　City and State

NOTICE: A copy of any notice of default and of any notice of sale will be sent to the address contained in this recorded request. If your address changes, a new request must be recorded.
Signature _____

Dated _____　　　_____

State of _____ **CALIFORNIA** _____

　　　　　　　　　　　　　　　　　} SS.　　_____

County of _____

On _____ before me,　　_____

_____

Notary Public, personally appeared _____

_____

personally known to me (or proved to me on the basis of satisfactory evidence) to be the person(s) whose name(s) is/are subscribed to the within instrument and acknowledged to me that he/she/they executed the same in his/her/their authorized capacity(ies), and that by his/her/their signature(s) on the instrument the person(s), or the entity upon behalf of which the person(s) acted, executed the instrument.
WITNESS my hand and official seal.

Signature _____

Notice of Sale

After recording the notice of default, a trustee must wait three months before recording a notice of trustee's sale if the loan is not reinstated by the borrower.

The notice of sale must contain a description of the property, and must be published in a newspaper of general circulation in the area where the property is located. The notice must appear at least once a week for 20 days, not more than 7 days apart, and must be posted publicly in the city where the sale will be held.

Foreclosure Facts

- Reinstatement period: until 5 days before the sale
- Trustee's sale may be held 20 days after notice of trustee's sale is issued
- Notice of sale must be published in local newspaper once weekly for 20 days prior to sale

The Sale

The sale is conducted at public auction, for cash, by the trustee, in the county where the property is located, approximately 4 months after the notice of default is recorded.

Foreclosure Time Frame Under a Trustee Sale

- Minimum of 3 months and 21 days

Until the auction bidding is over, the debtor or any junior lienholder may still redeem the property by paying off the defaulted loan in full, plus all fees, costs and expenses permitted by law. Reinstatement of the loan by bringing all delinquent payments up to date and paying all fees may be made at any time until 5 business days prior to the date of sale.

**Trustee Applies Foreclosure Sale
Proceeds in This Order:**

(1) Trustee's fees, costs and sale expenses

(2) Beneficiary—to satisfy the full amount of unpaid principal
and interest, charges, penalties, costs and expenses

(3) Junior lienholders in order of priority

(4) Debtor—any money left over

Anyone may bid at the auction, but the first lienholder, or holder of the debt being foreclosed, is the only one who may "credit bid," or bid the amount that is owed the holder on the defaulted loan without having to actually pay the money. All other bids must be in cash or cashier's checks.

The sale is made to the highest bidder, and the buyer receives a trustee's deed to the property. The debtor no longer has any right to redeem the foreclosed property.

Steps in a Trustee's Sale

• Beneficiary notifies trustee to foreclose

• Trustee records notice of default

• Reinstatement period (up to 5 days before the sale)

• Notice of trustee's sale and publication of date, time and
place of sale (3 weeks)

• Sale is held; highest cash bidder wins

• Trustee's deed is given to buyer (sale is final, borrower
has no right of redemption)

The sale is subject to certain liens of record that do not get eliminated by a foreclosure sale. That means the new buyer is responsible for payment of those liens.

> **Liens Not Eliminated by Foreclosure**
>
> • Federal tax liens
> • Assessments and real property taxes

Junior Lienholders

The sale of a property at the trustee's sale will extinguish the trust deed lien securing the debt to the beneficiary (lender) and will also extinguish any junior liens. That means the holder of a junior lien (a second, third, etc.), in order to protect his or her interest, must make a bid for the property, or possibly lose the right to collect on the loan if the sale amount is not enough for a pay-off on all trust deeds held against the property.

At this point, upon learning of the impending foreclosure on a trust deed senior to the one he or she holds, the junior lienholder has two choices: either stay silent and hope the proceeds from the foreclosure sale are enough to pay off the trust deed, or start his or her own foreclosure, which will then stop the first foreclosure that has already been filed.

If the junior lienholder chooses to file his or her own notice of default, he or she then has the right to claim the property after the statutory time period has passed, without having to bid against other hopeful buyers at the trustee's sale. The junior lienholder acquires the property subject to all loans senior to his or hers, with the obligation to keep them current or face foreclosure.

He or she now owns the property, and may either keep it until the property has regained its former value or try and sell it on the open market. Since it would not have brought enough at the foreclosure sale to pay off all liens, however, it probably still will not sell at a high enough price for the now owner, former lienholder, to get the investment returned.

The only thing to do is take a loss and sell it for whatever the market will allow, or hold the property, rent it out with a possible negative cash flow, until the market changes and the property has gained enough equity for a sale with a positive return.

Judicial Foreclosure

A beneficiary (lender) may choose a judicial foreclosure instead of the statutory trustee sale. That means instead of the automatic, defined by statute, 3 months and 21 days minimum foreclosure period, a lengthy court action may take place. The reason a beneficiary would choose a judicial foreclosure under a trust deed is that a deficiency judgment is allowed and the lender has the right to collect any unpaid amount through a deficiency judgment.

BENEFITS OF A TRUST DEED

A trust deed turns out to be an attractive alternative to a mortgage in some states. In locales where trust deeds are used, the benefits to both lender and borrower are numerous.

Benefits of a Trust Deed to a Lender

- In case of default, lender takes possession, collects rents
- Relatively short and simple foreclosure process
- Trustee holds title and can easily grant title to buyer at foreclosure sale
- No redemption after foreclosure
- A trust deed never expires

Benefits of a Trust Deed to a Borrower

- The property is the only security for the loan; no deficiency judgment is allowed in most cases. The borrower will only lose the property in question and other assets will be protected.

Whether a trust deed or mortgage is used to secure a promissory note, both lender and borrower have the full power of the law, depending on which state the property is in, to enforce their rights regarding repayment of a debt.

MORTGAGES

Most people are familiar with the word mortgage. A mortgage is a two-party instrument and is, in fact, a contract for a loan. The two parties are the mortgagor (borrower) and mortgagee (lender). This loan contract commonly is recorded against the real property.

Unfortunately, a default on the part of the mortgagor is the source of distress which states using trust deeds escape. A mortgagee (lender) in the Midwest, when faced with a default, (1) calls an attorney, and (2) files a lawsuit commonly known as a "judicial foreclosure." This is truly a lawsuit with all of its unpleasant ramifications, eventually resulting in a court-ordered marshal's or sheriff's sale, usually one to two years after the default. Not only is this a very lengthy and expensive process, it also involves the mortgagor's right to redeem the property. After the foreclosure sale, the mortgagor (borrower) has, usually, up to one year to redeem the property that was lost.

A mortgage is a financial instrument that is used to secure a property for the payment of a promissory note. It serves the same purpose as a trust deed by acting as the security for a debt. A mortgage becomes a lien against a described property until payment of the debt.

Do not get confused when you hear the word mortgage to describe some financial transactions. Trust deeds are commonly used in 14 states, even though you will hear reference to home mortgage, mortgage loan broker and mortgage banker in those states that, in fact, use trust deeds to secure loans.

Like a trust deed, a mortgage is a separate agreement from the promissory note, even while it is dependent on the note for its existence. As you recall, the promissory note is the evidence of the debt. The mortgage, then, is the security for the debt, just as the trust deed is the security in states where that document is used.

The promissory note can stand alone, without the mortgage as security. It would be a personal, unsecured note at that point. The mortgage, however, needs the note to validate its existence.

The actual mortgage includes the date of its execution, the borrower's name as mortgagor or giver of the mortgage, the name of the lender as the mortgagee, or the party who receives the mortgage. The debt and promissory note for which the mortgage provides security is identified, as well as the description of the property to be used as security for the loan.

The mortgage does not necessarily have to be against the property being purchased by the borrower. Commonly it is, but the property that is being mortgaged could be any property with the equity necessary to provide security for the loan.

A clause known as a *defeasance clause* is included in the mortgage. This provides for the defeat of the mortgage, or the determination of the property when the debt is paid in full. The wording would be "mortgage and the estate created hereby shall cease and be null and void" when the note is paid in full.

A Mortgage Contains:

- Date of signing
- Name of borrower as mortgagor, lender as mortgagee
- Reference to promissory note and amount of loan
- Description of property securing the loan
- Defeasance clause
- Covenants
- Notarized signature of borrower

There are two theories of how title follows a mortgaged property. In some states, the *title theory* is held, where the borrower is seen to deed the property being mortgaged to the lender at the time of signing the mortgage. In other states the *lien theory* asserts that the borrower gives only a lien right to the lender during the term of the loan. Some states follow the *intermediate theory* that says a mortgage is a lien unless the borrower defaults. The title then is automatically transferred to the lender. In any case, the borrower enjoys possession of the property during the full term of the mortgage no matter who is seen to hold title.

As part of the mortgage process, the borrower makes certain promises or covenants to the lender in the mortgage document. The borrower promises to pay the taxes, not to destroy or damage the improvements, to keep sufficient insurance against the property, and to maintain the property in good repair. There may or may not be an acceleration clause in the mortgage instrument, giving the lender the right to order payment of the loan in full if any of the conditions have been violated.

CHARACTERISTICS OF A MORTGAGE

A mortgage is held by the lender for the life of a loan, or until the borrower pays it off. There are some similarities to a trust deed, and some differences, as we shall see in the following examination of mortgages.

Parties

In a mortgage there are two parties: a *mortgagor* and a *mortgagee*. The mortgagor (borrower) receives a loan from the mortgagee (lender) and signs a promissory note and mortgage. The mortgage may become a lien in favor of the mortgagee until the debt is paid in full, or may be seen as the actual giving of title to the lender until repayment of the debt.

> **The Two Parties to a Mortgage are:**
>
> • Mortgagor (borrower)—giver of the mortgage
> • Mortgagee (lender)—receiver of the mortgage

Title

A mortgage may create a lien on real property or give actual *title* to the lender, depending on the legal attitude of the state where the property is located. Title may be vested in the borrower, or—like a trust deed where a deed of trust gives title (bare legal title) to a trustee—to the lender. In both cases, possession of the property remains with the borrower.

Statute of Limitations

The *Statute of Limitations* runs out on a note secured by a mortgage in four years. This means a lender must sue within four years of nonpayment to get his or her money back, or the mortgage expires.

Remedy for Default

The common *remedy* for default of a mortgage is judicial foreclosure, or a court action. If the mortgage contains a power of sale clause, a nonjudicial foreclosure is possible.

Reinstatement

Under a mortgage, a borrower in default may *reinstate* the loan by paying all delinquencies, plus all costs of the foreclosure action, at any time before the court approves the foreclosure.

MORTGAGE

THIS INDENTURE, made as of the _____ day of _____, 20__, by and between _____, (Mortgagor), and _____, (Mortgagee).

AMOUNT OF LIEN:

WHEREAS, Mortgagor is justly indebted to Mortgagee in the sum of _____ dollars ($ ____) and has agreed to pay the same, with interest thereon, according to the terms of a certain note (Note) given by Mortgagor to Mortgagee, which is attached hereto as Exhibit A.

DESCRIPTION OF PROPERTY SUBJECT TO LIEN:

NOW, THEREFORE, in consideration of the premises and the sum set forth above, and to secure the payment of the Secured Indebtedness as defined herein, Mortgagor by these presents does grant, bargain, sell and convey unto Mortgagee the property located at _____, more particularly described as:

Together with all buildings, structures and other improvements now or hereafter located on, above or below the surface of the property; and,

Together with all the common elements appurtenant to any parcel, unit or lot which is all or part of the Premises; and,

ALL the foregoing ecumbered by this Mortgage being collectively referred to herein as the Premises;

TO HAVE AND TO HOLD the Premises hereby granted to the use, benefit and behalf of the Mortgagee, forever. Conditioned, however, that if Mortgagor shall promptly pay or cause to be paid to Mortgagee, at its address listed in the Note, or at such other place, which may hereafter be designated by Mortgagee, its successors or assigns, with interest, the principal sum of _____ dollars ($_____) with final maturity, if not sooner paid, as stated in said Note unless amended or extended according to the terms of the Note executed by Mortgagor and payable to the order of Mortgagee, then these presents shall cease and be void, otherwise these presents shall remain in full force and effect.

COVENANTS OF MORTGAGOR

Mortgagor covenants and agrees with Mortgagee as follows:

Secured Indebtedness. This Mortgage is given as security for the Note and also as security for any and all other sums, indebtedness, obligations and liabilities of any and every kind arising, under the Note or this Mortgage, as amended or modified or supplemented from time to time, and any and all renewals, modifications or extensions of any or all of the foregoing (all of which are collectively referred to herein as the Secured Indebtedness), the entire Secured Indebtedness being equally secured with and having the same priority as any amounts owed at the date hereof.

(continued on next page)

Performance of Note, Mortgage, Etc. Mortgagor shall perform, observe and comply with all provisions hereof and of the Note and shall promptly pay, in lawful money of the United States of America, to Mortgagee the Secured Indebtedness with interest thereon as provided in the Note, this Mortgage and all other documents constituting the Secured Indebtedness.

Extent Of Payment Other Than Principal And Interest. Mortgagor shall pay, when due and payable, (1) all taxes, assessments, general or special, and other charges levied on, or assessed, placed or made against the Premises, this instrument or the Secured Indebtedness or any interest of the Mortgagee in the Premises or the obligations secured hereby; (2) premiums on policies of fire and other haZard insurance covering the Premises, as required herein; (3) ground rents or other lease rentals; and (4) other sums related to the Premises or the indebtedness secured hereby, if any, payable by Mortgagor.

Care of Property. Mortgagor shall maintain the Premises in good condition and repair and shall not commit or suffer any material waste to the Premises.

Prior Mortgage. With regard to the Prior Mortgage, Mortgagor hereby agrees to: (1) Pay promptly, when due, all installments of principal and interest and all other sums and charges made payable by the Prior Mortgage; (2) Promptly perform and observe all of the terms, covenants and conditions required to be performed and observed by Mortgagor under the Prior Mortgage, within the period provided in said Prior Mortgage; (3) Promptly notify Mortgagee of any default, or notice claiming any event of default by Mortgagor in the performance or observance of any term, covenant or condition to be performed or observed by Mortgagor under any such Prior Mortgage. (4) Mortgagor will not request nor will it accept any voluntary future advances under the Prior

Mortgage without Mortgagee's prior written consent, which consent shall not be unreasonably withheld.

DEFAULTS

Default. The occurrence of any one of the following events which shall not be cured within _____ days after written notice of the occurrence of the event, if the default is monetary, or which shall not be cured within _____ days after written notice, if the default is non-monetary, shall constitute an Event of Default: (1) Mortgagor fails to pay the Secured Indebtedness, or any part thereof, or the taxes, insurance and other charges, as herein before provided, when and as the same shall become due and payable; (2) Any material warranty of Mortgagor herein contained, or contained in the Note, proves untrue or misleading in any material respect; (3) Mortgagor materially fails to keep, observe, perform, carry out and execute the covenants, agreements, obligations and conditions set out in this Mortgage, or in the Note; (4) Foreclosure proceedings (whether judicial or otherwise) are instituted on any mortgage or any lien of any kind secured by any portion of the Premises and affecting the priority of this Mortgage.

Upon the occurrence of any Event of Default, the Mortgagee may immediately do any one or more of the following: (1) Declare the total Secured Indebtedness, including without limitation all payments for taxes, assessments, insurance premiums, liens, costs, expenses and attorney's fees herein specified, without notice to Mortgagor (such notice being hereby expressly waived), to be due and payable at once, by foreclosure or otherwise; (2) In the event that Mortgagee elects to

(continued on next page)

accelerate the maturity of the Secured Indebtedness and declares the Secured Indebtedness to be due and payable in full at once as provided for herein, or as may be provided for in the Note, then Mortgagee shall have the right to pursue all of Mortgagee's rights and remedies for the collection of such Secured Indebtedness, whether such rights and remedies are granted by this Mortgage, any other agreement, law, equity or otherwise, to include, without limitation, the institution of foreclosure proceedings against the Premises under the terms of this Mortgage and any applicable state or federal law.

MISCELLANEOUS PROVISIONS

Prior Liens.
Mortgagor shall keep the Premises free from all prior liens (except for those consented to by Mortgagee).

Notice, Demand and Request.
Every provision for notice and demand or request shall be deemed fulfilled by written notice and demand or request delivered in accordance with the provisions of the Note relating to notice.

Severability.
If any provision of this Mortgage shall, for any reason and to any extent, be invalid or unenforceable, the remainder of the instrument in which such provision is contained, shall be enforced to the maximum extent permitted by law.

Governing Law.
The terms and provisions of this Mortgage are to be governed by the laws of the State of _____. No payment of interest or in the nature of interest for any debt secured in part by this Mortgage shall exceed the maximum amount permitted by law.

Descriptive Headings.
The descriptive headings used herein are for convenience of reference only, and they are not intended to have any effect whatsoever in determining the rights or obligations of the Mortgagor or Mortgagee and they shall not be used in the interpretation or construction hereof.

Attorney's Fees.
As used in this Mortgage, attorneys' fees shall include, but not be limited to, fees incurred in all matters of collection and enforcement, construction and interpretation, before, during and after suit, trial, proceedings and appeals. Attorneys' fees shall also include hourly charges for paralegals, law clerks and other staff members operating under the supervision of an attorney.

Exculpation.
Notwithstanding anything contained herein to the contrary, the Note which this Mortgage secures is a non-recourse Note and such Note shall be enforced against Mortgagor only to the extent of Mortgagor's interest in the Premises as described herein and to the extent of Mortgagor's interest in any personalty as may be described herein.

IN WITNESS WHEREOF, the Mortgagor has caused this instrument to be duly executed as of the day and year first above written.

_____
Mortgagor

STATE OF)   COUNTY OF)

Subscribed and sworn before me this the _____ day of _____, 20____.

Witness my hand and seal.

_____ My commission expires:
Notary Public

Redemption

The right of redemption, or *equity of redemption* as it is known in those states using mortgages rather than trust deeds, usually allows a borrower in default to redeem the property for a specified time period before or after the foreclosure sale. Indeed, from the first sign of negligence in making the loan payments until the foreclosure sale occurs and the property is sold, the borrower can redeem the property by making up all sums that are due. In some states, the borrower has the right to redeem the property after the foreclosure sale by paying all sums due. All states recognize that even if a borrower defaults on the debt agreement, the borrower has the equity of redemption for a period of time defined by state statute.

Deficiency Judgment

A lender who forecloses against a defaulted mortgage may obtain a *deficiency judgment* against the debtor. Because a court action is required in order to foreclose against a mortgage, a deficiency judgment is allowed in some states. As you recall, a deficiency judgment may be filed against a borrower for the difference between the unpaid amount of the loan and the sale price if the proceeds are insufficient to satisfy the debt. If the court grants the judgment, the borrower is held responsible for the remaining amount of debt after the foreclosure sale. The lender may get a personal judgment against the borrower that will be effective for 10 years.

Satisfaction

Satisfaction of a mortgage, or payment in full, requires that the lender deliver the original note and mortgage to the party making the request. This release should be recorded to give public notice that the mortgage encumbrance has been paid in full.

Basic Differences Between Trust Deeds and Mortgages

Parties	Reinstatement
Title	Redemption
Statute of Limitations	Deficiency Judgment
Remedy	Satisfaction

FORECLOSURE UNDER A MORTGAGE

When the borrower and lender realize that a loan is not going to be repaid, because of some inability on the part of the borrower to make the payments, or to sell the property to pay off the amount borrowed, *foreclosure* is the lender's remedy for default on the loan.

In each state, specific foreclosure laws vary, but there are three general types of foreclosure proceedings. When the security instrument (either a trust deed or mortgage) conveys a power of sale to the lender in case of default, a *nonjudicial foreclosure* is allowed. A lender must request a court-ordered sale of the property after proving that the borrower has defaulted on the terms of the loan in states recognizing *judicial foreclosure*. Much less common, *strict foreclosure* allows a lender to get title to the property immediately upon default by the borrower and either sell the property or keep it to satisfy the debt.

Three Methods of Foreclosure

- Nonjudicial foreclosure—requires power of sale
- Judicial foreclosure—requires court-ordered sale
- Strict foreclosure—no judicial sale, not commonly used

In any case, if there is any money left over after a foreclosure sale the lender must return any proceeds in excess of the loan amount and certain fees to the borrower.

The foreclosure process used depends primarily on whether the state uses mortgages or deeds of trust for the purchase of real property. Generally, states that use mortgages conduct judicial foreclosures; states that use deeds of trust conduct non-judicial foreclosures. The principal difference between the two is that the judicial procedure requires court action.

Nonjudicial Foreclosure

The procedure where the lender conducts the sale of a mortgaged property without the involvement of a court is called *nonjudicial foreclosure*. Also known as *foreclosure by power of sale*, the process may be used as long as there is a clause in the mortgage, before it is executed, allowing it.

The lender directs the sale procedure to sell the property by first filing, or recording, a notice of default in the county where the property is located.

Next, the length of which is determined by state law or statute, is a waiting period during which the borrower can redeem the property by bringing the loan current, including taxes, insurance and any fees incurred by the foreclosure.

If the borrower is unable to cure the default, the lender sells the property at a public auction. If the state statute allows the borrower to redeem the property after the sale, he or she has up to a year in some cases to do so.

In some states, if the property does not sell at the public auction for the full amount of the loan or, in other words, there is a deficient amount realized at the sale, the lender has the remedy of a court action to claim the amount of the deficiency and obtain a deficiency judgment.

Judicial Foreclosure

To foreclose in accordance with the judicial procedure, a lender must prove that the mortgagor is in default. Once the lender has exhausted its attempts to resolve the default with the homeowner, the next step is to contact an attorney to pursue court action. A *judicial foreclosure* requires a lawsuit on the part of the lender. The attorney contacts the mortgagor to try to resolve the default. If the mortgagor is unable to pay off the default, the attorney files a lis pendens (action pending) with the court. The lis pendens gives notice to the public that a pending action has been filed against the mortgagor. A prospective buyer for the property would then be notified of the cloud on the title and could then proceed with the sale or not. The purpose of the court action is to provide evidence of a default and get the court's approval to initiate foreclosure.

Of the two common methods of foreclosure, the judicial foreclosure is more costly and time consuming. It may, however, provide for the recovery of that part of the loan that was not repaid by the sale of the property at a public foreclosure sale. When there is a deficient amount realized from a foreclosure sale, the lender can sue the borrower and get a deficiency judgment against all other assets of the borrower, causing the borrower to be personally responsible for repayment of the loan.

The judicial foreclosure is conducted by the county sheriff or by a referee appointed by the court. Anyone can bid on the property, for cash, including the borrower in default. In some cases, a cash deposit of 10% of the accepted bid is made at the sale, with the balance due 30 days later, upon closing. The lender who is foreclosing may bid up to the amount owed without having to pay cash if no one else makes a bid high enough.

In that case the lender would get the property back to hold or sell later, as they wish. The property would then be bank owned, or known as an REO or Real Estate Owned. If a buyer purchases the property for less than the total encumbrances, the junior liens go away. If the original borrower prevails in the bidding for the property, the junior liens remain on the property.

The successful bidder at the foreclosure sale, depending on which state the property is in, will get either a *referee's deed in foreclosure* or *sheriff's deed,* or a *certificate of sale.* The first two are special warranty deeds that give the buyer the title the borrower had at the time the original loan was made. The referee's deed or sheriff's deed are used primarily in states with

States Using Judicial and Nonjudicial Foreclosures

State	Judicial	Non-Judicial	State	Judicial	Non-Judicial
Alabama	X	X	Missouri		X
Alaska		X	Montana		X
Arizona		X	Nebraska	X	
Arkansas	X	X	Nevada		X
California		X	New Hampshire		X
Colorado		X	New Jersey	X	
Connecticut	X		New Mexico	X	
Delaware	X		New York	X	
District of Columbia		X	North Carolina		X
			North Dakota	X	
Florida	X		Ohio	X	
Georgia		X	Oklahoma	X	
Hawaii	X	X	Oregon		X
Idaho		X	Pennsylvania	X	
Illinois	X		Rhode Island		X
Indiana	X		South Carolina	X	
Iowa	X		South Dakota	X	
Kansas	X		Tennesee		X
Kentucky	X		Texas		X
Louisiana	X		Utah		X
Maine	X		Vermont	X	
Maryland	X		Virginia		X
Massachusetts	X		Washington		X
Michigan		X	West Virginia		X
Minnesota		X	Wisconsin	X	
Mississippi		X	Wyoming		X

no statutory redemption laws, where the buyer gets immediate possession of the property after the sale, which is final, with no redemption allowed to the buyer.

A certificate of sale is issued to the buyer at a foreclosure sale in states with statutory redemption laws. Depending on the state, the borrower has from one month to one year or more after foreclosure to redeem the property by paying off the judgment and reclaiming title to the property.

The buyer does not get possession of the property, in some states, until the redemption period is over.

Steps in a Judicial Foreclosure

- Lender files lawsuit against borrower and anyone else who has acquired an interest in the property after the mortgage being foreclosed was recorded

- Lender shows evidence of default of loan to court

- Lender asks for judgment instructing that:
    - ✓ The borrower's interest in the property be severed
    - ✓ The property to be sold at a public auction
    - ✓ The lender's demand to be paid from the sale

- Copy of complaint and summons delivered to defendants

- Lis pendens filed—informs public of litigation pending

- Public auction held, property sold to highest bidder

- Highest bidder receives sheriff's deed or certificate of sale

- Statutory redemption allowed in some states

Priority of Payment

A property may be used as the security for more than one loan. There may be a second or even a third mortgage against a property. These are known as junior mortgages. This is a common practice and poses no difficulty for the original lender as long as the borrower is willing to make the payments on all the loans and is able to do so. It becomes more than a nuisance, however, when a default occurs on one or more of the loans, and the property does not sell for an amount to cover all the loans against it at the foreclosure sale.

Comparison of Foreclosure Methods by State

State	Predominant Method of Foreclosure	Months to Complete Initial Action	Equitable Period of Redemption
ALASKA	Power of sale	3	None (A)
ARIZONA	Power of sale	4	None (B)
ARKANSAS	Power of sale	5	None (C)
CALIFORNIA	Power of sale	4	None (A)
COLORADO	Power of sale	2	2.5 mo. (D)
CONNECTICUT	Strict foreclosure	6	None (E)
DELAWARE	Judicial	9	None
DIST. OF COLUM	Power of sale	2	None
FLORIDA	Judicial)	6	None
GEORGIA	Power of sale	1	None
HAWAII	Judicial (F)	6	None (F)
IDAHO	Judicial (G)	6	6 mo. (G)
ILLINOIS	Judicial	6	6 mo. (H, I)
INDIANA	Judicial	7	3 mo. (J, K)
IOWA	Judicial	6	6 mo. (L)
KANSAS	Judicial	4	12 mo. (M)
KENTUCKY	Judicial	9	None (N)
LOUISIANA	Judicial	4	None
MAINE	Entry & possession	1	12 mo.
MARYLAND	Power of sale	2	None
MASSACHUSETTS	Power of sale	9	None
MICHIGAN	Power of sale	4	6 mo. (O)
MINNESOTA	Power of sale	3	6 mo. (P)
MISSISSIPPI	Power of sale	1	None
MISSOURI	Power of sale	2	None (Q)
MONTANA	Power of sale (R)	1	None (R)
NEBRASKA	Judicial	7	None (J, S)
NEVADA	Power of sale	5	None (T)
NEW HAMPSHIRE	Power of sale	2	None
NEW JERSEY	Judicial	6	None (U)
NEW MEXICO	Judicial	6	1 mo. (V)
NEW YORK	Judicial	8	None
NORTH CAROLINA	Power of sale	1	None
NORTH DAKOTA	Judicial	3	6 mo. (L)
OHIO	Judicial	8	None
OKLAHOMA	Judicial	6	None (W)
OREGON	Power of sale	9	None (X)
PENNSYLVANIA	Judicial	6	None
RHODE ISLAND	Power of sale	1	None
SOUTH CAROLINA	Judicial	5	None (U)
SOUTH DAKOTA	Judicial	6	6 mo. (L, Y, Z)
TENNESSEE	Power of sale	1	None (C)
TEXAS	Power of sale	3	None
UTAH	Power of sale	5	3 mo. (J, A1)
VERMONT	Strict foreclosure	1	6 mo. (A2)
VIRGINIA	Power of sale	2	None
WASHINGTON	Power of sale	5 (A3)	None
WEST VIRGINIA	Power of sale	2	None
WISCONSIN	Power of sale (A1)	3	12 mo. (A1)
WYOMING	Power of sale (A1)	3	3 mo. (A1)

Notes:

(A) Deed of trust. However, if there is a judicial foreclosure, there is a twelve-month redemption period.

(B) Judicial foreclosure under mortgage is also available. Time to complete would be four months followed by a six-month redemption. However, if property was abandoned, the redemption can be reduced to one month if so stated in the decree.

(C) Provided redemption rights have been expressly waived in the security instrument: if no waiver, redemption period is 12 months in Arkansas, 24 months in Tennessee.

(continued on next page)

(continued)

(D) Redemption period is five months on security instruments executed before July 1, 1965.

(E) Redemption (law date) depends entirely on the equity in the property. If little or no equity exists, there is a 30-day law date prior to completion; otherwise, length is determined by the court.

(F) Foreclosure by power of sale on entry and possession also available under deed of trust.

(G) For properties of more than 20 acres, redemption is twelve months. Power of sale foreclosure also available under trust deed.

(H) Statute permits both strict foreclosure (where value of property does not exceed 90% of debt) and foreclosure with consent of the mortgagor; in either case, the foreclosure sale is eliminated, the mortgagee waives deficiency judgment, and the decree vests title directly in the mortgagee subject to a three-month redemption period.

(I) Redemption is six months for sale if the judgment date is after January 1, 1982 (previously was twelve months from date of service).

(J) The redemption period precedes sale in Indiana, Nebraska (court stays sale on mortgagor's request), Oklahoma (without court appraisement), Wisconsin (if judicial foreclosure is used), and Utah (if foreclosure is by power of sale). In Nebraska redemption can be only between day of sale and confirmation of sale.

(K) On security instruments executed before July 1, 1975, redemption period is six months before sale, time to complete is then ten months with a twelve-month transfer time.

(L) If security instruments specifically provide for six-month redemption, period is twelve months. For Iowa, if the property was abandoned, redemption can be reduced to two months.

(M) Provided no suit is instituted for deficiency, redemption period is reduced to six months in cases of abandoned property or on purchase money mortgages with less than a third down.

(N) If foreclosure sale brings less than two-thirds of appraised value (court appraiser), there is a twelve-month redemption period.

(O) Redemption period is twelve months on security instruments dated prior to January 1, 1965. Redemption may be reduced if the property was abandoned.

(P) If deed is executed after July 1, 1967, the redemption is six months provided the deficiency judgment was waived.

(Q) Within ten days after sale, mortgagor may give notice of intention to redeem, including security deposit for taxes, interest, etc.; the redemption period is then twelve months.

(R) For estates of more than 15 acres, a mortgage is used and foreclosed judicially, one year redemption.

(S) Foreclosure by power of sale is available under a deed of trust, effective 1965. Time of completion then would be three months: no redemption following sale.

(T) Judicial foreclosure is available under a mortgage with a twelve month redemption following the sale.

(U) Provided no suit is instituted for deficiency; otherwise, redemption is six months. In South Carolina, the redemption is one month if a deficiency judgment was obtained.

(V) Provided mortgage specifically calls for shorter redemption period; otherwise, redemption period is six months.

(W) Provided sale is with court appraisement; otherwise, there is a six-month redemption period preceding the sale.

(X) If security instrument was executed prior to May 26, 1959, judicial foreclosure is necessary with a twelve-month redemption period following sale.

(Y) Foreclosure by power of sale with service is also available for properties of less than 40 acres.

(Z) Redemption period can be extended to 24 months upon filing of affidavit to mortgagor, including provision of accruing taxes, interest, etc.

(A1) Judicial foreclosure is also available. If used, the six-month redemption period precedes the sale. In Utah the six-month redemption would follow the sale. In Wyoming a three-month redemption follow the sale plus 30 days for successive lien holders.

(A2) For mortgages executed after April 1, 1968., the redemption period is six months from date of judgment unless a shorter period is granted per the complaint. Redemption is twelve months for mortgages executed before April 1, 1968.

(A3) Loan must be in default at least 120 days before day fixed for sale.

Compilation of State Legislature.

In many foreclosures, the proceeds of the sale do not pay all the debt; therefore a fair system of priorities for paying off holders of mortgages against the property was created. The debt with the highest priority is satisfied first from the proceeds of the sale, then the next highest priority debt is paid, then the next, and so on until either the sale proceeds have faded to nothing or all holders of debt relating to the property are contented with their payoff.

A lender would rather be in as senior a position as possible, regarding priority of recording for obvious reasons. Since the priority of a mortgage is determined by when it is recorded, the mortgage that is recorded first will be in first position to get paid if the borrower defaults. After that, the second mortgage to get recorded will get paid, and so on. The mortgage itself will not be identified as a first, second or third mortgage. The date and time of recording will be stamped by the county recorder on the document, and its priority will be determined by that imprint.

The logical outcome of this priority system of paying off holders of mortgages in case of foreclosure is that, sometimes, the property does not bring enough money at the foreclosure sale to satisfy all the creditors holding mortgages against the property. In those cases, the mortgages not paid off are eliminated. As a matter of fact, in some cases, there is not even enough money to pay the holder of the first mortgage off completely. That lender, then, must decide if it is worthwhile to pursue a deficiency judgment or not. If the amount is small enough, it probably would not be worth the cost of the lawsuit to recover the deficiency.

A majority of states allow the lender to obtain a deficiency judgment for any amount that is not recovered at the foreclosure sale. The judgment, if you recall, allows a lender to proceed against the borrower's other unsecured assets, if he or she has any.

Junior Lienholders

In a process much like what happens with a trust deed, the foreclosure sale of a property will extinguish the mortgage securing the debt to the mortgagee, or lender, and will also extinguish any junior mortgages. That means the holder of a junior lien (a second, third, etc.), in order to protect his or her interest, must make a bid for the property, or possibly lose the right to collect on the loan if the sale amount is not enough for a pay-off on all mortgages held against the property.

At this point, upon learning of the impending foreclosure on a mortgage senior to the one he or she holds, the junior lienholder has two choices:

either stay silent and hope the proceeds from the foreclosure sale are enough to pay off the mortgage, or start his or her own foreclosure, which will then stop the first foreclosure that has already been filed.

If the junior lienholder chooses to file a notice of default, he or she then has the right to claim the property after the statutory time period has passed, without having to bid against other hopeful buyers at the foreclosure sale. The junior lienholder acquires the property subject to all loans senior to his or her own, with the obligation to keep them current or face foreclosure.

The junior lienholder now owns the property, and may either keep it until the property has regained its former value or try and sell it on the open market. Since it would not have brought enough at the foreclosure sale to pay off all liens, however, it probably still will not sell at a high enough price for the, now owner, former lienholder, to get the investment returned.

CHAPTER QUIZ

1. The interest of a creditor (lender) in the property of a debtor (borrower) is called the:
   a. security interest
   b. evidence of the debt
   c. evidence of judgment
   d. trustor's interest

2. Which of the following is not mentioned in a trust deed?
   a. notice of deficiency
   b. name of trustor
   c. name of beneficiary
   d. address of property

3. Who is the lender?
   a. trustee
   b. trustor
   c. holder in due course
   d. beneficiary

4. Bare legal title is held by:

    a. beneficiary
    b. lender of record
    c. trustor
    d. trustee

5. The trustee may become involved in only two processes. What are they?

    a. making the loan and foreclosing
    b. making the loan and collecting the payments
    c. foreclosing and reconveying the loan
    d. qualifying the borrower and approving the loan

6. The Statute of Limitations runs out on a note secured by a mortgage in:

    a. four years
    b. five years
    c. six years
    d. seven years

7. The equity of redemption allows a borrower in default to:

    a. borrow against the property
    b. redeem the property for a specified time period before or after the foreclosure sale
    c. sell the property
    d. convey title to the property to a third party

8. Satisfaction of a mortgage requires which of the following?

    a. a default
    b. an acknowledgment
    c. assumption of the loan
    d. payment in full

9. A lender's remedy for default on a loan is:

    a. reconveyance
    b. deficiency judgment
    c. foreclosure
    d. forbearance

10. What is a junior lienholder?

    a. the holder of a first mortgage
    b. the holder of a second mortgage
    c. the holder of an encroachment
    d. an underage lender

ANSWERS

1. *a*
2. *a*
3. *d*
4. *d*
5. *c*
6. *a*
7. *b*
8. *d*
9. *c*
10. *b*

Mortgage Lenders

INTRODUCTION

Consumers use money and credit for the purpose of developing and acquiring real property. The environment of real estate mortgage financing is made up of the institutions that create and purchase instruments of finance, and the markets where they are transferred. Those institutions and markets facilitate the flow of funds in the financial system.

Institutions that make real estate loans are known as *financial intermediaries*. As the word "intermediary" indicates, these financial institutions stand between the suppliers and users of credit. They are conventional lenders who make money and credit available to borrowers.

Institutional lenders, such as commercial banks, thrifts including savings & loan associations, savings banks, mutual savings banks, and credit unions, life insurance companies, investment companies including mutual funds and Real Estate Investment Trusts (REITs) and pension funds are all financial intermediaries whose main job is to transfer money from the people who invest money to those who want to borrow it. Non-institutional lenders include mortgage bankers and mortgage brokers, investment companies, private individuals and non-financial institutions.

Financial Intermediaries

Institutional Lenders

- Commercial banks
- Thrifts
  - Savings & loan associations
  - Savings banks
  - Mutual savings banks
  - Credit unions
- Life insurance companies

Non-Institutional Lenders

- Mortgage bankers
- Mortgage brokers
- Investment companies
- Private individuals
- Non-financial institutions

As a liaison, the financial intermediary combines funds from many sources (individual savers, short-term or long-term investors) and adapts them into loans for the consumer. This process is called *intermediation*.

All mortgage lenders are financial intermediaries, even though they are not all depository institutions. A depository institution is one that accepts deposits in the form of savings accounts. Mortgage bankers, the originators of a majority of all residential loans, are not depository institutions. They make mortgage loans by borrowing from other institutions, and then selling the loans they originate to other institutions.

In today's sophisticated mortgage lending environment, the large percentage of loans are held either by the originator in its own portfolio, or sold on the secondary market. A few rare individuals do hold mortgage loans, but the majority of loans are held by institutions. The value of a mortgage loan to a buyer of that loan is related, in part, to the knowledge and skill of the financial intermediary who originated the loan at the consumer level.

INSTITUTIONAL LENDERS

An institutional lender is a financial intermediary or depository, such as a commercial bank, thrift or life insurance company that pools its depositors' money and then invests the fund in various ways, including trust deed and mortgage loans.

Commercial Banks

Commercial banks are the all purpose lenders. They make the widest range of loans, including loans for buying real estate, home equity loans, business loans and other short-term loans. Typically, though, a commercial bank will make short term, or interim, loans to finance construction. Long-term, take-out loans may be available after a construction loan is paid off.

Commercial banks manage consumer checking and savings accounts and certificates of deposit. Using those funds as well as resources borrowed from other intermediaries, commercial banks make loans to investment buyers, builders and businesses, making loans available to finance the nation's commerce and industry. Commercial banks are the largest originators of commercial real estate loans for the acquisition, development and construction of real estate projects.

The major type of lending activity funded by commercial banks is for short term (6 to 36 months) construction loans, even though they do make other types of loans as well.

Commercial banks may be chartered by the federal or state government. State-chartered commercial banks are regulated by the responsible state agency, but may be members of the Federal Reserve System. All federally chartered commercial banks must be members of the Federal Reserve System which supervises member commercial banks. Deposits are insured by the Federal Deposit Insurance Corporation (FDIC).

Thrifts

Thrifts are the largest single resource for residential mortgage credit. A thrift institution can be any one of the following major depositories of consumer savings.

Thrift Institutions

- Savings & loan associations
- Savings banks
- Mutual savings banks
- Credit unions

The form of ownership is the main difference between the savings and loan associations and mutual savings banks. The mutual savings bank is a cooperative form of ownership rather than a stock company like the savings and loan. Basically the two share the same trade association, the U.S. Savings and Loan League, and are supervised by the same government agency, the Office of Thrift Supervision. Deposits for both institutions are insured by the Federal Deposit Insurance Corporation (FDIC). Credit unions are limited by their charters to providing services for members of a particular organization, such as employees of fire departments, utilities, corporations or other specific group.

Savings & Loan Associations

Traditionally, savings and loan institutions have played a major role in the economy by pooling the savings of individuals to fund residential mortgages. The first customers of S&Ls were depositors as well as borrowers, and as their customer base grew, the S&L associations became a primary source of residential real estate loans.

Until the deregulation of the lending industry in 1980, the federally chartered S&Ls were required by federal regulation to hold at least 80% of their assets in residential loans to encourage lending on residential real estate. Special tax laws allowed owners of S&Ls to defer payment of income taxes on profits as long as the profits were held in surplus accounts and not distributed to those owners of the S&L. Limits were applied on the interest rate that could be paid on savings accounts, giving the savings and loan associations a dependable source of funds, at a fixed interest rate, which made possible long-term loans at reasonable rates.

The first indication of a problem came in the late 1970s, when a slow trickle became a deluge, as savers began to take their money out of S&Ls and put it in investments that paid a higher rate of interest. This process of *disintermediation* began as a result of uncontrolled inflation causing interest rates to soar to rates unseen in any market at any time anyone remembered. Because the S&Ls were restricted by law from offering competitive interest rates, depositors began to put their money in government securities, corporate bonds and money market funds offering them a greater return on their money.

The S&L had always counted on short-term deposits from savers and then loaned that money on long-term, fixed rate mortgage loans to borrowers. Their profit margin, however, was diminishing in a market where the S&L had to pay a higher interest rate to their depositors than they were getting on their long term loans. Since S&Ls could not compete with the higher returns from other sources, depositors began to drift away along with their money.

Depository Institution's Deregulation and Monetary Control Act: One of the main reasons for the flow of funds out of the S&L associations was deregulation of the industry. The Depository Institution's Deregulation and Monetary Control Act, approved in March 1980, permitted S&Ls to offer a much wider range of services than ever before. The deregulatory measures allowed savings and loan associations to enter the business of commercial lending, trust services and non-mortgage consumer lending. The Depository Institutions Deregulation and Monetary Control Act of 1980 allowed these sweeping changes, one of which was to raise deposit insurance from $40,000 to $100,000.

Many contend that this extension of insurance coverage encouraged savings and loan associations to engage in riskier loans than they might otherwise have sought. Even as the limits on insured deposits were raised, limitations on investments loans that savings institutions could make were relaxed. As a result, many S&Ls began making higher-risk loans on undeveloped land, real estate development loans and joint venture loans. S&Ls had been successful in the past because of the low-risk residential loans they had made, but now the new law permitted S&Ls to use savers' funds to get involved in higher-risk business ventures. Coupled with ill-trained administrators and managers, the "riverboat gambler" mentality of the S&Ls, in part, led to their ruin.

In addition to the problems of the S&Ls, the Federal Savings and Loan Insurance Corporation (FSLIC), the insurer who provided a recovery fund for depositors in the event of an S&L failure, eventually failed to keep up with the significant numbers of S&L institutions becoming insolvent. As a result, during the late 1970s and the 1980s, disintermediation and bad lending practices encouraged under deregulation caused a huge number of S&Ls to fail, and along with them, the FSLIC, which simply did not have enough funds to bail everyone out. It was time for the federal government to step in.

Prior to 1992, S&Ls were the largest private holder of residential mortgage debt, and were the largest originator of residential mortgages in the country. After the problems were encountered, that role was taken over by commercial banks as holders of mortgage loans, and mortgage bankers and commercial bankers as originators of mortgage loans.

After all is said and done, however, in terms of assets the savings and loan industry still ranks as the third largest financial institution in the United States. Only commercial banks and life insurance companies have greater assets.

The first few decades of the 19th Century saw increasing numbers of people move to urban areas of the United States. These individuals needed financial institutions where they could save funds at a profit with safety. They also needed to finance home purchases. Traditionally, individuals borrowed money for their home purchases from savings and loan associations.

It is believed that the first savings and loan association in the United States was formed in Philadelphia in 1831. It was patterned after similar institutions in England. The savings and loan industry grew rapidly. In response to this growth many states enacted laws for chartering and supervising savings and loan associations.

As the industry matured, two characteristics evolved. First was the use of long-term fixed mortgage home loans; the second was the accumulation of small long-term individual saving accounts. A savings and loan association during this time generally took deposits and made loans within the same community.

Savings and loan associations were looked upon as benevolent institutions providing a public service because of their function of encouraging savings and making home loans. Accordingly, they received favorable tax treatment. The Revenue Act of 1913, which set up the first permanent national income tax on corporations and individuals, exempted savings and loan associations from federal income tax.

The 1920s were a period of industrial expansion and high levels of personal income. Correspondingly, savings and loan associations grew substantially. The industry changed from small cooperatives to major financial institutions. With growth, savings and loan associations set up permanent offices and large staffs.

The stock market collapse of 1929 was the beginning of a deterioration of the economy resulting in a depression over the next several years. The poor economic environment was reflected in the financial operations of banks and financial entities which suffered the withdrawal of deposits and the failure of borrowers to make loan payments. Many financial institutions closed their doors, although the savings and loan industry had fewer failures than other monetary organizations.

Legislation was sponsored by the new administration in Washington D.C. to build the confidence of depositors in savings and loan associations. Important legislation included:

- *The Home Owner's Loan Act of 1933* provided for the first time, federal chartered savings and loan associations. The chartering and regulation of these entities was the responsibil-ity of a new organization, the Federal Home Loan Bank Board. The federal chartered savings and loan associations were required to be members of the Federal Home Loan Bank System and the Federal Savings and Loan Insurance Corporation.

- The Federal Savings and Loan Insurance Corporation (FSLIC) was another new organization that had the responsibility of insuring deposits within specific limits.

- *The Federal Home Loan Bank Act of 1932* set up the Federal Home Loan Bank System. Under the supervision of the Federal Home Loan Bank Board, the bank system is comprised of a three-member bipartisan body. Twelve regional banks were established to provide short- and long-term loans to savings and loan association members. The Federal Home Loan Bank System is patterned after the Federal Reserve System.

  The Federal Home Loan Bank of San Francisco is the 12th District bank that includes California, Arizona and Nevada.

- As the 1939 Internal Revenue Code again exempted their income from tax, favorable tax treatment continued for savings and loan associations.

Due to a scarcity of consumer goods and building materials during World War II, savings in all financial institutions, including savings and loan associations increased rapidly. Since the associations could not make a large amount of mortgage loans, they purchased government bonds.

After World War II, savings and loan associations enjoyed a high rate of growth in both deposits and loans made. As savings associations continued to develop, both in size and complexity, the financial community applied pressure to bring savings and loan associations under the federal income tax system, arguing equitable taxation.

Beginning in 1952, savings and loan associations were subject to federal income tax and filing requirements for the first time. However, the bad debt rules were so generous that few savings and loan associations incurred an income tax.

The Revenue Act of 1962 ended what appeared to be an income tax exemption enjoyed by savings and loan associations, although some favorable tax treatment did continue. The appearance of tax exemption was from a generous bad debt reserve. The reserve was based on a 20-year experience that included depression years. The bad debt provision substantially reduced the amount of taxable income.

The Tax Reform Act of 1969 subjected a greater amount of savings and loan associations' income to tax by including the following major provisions.

- Net bond gains were taxed as ordinary income. Under previous tax law, gains were taxed at capital gains rates and losses as ordinary income.

- The deduction for bad debts was reduced.

- The bad debt deduction in excess of experience was classified as a tax preference item. The Tax Reform Act of 1976 raised the minimum tax rate from 10% to 15% and the minimum tax rate exemption was reduced.

Steady growth in total assets and profitability allowed for the appearance of stability in the S&Ls during the 1970s, but during the 1980s, the industry struggled to survive, and the free-fall toward financial ruin and disgrace began, resulting in the well-known federal bailout.

Interest rates in 1979 and 1980 were extremely high. Savings and loan associations were in financial trouble as most of their loans were in long-term low interest mortgages while they had to pay high rates of interest to keep deposits. As we have seen, during these years the savings and loan associations were in a no-win situation. They had to pay rates of interest to depositors that were greater than they were getting in interest on the long-term mortgage loans, or lose their depositors. When they couldn't keep up with the demand to be competitive with other lending institutions, billions of dollars were withdrawn from savings and loan associations.

The S&L industry, by 1980, tried to solve its problems by winning federal government/regulatory approval for deregulation of depository institutions, in addition to creating accounting changes that differed from generally accepted accounting procedures. The industry also received regulatory consent to pursue high-yield/high-risk loans. Supervision of activities, however, did not follow these expanded lending practices. After a few profitable years, a lack of ethical practices coupled with negligent oversight by management caused vulnerable S&Ls to begin to collapse.

Because of this crisis, the most important legislation for the savings and loan industry in 50 years was enacted: the Garn-St. Germain Depository Institutions Act of 1982. This important act:

- Increased business opportunities for savings and loan associations. Traditionally federal savings and loan associations were limited in the investments they could make by type of investment and percent of assets loaned by type of investment.

- While the Act provided for more liberal investment guidelines, investment opportunities are still limited in comparison to other financial institutions. For example, the Act allowed for the increase in the amount of assets invested in nonresidential real estate from 20% to 40% of the association's total assets.

- Eliminated the advantage savings associations had over commercial banks. They previously could pay .25% more interest on deposits, which encouraged greater savings in saving and loan associations.

- Granted the Federal Home Loan Bank Board and the Federal Savings and Loan Insurance Corporation new powers to deal with financially troubled savings associations.

- Authorized emergency rescue programs to help troubled savings associations.

The second half of 1982 saw interest rates dropping and by year-end savings and loan associations were receiving more in interest income than the interest expense they paid on deposits. During 1981 and 1982 as many as 813 savings associations disappeared, however, most of which were merged into other institutions.

Savings and loan associations continued to fail during the 1980s and early 1990s for various reasons, including:

- Concentration of loans in a geographic region that was dominated by one industry and that industry was depressed. For example, Texas and Colorado are major energy states. Oil and gas companies were hurt by the fall in the price of oil in the early 1980s. This fall in prices caused high unemployment in the region. Unemployment caused defaults on residential loans and low occupancy for commercial rentals. Depressed real estate values greatly impacted savings and loan associations.

- The 1990s saw cutbacks in defense spending and military bases. Some geographic regions are dominated by this industry. The resulting unemployment during a weak economy lead to defaults in mortgages in the residential market that adversely impacted financial institutions.

- Concentration of investments that were adversely affected by the economy such as junk bonds.

- Fraud.

The Tax Reform Act of 1986 completed the downward spiral toward the end of prosperity and domination of mortgage lending for S&Ls. This act removed many of the tax benefits from real estate, which had made it an attractive investment. Because of the tax law changes, builders and developers could not sell their properties and many of the properties financed by S&Ls went back to the lenders through foreclosure.

Income from the foreclosed properties did not exist, and a careful look at earnings and loan portfolios by regulators showed that a catastrophe was developing. The National Association of REALTORS® (NAR), in review of the tangled web of financial misbehavior and bad business practices, assessed the situation as follows: "Deregulation and new investment powers made financial and managerial demands that most thrift executives had not considered. Speculative investment, a regulatory system that failed to exercise controls, basic mismanagement and unprecedented level of fraud, abuse and greed perpetrated by many thrift executives resulted in the inevitable legislative backlash."

After savings and loan associations had begun to engage in large-scale real estate speculation, financial failure of the institutions became rampant, with well over 500 forced to close during the 1980s. In 1989, after the FSLIC itself became insolvent, the Federal Deposit Insurance Corporation took over the FSLIC's insurance obligations, and the Resolution Trust Corporation was created to buy and sell defaulted savings and loan associations. The Office of Thrift Supervision was also created, in an attempt to identify struggling savings and loan organizations before it was too late. The U.S. government expects it will cost more than $500 billion over 30 years to bail out the savings and loan associations.

Financial Institutions Reform, Recovery and Enforcement Act (FIRREA):   The "inevitable legislative backlash" to the behavior of the savings and loan industry was the enactment by Congress of the Financial Institutions Reform, Recovery and Enforcement Act (FIRREA) in 1989.

This was an attempt to rebuild an industry that had disgraced itself by disregarding the welfare of consumers and nurturing greed and profiteering within the banking business.

Under FIRREA, the Office of Thrift Supervision (OTS) and the Housing Finance Board were authorized to oversee the savings and loan regulation responsibilities that had belonged to the Federal Home Loan Bank Board (FHLBB) under the old system. The Federal Deposit Insurance Corporation (FDIC) now insures deposits in all federally chartered banks and savings institutions up to $100,000 per account for commercial and savings banks. The FDIC also supervises the Savings Association Insurance Fund (SAIF) and the Resolution Trust Corporation (RTC). Other new government agencies were created to unravel the banking crisis and regulate banking transactions in the future.

Agencies Created For Bank Reorganization Under FIRREA

Office of Thrift Supervision (OTS)

The Office of Thrift Supervision (OTS) is the primary regulator of all federally chartered and many state-chartered thrift institutions, which include savings banks and savings and loan associations. OTS was established as a bureau of the U.S. Department of the Treasury on August 9, 1989, and has four regional offices located in Jersey City, Atlanta, Dallas and San Francisco. OTS is funded by assessments and fees levied on the institutions it regulates.   *http://www.ots.treas.gov*

(continued on next page)

(continued)

Agencies Created For Bank Reorganization Under FIRREA

Federal Deposit Insurance Corporation (FDIC)

A federal agency created by Congress to insure the deposits of federally chartered banks. The insurance is financed through premiums charged the financial institution, and each insured account is covered up to $100,000.

The previously existing FDIC operates two new separate insurance funds: the Bank Insurance Fund (BIF) for institutions previously covered under the FDIC, and the Savings Association Insurance Fund (SAIF) for those institutions formerly covered under the dissolved Federal Savings and Loan Insurance Corporation (FSLIC). The FDIC was transferred from the Federal Reserve Bank to the Treasury Department, from where it watches over member banks and savings institutions, arriving regularly for examinations.

Savings Association Insurance Fund (SAIF)

A deposit insurance fund for savings and loan associations administered by the Federal Deposit Insurance Corporation. This fund collects premiums to produce the money needed to insure accounts at savings banks. It assumed the functions of the Resolution Trust Corporation (RTC) in 1995.

Resolution Trust Corporation (RTC)

A corporation formed by Congress in 1989 to replace the Federal Savings and Loan Insurance Corporation and respond to the insolvencies of about 750 savings and loan associations. As receiver, it sold assets of failed S&Ls and paid insured depositors. In 1995 its duties, including insurance of deposits in thrift institutions, were transferred to the Savings Association Insurance Fund.

Federal Housing Finance Board (FHFB)

Mortgage lending by the 25 regional Federal Home Loan Banks is supervised by the FHFB, replacing the now lifeless Federal Home Loan Bank Board (FHLBB). If a savings bank can't meet "Qualified Thrift Lender" (QTL) guidelines, it may not borrow funds from any of the Federal Home Loan Banks. The FHFB may close a troubled bank and transfer management of the institution to the Resolution Trust Corporation (RTC).

Even though the market share of S&Ls has decreased from the time they dominated the residential mortgage market, S&Ls are still a powerful force in mortgage lending. In spite of all the problems over the past 20 years, the industry is still active in both the primary and secondary money markets. Those surviving institutions are still a major source of mortgage money and, once again, place a major emphasis on residential lending.

Savings Banks

Savings banks have been described as distinctive types of thrift institutions, behaving sometimes like commercial banks and sometimes like S&Ls. Lending practices for savings banks are cyclical, depending on saver's diligence in depositing funds.

When lending institutions were being established in the first part of the 19th Century, the average income worker, who was not wealthy but wanted to save money, was mostly ignored as far as investments went. Savings banks were established to encourage savings by people who did not have a serious amount of disposable income after their living expenses, but who did want to invest in their future.

At the beginning, savings banks were mutual organizations, relying on their customer's savings to provide all the capital they needed to be successful, and did not sell stock in the company to shareholders. In order to be competitive with other lending institutions after deregulation in the mid-1990s, savings banks became stock institutions, raising more capital and changing their image.

The difference between banks that are mutual organizations and those that are stock institutions is that all depositors share ownership in the mutual savings bank that is managed by a board of trustees. A stock company is managed by a board of directors who represent stockholders of the bank.

While savings banks are authorized to make mortgage loans, most specialize in consumer and commercial loans. However, they are active in purchasing low-risk FHA/VA and conventional mortgages from other mortgage lenders and mortgage bankers. Since most savings banks are located primarily in the capital-surplus areas of the northeast and possess more funds than are needed locally, savings banks play an important part in the savings-investment cycle by purchasing loans from areas that are capital deficient. This flow of funds from areas with excess funds to areas with scarce resources helps to stimulate a healthy national financial environment.

PROFILE OF STATE-CHARTERED SAVINGS AND LOAN ASSOCIATIONS (In millions of dollars)				
PERIOD ENDING	**12/31/2000**	**12/31/2001**	**12/31/2002**	**03/31/2003**
Number of Savings and Loan Associations	3	1	1	1
Loans & Leases (Net)*	635.8	277.8	302.1	304.6
Reserve for loans	5.3	1.6	1.9	2.0
Total Assets	1,315.6	305.6	337.6	342.0
Total Deposits	1,109.2	204.2	214.2	220.9
Total Equity Capital	116.6	22.6	26.9	28.1
Noncurrent Loans & Leases**	2.2	0.3	0.0	0.0
Total Past Due Loans & Leases***	2.8	0.3	0.0	0.1
Other Real Estate Owned	0.5	0.0	0.0	0.0
Interest Earned	87.3	22.8	21.4	5.1
Interest Expense	43.4	12.8	9.2	3.1
Net Interest Income	43.9	10.0	12.2	2.0
Noninterest Income	7.0	1.3	1.3	0.5
Loan Loss Provision	0.5	0.2	0.2	0.0
Noninterest Expense	25.2	4.8	5.2	1.4
Net Income	15.5	3.7	4.8	1.3
Return on Assets#	1.18	1.23	1.41	1.48
Return on Equity#	13.26	16.53	17.77	18.02
Net Interest Margin#	3.34	3.26	3.62	2.35
Loans & Leases/Deposits	57.32	136.03	141.01	137.89
Loans & Leases/Assets	48.33	90.88	89.49	89.08
LLR/Total Loans	0.83	0.57	0.62	0.66
Equity Capital/Assets	8.86	7.41	7.95	8.22
Noncurrent Loans&Leases/Total Loans&Leases**	0.34	0.10	0.00	0.00
Tot. Past Due Loans&Leases/Total Loans&Leases	0.44	0.10	0.00	0.02
Reserves for Loans/Noncurrent Loans&Leases**	245.11	586.03	-	-

* Net of unearned income.

** Noncurrent loans & leases are loans & leases past due 90 days or more and nonaccruals.

*** Includes noncurrent loans & leases plus loans & leases 30-89 days delinquent.

Aggregate, annualized return

Mutual Savings Banks

Mutual savings banks are owned by the depositors whose return on their investment is determined by how successful the bank's investment strategies are. They are located mostly in the northeast states. Depositors in mutual savings banks share in the earnings of the bank after expenses, reserves and contributions to surplus. Recently, mutual savings banks have been permitted to convert to savings bank status.

Credit Unions

A credit union is an association whose members usually have the same type of occupation. The members join together for mutual benefit by saving money in their own bank and receiving better interest rates. Both secured and unsecured loans are made at rates lower than other lenders can offer. Because of the low overhead and other costs of doing business, credit unions are a growing source of funds for consumers. They are supervised by the National Credit Union Association Board (NCUAB) and deposits are insured by the federally insured National Credit Union Share Insurance Fund.

Insurance Companies

Insurance companies generally invest in real estate by making large commercial loans to developers and builders. They don't usually get involved with the single home residential market, but can buy loans from mortgage companies and invest in government insured or guaranteed loans. Life insurance companies, in particular, receive regular, periodic payments from customers in return for assurance that any loss would be covered if certain described events occur for which the customer is insured. The insurance company needs to invest the funds to build up its reserves for the occasion when it does have to pay a claim. Commercial real estate is a good, long-term investment for insurance companies because of the long time line of their investment goals.

NON-INSTITUTIONAL LENDERS

In addition to institutional lenders, there is another group of lenders referred to as non-institutional lenders. This group includes mortgage companies and private individuals, as well as others—like pension funds and title companies—who are non-financial lenders.

Top 100 Federal Credit Unions
By Total Assets

NAME	CITY	STATE	2003 MAR. ASSETS	2002 DEC. ASSETS	RANK '03	RANK '02
NAVY	MERRIFIELD	VA	$18,560,685,512	$17,573,419,565	1	1
PENTAGON	ALEXANDRIA	VA	$5,773,031,878	$5,175,320,825	2	2
ORANGE COUNTY TEACHERS	SANTA ANA	CA	$4,248,215,758	$4,005,666,091	3	3
AMERICAN AIRLINES	DFW AIRPORT	TX	$3,985,246,229	$3,882,663,512	4	4
SUNCOAST SCHOOLS	TAMPA	FL	$3,737,203,844	$3,529,008,372	5	5
KINECTA	MANHATTAN BEACH	CA	$3,070,896,489	$2,996,768,650	6	6
SECURITY SERVICE	SAN ANTONIO	TX	$2,970,188,375	$2,743,157,679	7	7
ESL	ROCHESTER	NY	$2,428,979,345	$2,322,203,071	8	8
ALASKA USA	ANCHORAGE	AK	$2,222,335,489	$2,160,096,919	9	9
RANDOLPH-BROOKS	UNIVERSAL CITY	TX	$1,995,097,274	$1,930,253,386	10	10
DIGITAL	MARLBOROUGH	MA	$1,971,177,162	$1,799,762,650	11	11
DESERT SCHOOLS	PHOENIX	AZ	$1,853,200,283	$1,754,849,019	12	12
UNITED NATIONS	NEW YORK	NY	$1,672,471,464	$1,621,844,193	13	13
ADDISON AVENUE	PALO ALTO	CA	$1,659,974,064	$1,621,446,084	14	14
DFCU FINANCIAL	DEARBORN	MI	$1,640,880,236	$1,506,385,512	15	18
LOCKHEED	BURBANK	CA	$1,639,294,488	$1,528,544,306	16	16
HUDSON VALLEY	POUGHKEEPSIE	NY	$1,604,163,705	$1,494,773,889	17	20
BANK FUND STAFF	WASHINGTON	DC	$1,588,163,798	$1,554,014,075	18	15
ENT	COLORADO SPRING	CO	$1,582,205,630	$1,482,913,650	19	21
MISSION	SAN DIEGO	CA	$1,578,701,552	$1,474,244,380	20	22
TEACHERS	FARMINGVILLE	NY	$1,564,531,143	$1,434,855,156	21	24
POLICE & FIRE	PHILADELPHIA	PA	$1,552,610,180	$1,498,444,078	22	19
SAN ANTONIO	SAN ANTONIO	TX	$1,539,456,231	$1,525,639,300	23	17
BETHPAGE	BETHPAGE	NY	$1,538,960,221	$1,461,709,975	24	23
REDSTONE	HUNTSVILLE	AL	$1,497,343,115	$1,414,926,681	25	25
GTE	TAMPA	FL	$1,461,201,852	$1,295,467,492	26	27
VISIONS	ENDICOTT	NY	$1,393,108,593	$1,339,334,334	27	26
NWA	APPLE VALLEY	MN	$1,367,138,478	$1,290,198,484	28	28
AFFINITY	BASKING RIDGE	NJ	$1,297,529,849	$1,191,610,234	29	29
MACDILL	TAMPA	FL	$1,264,635,175	$1,157,269,382	30	31
TINKER	TINKER AFB	OK	$1,223,937,415	$1,175,271,116	31	30
TOWER	LAUREL	MD	$1,221,895,563	$1,118,310,876	32	33
COASTAL	RALEIGH	NC	$1,221,199,722	$1,154,366,808	33	32
ARIZONA	PHOENIX	AZ	$1,174,852,885	$1,083,409,669	34	34
KERN SCHOOLS	BAKERSFIELD	CA	$1,105,893,129	$1,026,428,718	35	36
IBM MID AMERICA EMPLOYEES	ROCHESTER	MN	$1,097,350,829	$1,054,202,728	36	35
STATE EMPLOYEES	ALBANY	NY	$1,040,450,004	$1,009,984,004	37	37
NORTHWEST	HERNDON	VA	$1,032,897,685	$968,367,248	38	38
MICHIGAN STATE UNIVERSITY	EAST LANSING	MI	$1,024,533,532	$929,757,196	39	39
FOUNDERS	LANCASTER	SC	$944,571,696	$904,195,158	40	40
AEDC	TULLAHOMA	TN	$929,647,504	$886,531,998	41	41
MERCK EMPLOYEES	RAHWAY	NJ	$925,207,807	$857,116,764	42	45
TRULIANT	WINSTON SALEM	NC	$912,616,153	$870,423,898	43	42
LANGLEY	HAMPTON	VA	$893,555,463	$865,295,086	44	44
POLISH & SLAVIC	BROOKLYN	NY	$890,037,825	$868,565,415	45	43
SOUTH CAROLINA	NORTH CHARLESTO	SC	$887,099,391	$856,644,409	46	46
ALLEGACY	WINSTON-SALEM	NC	$885,876,701	$849,279,097	47	47
CHARTWAY	VIRGINIA BEACH	VA	$856,723,132	$835,506,132	48	48
AFFINITY PLUS	ST. PAUL	MN	$828,927,892	$792,505,042	49	49
KEESLER	BILOXI	MS	$828,444,101	$775,878,647	50	52
MEMBERS 1ST	MECHANICSBURG	PA	$827,017,805	$781,341,246	51	50
SANDIA LABORATORY	ALBUQUERQUE	NM	$806,736,075	$768,726,110	52	53
AMERICAN EAGLE	EAST HARTFORD	CT	$806,402,028	$776,520,989	53	51
NASSAU EDUCATORS FCU	WESTBURY	NY	$786,223,477	$738,787,416	54	55
EGLIN	FT. WALTON BEAC	FL	$782,694,840	$767,847,337	55	54
CHEVRONTEXACO	OAKLAND	CA	$764,182,159	$705,520,659	56	56
ROBINS	WARNER ROBINS	GA	$744,521,538	$685,478,615	57	58

Top 100 Federal Credit Unions
By Total Assets (con't.)

NAME	CITY	STATE	2003 MAR. ASSETS	2002 DEC. ASSETS	RANK '03	'02
CENTRAL FLORIDA EDUCATORS	ORLANDO	FL	$741,145,695	$691,531,453	58	57
GREYLOCK	PITTSFIELD	MA	$713,884,102	$680,847,443	59	59
DM	TUCSON	AZ	$709,580,102	$678,906,840	60	60
NEVADA	LAS VEGAS	NV	$700,375,772	$678,087,084	61	61
ORNL	OAK RIDGE	TN	$687,089,781	$671,479,796	62	62
ANDREWS	SUITLAND	MD	$668,925,897	$635,979,522	63	65
XEROX	EL SEGUNDO	CA	$664,929,932	$636,448,201	64	64
OPERATING ENGINEERS LOCAL UNION #3	DUBLIN	CA	$661,016,584	$653,173,918	65	63
STATE DEPARTMENT	ALEXANDRIA	VA	$654,401,947	$634,439,298	66	66
HAWAII STATE	HONOLULU	HI	$653,866,830	$631,713,078	67	67
APPLE	FAIRVAX	VA	$634,796,014	$598,457,892	68	70
US AIRWAYS	MOON TOWNSHIP	PA	$632,270,972	$613,543,063	69	68
TYNDALL	PANAMA CITY	FL	$631,836,143	$610,310,339	70	69
NUVISION FINANCIAL	HUNTINGTON BEAC	CA	$626,558,844	$595,776,717	71	71
NEW MEXICO EDUCATORS	ALBUQUERQUE	NM	$623,324,511	$590,710,007	72	73
MIDFLORIDA	LAKELAND,	FL	$621,634,735	$575,960,980	73	76
PEN AIR	PENSACOLA	FL	$617,960,170	$554,867,294	74	80
F & A	MONTEREY PARK	CA	$616,525,866	$593,276,031	75	72
U OF C	BOULDER	CO	$612,164,977	$586,311,017	76	74
CAL TECH EMPLOYEES	LA CANADA	CA	$608,566,733	$577,010,153	77	75
NASA	BOWIE	MD	$602,233,769	$574,243,687	78	77
HAWAIIUSA	HONOLULU	HI	$598,062,453	$567,523,873	79	78
ADVANCIAL	DALLAS	TX	$589,574,821	$565,428,569	80	79
UNIVERSITY	AUSTIN	TX	$589,125,844	$545,872,257	81	83
IBM SOUTHEAST EMPLOYEES	BOCA RATON	FL	$586,554,391	$552,613,261	82	81
UNITED SERVICES OF AMERICA	SAN DIEGO	CA	$585,425,591	$526,032,880	83	89
GENERAL ELECTRIC	TROY	MI	$577,232,265	$536,738,593	84	86
EVENDALE EMPLOYEES	CINCINNATI	OH	$567,208,858	$539,298,804	85	85
MAX	MONTGOMERY	AL	$566,654,391	$550,793,449	86	82
HIWAY	ST. PAUL	MN	$563,423,534	$532,907,759	87	88
ELI LILLY	INDIANAPOLIS	IN	$560,674,953	$534,573,821	88	87
FIBRE	LONGVIEW	WA	$551,928,297	$542,327,031	89	84
LOS ANGELES POLICE	VAN NUYS	CA	$544,371,039	$516,621,464	90	91
J. S. C.	HOUSTON	TX	$535,231,222	$503,583,959	91	93
USALLIANCE	RYE.	NY	$533,492,754	$518,698,158	92	90
CITADEL	THORNDALE	PA	$531,829,667	$507,717,936	93	92
SUFFOLK	MEDFORD	NY	$531,526,844	$474,035,610	94	103
AMERICA'S FIRST	BIRMINGHAM	AL	$531,115,542	$496,971,655	95	97
SOUTH FLORIDA EDUCATIONAL	MIAMI	FL	$529,205,731	$502,234,671	96	94
ROCKLAND	ROCKLAND	MA	$524,184,347	$499,252,124	97	96
LOCKHEED GEORGIA EMPLOYEES	MARIETTA	GA	$524,092,791	$501,140,866	98	95
CORNING	CORNING	NY	$513,718,678	$493,671,613	99	98
KITSAP COMMUNITY	BREMERTON	WA	$513,055,183	$490,357,939	100	100

Mortgage Bankers and Brokers

Mortgage bankers originate the majority of residential mortgage loans. These individuals act as financial intermediaries by connecting borrowers and lenders. The name, mortgage banker, sounds like an institution that accepts deposits, but in fact a mortgage banker is a borrower himself, using other people's money in the course of being a financial intermediary.

A *mortgage banker* is similar to a *mortgage broker,* but with a major difference. A mortgage broker originates a loan by taking the application from a borrower and selling that unclosed loan to another mortgage lender. The mortgage broker then has no other concern with that loan once he has sold it and been paid. Mortgage bankers, however, sell all of the mortgages they originate and close and continue to service the loan after the sale.

Mortgage bankers, then, make mortgage loans to consumers and sell them to institutional investors. Some mortgage companies have funds of their own, and others act as a go-between for the institutions who have the money and the borrowers who need it.

Many mortgage bankers get their funding from commercial banks on short-term lines of credit while arranging to sell pools of loans they have originated. The process of assembling into one package a number of mortgage loans, prior to selling them to an investor, is called *warehousing.* The sale of these loan packages provides added capital with which to make more loans, which can then be packaged and sold, thus repeating the cycle.

About Mortgage Bankers and Brokers

- Mortgage bankers lend their own funds, borrow funds from other intermediaries, service their loans, as well as broker loans for others.
- Mortgage brokers mainly put borrowers and lenders together, and do not normally lend their own money, or service loans.

The mortgage banker often acts as a mover of funds from one area of the country with an abundance of money to be loaned, to another area that is capital deficient.

The biggest role of mortgage companies, however, is to originate and service loans which they then sell in the secondary mortgage market. As the person in the middle who stirs the pot, the mortgage banker is careful to follow guidelines established by those who will be buying the loans.

Generally, a mortgage company prefers loans that are most readily saleable in the secondary market, such as government-insured or government-guaranteed mortgages (FHA, VA), or conventional mortgages for which it has advance purchase commitments.

When a borrower applies for a loan from a mortgage broker or banker, there are certain procedures followed to assure the loan will be saleable in the secondary market.

Loan Application Procedures

- The customer fills out a loan application.
- A credit report is ordered.
- The subject property is appraised.
- The application package, including application form, borrower's financial statement, appraisal and copy of the sale agreement, presented to the investor.
- The investor decides whether or not to accept.
- Approval is sent to the mortgage company.
- When loan conditions are met, the mortgage banker sends funds to escrow for closing.
- After closing, documents are sold to the investor and the mortgage banker services the loan (accepts and keeps track of payments, tracks the life of the loan).

Investment Companies

Pooling the funds of many investors, these companies invest in a portfolio of assets. The investment companies might specialize in investing in certain types of investments or industries, such as income stocks or growth stocks or Real Estate Investment Trusts (REITs).

An REIT is another way private individuals can operate in the real estate market as investors, by joining together, each with a small amount of capital, to pool their resources to buy real estate, with the risk of loss spread out among the investors. REITs invest in an assorted mix of real estate and mortgage investments as a group, with a minimum of 100 investors required. There are serious legal requirements to qualify as a trust and for special tax treatment.

Essentially a creation of the Internal Revenue Code, an REIT may be a real estate company or a group of individuals that has chosen to qualify under certain tax provisions to become an entity that distributes to its shareholders the greater part of its profits generated from the sale of its properties. The REIT itself does not pay taxes on its profits, but individual members of the trust are taxed, at their own tax rates, on the dividends distributed to them.

REIT Requirements

Assets

- At least 75% of the value of a REIT's assets must consist of real estate assets, cash and government securities.

- Not more than 5% of the value of the assets may consist of the securities of any one issuer if the securities are not includable under the 75% test.

- A REIT may not hold more than 10% of the outstanding voting securities of any one issuer if those securities are not includable under the 75% test.

Income

- At least 95% of the entity's gross income must be derived from dividends, interest, rents or gains from the sale of certain assets.

- At least 75% of gross income must be derived from rents, interest on obligations secured by mortgages, gains from the sale of certain assets or income attributable to investments in other REITs.

- Not more than 30% of the entity's gross income can be derived from sale or disposition of stock or securities held for less than 6 months or real property held for less than 4 years other than property involuntarily converted or foreclosed on.

Distribution of Income

- Distributions to shareholders must equal or exceed the sum of 95% of REIT taxable income.

(continued on next page)

REIT Requirements *(continued)*

Stock and Ownership

- Shares in a REIT must be transferable and must be held by a minimum of 100 persons.

- No more than 50% of REIT shares may be held by five or fewer individuals during the last half of a taxable year.

Private Individuals

Private individuals can be lenders, also. The most common way is by carrying back a trust deed on the sale of their own home, or they can go through a mortgage broker, who will then find them a borrower. Usually, private loans are short term, with the main motivation of the lender being safety of the loan, and a high return on the investment.

Non-Financial Institutions

Universities, pension funds, trust departments of banks, title companies and mortgage investment companies all hold real estate loans as investments.

CHAPTER QUIZ

1. Institutions that make real estate loans are known as:

    a. financial intermediaries
    b. hypothecators
    c. disintermediators
    d. trustees

2. Which of the following is the all purpose lender?

    a. savings banks
    b. insurance companies
    c. commercial banks
    d. mortgage bankers

3. The largest single resource for residential mortgage credit is:

    a. commercial banks
    b. private individuals
    c. thrifts
    d. insurance companies

4. One of the following is not a thrift institution.

    a. savings & loan associations
    b. mortgage bankers
    c. mutual savings banks
    d. credit unions

5. One of the main reasons for the flow of funds out of the S&L associations in 1980 was:

    a. deregulation of the industry
    b. intermediation
    c. tighter controls and regulation
    d. high interest rates being paid by the S&Ls

6. What was the most important legislation enacted for the savings and loan industry in the second half of the 20th Century?

    a. the Tax Reform Act of 1969
    b. the Garn-St. Germain Depository Institutions Act of 1982
    c. the Depository Institution's Deregulation and Monetary Control Act of 1980
    d. the Financial Institutions Reform, Recovery and Enforcement Act (FIRREA) in 1989

7. The type of institution owned by the depositors whose return on their investment is determined by the success of the bank's investment strategy:

    a. mutual savings bank
    b. commercial bank
    c. S&L
    d. savings bank

8. What institution invests in real estate by making large commercial loans to developers and builders?

    a. mutual savings banks
    b. credit unions
    c. commercial banks
    d. insurance companies

9. Who makes mortgage loans to consumers and sells them to institutional investors?

    a. credit unions
    b. mortgage brokers
    c. private individuals
    d. mortgage bankers

10. The process of assembling into one package a number of mortgage loans, prior to selling them to an investor, is called:

    a. warehousing
    b. itemizing
    c. underwriting
    d. pledging

ANSWERS

1. *a*
2. *c*
3. *c*
4. *b*
5. *a*
6. *b*
7. *a*
8. *d*
9. *d*
10. *a*

7

*chapter
seven*

The Mortgage Market

INTRODUCTION

In the aftermath of a decade of negative forces at work in the economy during the 1980s, the real estate industry, and particularly government-regulated financial institutions that supplied most of the funds, had to find new ways to compete and serve the consumer.

These government-regulated depository institutions, known as *financial intermediaries* (savings banks, commercial banks, credit unions and mutual savings banks), lost customers—and their savings accounts—to the un-regulated non-depository institutions such as the uninsured money-market funds. As we have seen in the previous chapter, the reason was: customers could get a higher interest rate on their savings from the unregulated institutions than the regulated lenders were allowed to pay under the law.

As you recall, the process of depositors removing funds from savings is called *disintermediation*. That savings account money was what the financial institutions used to make home loans. The less available money there was, like all scarce goods, the more it cost. And the more it cost, the fewer there were who could afford it. The downward free-fall of the economy fed upon itself.

Institutional lenders holding existing, low-interest-rate loan portfolios that were declining in value could not make enough new higher-interest-rate loans to make up for their losses. There were several reasons for their lack of profits. As we have seen, money was disappearing from personal savings accounts and interest rates were rising. Potential home buyers could not qualify for the high monthly payments required on the new loans, nor could they come up with the down payment to buy the expensive new homes whose prices were inflated by rapid appreciation.

Home ownership often was postponed by the crisis in the banking industry, which caused a crisis in the real estate industry. If no one could buy, no one could sell. Builders and developers stopped operations and the economy was stuck. Tight money and credit, plus high interest rates, made money scarce for mortgage loans and made it expensive in the nation's financial services marketplace. The viable borrowers had to compete for whatever funds were available, and had to pay top dollar.

Deregulation is a process where financial institutions that formerly had been restrained in their lending activities by the law, are allowed to compete freely for profits in the marketplace. Controls on lending practices still exist, but loans can now be marketed competitively by all lending institutions.

Now the question was how to make mortgage funds available and affordable to the consumer, and allow financial institutions to make a profit. The deregulation efforts of the federal government, along with alternative mortgage plans, have worked together to restructure the housing finance system throughout the nation.

Traditionally, fixed-rate loans have been the only choice for a home buyer. In an attempt to offer alternatives to consumers, and renew their faith in their ability to borrow money for homes, lenders found new ways to make loans consumer friendly.

What lenders offered were newly designed Variable Rate Mortgages (VRMs) that made it possible for everyone to win. Lenders could offer loans at a rate that was affordable to the borrower, yet not be tied to that original interest rate for the life of the loan. They were loans connected to movable indexes that reflected changes in the economy, and allowed a safety net for the lending institutions. Lenders wouldn't be stuck with old, unprofitable, low-interest-rate loans, and could be reasonably sure that the new loans would stimulate the real estate industry by creating new buyers, which in turn would create more borrowers.

As the banking industry continued to correct itself with more alternatives for borrowers, the Adjustable Rate Mortgage (ARM) was offered as an improvement on the VRM loans. The ARM allows for the interest rate to adjust periodically in relationship to a predetermined index plus a pre-established margin. For example, if a loan was tied to an index, such as a Treasury bill rate, and that rate was 5% at the time the loan was originated, the interest rate on the loan might be quoted as 5% plus a margin of 2%, to make the interest rate to the consumer 7% upon origination of the loan.

Generally, the way adjustable rate financing works to the benefit of the bankers is that it allows, contractually, for an inflow of extra cash during times of tight money and higher interest rates. In other words, the borrower's payments will increase because the interest rate will go up, therefore more money will flow into the financial institution.

Historically, the role of financial institutions has been intertwined with that of real estate in ways that may or may not benefit all parties. What has taken place during the past decade is a learning curve toward mutually acceptable goals by bankers and consumers alike.

THE NATIONAL ECONOMY

The economic system in America is a mixed capitalistic system. The government is asked by its citizens to influence the general economic direction, and assure reasonable, stable competition. However, private citizens have the right to own, control and dispose of property and make the majority of decisions about the overall economy themselves. Our economy is the result of millions of decisions we all make every day about producing, earning, saving, investing and spending.

Real Estate's Four Major Roles in the U.S. Economy

Net Worth
Real estate in the form of land and improvements makes up a very large portion of the total net worth of the United States as a nation (not to be confused with the government).

Income Flow
As we see from the circular flow chart of our economy, money is paid for the use of real estate and for the raw materials, labor, capital and management used in construction work of all kinds.

Major Employer

The real estate industry (brokerage, construction, management, finance) is a major employer in this country. It provides employment for a large segment of the population, accounting for billions of dollars in national income.

Appreciation and Inflation

In recent years appreciation in the value of real estate has overtaken the annual rate of inflation and is the single largest indicator of inflation. As the value of the dollar has decreased, passbook savings accounts and other forms of financial savings have lost their appeal as ways to save and invest for the future. Real estate has become a major means by which people save. Particularly in California where property has historically appreciated at such an alarmingly fast rate, it has been common for homeowners to consider their home as "money in the bank."

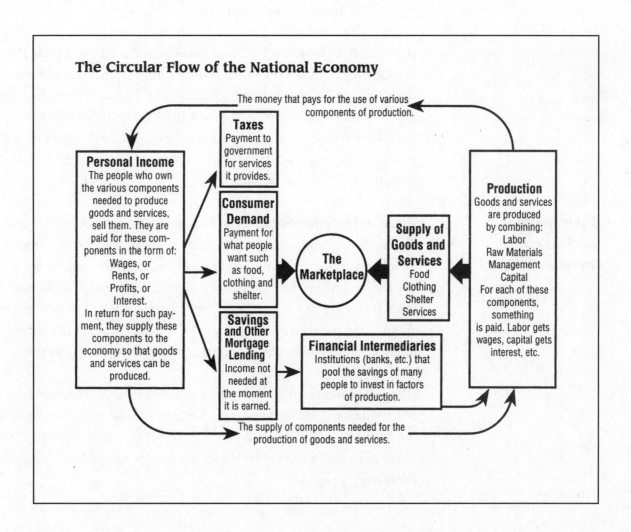

The Circular Flow of the National Economy

THE FEDERAL RESERVE BANK SYSTEM (THE FED)

The Federal Reserve Bank System (the Fed) is the nation's central bank, whose job it is to regulate the flow of money and credit to promote economic growth with stability. The Fed develops national *monetary policy* and shares responsibility with the 12 Federal Reserve Banks for applying that policy and setting money supply goals.

Today the Federal Reserve's duties fall into four general areas:

- Conducting the nation's monetary policy

- Supervising and regulating banking institutions and protecting the credit rights of consumers

- Maintaining the stability of the financial system

- Providing certain financial services to the U.S. government, the public, financial institutions and foreign official institutions.

In an effort to avoid the peaks and valleys of the business cycle that cause liquidity and credit crises, the Fed monitors changing economic conditions and applies appropriate controls. The Fed influences the supply of money and credit available, thus controlling the behavior of lenders and borrowers. These controls are far reaching, often affecting interest rates, jobs and economies worldwide. To accomplish its goals, the Fed uses three basic tools.

Basic Tools of the Federal Reserve System

Reserve Requirements: The Fed increases or decreases the amount of money in circulation by raising or lowering reserve requirements for member banks. A certain percentage of each deposit must be set aside as a reserve, and when the Fed requires a larger reserve, the banks have less to lend, thus interest rates increase while borrowing and spending decrease. By lowering the reserve requirement, the banks have more money to lend, interest rates may decrease, and borrowing and spending increase.

Discount Rates: This is the interest rate a bank is charged by the Fed to borrow money. A decrease in the discount rate allows more bank borrowing from the Fed. Bank borrowing increases money available for lending. Raising the discount rate produces less money available for lending to the consumer.

Open Market Operations: The Fed also buys and sells government securities to influence the amount of available credit. When the Fed buys securities, more money is available in the banks to lend. When the Fed sells securities, the opposite is true. The open-market operations process is the most flexible and widely used technique for expanding or slowing the economy.

Three Tools of the Fed to Regulate the Money Supply

- Reserve requirements
- Discount rate
- Open market operations

History of the Federal Reserve System

1775–1791: U.S. Currency in the Beginning

To finance the American Revolution, the Continental Congress printed the new nation's first paper money. Known as "continentals," the currency notes were issued in such quantity they led to inflation, which, though mild at first, rapidly accelerated as the war progressed. Eventually, people lost faith in the notes, and the phrase "Not worth a continental" came to mean "utterly worthless."

1791–1811: First Attempt at Central Banking

At the urging of Treasury Secretary Alexander Hamilton, Congress established the First Bank of the United States, headquartered in Philadelphia, in 1791. It was the largest corporation in the country and was dominated by big banking and money interests. Many agrarian-minded Americans uncomfortable with the idea of a large and powerful central bank opposed it. By 1811 when the bank's 20-year charter expired, Congress refused, by one vote, to renew it.

1816–1836: A Second Try Fails

By 1816 the political climate was once again inclined toward the idea of a central bank; by a narrow margin, Congress agreed to charter the Second Bank of the United States. But when Andrew Jackson, a central bank foe, was elected president in 1828, he vowed to kill it. His attack on its banker-controlled power touched a popular nerve with Americans, and when the Second Bank's charter expired in 1836, it was not renewed.

1836–1865: The Free Banking Era

State-chartered banks and unchartered *free banks* took hold during this period, issuing their own notes, redeemable in gold or specie (coined money). Banks also began offering demand deposits to enhance commerce. In response to a rising volume of check transactions, the New York Clearinghouse Association was established in 1853 to provide a way for the city's banks to exchange checks and settle accounts.

1863: National Banking Act

During the Civil War the National Banking Act of 1863 was passed, providing for nationally chartered banks, whose circulating notes had to be backed by U.S. government securities. An amendment to the act required taxation on state bank notes but not national bank notes, effectively creating a uniform currency for the nation. Despite taxation on their notes, state banks continued to flourish due to the growing popularity of demand deposits, which had taken hold during the Free Banking Era.

1873–1907: Financial Panics Prevail

Although the National Banking Act of 1863 established some measure of currency stability for the growing nation, bank runs and financial panics continued to plague the economy. In 1893 a banking panic triggered the worst depression the United States had ever seen, and the economy stabilized only after the intervention of financial mogul J.P. Morgan. It was clear that the nation's banking and financial system needed serious attention.

1907: A Very Bad Year

In 1907 a bout of speculation on Wall Street ended in failure, triggering a particularly severe banking panic. J.P. Morgan was again called upon to avert disaster. By this time most Americans were calling for reform of the banking system, but the structure of that reform was cause for deep division among the country's citizens. Conservatives and powerful money trusts in the big Eastern cities were vehemently opposed by so-called progressives. But there was a growing consensus among all Americans that a central banking authority was needed to ensure a healthy banking system and provide for an elastic currency.

1908–1912: The Stage is Set for Decentralized Central Bank

The Aldrich-Vreeland Act of 1908, passed as an immediate response to the panic of 1907, provided for emergency currency issues during crises.

It also established the National Monetary Commission to search for a long-term solution to the nation's banking and financial problems. Under the leadership of Senator Nelson Aldrich, the commission developed a banker-controlled plan. William Jennings Bryan and other progressives fiercely attacked the plan; they wanted a central bank under public, not banker, control. The 1912 election of Democrat Woodrow Wilson killed the Republican Aldrich plan, but the stage was set for the emergence of a decentralized central bank.

1912: Woodrow Wilson as Financial Reformer

Though not personally knowledgeable about banking and financial issues, Woodrow Wilson solicited expert advice from Virginia Representative Carter Glass, soon to become the chairman of the House Committee on Banking and Finance, and from the committee's expert adviser, H. Parker Willis, formerly a professor of economics at Washington and Lee University. Throughout most of 1912, Glass and Willis labored over a central bank proposal, and by December 1912 they presented Wilson with what would become, with some modifications, the Federal Reserve Act.

1913: The Federal Reserve System is Born

From December 1912 to December 1913 the Glass-Willis proposal was hotly debated, molded and reshaped. By December 23, 1913, when President Woodrow Wilson signed the Federal Reserve Act into law, it stood as a classic example of compromise—a decentralized central bank that balanced the competing interests of private banks and populist sentiment.

1914: Open for Business

Before the new central bank could begin operations, the Reserve Bank Organizing Committee, comprised of Treasury Secretary William McAdoo, Secretary of Agriculture David Houston, and Comptroller of the Currency John Skelton Williams, had the arduous task of building a working institution around the bare bones of the new law. But by November 16, 1914, the 12 cities chosen as sites for regional Reserve Banks were open for business, just as hostilities in Europe erupted into World War I.

1914–1919: Fed Policy During the War

When World War I broke out in mid-1914, U.S. banks continued to operate normally, thanks to emergency currency issued under the Aldrich-Vreeland Act of 1908. But the greater impact in the United States came from the Reserve Banks' ability to discount banker's acceptances. Through this mechanism, the United States aided the flow of trade goods to Europe, indirectly helping to finance the war until 1917, when the United States officially declared war on Germany and financing our own war effort became paramount.

1920s: The Beginning of Open Market Operations

Following World War I, Benjamin Strong, head of the New York Fed from 1914 until his death in 1928, recognized that gold no longer served as the central factor in controlling credit. Strong's aggressive action to stem a recession in 1923 through a large purchase of government securities gave evidence of the power of open market operations to influence the availability of credit in the banking system. During the 1920s the Fed began using open market operations as a monetary policy tool. During his tenure, Strong also elevated the stature of the Fed by promoting relations with other central banks, especially the Bank of England.

1929–1933: The Market Crash and the Great Depression

During the 1920s Virginia Representative Carter Glass warned that stock market speculation would lead to dire consequences. In October 1929 his predictions seemed to be realized when the stock market crashed, and the nation fell into the worst depression in its history. From 1930 to 1933 nearly 10,000 banks failed, and by March 1933 newly inaugurated President Franklin Delano Roosevelt declared a bank holiday, while government officials grappled with ways to remedy the nation's economic woes. Many people blamed the Fed for failing to stem speculative lending that led to the crash, and some also argued that inadequate understanding of monetary economics kept the Fed from pursuing policies that could have lessened the depth of the Great Depression.

1933: The Depression's Aftermath

In reaction to the Great Depression, Congress passed the Banking Act of 1933, better known as the Glass-Steagall Act, calling for the separation of commercial and investment banking and requiring use of government securities as collateral for Federal Reserve notes. The act also established the Federal Deposit Insurance Corp. (FDIC), placed open market operations under the Fed and required bank holding companies to be examined by the Fed, a practice that was to have profound future implications, as holding companies became a prevalent structure for banks over time. Also, as part of the massive reforms taking place, Roosevelt recalled all gold and silver certificates, effectively ending the gold and any other metallic standard.

1935: More Changes to Come

The Banking Act of 1935 called for further changes in the Fed's structure, including the creation of the Federal Open Market Committee (FOMC) as a separate legal entity, removal of the Treasury Secretary and the Comptroller of the Currency from the Fed's governing board, and establishment of members' terms at 14 years. Following World War II, the Employment Act added the goal of promoting maximum employment to the list of the Fed's responsibilities. In 1956 the Bank Holding Company Act named the Fed as the regulator for bank holding companies owning more than one bank, and in 1978 the Humphrey-Hawkins Act required the Fed chairman to report to Congress twice annually on monetary policy goals and objectives.

1951: The Treasury Accord

The Fed largely supported the Treasury's *fiscal policy* goals from its founding in 1913 to the years up to and following World War II. When the Korean Conflict broke out in 1951, Fed chairman William McChesney Martin again faced pressure from the Treasury to maintain low interest rates to help provide funds for the new conflict. Martin, however, worked closely with the Treasury to break the long-standing practice of supporting government bond interest rates. Since then the Fed has remained staunchly independent in its use of open market operations to support its monetary policy goals.

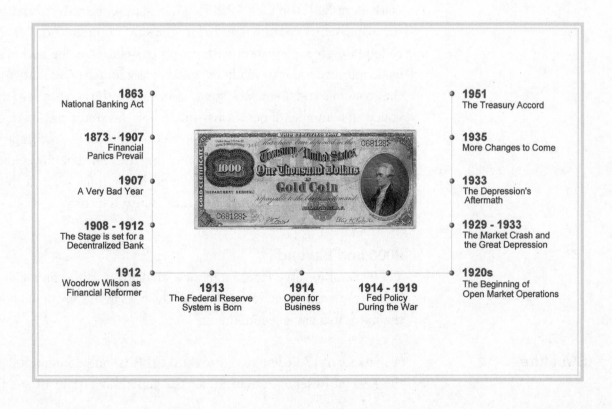

1970s–1980s: Inflation and Disinflation

The 1970s saw inflation skyrocket as producer and consumer prices rose, oil prices soared and the federal deficit more than doubled. By August 1979, when Paul Volcker was sworn in as Fed chairman, drastic action was needed to break inflation's stranglehold on the U.S. economy. Volcker's leadership as Fed chairman during the 1980s, though painful in the short term, was successful overall in bringing double-digit inflation under control.

1980: Setting the Stage for Financial Modernization

The Monetary Control Act of 1980 required the Fed to price its financial services competitively against private sector providers and to establish reserve requirements for all eligible financial institutions. The act marks the beginning of a period of modern banking industry reforms. Following its passage, interstate banking proliferated, and banks began offering interest-paying accounts and instruments to attract customers from brokerage firms. Barriers to insurance activities, however, proved more difficult to circumvent. Nonetheless, momentum for change was steady, and by 1999 the Gramm-Leach-Bliley Act was passed, in essence overturning the Glass-Steagall Act of 1933 and allowing banks to offer a menu of financial services, including investment banking and insurance sales.

1990s: The Longest Economic Expansion

Two months after Alan Greenspan took office as Fed chairman, the stock market crashed—on Oct. 19, 1987. In response, he ordered the Fed to issue a one-sentence statement before the start of trading on Oct. 20: "The Federal Reserve, consistent with its responsibilities as the nation's central bank, affirmed today its readiness to serve as a source of liquidity to support the economic and financial system." Since then, the Fed has used monetary policy on a number of occasions—including the credit crunch of the early 1990s and the Russian default on government bonds—to keep potential financial problems from adversely affecting the real economy. Greenspan's tenure has been marked by generally declining inflation and the longest peacetime economic expansion in our country's history.

2000 and Beyond

The Federal Reserve faces many new challenges in the financial services industry: deregulation, technological advances in the payments system and the move to a global economy.

Structure

A network of 12 Federal Reserve Banks (FRBs) and 25 branches make up the Federal Reserve System under the general oversight of the Board of

Governors (BOG) in Washington, D.C. Reserve Banks are the operating arms of the central bank. They serve other lending institutions, the U.S. Treasury and, indirectly, the public. A Reserve Bank is often called the banker's bank, storing currency and coin, and processing checks and electronic payments. Reserve Banks also supervise commercial banks in their regions. As the bank for the U.S. government, Reserve Banks handle the Treasury's payments, sell government securities and assist with the Treasury's cash management and investment activities.

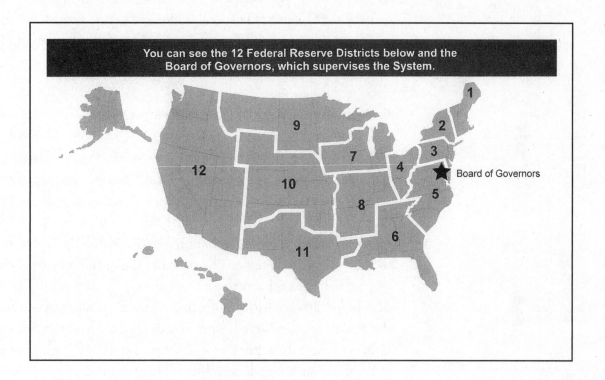

Additionally, Reserve Banks conduct research on regional, national and international economic issues. Research plays a critical role in bringing broad economic perspectives to the national policy-making arena, and supports Reserve Bank presidents who all attend meetings of the Federal Open Market Committee (FOMC).

Each Reserve Bank's board of directors oversees the management and activities of the district bank. Reflecting the diverse interests of each district, these directors contribute local business experience, community involvement and leadership. The board imparts a private-sector perspective to the Reserve Bank. Each board appoints the president and first vice president of the Reserve Bank, subject to the approval of the Board of Governors.

All member banks hold stock in Reserve Banks and receive dividends. Unlike stockholders in a public company, however, banks cannot sell or trade their Fed stock.

Reserve Banks interact directly with banks in their districts through examinations and financial services and bring important regional perspectives that help the entire Federal Reserve System do its job more effectively.

It's no wonder many people have a difficult time describing the Federal Reserve, a complex organization of paradoxes. The Federal Reserve has both private and public elements, centralized and decentralized authority, and operates independently within the government under the general oversight of Congress. The Fed's unique structure provides accountability, while avoiding centralized, governmental control of banking and monetary policy.

Federal Open Market Committee (FOMC)

The Federal Open Market Committee (FOMC) establishes the goals of monetary policy. To achieve this success, the Fed uses a variety of methods to gauge the impact of its policies on the nation's economy. But the 12 Reserve Banks play critical roles, too. After each meeting, the FOMC issues a directive to the Open Market Desk at the New York Fed. This directive sets out some general objectives that the FOMC wishes the Open Market Desk to achieve—easing, tightening or maintaining the growth of the nation's money supply. To achieve these goals, the Open Market Desk each day buys or sells Treasury securities in the open market. While policy deliberations of the FOMC are conducted in private, the Fed has always made its decisions known to the public. Beginning in 1994, the FOMC began announcing its policy decisions immediately after making them.

Research economists at all 12 Reserve Banks, as well as economists at the Board of Governors, contribute to the policy-making process. Generally speaking, Reserve Banks are monitoring the unique economies of their districts and studying relationships among national economic indicators. Their primary duty is to prepare their Reserve Bank president for his or her participation in FOMC deliberations. They also collect loan and deposit data from banks and bank holding companies used in analyzing regional and national bank performance, credit demand and other banking topics.

Board of Governors (BOG)

When creating the Federal Reserve, one of Congress' paramount concerns was to address the nation's banking panics. This short-term need led to one of the Fed's three main responsibilities: to foster safe, sound and competitive practices in the nation's banking system.

To accomplish this, Congress gave the Fed responsibility to regulate the banking system and supervise certain types of financial institutions. What's the difference between these two? Bank regulation refers to the written rules that define what acceptable behavior is for financial institutions. The Board of Governors carries out this responsibility. Bank supervision refers to the enforcement of these rules. The 12 Reserve Banks carry out this responsibility, supervising state-chartered member banks, the companies that own banks (bank holding companies) and international organizations that do banking business in the United States. For the Fed, supervising banks generally means one of three duties: establishing safe and sound banking practices, protecting consumers in financial transactions, and ensuring the stability of U.S. financial markets by acting as lender of last resort. The common goal of all three duties, however, is the same: to minimize risk in the banking system.

Bank Supervision Includes:

- Establishing safe and sound banking practices
- Protecting consumers in financial transactions
- Ensuring the stability of U.S. financial markets by acting as lender of last resort

---

Another Fed goal is to protect consumers in lending and deposit transactions. Congress has given the Fed broad power to make, interpret and enforce laws that protect consumers from lending discrimination and inaccurate disclosure of credit costs or interest rates.

Perhaps the most important supervisory responsibility of all, however, is to respond to a financial crisis by acting as lender of last resort for the nation's banking system. Through its discount window, the Fed lends money to banks so that a shortage of funds at one institution does not disrupt the flow of money and credit in the entire banking system. Typically, the Fed makes loans to satisfy a bank's unanticipated needs for short-term funds. But the Fed also makes longer-term loans to help banks manage seasonal fluctuations in their customers' deposit or credit demands.

Providing Financial Services

The Federal Reserve is also charged with the critical task of providing a safe and efficient method of transferring funds throughout the banking system. Reserve Banks and their branches carry out this mission, offering payments services to all financial institutions in the United States, regardless of size or location. Hand in hand with that mission is the obligation to improve the payments system by encouraging efficiency and technological advances.

Essentially, a Reserve Bank serves as a bankers' bank, offering a wide variety of payments services. It distributes currency and coin, processes checks and offers electronic forms of payment. The Fed competes with the private sector in its financial services to foster competition in the marketplace, and promote innovation and efficiency in the payments system. It does not seek to make a profit from its participation; it sets prices only to recover costs.

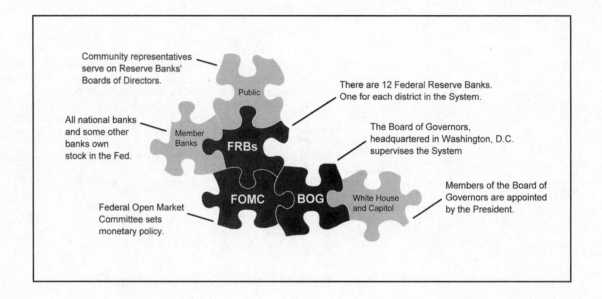

Regional Reserve Banks are responsible for meeting public demand for currency and coin within their districts. In addition, Reserve Banks also process commercial checks. Every day billions of dollars are transferred electronically among U.S. financial institutions. The Reserve Banks provide two electronic payment services: funds transfer and the *automated clearing house*, or *ACH*. The funds transfer service provides a communications link among financial institutions and government agencies. The ACH provides a nationwide network to exchange paperless payments among financial institutions and government agencies. The ACH accommodates a wide range of recurring corporate and consumer transactions, such as payroll deposit, electronic bill payment, insurance payments and Social Security disbursements.

The Life of a Check

Let's say that you have saved your money over the past few months to buy a new CD player. Today, you finally found the one that you want on sale for $100 at a local electronics store. Instead of carrying $100 in cash, you brought your checkbook. You write a check from an account you have at your financial institution to pay for the CD player. Checks are written orders that tell your financial institution to transfer funds from your account to the account of an individual or business that receives your check.

Now, it seems like the transaction is complete. Not quite. You look at your account online just after writing the check and notice that the $100 is still there. How does the store receive $100 from your account?
Let's see how this transaction takes place.

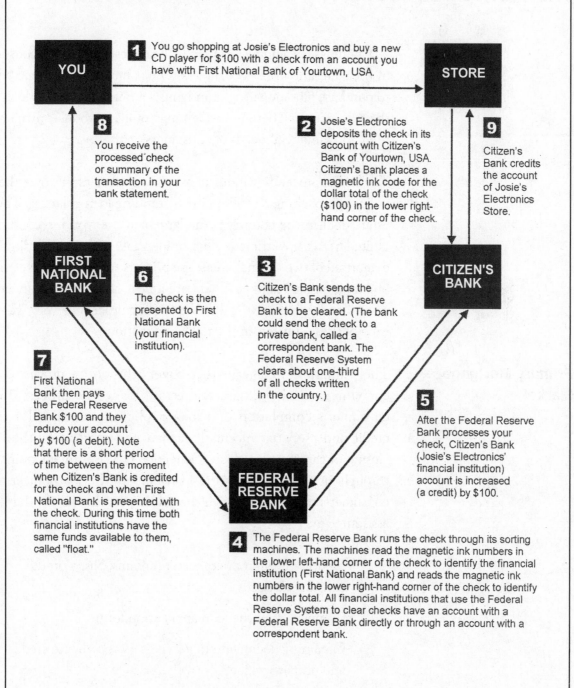

YOU

1 You go shopping at Josie's Electronics and buy a new CD player for $100 with a check from an account you have with First National Bank of Yourtown, USA.

STORE

8 You receive the processed check or summary of the transaction in your bank statement.

2 Josie's Electronics deposits the check in its account with Citizen's Bank of Yourtown, USA. Citizen's Bank places a magnetic ink code for the dollar total of the check ($100) in the lower right-hand corner of the check.

9 Citizen's Bank credits the account of Josie's Electronics Store.

FIRST NATIONAL BANK

6 The check is then presented to First National Bank (your financial institution).

3 Citizen's Bank sends the check to a Federal Reserve Bank to be cleared. (The bank could send the check to a private bank, called a correspondent bank. The Federal Reserve System clears about one-third of all checks written in the country.)

CITIZEN'S BANK

7 First National Bank then pays the Federal Reserve Bank $100 and they reduce your account by $100 (a debit). Note that there is a short period of time between the moment when Citizen's Bank is credited for the check and when First National Bank is presented with the check. During this time both financial institutions have the same funds available to them, called "float."

5 After the Federal Reserve Bank processes your check, Citizen's Bank (Josie's Electronics' financial institution) account is increased (a credit) by $100.

FEDERAL RESERVE BANK

4 The Federal Reserve Bank runs the check through its sorting machines. The machines read the magnetic ink numbers in the lower left-hand corner of the check to identify the financial institution (First National Bank) and reads the magnetic ink numbers in the lower right-hand corner of the check to identify the dollar total. All financial institutions that use the Federal Reserve System to clear checks have an account with a Federal Reserve Bank directly or through an account with a correspondent bank.

In addition to serving as the bankers' bank, the Federal Reserve System acts as banker for the U.S. government. Federal Reserve Banks maintain accounts for the U.S. Treasury; process government checks, postal money orders and U.S. savings bonds; and collect federal tax deposits. Reserve Banks also sell new Treasury securities, service outstanding issues and redeem maturing issues.

THE MORTGAGE MARKET

The purchase of a home is generally the largest acquisition consumers make in their lifetime. Most consumers do not have the financial wherewithal to purchase a home outright and must obtain a real estate loan to finance the transaction. There is a wide range of loan products available to meet the varied financial needs of consumers.

The real estate lending industry has grown substantially over the past years and is approaching $4 trillion in outstanding loan balances. The total real estate debt in the country is the largest in the world, second only to the United States government. The residential real estate lending industry is comprised of two distinct areas: the primary mortgage market and the secondary mortgage market. There are a host of other ancillary entities that service and support the real estate lending process as well. We will discuss each of these subjects in the following section.

Primary Mortgage Market

The primary mortgage market covers the entire process a consumer encounters in obtaining a real estate loan. The process includes the consumer's completion of a loan application form, validation of the credit and property information, loan underwriting by the lender and closing of the mortgage loan. Generally, the consumer's primary contact throughout this process is the loan officer. The loan officer acts as the consumer's navigator through the primary market labyrinth and provides assistance in:

- Identifying appropriate loan programs, based on the consumer's needs
- Completion of the loan application form
- Obtaining documentation necessary to validate credit and property value

•Compiling supporting information in a package suitable
to submit to lenders

•Communications between the lender and the consumer

Historically, the process of obtaining a loan has taken several weeks to complete. In the future, this time frame is expected to improve dramatically as the application process, credit validation and loan underwriting become more automated. Some industry experts believe that in the near future, the primary market process will be completed in hours and days rather than weeks and months.

Secondary Mortgage Market

America has a secondary mortgage market that attracts capital from around the world to finance a wide range of mortgage products designed specifically to make homeownership affordable and accessible. No other country has a comparable secondary market.

This important market is the foundation of the lending process and an essential part of our national economy's health. The secondary market's main function is to get the money to primary lenders who then loan it to consumers, who make loan commitments which are then sold on the secondary market, with the money paid back into the primary market.

The secondary mortgage market consists of the system of lending institutions such as thrifts or mortgage bankers, private investors and government credit agencies that buy pools of existing loans from loan-originator sellers (primary markets). They later buy from—and sell to—each other the existing mortgage loans originated in the primary mortgage market.

Participants in the secondary market who purchase existing mortgages do not originate the loans, but buy them with funds they have acquired by issuing bonds or other types of debt instruments. The mortgages they buy are used as security for those debt instruments. The debt issue, then, known as a mortgage-backed or *mortgage related security* (MRS), is collateralized by the mortgages that have been bought in the secondary market. These mortgage-backed securities also are bought and sold in the secondary market.

The original source of the funds used to buy the mortgage-backed securities is investors who purchase the securities from the secondary market agency or company. That agency then uses the funds from the investor to buy more mortgages—for example, from a savings and loan or mortgage banker. The savings and loan or originator of the loan uses the funds they receive from the sale of the loan to originate more mortgage loans. Consumers and the entire economy benefit by the investors supplying the funds that end up, eventually, as home loans to consumers.

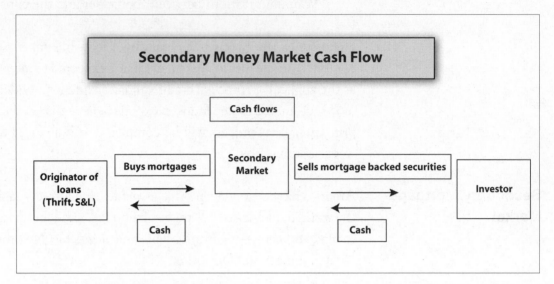

The secondary mortgage market exists because of the need, by thrifts and other financial institutions, to have the ability to sell their assets quickly when they need more money, particularly in a market where consumers are demanding more home loans. In the past, the bulk of a financial institution's resources consisted of depositor's funds which were tied up in long-term mortgage loans. These were not particularly convenient as a source for quick money because of the perceived risk of default or unsoundness by creditors who might be located a continent away from the collateral of the loan in question. To make matters worse, there would be an area of the country with a greater supply of capital, in the form of deposits, resulting in excess money with nowhere to spend it, and another area of the country with a greater demand for mortgage loans, but no money to lend because of lack of deposits. Because lending institutions were unable to buy and sell mortgages easily, the supply and demand for money was always out of sync.

The solution was to create a money market where loans could be bought and sold without difficulty, so funds could be moved to a capital needy area from one with abundant funds. By encouraging financial institutions in capital-surplus areas to purchase mortgages from financial institutions in capital-deficient areas, the volatile, inconsistent flow of cash that had led to insecurity and financial crisis for mortgage lenders faded to a memory.

The Three Major Participants in the Secondary Mortgage Market

Federal National Mortgage Association (FNMA or Fannie Mae): Fannie Mae is a private, shareholder-owned company that works to make sure mortgage money is available for people in communities all across America. Fannie Mae does not lend money directly to home buyers. Instead, it works with lenders to make sure they don't run out of mortgage funds, so more people can achieve the dream of homeownership.

Fannie Mae is the country's second largest corporation, in terms of assets, and the nation's largest source of financing for home mortgages. It is one of the largest financial services corporations in the world. And with approximately 4,700 dedicated employees, it is also one of the world's most productive corporations.

Fannie Mae stock (FNM) is actively traded on the New York Stock Exchange and other exchanges and is part of the Standard & Poors' 500 Composite Stock Price Index.

Created by Congress in 1938 to bolster the housing industry in the aftermath of the Great Depression, Fannie Mae was part of the Federal Housing Administration (FHA) and authorized to buy only FHA-insured loans to replenish lenders' supply of money.

In 1968, Fannie Mae became a private company operating with private capital on a self-sustaining basis. Its role was expanded to buy mortgages beyond traditional government loan limits, reaching out to a broader cross-section of Americans.

Today, Fannie Mae operates under a congressional charter that directs it to channel its efforts into increasing the availability and affordability of homeownership for low-, moderate- and middle-income Americans. Yet Fannie Mae receives no government funding or backing, and is one of the nation's largest taxpayers as well as one of the most consistently profitable corporations in America.

Fannie Mae is committed to the American dream of homeownership by expanding opportunities for homeownership and by helping lenders reach out and serve more first-time homebuyers.

Fannie Mae's Three-phase American Dream Commitment

1. Expand access to homeownership for millions of first-time home buyers and help to raise the minority homeownership rate to 55% with the ultimate goal of closing the homeownership gaps entirely.

2. Make homeownership and rental housing a success for millions of families at risk of losing their homes.

3. Expand the supply of affordable housing where it is needed most.

Originally created as a secondary market for *FHA-insured* and *Veterans Administration-guaranteed* loans and the private residential mortgage market, Fannie Mae supports the secondary mortgage market by issuing mortgage-related securities and purchasing mortgages. Fannie Mae buys loans from lenders who conform to FNMA guidelines, and by doing so, puts mortgage money back into the system so lenders can make more loans. FNMA is the largest investor in the secondary market. In 1968 FNMA was divided into two separate systems: FNMA and GNMA. FNMA became a privately owned corporation, while GNMA remained government owned.

Government National Mortgage Association (GNMA or Ginnie Mae):
Ginnie Mae was created in 1968 as a wholly owned corporation within the Department of Housing and Urban Development (HUD). Its purpose was—and is—to serve low- to moderate-income homebuyers.

HISTORY OF CONFORMING FANNIE MAE & FREDDIE MAC LOAN LIMITS

Year	One Family ($)	Two Family ($)	Three Family ($)	Four Family ($)	As Listed in HSH Reports
2007	417,000	533,850	645,300	801,950	417
2006	417,000	533,850	645,300	801,950	417
2005	359,650	460,400	556,500	691,600	359
2004	333,700	427,150	516,300	641,650	333
2003	322,700	413,100	499,300	620,500	322
2002	300,700	384,900	465,200	578,150	300
2001	275,000	351,950	425,400	528,700	275
2000	252,700	323,400	390,900	485,800	252
1999	240,000	307,100	371,200	461,350	240
1998	227,150	290,650	351,300	436,600	227
1997	214,600	274,550	331,850	412,450	214
1996	207,000	264,750	320,050	397,800	207
1995	203,150	259,850	314,100	390,400	203
1994	203,150	259,850	314,100	390,400	203
1993	203,150	259,850	314,100	390,400	203
1992	202,300	258,800	312,800	388,800	202
1991	191,250	244,650	295,650	367,500	191
1990	187,450	239,750	289,750	360,150	187
1989	187,600	239,950	290,000	360,450	187
1988	168,700	215,800	260,800	324,150	168
1987	153,100				153
1986	133,250				133
1985	115,300				115
1984	114,000				114
1983	108,300				108
1982	107,000	136,800	165,100	205,300	107
1981	98,500	126,000	152,000	189,000	98
1980	93,750				93

Note: Maximum loan amounts are 50% higher in Alaska and Hawaii.

Source: FNMA, FHLMC

The National Housing Act was enacted on June 27, 1934, as one of several economic recovery measures. It provided for the establishment of a Federal Housing Administration (FHA) to be headed by a Federal Housing Administrator. Title II of the Act provided, as one of the principal functions of the FHA, for the insurance of home mortgage loans made by private lenders.

Title III of the Act provided for the chartering of national mortgage associations by the Administrator. These associations were to be private corporations regulated by the Administrator, and their chief purpose was to buy and sell the mortgages to be insured by FHA under Title II. Only one association was ever formed under this authority. It was formed on February 10, 1938, as a subsidiary of the Reconstruction Finance Corporation, a government corporation. Its name was National Mortgage Association of Washington, and this was changed that same year to Federal National Mortgage Association.

By amendments made in 1948, the charter authority of the Administrator was repealed and Title III became a statutory charter for the Federal National Mortgage Association. By revision of Title III in 1954, Fannie Mae was converted into a mixed-ownership corporation, its preferred stock to be held by the government and its common stock to be privately held. It was at this time that Section 312 was first enacted, giving Title III the short title of Federal National Mortgage Association Charter Act.

By amendments made in 1968, the Federal National Mortgage Association was partitioned into two separate entities, one to be known as Government National Mortgage Association (Ginnie Mae), the other to retain the name Federal National Mortgage Association. Ginnie Mae remained in the government, and Fannie Mae became privately owned by retiring the government-held stock. Ginnie Mae has operated as a wholly owned government association since the 1968 amendments.

Established as a government corporation within the Department of Housing and Urban Development (HUD) to participate in the secondary mortgage market, Ginnie Mae supports the secondary mortgage market by guaranteeing *pass-through securities* originated by the VA and FHA. Pass-through securities allow the investors an undivided interest in a pool of mortgages. The investor has an ownership position in the mortgages, receiving regular payments of principal and interest on the mortgages just as if he or she were the originating lender. The underlying loans are guaranteed against default by the FHA and VA, and Ginnie Mae guarantees the timely payment on the loans in the pool. Ginnie Mae does not buy mortgages or issue securities, but acts in a support role to other participants in the secondary market.

Federal Home Loan Mortgage Corporation (FHLMC or Freddie Mac): Freddie Mac is a shareholder-owned corporation whose people are dedicated to improving the quality of life by making the American dream of decent, accessible housing a reality. This mission is accomplished by linking Main Street to Wall Street—purchasing, *securitizing* and investing in home mortgages, and ultimately providing homeowners and renters with lower housing costs and better access to home financing. Since its inception, Freddie Mac has financed one out of every six homes in America.

Freddie Mac buys residential mortgages and funds them in the capital markets in one of two ways—using mortgage-backed securities or a variety of debt instruments. By bringing efficiency to the securities markets, Freddie Mac lowers funding costs, making housing more affordable for the nation's families and increasing shareholder value.

Freddie Mac was created to increase the availability of mortgage credit by developing and maintaining a nationwide secondary market for residential conventional mortgage loans. Approved existing mortgage loans are bought and resold to individual investors or financial institutions.

Freddie Mac conducts its business by buying mortgages that meet the company's underwriting and product standards from lenders, packaging the mortgages into securities and selling the securities—guaranteed by Freddie Mac to investors, such as insurance companies and pension funds. About half of all new single-family mortgages originated today are sold to secondary market conduits.

Mortgage lenders use the proceeds secured from selling loans to Freddie Mac to fund new mortgages, constantly replenishing the global pool of funds available for lending to homebuyers and apartment owners.

Just as stock and bond markets have put investor capital to work for corporations, the secondary mortgage market puts private investor capital to work for homebuyers and apartment owners, providing a continuous flow of affordable funds for home financing.

For the most part, the process is invisible to borrowers and renters. But because Freddie Mac exists, millions of people have benefited from lower monthly mortgage payments and better access to home financing.

HOW THE INDUSTRY WORKS

1 Prospective homebuyer applies for a mortgage loan through a mortgage lender, mortgage broker, credit union or even on-line. Automated underwriting systems like Loan Prospector can evaluate a homebuyer's credit, collateral, and capacity to repay against the loan requirements and respond within minutes.

2 Mortgage lender packages the loans it has made and sells those packages to the secondary market (Freddie Mac). The lender uses the proceeds of the sale to make new loans to other homebuyers.

3 Freddie Mac sells notes backed by the mortgage loans it has purchased to securities investors. It uses the funds from the security sales to purchase more mortgage loans from lenders across the country.

Secondary Mortgage Market

Federal National Mortgage Association (Fannie Mae)

- Issues stock to general public
- Provides adjustable-rate mortgages
- Issues mortgage-backed securities

Government National Mortgage Association (Ginnie Mae)

- Guarantees securities issued by FHA-approved home mortgage lenders

Federal Home Loan Mortgage Corporation (Freddie Mac)

- Issues stock to general public
- Buys and resells residential conventional mortgage loans

About Loan Markets

- The primary mortgage market initiates loans directly with borrowers.
- The secondary mortgage market buys and sells existing loans which have originated in the primary market.

Ancillary Services

There are many ancillary services that support the mortgage lending process. Some of the more visible are:

Real Estate Broker and Real Estate Sales Associate

These professionals assist consumers in the buying and selling of real estate. The real estate professional, usually the first contact consumers have when deciding on a real estate loan, in turn will refer clients to a mortgage specialist.

Title Company
Title companies perform a title search on the property and issue a title policy for the lender and the purchaser to insure that there is a valid mortgage lien against the property and title is clear.

Closing Agent
This entity facilitates the closing of a mortgage loan by acting as an impartial third party. The closing agent can be an escrow company, an attorney or title company agent depending on the region.

Appraiser
This professional evaluates the market value of real estate for the buyer and the lender.

Credit Reporting Agency
These companies research the credit records of consumers and memorialize the findings in a factual credit report. They have access to databases that store credit information on most consumers in the country. Additionally, they search the public records for derogatory items that may have been filed against a consumer, such as judgments, bankruptcies and liens. Frequently, credit reporting agencies will research other items, such as place of employment, banking relationships and previous residency.

Private Mortgage Insurance Company (PMI)
When the loan exceeds 80% of the value of the property, lenders usually require private mortgage insurance that insures the lender in the event a borrower defaults and the property ends up in foreclosure. There are a small number of companies that provide this insurance. Usually borrowers pay for this insurance as part of the monthly payment.

Hazard Insurance Company
Lenders require hazard insurance that covers the outstanding loan on the property. There are many casualty insurance companies that provide hazard insurance. In most cases, the lender is the loss payee on the policy and will receive the proceeds on a claim. The proceeds then will be used to pay for the repairs.

REAL PROPERTY LOAN LAW

The Real Estate Law requires anyone negotiating a loan to have a real estate license. In the past, abuses have occurred in the form of excessive commissions, inflated costs and expenses, the negotiating of short-term loans with large balloon payments, and misrepresentation or concealment of material facts by licensees negotiating these loans.

As a result of this mistreatment of consumers by some corrupt agents, legislation was passed to correct the situation. The Real Property Loan Law now applies to loans secured by first trust deeds under $30,000 and by junior trust deeds under $20,000.

The law requires anyone negotiating a loan to provide a Mortgage Loan Broker's Statement (sometimes called a Mortgage Loan Disclosure Statement) to a prospective borrower, with information concerning all important features of a loan to be negotiated for the borrower.

From time to time, a real estate agent, as part of a transaction, will be involved in negotiating a loan for the borrower. A completed Mortgage Loan Disclosure Statement must be presented to the prospective borrower, and the borrower must sign the statement prior to signing loan documents.

A real estate broker negotiating or making loans subject to the Real Property Loan Law is limited by law in the amount that may be charged as a commission.

Maximum Commissions Allowed Under Real Property Loan Law

First Trust Deeds

- 5% of loan amount if term is less than 3 years
- 10% of loan amount if term is 3 years or more

Second or other Junior Trust Deeds

- 5% of loan amount if term is less than 2 years
- 10% of loan amount if term is at least 2 years, but less than 3 years
- 15% of loan amount if term is 3 years or more

On loans $30,000 and over for first trust deeds, and $20,000 or more for junior trust deeds, the broker may charge as much as the borrower will agree to pay.

No balloon payment is allowed for loans on owner-occupied homes where a broker has been involved in the negotiation if the term is six years or less. This requirement does not apply when a seller carries back a trust deed as part of the purchase price.

About Loans

- A conventional loan is a loan that is not a government sponsored or private loan.

PERSONAL PROPERTY SECURED TRANSACTIONS

A *security agreement* is the device commonly used to secure a loan on personal property, much as a trust deed secures a loan on real property. As you recall, personal property is something that is movable, and is not real property. Jewelry and bulk items—such as retail inventory, autos and boats—are examples of personal property that might be used to secure a debt. The security agreement is the document used to create the security interest in personal property.

To protect, or "perfect"—as it is called, the interest created by the security agreement, or prevent the security from being sold or liened by someone else, a *financing statement* must be filed. A security interest is "perfected" when it has "attached"—or finalized, and the financing statement has been properly recorded in the office of the Secretary of State in Sacramento or the appropriate county recorder.

A Security Interest "Attaches" When:

- There is agreement by the parties
- Value has been given
- The debtor has acquired rights in the collateral

The financing statement is only the form used to record the debt, not actual evidence of the debt. The security agreement contains all the details of the agreement, and is the document that describes the obligation. Once the interest created by the security agreement is perfected, the secured party's interest is protected against the debtor's other creditors.

CHAPTER QUIZ

1. The process of depositors removing funds from savings is called:

     a. disintermediation
     b. reapportionment
     c. intermediation
     d. disinterment

2. A process where financial institutions that formerly had been restrained in their lending activities by the law, were allowed to compete freely for profits in the marketplace:

     a. intermediation
     b. hypothecation
     c. deregulation
     d. steering

3. The economic system in America is a:

     a. socialistic system
     b. mixed capitalistic system
     c. Keynes economic system
     d. checks and balance system

4. What banking agency develops national monetary policy and shares responsibility with 12 member banks for applying that policy and setting money supply goals?

     a. Federal Deposit Insurance Corporation (FDIC)
     b. Federal Reserve System (the Fed)
     c. Housing and Urban Development (HUD)
     d. Federal National Mortgage Association (FNMA)

5. Which of the following is not a tool of the Fed in regulating the economy?

    a. discount rate
    b. reserve requirement
    c. regulation of the secondary money market
    d. open market operations

6. The primary mortgage market is where lenders make mortgage loans directly to:

    a. Federal National Mortgage Association (FNMA)
    b. citizens with disabilities
    c. other lenders
    d. borrowers

7. All of the following are government agencies except:

    a. Federal National Mortgage Association (FNMA)
    b. Government National Mortgage Association (GNMA)
    c. Federal Reserve System (the Fed)
    d. Department of Housing and Urban Development (HUD)

8. Which of the following does not participate in the secondary market as a major player?

    a. Federal Reserve System (the Fed)
    b. Federal National Mortgage Association (FNMA)
    c. Government National Mortgage Association (GNMA)
    d. Federal Home Loan Mortgage Corporation (FHLMC)

9. The Real Estate Law requires anyone negotiating a loan to have:

    a. a real estate license
    b. a loan negotiator license
    c. a securities license
    d. an appraiser license

10. The instrument commonly used to secure a loan on personal property is known as a:

    a. pledge agreement
    b. financing statement
    c. security agreement
    d. trust deed

ANSWERS

1. *a*
2. *c*
3. *b*
4. *b*
5. *c*
6. *d*
7. *a*
8. *a*
9. *a*
10. *c*

8

chapter eight

Mortgage Insurance and Government Participation in Finance

INTRODUCTION

Insurance in general is intended to spread any loss from a particular peril over a large insured group. Mortgage default insurance is a special form of insurance designed to insure a portion of a mortgage. The lender is insured against losses that result when a borrower defaults on a mortgage loan and the loan must be foreclosed by the lender. There are three basic default insurance plans: Veterans Administration (VA), Federal Housing Administration (FHA) and Private Mortgage Insurance (PMI). The plans differ in terms of eligibility requirements, costs, loan limits, underwriting procedures and coverage.

TYPES OF MORTGAGE DEFAULT INSURANCE

The four types of mortgage default insurance are: partial coverage, full coverage, coinsurance and self-insurance. The lender is insured, with all types, in case of default on the part of a borrower.

Types of Mortgage Default Insurance

Partial Coverage

- The insurer will cover losses up to a certain percentage of the original loan amount. If the loan amount is $100,000, and the insurer will protect against a 20% loss, then any claims up to $20,000 will be covered.

Full Coverage

- All lender losses are protected.

Coinsurance

- There is a limit on the maximum amount of coverage. The insurer will pay all losses up to a certain percentage of the loan amount, and any loss beyond an agreed upon dollar amount will be shared in the same ratio between the lender and the insurer. Again, if the loan amount is $100,000, and the insurer will protect against a 20% loss, then any claims up to $20,000 will be covered. If the loss is $30,000, the lender will pay the first $20,000 and 20% or $2,000 of the remainder.

Self-Insurance

- The entire risk is held by the lender.

In most cases, the lender does not bear the cost to purchase mortgage insurance. If the loan is insured by FHA or is private mortgage insurance (PMI), the borrower is debited; if the loan is guaranteed by the VA, the federal government bears the burden of cost.

With most loans where mortgage default insurance is required, the insurance is a contingency of funding the loan. The costs to the borrower vary, depending on the agency issuing the loan. With a VA loan, the borrower pays a funding fee at the beginning of the loan process. The borrower is charged an up-front fee as well as a yearly premium on FHA and other loans requiring PMI. In most cases, conventional loans with a loan-to-value ratio greater than 80% also require private mortgage insurance.

GOVERNMENT INSURANCE

The two federal agencies that participate in real estate financing are the Federal Housing Administration (FHA) and the Veterans Administration (VA). The FHA is a full coverage insurance program, covering all losses a lender might incur. The VA is a partial insurance plan covering losses up to a certain percentage of the loan amount. Together, they make it possible for people to buy homes they would never be able to purchase without government involvement.

The California Farm and Home Purchase Program, or Cal-Vet loan (California), is a state program that helps eligible veterans. The United States Department of Veterans Affairs guarantees some Cal-Vet loans, and on some loans the Cal-Vet program purchases private mortgage insurance. In both cases a loan guaranty fee will be charged to the borrower, which is between 1.25% and 2% of the loan amount depending on the down payment. Under certain circumstances the fee may be added to the loan amount. This is a one-time fee, and will not affect the interest rate or monthly installment unless it is financed in the loan. There is no fee if the down payment is 20% or more.

Federal Housing Administration (FHA)

The FHA program, a part of HUD since 1934, has caused the greatest change in home mortgage lending in the history of real estate finance. The FHA was established to improve the construction and financing of housing.

Consumers as well as real estate licensees should become familiar with the operation, purposes and advantages of the program to best take advantage of what the program offers. Regulations change from time to time, and up-to-date information on loan programs is usually available through a mortgage broker who specializes in government insured or guaranteed loans, or on the HUD website.

The FHA does *not* make loans. It *insures* loans made by authorized lending institutions such as banks, savings banks and independent mortgage companies. As long as FHA guidelines are used in funding the loan, the FHA, upon default by the borrower, insures the lender against loss. If the borrower does default, the lender may foreclose and the FHA will pay cash up to the established limit of the insurance.

Any consumer may qualify for an FHA loan. A borrower does not apply to the FHA for a mortgage loan, but application is made through an approved lender who processes the application and submits it to FHA for approval.

The lender is protected, in case of foreclosure, by charging the borrower a fee for an insurance policy called Mutual Mortgage Insurance. The insurance requirement is how the FHA finances its program. The premium may be financed as part of the loan or paid in cash at the close of escrow.

The FHA will make a variety of types of loans. Borrowers can get qualified for an FHA loan before a builder starts construction, enabling both borrower and builder to count on the completion of the transaction. Reverse annuity loans allow borrowers to convert equity into a monthly income or line of credit. A borrower must be at least 62 years of age, own the property, occupy it as a principal residence and join a special FHA consumer information session. There are no income qualifications for this type of loan, and no repayment as long as the borrower occupies the home as a principal residence. This program is available for properties of one-to-four units.

The FHA insures the full amount of a loan when there is a default and foreclosure. There are maximum loan amounts that the FHA will loan, however, depending upon where the property is located, in order to manage the risk of default. Before approving a borrower, the FHA takes into consideration the borrower's income, credit and work history, funds available for settlement and monthly housing expense. Any qualified resident of the United States may obtain an FHA loan as long as the property will be the borrower's principal residence and is located in the United States. U.S. citizenship is not a requirement.

The lender may negotiate the interest rate with the borrower and may charge points (1 point is 1% of the loan) which can be paid by either the buyer or seller.

Section 203-B

The FHA offers financing on the purchase or construction of owner-occupied residences of one-to-four units under Section 203-B. This program offers 30 year, fixed-rate, fully amortized mortgages.

Section 245 GPM

A graduated payment mortgage (GPM) is offered by the FHA to borrowers who might have trouble qualifying for regular loan payments, but who expect their income to increase. Payments for the first five years are low, and cover only part of the interest due, with the unpaid amount added to the principal balance. After that time the loan is recalculated, with the new payment remaining steady for the term of the loan.

Veterans Administration (VA)

The Veterans Administration does *not* make loans. It *guarantees* loans made by an approved institutional lender, much like the FHA. The main differences between the two government programs are: Only an eligible veteran may obtain a VA loan, and the VA does not require a down payment up to a certain loan amount. Both programs were created to assist people in buying homes when conventional loan programs did not fit their needs.

These loans are made by a lender, such as a mortgage company, savings and loan or bank. VA's guaranty on the loan protects the lender against loss if the payments are not made, and is intended to encourage lenders to offer veterans loans with more favorable terms. The amount of guaranty on the loan depends on the loan amount and whether the veteran used some entitlement previously.

With the current maximum guaranty, a veteran who hasn't previously used the benefit may be able to obtain a VA loan up to $417,000 with no down payment, depending on the borrower's income level and the appraised value of the property. A local VA office can provide more details on guaranty and entitlement amounts.

When a veteran finds a house he or she wants to purchase, a VA approved conventional lender will take the loan application and process the loan according to VA guidelines.

A veteran must possess a Certificate of Eligibility, which is available from the Veteran's Administration, before applying for a VA loan. The certificate will show the veteran's entitlement, or right to obtain the loan.

Five Easy Steps to a VA Loan

(1) Apply for a "Certificate of Eligibility." A veteran who doesn't have a certificate can obtain one easily by completing VA Form 26-1880, Request for a Certificate of Eligibility for VA Home Loan Benefits, and submitting it to one of the Eligibility Centers with copies of his or her most recent discharge or separation papers covering active military duty since September 16, 1940, which show active duty dates and type of discharge.

(2) Decide on a home the buyer wants to acquire and sign a purchase agreement.

(3) Apply to a VA approved mortgage lender for the loan. While the appraisal is being done, the lender (mortgage company, savings and

loan, bank, etc.) can be gathering credit and income information. If the lender is authorized by VA to do automatic processing, upon receipt of the VA appraisal, the loan can be approved and closed without waiting for VA's review of the credit application. For loans that must first be approved by VA, the lender will send the application to the local VA office, which will notify the lender of its decision.

(4) The lender orders an appraisal, known as *Certificate of Reasonable Value (CRV)*, from VA. A loan can't exceed the value established by the CRV. Most VA regional offices offer a "speed-up" telephone appraisal system.

(5) Close the loan and the buyer moves in.

A major benefit of a loan guaranteed by the Veterans Administration is that no down payment is required for some VA loans. There is a maximum loan amount allowed for a no-down- payment transaction, and a formula to establish the amount of down payment for a larger loan amount.

If a veteran sells his or her home, and the buyer gets a new loan which pays off the old VA loan, the veteran may restore eligibility and apply for a new VA loan.

If a veteran sells his or her home and the buyer takes it "subject to" the existing VA loan, the veteran remains personally liable for the loan. A VA loan is a purchase-money loan that may result in a deficiency judgment in the case of foreclosure, and the original borrower (the veteran) would be liable for the deficient amount.

Maximum loan amounts vary in different areas of the state depending on local economies. There is no maximum sales price a veteran may pay.

Certain specific criteria apply to these loans, however. All property secured by a VA loan must be owner-occupied. Points charged to the seller, and interest rates, are subject to change depending on economic conditions. No prepayment penalty is allowed on a VA loan. The seller usually pays loan discount points, unless the loan is a refinance.

There are a variety of loan types available, including fixed-term loans, adjustable-rate loans and graduated payment loans.

VA Financing—A Good Deal for Veterans

More than 29 million veterans and service personnel are eligible for VA financing. Even though many veterans have already used their loan benefits, it may be possible for them to buy homes again with VA financing using remaining or restored loan entitlement.

Before arranging for a new mortgage to finance a home purchase, veterans should consider some of the advantages of VA home loans.

- Most important consideration, no down payment is required in most cases.

- Loan maximum may be up to 100% of the VA-established reasonable value of the property. Due to secondary market requirements, however, loans generally may not exceed $240,000.

- Flexibility of negotiating interest rates with the lender.

- No monthly mortgage insurance premium to pay.

- Limitation on buyer's closing costs.

- An appraisal which informs the buyer of property value.

- Thirty-year loans with a choice of repayment plans:

  - Traditional fixed payment (constant principal and interest; increases or decreases may be expected in property taxes and homeowner's insurance coverage).

  - Graduated Payment Mortgage (GPM)—low initial payments which gradually rise to a level payment starting in the sixth year.

  - Growing Equity Mortgage (GEM)—in some areas; gradually increasing payments with all of the increase applied to principal, resulting in an early payoff of the loan.

- For most loans for new houses, construction is inspected at appropriate stages to ensure compliance with the approved plans, and a 1-year warranty is required from the builder that the house is built in conformity with the approved plans and specifications. In those cases where the builder provides an acceptable 10-year warranty plan, only a final inspection may be required.

- An assumable mortgage, subject to VA approval of the assumer's credit.

• Right to prepay loan without penalty.

• VA performs personal loan servicing and offers financial counseling to help veterans avoid losing their homes during temporary financial difficulties.

Summary of Facts about VA Loans

• No down payment required in some cases

• Certificate of Eligibility required

• Loan amount may not be more than the appraised value

• Certificate of Reasonable Value (VA appraisal) required

• Property must be owner occupied

• Seller usually pays discount points

• No maximum sales price

California Veteran Loans (Cal-Vet)

The California Department of Veterans Affairs administers the Cal-Vet loan program to assist California veterans in buying a home or farm. Unlike other government financing, the Cal-Vet program funds and services its own loans. Funds are obtained through the sale of State General Obligation Bonds.

Upon application for a Cal-Vet loan and approval of the borrower and property, the Department of Veterans Affairs purchases the property from the seller, takes title to the property and sells to the veteran on a contract of sale. The department holds legal title, with the veteran holding equitable title, until the loan is paid off. The veteran has an obligation to apply for life insurance, with the Department of Veterans Affairs as beneficiary, to pay off the debt in case of the veteran's death.

• A veteran does not get title to property bought with a Cal-Vet loan until the loan is paid in full.

Cal-Vet has expanded eligibility so that most veterans (including those now on active duty) wanting to buy a home in California are eligible, subject to financial qualification and available bond funds. There are certain restrictions for peacetime-era veterans.

The good news about Cal-Vet is the money a veteran can save with low interest rates, low down payment and easier qualification. Best of all, this program is available to a qualified veteran at no cost to California taxpayers. Here are some of the attractive features of the Cal-Vet loan.

- Low interest rate
- Even lower rate for qualified first-time home buyers
- Low down payment (lower case)
- Loans up to $521,250
- Subsequent eligibility—use the loan again
- Home and loan protection plans

Interest Rates

Interest rates for new loans are reviewed frequently to insure that the rates offered are below market. Interest rates are subject to change without notice. Current rates are posted on the Cal-Vet website. A borrower's rate is *locked in* as of the date he or she applies, and if rates are reduced while the loan is being processed, the veteran will receive the benefit of the lower rate. While technically a flexible rate, there is a 1/2% cap on increases during the term of the loan.

Low Down Payment

The veteran's out-of-pocket investment is minimal with the low down payment requirement. A borrower will invest as little as 2 or 3% of the purchase price or appraised value, whichever is less, as the down payment.

Maximum Loans up to $521,250

This loan maximum works well in nearly every California market, and is higher than some other government loan programs. The loan maximum for residential properties is $521,250; up to $125,000 for mobile homes in rental parks and $781,875 for farm properties. First-time homebuyer loans have lower purchase price limits in some counties.

Loan Fees

Cal-Vet obtains a loan guaranty on all loans, using either a guaranty from the United States Department of Veterans Affairs, or private mortgage insurance. A borrower also will be charged a loan origination fee (common with most loans) of 1% of the loan amount. This fee must be paid in escrow.

No Monthly Private Mortgage Insurance Premium

Most traditional lenders require a Private Mortgage Insurance (PMI) Premium on loans that exceed an 80% loan-to-value ratio. Cal-Vet helps veteran-borrowers by charging a guarantee fee at the close of escrow, which eliminates the monthly PMI premium.

Expanded Eligibility

Most veterans planning to buy a home in California are eligible; there is no prior residency requirement. Eligible veterans must meet federal rules regarding the use of the bonds funds. Cal-Vet has several bond fund sources for veterans who served during a wartime era, regardless of when they served. Veterans whose service was during peacetime are eligible, but must meet the requirements for use of Revenue Bonds funds.

Peacetime-era veterans must be first-time homebuyers and meet income and purchase price limitations. Veterans must have received a discharge under honorable conditions, and provide a copy of their DD-214 or release from active duty. If a veteran is currently serving on active duty, he or she can provide a Statement of Service to verify qualifying dates and character of service.

Reusable Loans

A veteran may obtain a new Cal-Vet loan each time he or she decides to purchase a different residence. It may be used again and again as long as the previous loan has been paid off.

Home and Loan Protection Plans

In an effort to ensure that a veteran's investment is safe and sound, Cal-Vet provides comprehensive protection for a veteran and his or her family. No other lender offers protection against natural disasters like Cal-Vet. While thousands of Californians have lost everything in natural disasters like floods and earthquakes, Cal-Vet loan holders have full replacement cost coverage for their homes, keeping disaster in check. A Cal-Vet homeowner is fully protected against floods and earthquake damage with a Cal-Vet financed home. Cal-Vet's deductible is a low $500 on flood claims, and $500 or 5% of the coverable loss (whichever is greater) on earthquake and mudslide claims.

The Cal-Vet loan also includes fire and hazard insurance coverage. There is a guaranteed replacement cost coverage on the home, with low premiums and a $250 deductible. With the Cal-Vet loan a veteran receives limited guaranteed life insurance in an amount to make the principal and interest payments for 1 to 5 years, depending on his or her health status at the time the loan is originated. Optional coverage is offered by the insurance carrier including additional life insurance for the veteran, life insurance for the spouse, and disability insurance. Applicants must be under the age of 62 when their loan is funded to receive the life insurance coverage.

Loan Processing

A veteran may process the loan through the local Cal-Vet office or with a Cal-Vet approved mortgage broker. A real estate agent or broker may coordinate the entire process with Cal-Vet, just as they would do with loans from other lenders. Loan processing functions have been centralized to provide consistent and timely processing. Cal-Vet commonly closes most loans within 30 days from receipt of the application.

Summary of Facts about Cal-Vet Loans

- The Department of Veterans Affairs buys the home selected by the veteran and sells it to him or her, using a contract of sale (land contract). The state is the vendor and the veteran becomes the vendee. Title is held by the California Department of Veterans Affairs until the loan is paid off.

- Qualified veterans living in California are eligible for Cal-Vet loans, regardless of where they were born or where they lived when they entered military service. A veteran who accepted a benefit from another state can be eligible for a Cal-Vet loan. A 17-year-old California veteran is eligible, and can sign Cal-Vet documents.

- Eligibility is returned to the veteran after an original loan is paid in full.

- **The same person could be eligible for an FHA, a VA and a Cal-Vet loan.**

PRIVATE MORTGAGE INSURANCE (PMI)

Private Mortgage Insurance (PMI) is extra insurance that lenders require from most homebuyers who obtain loans that are more than 80% of their new home's value. In other words, buyers with less than a 20% down payment are normally required to pay PMI.

Benefits of PMI

PMI plays an important role in the mortgage industry by protecting a lender against loss if a borrower defaults on a loan and by enabling borrowers with less cash to have greater access to homeownership. With this type of insurance, it is possible for a borrower to buy a home with as little as a 3% to 5% down payment. This means that a consumer can buy a home sooner without waiting years to accumulate a large down payment.

New PMI Requirements

A relatively new federal law, The Homeowner's Protection Act (HPA) of 1998, requires lenders or servicers to provide certain disclosures concerning PMI for loans secured by the consumer's primary residence obtained on or after July 29, 1999. The HPA also contains disclosure provisions for mortgage loans that closed before July 29, 1999. In addition, the HPA includes provisions for borrower-requested cancellation and automatic termination of PMI.

Why a Change in PMI Requirements?

In the past, most lenders honored consumers' requests to drop PMI coverage if their loan balance was paid down to 80% of the property value and they had a good payment history. However, consumers were responsible for requesting cancellation and many consumers were not aware of this possibility. A consumer had to keep track of the loan balance to know if there was enough equity, then had to request that the lender discontinue requiring PMI coverage. In many cases, people failed to make this request even after they became eligible, and they paid unnecessary premiums ranging from $250 to $1,200 per year for several years. With the new law, both consumers and lenders share responsibility for how long PMI coverage is required.

The Homeowner's Protection Act (HPA) of 1998

Generally, the HPA applies to *residential mortgage transactions* obtained on or after July 29, 1999, but it also has requirements for loans obtained before that date. This new law does not cover VA and FHA government-guaranteed loans. In addition, the new law has different requirements for loans classified as "high-risk."

Although the HPA does not provide the standards for what constitutes a "high risk" loan, it permits Fannie Mae and Freddie Mac to issue guidance for mortgages that conform to secondary market loan limits. Fannie Mae and Freddie Mac are corporations chartered by Congress to create a continuous flow of funds to mortgage lenders in support of homeownership. As of November 28, 2006, mortgages in amounts of $417,000 or less are considered conforming loans. For non-conforming mortgages, the lender may designate mortgage loans as "high risk."

There are four requirements for a transaction to be considered a residential mortgage transaction: (1) a mortgage or deed of trust must be created or retained; (2) the property securing the loan must be a single-family dwelling; (3) the single-family dwelling must be the primary residence of the borrower; and (4) the purpose of the transaction must be to finance the acquisition, initial construction or refinancing of that dwelling.

How Does a Borrower Cancel or Terminate PMI?

Under the Homeowners Protection Act (HPA), a borrower has the right to request cancellation of PMI when he or she pays down a mortgage to the point that it equals 80% of the original purchase price or appraised value of the home at the time the loan was obtained, whichever is less. The borrower also needs a good payment history, meaning that he or she has not been 30 days late with the mortgage payment within a year of the request, or 60 days late within 2 years. The lender may require evidence that the value of the property has not declined below its original value and that the property does not have a second mortgage, such as a home equity loan.

Automatic Termination

Under HPA, mortgage lenders or servicers must automatically cancel PMI coverage on most loans, once a borrower pays down the mortgage to 78% of the value, as long as the borrower is current on the loan. If the loan is delinquent on the date of automatic termination, the lender must terminate the coverage as soon thereafter as the loan becomes current. Lenders must terminate the coverage within 30 days of cancellation or the automatic termination date, and are not permitted to require PMI premiums after this date. Any unearned premiums must be returned to the borrower within 45 days of the cancellation or termination date.

For high risk loans, mortgage lenders or servicers are required to automatically cancel PMI coverage once the mortgage is paid down to 77% of the original value of the property, provided the borrower is current on the loan.

Final Termination

Under HPA, if PMI has not been canceled or otherwise terminated, coverage must be removed when the loan reaches the midpoint of the amortization period. On a 30-year loan with 360 monthly payments, for example, the chronological midpoint would occur after 180 payments. This provision also calls for the borrower to be current on the payments required by the terms of the mortgage. Final termination must occur within 30 days of this date.

What Disclosures Does the Homeowners Protection Act (HPA) Require?

For Loans Obtained On or After July 29, 1999

The HPA has established three different times when a lender or servicer must notify a consumer of his or her rights. Those times are at loan closing, annually, and upon cancellation or termination of PMI.

The content of these disclosures varies depending on whether: (1) PMI is "borrower-paid PMI" or "lender-paid PMI," (2) the loan is classified as a "fixed rate mortgage" or "adjustable rate mortgage," or (3) the loan is designated as "high risk" or not.

At loan closing, lenders are required to disclose all of the following to borrowers:

- The right to request cancellation of PMI and the date on which this request may be made.

- The requirement that PMI be automatically terminated and the date on which this will occur.

- Any exemptions to the right to cancellation or automatic termination.

- A written initial amortization schedule (fixed-rate loans only).

Annually, a mortgage loan servicer must send borrowers a written statement that discloses:

- The right to cancel or terminate PMI.

• An address and telephone number to contact the loan servicer to determine when PMI may be canceled.

When the PMI coverage is canceled or terminated, a notification must be sent to the consumer stating that:

• PMI has been terminated, and the borrower no longer has PMI coverage.

• No further PMI premiums are due.

The obligation for providing notice of cancellation or termination is with the servicer of the mortgage.

For Loans Obtained Before July 29, 1999

An annual statement must be sent to consumers whose mortgages were obtained before July 29, 1999. This statement should explain that under certain circumstances PMI may be canceled (such as with consent of the mortgagee). It should also provide an address and telephone number to contact the loan servicer to determine whether PMI may be canceled.

The HPA's cancellation and automatic termination rules do not apply to loans made before July 29, 1999.

Although parts of the new law apply only to loans obtained on or after July 29, 1999, many lenders report that they plan to follow the HPA's requirements for both new and existing loans. Making a call to your mortgage loan servicer will help you understand exactly how the law applies to you and your mortgage.

What if the Value of the Home Has Increased?

When making mortgage payments, most of the payments during the first few years are finance charges. Therefore, it can take 10 to 15 years to pay down a loan to reach 80% of the loan value. If the home prices in the area are rising quickly, the borrower's property value may increase so that it can reach the 80% mark a lot faster. The property value could also increase due to home improvements that the borrower makes to the home.

If a borrower thinks that the home value has increased, he or she may be able to cancel PMI on the mortgage. Although the new law does not require a mortgage servicer to consider the current property value, a borrower should contact the lender to see if there is willingness to do so. Also, a borrower should be sure to ask what documentation may be required to demonstrate the higher property value.

CHAPTER QUIZ

1. Which of the following is not one of the three basic default insurance plans?

   a. Department of Housing and Urban Development (HUD)
   b. Veterans Administration (VA)
   c. Federal Housing Authority (FHA)
   d. Private Mortgage Insurance (PMI)

2. The four types of mortgage default insurance include all except:

   a. partial coverage
   b. full coverage
   c. coinsurance
   d. amortized coverage

3. The Federal Housing Administration (FHA):

   a. guarantees loans
   b. pledges loans
   c. insures loans
   d. endorses

4. Who may obtain a Federal Housing Administration (FHA) loan?

   a. any citizen who qualifies
   b. a veteran
   c. a retiree
   d. all of the above

5. The Veterans Administration (VA):

   a. underwrites loans
   b. insures loans
   c. warrantees
   d. guarantees loans

6. Who may obtain a Veterans Administration (VA) loan?

   a. eligible citizens
   b. eligible veterans
   c. eligible retirees
   d. any citizen

7. A Veterans Administration (VA) appraisal is called:

    a. certificate of reasonable value (CRV)
    b. estimate of value (EV)
    c. guarantee of value (GV)
    d. instrument of certain value (ICV)

8. Who administers the Cal Vet program?

    a. the California Department
       of Veterans Affairs
    b. Veterans Administration (VA)
    c. Department of Housing and Urban
       Development (HUD)
    d. Real Estate Commissioner

9. Who holds legal title to the property under a Cal Vet loan?

    a. the veteran
    b. Veterans Administration (VA)
    c. California Department of
       Veterans Affairs
    d. Department of Housing and Urban
       Development (HUD)

10. Buyers with less than _____ percent down payment are normally required to pay PMI:

    a. 5%
    b. 10%
    c. 15%
    d. 20%

ANSWERS

1. *a*
2. *d*
3. *c*
4. *d*
5. *d*
6. *b*
7. *a*
8. *a*
9. *c*
10. *d*

Real Estate as an Investment

INTRODUCTION

An investment is the outlay of money with the reasonable expectation of profit. Individuals, businesses and institutions are all known to invest some discretionary portion of the money they earn. Real estate is among their investment choices, which might also include stocks; corporate bonds; local, state and U.S. government securities; tangibles such as precious metals, art and jewelry; savings accounts; certificates of deposit; individual retirement accounts and commercial paper. Investors will commit their limited investment dollars, however, only if the benefits equal or exceed the benefits associated with other investment opportunities. Investing in real estate is a convenient and reliable choice when other sources for investment are not profitable or productive.

Real estate investment presents both distinctive problems and special opportunities. Real estate is a restricted, non-liquid investment opportunity; stationary, sometimes scarce, durable and physically real. It is not always easy to own buildings requiring maintenance, tenants, retrofitting and security, and that are subject to fire, earthquakes and advantages and disadvantages of a particular locality.

Since real estate is extremely dependent on local conditions, consumers should invest in real property only if they are knowledgeable of local real estate values—including the local economy, market conditions, political environment and building controls. All of these factors can be critical to the success or failure of an investment.

WHY INVEST IN REAL ESTATE

Most consumers have certain expectations for their financial future when they invest their hard earned money. Investment opportunities are myriad and can be glamorous, sophisticated, exotic or commonplace. The careful investor in real estate must decide whether the benefit of putting his or her money in a non-liquid asset such as an apartment building or commercial shopping center is as great as with other types of investments, such as the stock market or bank certificates of deposit. Is the return on the real estate high enough to be worth the extra risk involved in tying up the money for an extended period of time? What are the local market conditions, and how are they likely to change over the course of two, five or ten years? It is certainly easier, and in many ways safer, to rely instead on other types of investments. For instance, investing in certificates of deposit requires little work, is easy to understand and historically has provided a conservative, but steady, return.

Basic Facts about Investing in Real Estate

- An introduction to creative real estate investment must begin with an understanding of the process. For the average consumer, real estate investing is the most common and effective method of building wealth aside from ordinary income derived from a regular paying job.

- Many programs and methods are available for consumers to build a real estate investment portfolio, regardless of income, credit, assets, gender, race or education.

- Many beginning real estate investors lose money. Those investors who do succeed sometimes have a little luck on their side; but they all tend to have a common trait: knowledge.

The biggest barrier to thriving as a real estate investor, for the average consumer, has always been and continues to be lack of knowledge. Familiarity with alternative finance resources and knowledge of tactics is essential to maintaining positive investment practices throughout the life of the venture.

There is basically only one reason for investing in real estate and that is profit. It may not be immediate profit, as in some investments, but for the long haul the profit will be there. Buying real estate can often lead to a return on investment (ROI) that is much greater than the return on other conservative investments. This is because real estate projects provide three ways to make a return on the initial investment. Added together, these three types of return on investment can add up to a substantial total return—one that validates the greater risk and involvement.

Types of Return on Investment (ROI)

The three types of return on investment (ROI) found in a real estate investment are cash flow, return on taxes and appreciation.

Cash Flow

Cash flow is the amount returned to an investor as cash after expenses, including debt service (mortgage payment). It represents the most direct type of return, since it is money an investor can see almost immediately. Some good investments do not have a positive cash flow at first, but the investment may be justified by the return from the other two ROIs.

Return on Taxes

Some investors, especially those in higher tax brackets, are less concerned with cash return than they are with the tax advantages of real estate investment. Income property provides tax shelter by allowing the investor to deduct, on an annual basis, the interest on the loan, property taxes, insurance, management, maintenance and utilities. Loss on the sale of income property may also be deducted. Another benefit of investing in income producing property is allowed depreciation. Depreciation may not be taken on a personal residence, but investment property must be depreciated according to a formula determined by the Internal Revenue Service (IRS).

The tax laws reward an investor for the financial risk taken and benefit the economy from the investment by allowing the taxpayer to reduce tax liability in numerous ways. As long as an investment is income producing, such as apartment buildings or commercial property, certain reductions in tax liability are allowed.

One of the most important tax benefits of income property ownership is the depreciation allowance. While a homeowner can exclude a certain amount of profit from being taxed, the owner of income property may not. However, the investor must claim depreciation and other deductions which will reduce the tax bill beyond that which is allowed a homeowner.

Depreciation for tax purposes is not based on actual deterioration, but on the calculated useful life of the property. The theory is that improvements, not land, deteriorate and lose their value. A building is thought to have a certain number of years where it can generate an income and after that is no longer a practical investment. The investor is compensated for the loss by being allowed to deduct a certain dollar amount each year based on the useful life of the property until, on paper at least, the property no longer has any value as an investment.

However, tax laws regarding depreciation change so often, it is advisable for the reader to check current IRS rules for calculating depreciation.

The common method used to determine the dollar amount per year that will be deducted is straight line depreciation, where the same amount is deducted every year over the depreciable life of a property. In calculating depreciation, the value of the improvements is divided by the depreciable life of the property, to arrive at the annual dollar amount that can be claimed as depreciation and thus deducted as such. Here is how it works.

To Calculate Depreciation

- Determine what the IRS allowance for the depreciable life of a residential income property is by checking current tax law. For our purposes let's assume it is 27½ years.

- Subtract the value of the land from the value of the property to determine the value of the building. The value of the land can be calculated from the tax assessor's bill or by using the value of similar parcels.

Value of property	$400,000
Value of land	– 160,000
Value of building	$240,000

- $240,000 divided by 27½ years = $8,727 annual depreciation allowance

When the owner of income producing property sells the property, the amount depreciated over the years will be subtracted from their cost basis to determine their tax liability or capital gain. Also, when the property is sold, the new owner is allowed to begin depreciating the building as if it were new, based on the new sales price.

The gain on an income producing property is calculated much like that for a personal residence, except any depreciation that has been claimed over the years must be subtracted from the cost basis. This means the dollar amount that has been deducted for depreciation over the time of property ownership, after the cost of any improvements has been added to the purchase price, must be subtracted from the cost basis to arrive at the adjusted cost basis. The amount of taxable gain is then calculated by subtracting the adjusted cost basis from the selling price, less the expenses of sale (commission).

To Calculate the Amount of Capital Gain on Income Property

Purchase price (cost basis)	$600,000
Improvements	+100,000
	$700,000
Depreciation claimed	−75,000
Adjusted cost basis	$625,000
Selling price	$900,000
Expenses of sale (commission)	−54,000
Adjusted selling price	$846,000
Adjusted cost basis	−625,000
Capital gain (profit)	$221,000

Unlike a primary residence where a certain amount of gain may be excluded from being taxed, taxes are owed on any profit made whenever income producing property is sold. However, there are ways an investor may legally defer the gain to a later time.

Installment Sale: An installment sale is one where payments are made, by the buyer to the seller, over a period of more than one year. This is one way capital gain and the tax payments owed can be spread out over a period of time. Part of the tax liability can be deferred by the seller taking back a note and trust deed, or an all inclusive trust deed or contract of sale, with monthly payments. Only the amount of the gain that is collected in the tax year is taxable income and the tax due on the rest can be deferred until collected. Once again, the reader should check current tax laws about installment sales.

Tax-Deferred Exchange (1031 Exchange):   Sometimes called a "tax-free" exchange, this method of deferring tax liability allows an investor to exchange a property for a "like" property, and defer the gain until the property is sold. It is not really a tax-free exchange. The taxes are simply put off until a later date.

Most real property qualifies as "like" property, as long as it is held as an investment. It may be an apartment building, a commercial building, a business or raw land. However, a personal residence would not qualify as a "like" property in an exchange with investment property.

If equities are not equal in two properties being exchanged, money or anything of value (cars, boats, stocks, furniture) other than like-kind property, may be put in by the investor who is "trading up" to balance the equities. This extra cash or non-like property put into an exchange is known as *boot*.

In the example below, to qualify for a tax-deferred exchange, Investor A needs to add $50,000 (boot) to the sale to make the equities match. Investor A would have no tax liability on the sale and Investor B would be taxed on the amount of the boot received in the year of the sale (if he or she realized a gain from the sale). If the amount of the boot exceeds the amount of the gain, tax liability is limited to the amount of the gain.

Investor A:	Property value	$400,000
	Encumbrances	– 50,000
	Equity	$350,000
Investor B:	Property value	$600,000
	Encumbrances	– 200,000
	Equity	$400,000

In calculating the gain on each property, the cost basis of the property being exchanged becomes the cost basis of the property being acquired, if no boot is given or received, and the cost basis follows the taxpayer through subsequent exchanges or sales. The profit or taxable gain is determined by subtracting the adjusted cost basis from the exchange value of the property.

Tax-deferred exchanges can become very complicated. An accountant should be consulted before entering into the sale of a tax-deferred property. In this text, our discussion is mainly an overview of the subject. We recommend that you study the topic further if you find it of interest.

Appreciation

The greatest return on investment is typically from appreciation, which is the continuing increase in the value of a property due to higher market value each year. Properties can have significant increases in value over time due to various forces such as high demand, low interest rates, inflation or change in the economy.

The relatively high ROI due to appreciation represents one of the primary reasons for investing in real estate. However, this return is realized only on the sale of the property, and may be dependent on an investor being able to tie up his or her money for an extended period of time. Real estate investing is not for those who need a regular, predictable return on their investment. But it can be very rewarding for those who can invest relatively large amounts and wait for favorable selling conditions.

Factors in a Decision to Invest in Real Estate

- Location
- Financial and political stability of controlling authority (city or county)
- Redevelopment, potential general city plan, zoning or restriction changes
- Rent control
- Price—is cash necessary
- Terms and financing—seller names price, buyer names terms
- Context—find worst building in best district
- Condition—look for cosmetic problems, not structural

(continued on next page)

**Factors in a Decision to
Invest in Real Estate** *(continued)*

- Demand—what is the competition among buyers

- Competition—what are new properties coming on market, will they improve your property and make it more valuable

- Existing leases—are they good or bad

- Existing operating expenses

- Cost to rehab

- Replacement cost—compare with new construction

- Higher and better use—will market allow for better cash flow

- Zoning—how restrictive

- Historic tax credits—consider as "frosting on the cake"

- Motives of seller—why are they selling (ask them)

- Availability of investors—prepare a feasibility analysis to show them

- Economic cycle—is the timing good, or is there a down-swing

- Appraised value—independent appraisal (don't base on insured or assessed values)

INVESTMENT PROCESS

An introduction to real estate investment must begin with an understanding of the process. The process for acquiring investment property is similar to buying a home, but a different type of due diligence is involved, as well as an increased awareness and acceptance of the risk involved. The typical home buyer does not necessarily see the purchase of a primary residence in terms of risk, and rightly so. All a consumer has to think about in the purchase of a home, aside from qualifying for the loan and making the payments, are the intangible benefits of home ownership which allow a consumer to purchase a home without having to think about cash flow, depreciation, tenant issues or capitalization rates.

The successful investor must understand the nature of real estate investment, that it is vastly different from buying his or her personal residence and must be knowledgeable and thorough in each stage of the process of acquiring investment property.

Stages of the Investment Process

- Preparation and planning
- Gathering resources
- Targeting the right property
- Negotiating terms
- Closing the purchase and taking over the property

Preparation and Planning

Everyone is familiar with the saying "people don't plan to fail, they fail to plan." That is especially true with real estate investing. Real estate investing is entrepreneurship; it is running a business. A consumer's chances for business success will always be greater if he or she makes adequate preparations and plans before launching a new venture.

The first preparatory steps should be to clarify the investment objectives. Personal goals and plans will influence what the investor decides to pursue. If the goal is strong positive cash flow, then the target property and the process selected would be different than if the chosen goal is resale value.

Investment Goals

- Clarify goals
- Prepare for the investment
- Prepare finances
- Develop a written plan
- Create the business
- Determine preferences and priorities

Clarify Goals

The very first step for any aspiring real estate investor is to clarify goals and objectives. The goals will determine what tactics an investor will use and what properties he or she will choose or reject. These reflections should not be left to daydreams and mental notes. They should be written down along with answers and considerations.

Can an investor acquire ten units or 50 units in a year's time? It's very do-able, although the challenges will differ according to the investor's financial and credit situation and the type of property selected by the investor. Will it be easy? No, probably not. A consumer must be willing to invest 20 to 40 hours a week searching for just the right property to fit his or her goals. With relatively stable personal finances the route will be much easier, but the investor still needs to clarify goals or complete an investment analysis questionnaire to make sure the goals are realistic. The right answers are the truly honest ones, regardless of how difficult the truth. The wrong answers are the ones that stray from the truth. Here are a few questions the investor should consider about goals before making an investment in real estate.

Personal Investment Analysis Questionnaire

- Where would I like to be financially and personally next year? How about five years from now?

- How can investing in real estate help me with meeting those goals?

- Are there other investments or projects that I want to pursue in the near future?

- What are my current liabilities? Are there more coming in the future, such as college costs for children?

- Do I want my real estate investments to build my wealth? Or do I want it to simply add a little more to my other income sources?

- Where on my priority scale will I place my real estate investments? Obviously, it should come after my family and basic needs.

- How much time do I have available to spend on real estate investments?

- Do I want real estate investing to become my full time or primary employment? Or do I want to make it a side hobby to my full-time job?

- What do I want from my short-term real estate investments? Cash flow to improve my income situation? Resale profits to put into other investments? Collateral with self-liquidating liabilities that will improve my asset situation after retirement?

This last question is perhaps the most important one that a new investor must answer before moving on to other preparatory steps. For example, if the investor is seeking to increase cash flow, the properties selected probably will be much different than if the goal were to make investments that can be cashed in for profits upon retirement.

Mia had no real income to speak of, but had excellent credit. In four months, she bought four properties with no money down and no closing costs. She sold all the properties less than 12 months later for total net profits of about $110,000. Unfortunately, she waited and bought her first property over five months after attending a real estate investor's seminar—even though she was immediately pre-approved for 100% mortgage financing and started shopping right away.

Why the delay? She kept forgetting her stated goals. She wanted properties that would generate positive cash flow, so that she would not have to spend any money subsidizing those investments. She was looking for positive cash-flow properties!

Unfortunately, the real estate agents she was using did not know how to calculate positive cash flow. She would tell them that she was looking for 2- to 4-unit properties with positive cash flow, and her agents would simply print out all the 2- to 4-unit properties in the areas she identified, regardless of how much profit they were generating. She would then compound the problem by falling in love with a property, even though it was a money loser. She needed a reminder of the importance of sticking to her business plan (with its stated objectives); but the cycle kept repeating itself.

Finally, she was able to buy a property that fit her plans. When she began to understand the whole process and the importance of maintaining her goals, buying subsequent properties was easy. The first five months shopping for qualified property was just part of her learning curve.

Prepare for the Investment

Sometimes real estate investing is easier for those who have had entrepreneurial experience, starting or running their own business. Investors with entrepreneurial experience are more aware of the emotional and mental needs of running a business.

The truth is, however, that anyone armed with the proper resources and knowledge can build wealth in real estate. To obtain some of the experiences of seasoned entrepreneurs, beginning real estate investors must take the time to prepare themselves for this new venture.

Preparing for the Investment

It's Business

- It's inevitable that entrepreneurs invest their emotions, as well as their capital and energies, into their business. However, successful entrepreneurs all have the ability to separate business decisions from personal ones. This doesn't mean that an investor should abandon his or her ethics, morality, conscience, values or principles. It is rather an acknowledgment that investing is essentially like playing a game: it's only a game. At the end of the game, win or lose, the investor goes home and, if he or she is lucky, will play another game the next day or week. And if the investor is very good, this game will eventually support a desired lifestyle. Of course, it's very hard to separate business from personal life if personal well-being is entirely dependent on business. That's the challenge facing all beginning real estate investors.

Business Space

- Even while working from home, which is common for beginning investors, the individual should try to set aside a room or desk at which business is conducted. The investor should try to avoid having business papers spill over into other areas of the home, and vice versa. If an office can be set up in a separate room, that would be great. However, an investor can do just as well with a desk in the corner of a bedroom. Regardless of where the office is situated, though, it should be kept away from television or traffic that could distract and interfere with efficiency.

Organized Systems

- Real estate investing will involve a great deal of paperwork and records, especially at the beginning as the investor shops for and buys more properties. If investors are actively managing their own properties, the demands on a filing system are even greater. There will be leases and tenant records, as well as property records and contracts, and files for service providers. Perhaps the most important items to save are receipts; it may be surprising to see the amount of deductions and tax savings available to real estate investors. A decent computer and software system, with an office suite of administrative programs, such as Microsoft Office, is also a must. Tasks may be automated and communications sent electronically, saving time and possibly money. The computer is also important to send and receive faxes, as well as send and receive important business email.

(continued on next page)

Preparing for the Investment   *(continued)*

Self-Discipline

- Successful entrepreneurship requires self-discipline to do what needs to be done when it needs to be done. Self-discipline isn't necessarily genetic, and it can be learned. Moreover, self-discipline is aided by structure, such as having an office area set aside. Another structural tool to consider is to schedule specific times to take care of tasks.

Avoid Bad Habits

- Perhaps the biggest bad habit consumers need to conquer is procrastination. Receipts should go directly into the receipt box, not dropped on the dresser with the idea of filing it later. Successful investors should get in the habit of doing tasks now or as soon as possible. A "to-do" list may help.

Patience

- Business requires patience. If an investor is constantly stressed by entrepreneurship, there are a couple of probable conclusions: either the investor is doing it wrong or is not meant to be an entrepreneur. Things can and do go wrong; but that's one of the wonderful opportunities that entrepreneurship offers, the chance to learn and improve.

Perspective

- When serious decisions are required, it always helps to remember objectives, goals and plans. Keep a perspective on the big picture, while concentrating on the immediate tasks.

Prepare Your Finances

The great thing about real estate investing is that the strengths of selected properties can overcome weaknesses in an investor's personal income, assets and credit. At a certain point, such as if the property in question is larger than four units, a lender is only mildly curious about the buyer. Primarily, the lender wants to make sure the property supports itself, not counting the strength of the investor's financial statement. Nonetheless, each person still needs to prepare all of the important financial papers. First of all, it helps the investor to know exactly what his or her strengths and weaknesses are. Secondly, the mortgage lender will require them.

Prepare Multiple Copies of the Following Documents

(1) Complete tax returns for the past 3 years

(2) W-2s for the past 3 years

(3) The most recent two statements for all bank and asset accounts

(4) Legible photocopy of driver's license and social security card

(5) Letter of explanation for credit problems

(6) Supporting documents for credit issues, such as bankruptcy papers and judgment decrees

(7) Renters: landlord contact information (to verify rent history) and copies of canceled rent checks for the past 12 months

Again, the investor should only provide copies. Originals should not be released unless absolutely necessary. A mortgage loan officer can assist in clarifying what is needed, as well as reviewing the investor's credit report and arranging a mortgage pre-approval.

Develop a Written Business Plan

A real estate investor has now become an entrepreneur. Nothing helps to increase the chances of success for beginning entrepreneurs better than a good business plan. This plan need not be extravagant or written in stone. At the very least, the investor should lay out goals and basic game plan. What types of properties or investments sound good? How much can the investor afford to invest? What resources, contingencies and assistance are at his or her disposal? What are personal strengths and weaknesses?

Real estate investing is about acquiring and owning a business, which also happens to be a property. The right business decision during the preparatory stage can save the investor thousands of dollars and an enormous amount of grief.

**Issues to Consider When Establishing a
Real Estate Investing Business**

Partners

• One of the first issues an investor should consider is whether to do this alone, or partner with key people. If time

(continued on next page)

**Issues to Consider When Establishing a
Real Estate Investing Business**   *(continued)*

Partners   *(continued)*

and resources are limited, a partnership definitely should be considered. Of course, an investor needs partners that can be trusted, and a well-designed (by a professional, not the investor) partnership agreement to reinforce that trust. Partners who can complement an investor's skills and resources should be selected. For example, if a partnership is a four-person team, one partner could handle the financing responsibilities; one partner might be a real estate agent who guides the property search, acquisition and leasing; another partner might manage the fiscal and administrative operations; and the fourth partner could have intensive contractor experience to guide the work and understand properties structurally. Everyone could be involved in cleaning and repair work.

Business Mail and Phone

• If the investor is working out of a home office, there should be an offsite post office box or local mail-store box to receive business mail to avoid the problem of tenants and clients contacting the investor at home. Use this mailbox address on all correspondence. Also, the investor should set up a separate business phone line, and have a cell phone as well.

Determine Preferences and Priorities

As per the business plan, it is now time for the investor to focus on tactics. Specifically, what will be the initial target properties and areas? The investor must be prepared to answer why those targets were selected. Are they three units close to home or a condominium conversion project downtown? Both can be good investments—for the right person at the right time. However, the real question is what the investor is ready and able to pursue.

It goes without saying that adequate preparation will save time, aggravation and money; and this is especially true of buying real estate. After the investor has completed preparations, it is now time to begin shopping.

To further highlight the importance of adequate preparations, consider that the most successful real estate investors all make detailed analysis and plans before embarking on any venture. Detailed feasibility studies are the minimum preparations taken by experienced investors. In many cases, only a fraction of the considered projects (after feasibility studies and preparations are completed) are actually launched.

Successful real estate investing is very demanding. An investor may have to look at 25 properties before finding one that will meet investment parameters and allow the investor to make an offer. Furthermore, out of every four offers, the investor may only complete one purchase. That's actually not too bad for beginning investors. As the investor gets more experienced or works with more experienced agents, it may mean only having to look at 10 properties before finding a good one on which to make an offer.

Gathering Resources

A real estate investor should not go on the journey alone. The real estate industry has agents and resources at an investor's disposal during the entire investment process. Before starting, however, an investor should identify the key individuals as resources who will be there for much of the process. It is best to establish the relationship before starting, when possible, so that their assistance will be available when the time comes.

Because of the large amount of money involved with mortgages and real estate transactions, many agents, representatives, service providers and individuals become involved to protect the interests of the investor as well as other parties to a transaction.

Common Service Providers for the Real Estate Investment Process

- Attorney
- Real estate agent
- Loan officer
- Property inspector
- Insurance agent
- Appraiser
- Closing or escrow agent
- Accountant

Attorney

Real estate investors need experienced attorneys with a background in commercial and investment real estate. It also helps if they or someone in their firm also can provide the investor with business planning assistance.

Investors should not assume that attorneys who help purchase homes are qualified to be investment attorneys.Real estate closings on the purchase of homes are heavily regulated and highly standardized. So much so, that practically any attorney can handle the typical home closing without any problems. If there are any questions, they can always turn to the closing agent, usually a representative of the title company, who is well-trained in residential closings. Investment properties have a different focus altogether.

Another point to remember is that good attorneys cost more. Experienced investment property attorneys will cost much more than regular residential property attorneys. But they are worth it.

If an investor wants to lower closing costs to the absolute minimum, attorney fees is not the area to look for bargains. Yes, the investor may save $200 by going with a cheaper attorney, but an experienced attorney's knowledge and experience can save thousands of dollars. The investor should find an experienced real estate attorney with investment property forte, and consider it a smart investment.

It may surprise some people to learn that they do not need an attorney to handle closings. Legally, anyone can do it without professional assistance. But both the buyer and seller will typically have attorney representation in some states. In other states buyer and seller will be represented by an escrow holder who will be a dual agent dealing with both parties. In most cases, however, communication between the two parties is usually only done between the attorneys, escrow holders or real estate agents. In locales where an attorney acts as closing agent, it is the attorney's responsibility to protect client's legal and financial interests. The buyer's attorney will review all documents involved with the purchase transaction, from the purchase agreement and loan good faith estimate disclosure to the closing's final settlement statement.

At the closing, the buyer's attorney will review the dozens of legal documents and disclosures that must be signed by the buyer. The buyer's attorney will explain each document to the buyer before it is signed. Also, both attorneys will calculate and verify the final transaction figures prior to concluding the closing.

In the case where an escrow holder acts as the closing agent, the same events occur as when an attorney closes the transaction, with the escrow holder explaining any disclosures that have not been explained by the real estate agent, overseeing signing of loan documents, calculating closing costs and preparing closing statements.

Real Estate Agent

Real estate agents are generally free for the buyer/investor, so why not use them. Fortunately, there are real estate agents who are well equipped to help an investor find suitable investment properties. They have had training in locating profitable investment properties and experience in the successful acquisition of such properties.

An investor should look for an experienced and well-informed real estate agent when he or she starts interviewing agents. A salesperson or broker possessing certain investment designations such as CCIM *(Certified Commercial Investment Member of the Commercial Investment Institute)* would be a particularly valuable asset to an investor. The CCIM designation is awarded by the Commercial Investment Real Estate Council, an affiliate of the National Association of REALTORS®, representing the real estate industry's highest professional and ethical standards. For a real estate investment broker to earn the CCIM designation, the member must have experienced and completed a rigorous series of professional courses and passed a comprehensive final examination, along with having submitted a resume of transactions showing a certain depth of experience. The CCIM designation is rapidly growing in recognition as the hallmark of a truly experienced professional in the field of commercial investment real estate brokerage.

Agent vs. Broker: Real estate agents cannot operate independently; they must work for a broker. Only a real estate broker can own and operate a real estate office. Real estate agents who take further training and pass the state broker exam can become real estate brokers. Until then, they can only list real estate or assist buyers if they work through a broker. From the point of view of an investor, the only difference is that a real estate broker may possess more knowledge or experience than a salesperson, and thus be more helpful in a transaction. There are many salespersons, however, who are extremely knowledgeable—even specialists in investment properties—who would be the perfect candidate to help an investor find properties that matched objectives.

Buyer's Broker: Some buyers may select a more specialized agent, called a buyer's broker. The certified buyer's broker has only recently become a more focused service and should not be confused with other real estate agents or brokers. The buyer's broker represents only the buyer and has no allegiance to the seller. The buyer will pay the buyer's broker for his or her service. Because the buyer's broker does not depend on seller paid commission, the buyer's broker will look at properties that might not be listed on the Multiple Listing Service (MLS). Increasingly, buyer's brokers are common in commercial real estate transactions.

Listing Agent: The listing agent is the real estate agent or broker responsible for selling the property. The agent works for and represents the seller. The name derives from the agent's primary task of listing the property for sale, usually through the local Multiple Listing Service (MLS). When a buyer finds a worthy property, the buyer's broker or real estate agent will approach the listing agent to make an offer, arrange preliminary inspections and negotiate a final price. The listing agent shares the property's sales commission with the buyer's real estate agent. An investor needs to keep in mind that the listing agent has a fiduciary duty to carry out the best interests of the seller, and the buyer's interest might not be first priority, beyond being honest and truthful as required by real estate law. It might be more profitable for an investor to make an offer through his or her own agent rather than depending on a listing agent to represent both buyer and seller as a dual agent.

Loan Officer

The lender's representative is typically the loan officer, although the applicant may also have to communicate with the loan processor or underwriter. It is the loan officer's responsibility to initially pre-qualify and pre-approve the buyer's mortgage loan application, as well as eventually obtaining final approval and coordinating the loan closing for the purchase mortgage loan. Because of the money and myriad government regulations involved, loan officers must provide the borrower with a good deal of information. By the same token, the loan officer must gather numerous borrower documents to support and process the application. But the loan officer also often acts as an informal advisor for the borrower, as the lender has a vested interest in the borrower's success.

Not all loan officers and lenders are alike, although most lenders tend to eventually sell their loans to investors that have nothing to do with the initial transaction. Banks may lend their own money, but usually sell the loan (through Fannie Mae and Freddie Mac) to the secondary mortgage market so that they can replenish their cash supply and make a profit on initiating the loan. Mortgage companies usually broker to dozens of banks from across the country. This allows mortgage brokers to work with more challenged borrowers, who may have a difficult time with the conservative parameters of most banks.

A consumer seeking a standard home loan or even a standard investment loan (on one-to-four units), with the usual down payment requirements and restrictions, can go to practically any bank or mortgage company for the financing. If an investor is looking for creative financing, such as a no money down, 100% mortgage, for investment (rental) properties, however, he or she will probably work with a mortgage broker with ties to specialized lenders. There are considerably more lenders willing to make loans on one-to-four units than there are for larger properties with increased investment risks. Those risks might include no seller obligation for transfer disclosures about the condition of the property, as well as no protection under RESPA (Real Estate Settlement Procedures Act) rules for properties with more than four units.

Property Inspector

The property inspector is different from the appraiser. The inspector is typically an option available to the buyers, so they don't have to conduct an actual inspection of the property if they do not want to pay for one. But an investor would be unwise not to take advantage of this option. Actually, it would be a huge mistake not to have an investment property fully inspected before purchasing the property.

The property inspector will conduct a thorough examination of the property for defects, operating efficiency and overall condition. Among other things, the inspector will check heating, cooling, plumbing and electrical systems, as well as the building's structure. It is also a good idea to accompany the inspector if the investor is a first-time buyer, as it may be the first and only opportunity to learn such practicalities as restarting a furnace, locating the fuse box and checking the primary water valves.

Insurance Agent

At the typical closing, the buyer must provide proof of paid hazard insurance coverage for one full year. This is a common mortgage loan requirement and it is advisable for the buyer to use a respectable insurance company in the area of the property, as the buyer will want the insurance agent nearby if there is a problem. The agent will have to review the property briefly to confirm acceptable condition, though properties with serious defects may have a more difficult time obtaining affordable insurance coverage.

Appraiser

The appraiser determines an approximate fair market value for the subject property, based on a review and analysis of recorded data about that property and its locale. The lender will normally order the appraisal. Although the lender must approve the appraiser, the buyer sometimes has an option regarding selection of an independent appraiser.

The appraiser is separate and distinct from the real estate inspector, because the appraiser's focus is on the market value. In most cases, the appraiser assumes that the property is in normal working condition and only visits the subject property briefly.

When visiting the property, the appraiser will take floor and lot measurements, as well as photograph the property and neighborhood. The appraiser will also use the visit to confirm the property's condition. The appraiser usually will not calculate any major adjustments based on the property's condition unless the property shows visible deterioration or contains major value-inflating improvements. Still, improvements can only increase the property value so much—the neighborhood has the anchoring influence on the appraised value.

Closing Agent

A closing agent, who may be a representative of the title company or an escrow holder, will conduct the closing. In some locales or situations, however, the seller's attorney will act as the closing agent. The closing agent will prepare many of the closing documents, although the lender's document preparation department or provider usually packages the mortgage loan documents and disclosures.

The buyer should expect to sign numerous legal documents and disclosures. The seller will only need to sign a few documents and often skips the closing, as the seller's attorney is the only person necessary to represent the seller in some states. The closing agent will gather final transaction calculations from both attorneys and collect any necessary funds from the buyer, seller and lender. Once all documents are signed, the closing agent will notarize them and prepare them for recording with the county. After a final review and check with the lender, the closing agent will then disburse funds to the seller, attorneys, real estate agents, service providers, lien holders (to be paid off) and buyers, as required by the transaction.

Accountant

A knowledgeable tax accountant becomes invaluable when it is time to prepare tax returns. An investor and entrepreneur will have many tax advantages available but will probably need a professional to find and apply these tax deductions and benefits. There are many tax reporting software programs available today that can automatically locate many of these deductions and savings, but a Certified Public Accountant (CPA) can help the investor look at the bigger, long-term picture and plan appropriately.

Targeting the Right Property

The investor is now ready to begin shopping. Normally, the investor would not be committed to any obligation during a shopping process, so keeping an open mind is important to acquiring a property that is consistent with one's goals. It is not uncommon for the successful investor to change decisions a few times, each time getting closer to the property that is exactly right.

> ### Steps to Locating the Right Property
>
> • Review the business plan
> • Obtain loan pre-approval
> • Obtain available property listing
> • Visit and inspect prospective properties
> • Prioritize preferences

Review the Business Plan

A business plan is useless unless the investor actually applies it. Whenever a person starts to feel off-course, the first move should be to review the business plan. As the investor begins shopping, it is particularly important to recall special goals, priorities, preferences and minimum requirements.

As mentioned earlier, an investor's goals and plans will determine which properties are right. Instead of having to look at thousands of prospective investments, the business plan should be the focus for the search. The investor should also share the business plan with the key people assisting in the acquisition, especially the real estate agent, loan officer and accountant. As the investor starts shopping for property, that is the time to make sure the real estate agent understands the selected investment strategy and objectives.

Obtain Loan Pre-Approval

The fact is that a consumer is not really considered a serious buyer—let alone investor—unless he or she has funds backing up inquiries and offers. A loan pre-approval certificate is a powerful tool. It means that a buyer can close sooner and more assuredly than someone without a loan commitment, and delays mean additional headaches and expenses for the seller. There are two landmarks in obtaining preliminary mortgage financing that all prospective investors should understand.

- *Pre-Qualification:* The minimum certification that most sellers will want is a pre-qualification. However, the pre-qualification carries no obligation from the lender. The pre-qualification usually entails a quick credit and income analysis conducted by the loan officer. In most cases, the borrower has yet to complete the loan application. Still, the pre-qualification certificate will often suffice for most listing agents.

- *Pre-Approval:* The pre-approval involves the processing of a full loan application, with most of the required borrower documents attached. The pre-approval is a preliminary approval and does carry significantly more weight than the pre-qualification. The preliminary approval is usually conditioned on the borrower finding an acceptable (to the lender) property, maintaining credit qualifications and providing any other items required by the lender.

Depending on the property desired, it may be easy to obtain a pre-qualification and/or pre-approval. A buyer must complete a pre-approval questionnaire and either email, fax or mail the completed form to a loan representative. Normally the lender can give a pre-qualification in a few minutes after checking the buyer's credit and analyzing the buyer's income, and can then prepare an application package for the pre-approval.

If the property in question is a large investment property, pre-approval may not be available to the buyer, since the lender is going to look at the property more than the buyer in evaluating the risk involved in making the loan.

If an investor wants to shop around with different lenders, he or she needs to realize that there is a right way and a wrong way to do it. Following the wrong way can severely damage the investor's credit, because every time any creditor requests a credit report—for a pre-qualification or pre-approval—the investor's credit record will indicate an inquiry and each inquiry has the potential to lower the investor's FICO® or credit score by 10 to 20 points. Shopping around for the best deal is smart, but after the sixth creditor an investor may discover a personal credit grade that has dropped from an A to a B, thereby jeopardizing the mortgage financing.

The right way to shop around is for the investor to obtain a credit report from all three credit reporting bureaus, TransUnion, Experian and CBI/Equifax. This can be done on line. Also, the credit reports should indicate the investor's FICO® credit score.

As an investor shops around for a pre-qualification, the process should be to tell the loan officers not to request a credit report and give them a copy instead. That is more than sufficient for a pre-qualification, and such credit reports are good for up to 60 to 90 days. Once the investor applies for a pre-approval or a full approval, the lender will then have to request its own credit report.

Obtain Available Property Listings

Armed with a business plan and loan approval, an investor is ready to begin some serious shopping. The next stop should be with a professional real estate agent, who can identify the properties that meet the investor's required criteria and who has access to the Multiple Listing Service (MLS). A real estate agent can generate a computer print-out of properties that provides a wealth of information about each property, including rental income and operating expenses. The investor should review the data offered and prioritize all of the listings using the business plan as guide.

Not all for sale properties are listed through brokers. Many sellers try to market their properties themselves in order to avoid paying the 5% to 6% commission they would otherwise have to pay to list with an agent. Unfortunately, considering those properties as purchase prospects will require more legwork from investors—unless they use a buyer's broker.

Still, for-sale-by-owner (FSBO) properties are too important to ignore. An investor's best bet is to spend a couple of hours scouring the real estate classified ads for such properties. The investor should telephone the sellers of interesting properties and conduct a preliminary analysis over the phone, get more information about the property, its expenses and its income potential, as well as discovering the seller's motivation. In some cases, an investor may be able to negotiate creative transactions with the seller.

Visit and Inspect Prospective Properties

The investor should drive by each of the preferred properties at least once before seriously previewing them. Prior to actually visiting any properties, the organized investor will have analyzed each one for its potential, and then prioritize each property according to its compatibility with the investor's goals. After the investor has done all the homework on the properties, it is time to visit only those that meet the investment requirements. Only then should the real estate agent make the appointment to preview those properties.

PROPERTY INSPECTION CHECKLIST

Property Address	Date & Time of Visit

NEIGHBORHOOD

Area Type: ☐ Urban ☐ Suburban ☐ Rural	Prominent Use: ☐ Residential ☐ Commercial ☐ Industrial ☐ Other:		General Condition: ☐ Excellent ☐ Stable ☐ Fair ☐ Distressed ☐ Awful	Traffic: ☐ Heavy ☐ Medium ☐ Light
Noise: ☐ Loud ☐ Medium ☐ Quiet	Lighting: ☐ Well Lit ☐ Fair ☐ Poorly Lit ☐ None	Nearby Homes: ☐ Excellent ☐ Good ☐ Fair ☐ Distressed	Neighbors: ☐ Seniors ☐ Families ☐ Young Singles ☐ Other	
Schools: ☐ < ½-mile ☐ ½-1 mile ☐ > 1 mile	Shopping: ☐ < ½-mile ☐ ½-1 mile ☐ > 1 mile	Public Transportation: ☐ < ½-mile ☐ ½-1 mile ☐ > 1 mile	Church: ☐ < ½-mile ☐ ½-1 mile ☐ > 1 mile	Parks: ☐ < ½-mile ☐ ½-1 mile ☐ > 1 mile
Gym, Recreation Ctr: ☐ < ½-mile ☐ ½-1 mile ☐ > 1 mile	Hospital/Medical: ☐ < ½-mile ☐ ½-1 mile ☐ > 1 mile	Employment: ☐ < ½-mile ☐ ½-1 mile ☐ > 1 mile	Highways & Major Streets: ☐ < ½-mile ☐ ½-1 mile ☐ > 1 mile	Entertainment: ☐ < ½-mile ☐ ½-1 mile ☐ > 1 mile

Comments:

PROPERTY SITE & LOT

Lot Size	Topography: ☐ Flat ☐ Sloping ☐ Hilly ☐ Other:	Location on Block: ☐ Corner ☐ Middle ☐ Other:	Driveway: ☐ None ☐ Good ☐ Fair ☐ Damaged	Sidewalk: ☐ Excellent ☐ Good ☐ Fair ☐ Awful
Alley: ☐ None ☐ Good ☐ Fair ☐ Damaged	Patio: ☐ None ☐ Good ☐ Fair ☐ Damaged	Visible Encumbrances: ☐ None ☐ Yes:	Visible Easements: ☐ None ☐ Yes:	Pool: ☐ None ☐ Good ☐ Fair ☐ Damaged
Fence: ☐ None ☐ Good ☐ Fair ☐ Damaged	Landscaping: ☐ None ☐ Good ☐ Fair ☐ Damaged	Description of Landscaping & Exterior Site Elements		
Parking Type: ☐ None ☐ Garage ☐ Paved ☐ Unpaved	Parking Condition: ☐ NA ☐ Excellent ☐ Good ☐ Poor	Description of Exterior Parking Elements (paving, striping, carports, etc.)		

Comments:

BUILDING EXTERIOR

Building Style:	Levels/Stories:	Finish Type: ☐ Brick ☐ Vinyl ☐ Wood ☐ Other:	Finish Condition: ☐ Excellent ☐ Good ☐ Fair ☐ Damaged	Curb Appeal: ☐ Excellent ☐ Good ☐ Fair ☐ Poor
Front Wall Condition: ☐ Excellent ☐ Good ☐ Damaged:	Side Wall 1 Condition: ☐ Excellent ☐ Good ☐ Damaged:	Side Wall 2 Condition: ☐ Excellent ☐ Good ☐ Damaged:	Rear Wall Condition: ☐ Excellent ☐ Good ☐ Damaged:	
Front Windows Condition: ☐ Excellent ☐ Good ☐ Poor/Damaged:	Side 1 Windows Condition: ☐ Excellent ☐ Good ☐ Poor/Damaged:	Side 2 Windows Condition: ☐ Excellent ☐ Good ☐ Poor/Damaged:	Rear Windows Condition: ☐ Excellent ☐ Good ☐ Poor/Damaged:	
Front Storm Windows: ☐ None ☐ Good ☐ Fair ☐ Damaged:	Side 1 Storm Windows: ☐ None ☐ Good ☐ Fair ☐ Damaged:	Side 2 Storm Windows: ☐ None ☐ Good ☐ Fair ☐ Damaged:	Rear Storm Windows: ☐ None ☐ Good ☐ Fair ☐ Damaged:	
Front Window Screens: ☐ None ☐ Good ☐ Fair ☐ Damaged:	Side 1 Window Screens: ☐ None ☐ Good ☐ Fair ☐ Damaged:	Side 2 Window Screens: ☐ None ☐ Good ☐ Fair ☐ Damaged:	Rear Storm Window Screens: ☐ None ☐ Good ☐ Fair ☐ Damaged:	
Front Door Type: ☐ Glass ☐ Metal ☐ Wood ☐ Other:	Front Door Condition: ☐ Excellent ☐ Good ☐ Damaged:	Front Intercom: ☐ None ☐ Good ☐ Fair ☐ Damaged:	Front Security Camera: ☐ None ☐ Good ☐ Damaged:	Front Door Lighting: ☐ Excellent ☐ Good ☐ Fair ☐ None
Front Door Lock: ☐ Excellent ☐ Good ☐ Fair ☐ Damaged	Inner Front Door Type: ☐ None ☐ Glass ☐ Metal ☐ Wood ☐ Other:	Inner Front Door Condition: ☐ Excellent ☐ Good ☐ Damaged:	Inner Front Door Lock: ☐ Excellent ☐ Good ☐ Fair ☐ Damaged	Foyer/Inner-Door Light: ☐ Excellent ☐ Good ☐ Fair ☐ None
Front Lighting: ☐ Excellent ☐ Good ☐ Poor/None:	Gutters: ☐ None ☐ Excellent ☐ Good ☐ Damaged:	Downspout: ☐ None ☐ Excellent ☐ Good ☐ Damaged:	Chimney: ☐ None ☐ Excellent ☐ Good ☐ Damaged:	
Rear Door Type: ☐ Glass ☐ Metal ☐ Wood ☐ Other:	Rear Door Condition: ☐ Excellent ☐ Good ☐ Damaged:	Rear Door Lock: ☐ Excellent ☐ Good ☐ Fair ☐ Damaged	Rear Door Access: ☐ NA ☐ Restricted ☐ Open	Rear Door Lighting: ☐ Excellent ☐ Good ☐ Fair ☐ None
Eaves: ☐ Excellent ☐ Good ☐ Poor/Damaged:	Roof Style: ☐ Flat ☐ Pitched ☐ Other:	Roofing Type: ☐ Sheet ☐ Shingle ☐ Tar ☐ Other:	Roof Condition: ☐ Excellent ☐ Good ☐ Fair ☐ Poor/Damaged:	

(continued on next page)

(continued)

Additional Comments About Roof:

| Sprinklers: ☐ NA ☐ Good ☐ Damaged: | Garage: ☐ NA ☐ Good ☐ Damaged: | Garage Door: ☐ None ☐ Good ☐ Damaged: | Exterior Lights: ☐ Excellent ☐ Good ☐ Fair ☐ None | Ext. Electrical Outlets: ☐ None ☐ Good ☐ Damaged: |

Comments:

INTERIOR (General)

Interior Square Footage	Total # of Rental Units:	# of Studios/Efficiency:	# of 1-Bedrooms:	# of 2-Bedrooms:	# of 3+ Bedrooms:

| Foyer: ☐ None ☐ Yes, Size: | Foyer Condition: ☐ NA ☐ Good ☐ Fair ☐ Poor | Lobby: ☐ None ☐ Yes, Size: | Lobby Condition: ☐ NA ☐ Good ☐ Fair ☐ Poor | Mgmt Office: ☐ None ☐ Yes, Size: | Office Condition: ☐ NA ☐ Good ☐ Fair ☐ Poor |

1st Hall Floor Type: ☐ Wood ☐ Carpet ☐ Tile ☐ Other:	1st Hall Floor Condition: ☐ Good ☐ Fair ☐ Damaged:	1st Hall Wall/Ceiling Type: ☐ Paint ☐ Wallpaper ☐ Stucco ☐ Other:	1st Hall Wall/Ceiling Cond.: ☐ Good ☐ Fair ☐ Damaged:	1st Hall Lighting: ☐ Good ☐ Fair ☐ Poor
2nd Hall Floor Type: ☐ Wood ☐ Carpet ☐ Tile ☐ Other:	2nd Hall Floor Condition: ☐ Good ☐ Fair ☐ Damaged:	2nd Hall Wall/Ceiling Type: ☐ Paint ☐ Wallpaper ☐ Stucco ☐ Other:	2nd Hall Wall/Ceiling Cond.: ☐ Good ☐ Fair ☐ Damaged:	2nd Hall Lighting: ☐ Good ☐ Fair ☐ Poor
3rd Hall Floor Type: ☐ Wood ☐ Carpet ☐ Tile ☐ Other:	3rd Hall Floor Condition: ☐ Good ☐ Fair ☐ Damaged:	3rd Hall Wall/Ceiling Type: ☐ Paint ☐ Wallpaper ☐ Stucco ☐ Other:	3rd Hall Wall/Ceiling Cond.: ☐ Good ☐ Fair ☐ Damaged:	3rd Hall Lighting: ☐ Good ☐ Fair ☐ Poor
# of Staircases:	Staircase Condition: ☐ Good ☐ Fair ☐ Damaged:	Staircase Lighting: ☐ Good ☐ Fair ☐ Poor	Secured access: ☐ Yes ☐ No	Fire Doors: ☐ Yes ☐ No
# of Mgmt. Closets:	Closet Condition: ☐ Good ☐ Fair ☐ Damaged:	Closet Lighting: ☐ Good ☐ Fair ☐ Poor/None	Attic: ☐ None ☐ Yes, Size:	Attic Condition: ☐ Good ☐ Fair ☐ Damaged:
Basement: ☐ None ☐ Yes, Size:	Basement Condition: ☐ Finished ☐ Unfinished ☐ Damaged:	Basement Lighting: ☐ Good ☐ Fair ☐ Poor/None	Attic Walls: ☐ Good ☐ Fair ☐ Damaged:	Basement Floor: ☐ Good ☐ Fair ☐ Damaged:
Mechanical Room: ☐ None ☐ Yes, Size:	Mech Room Condition: ☐ Good ☐ Fair ☐ Poor:	Mech Room Lighting: ☐ Good ☐ Fair ☐ Poor/None	Laundry Room: ☐ None ☐ Yes, Size:	Laundry Rm. Condition: ☐ Good ☐ Fair ☐ Damaged:
Fire Sprinklers: ☐ None ☐ Good ☐ Damaged:	Fire Extinguishers: ☐ None ☐ Good ☐ Insufficient:	Fire Alarm System: ☐ None ☐ Good ☐ Damaged:	Smoke Detectors: ☐ None ☐ Good ☐ Insufficient	Emergency Lighting: ☐ None ☐ Good ☐ Insufficient

Comments:

MECHANICALS

Furnace Type: ☐ None ☐ Boiler ☐ Hot Water ☐ Steam ☐ Electric ☐ Gas	Furnace Condition: ☐ New ☐ Good ☐ Fair ☐ Damaged:	Hot Water Heater: ☐ None ☐ Good ☐ Fair ☐ Damaged:	Hot Water Tank: ☐ None ☐ Good ☐ Fair ☐ Damaged:
Radiators: ☐ None ☐ Good ☐ Fair ☐ Damaged:	Heating Ducts: ☐ None ☐ Good ☐ Fair ☐ Damaged:	Space Heaters: ☐ None ☐ Good ☐ Fair ☐ Damaged:	A/C Unit: ☐ None ☐ Good ☐ Fair ☐ Damaged:
A/C Ducts: ☐ None ☐ Good ☐ Fair ☐ Damaged:	Electric Service Control: ☐ Fuse Box ☐ Circuit-Breaker Panel	Electric Wiring: ☐ Good ☐ Fair ☐ Needs Upgrade	Elevators: ☐ None ☐ Good ☐ Damaged:	Elevator Lighting: ☐ Good ☐ Fair ☐ Poor

Comments:

INTERIOR (Individual Units)

Unit 1 Type: ☐ Studio ☐ 1BR ☐ 2BR ☐ Other:	Unit 1 Size	Unit 1 Kitchen: ☐ Excellent ☐ Good ☐ Poor/Damaged:	Unit 1 Kitchen Equipment: ☐ Refrigerator ☐ Stove ☐ Oven ☐ Microwave ☐ Other:	Unit 1 Bathroom: ☐ Excellent ☐ Good ☐ Poor/Damaged:
Unit 1 Floor Types: ☐ Wood ☐ Carpet ☐ Tile ☐ Other:	Unit 1 Floor Condition: ☐ Good ☐ Fair ☐ Damaged:	Unit 1 Wall/Ceiling Type: ☐ Paint ☐ Wallpaper ☐ Stucco ☐ Other:	Unit 1 Wall/Ceiling Cond.: ☐ Good ☐ Fair ☐ Damaged:	Unit 1 Lighting: ☐ Excellent ☐ Good ☐ Fair ☐ Poor
Unit 1 Living Room: ☐ Excellent ☐ Good ☐ Poor/Damaged:	Unit 1 Bedrooms: ☐ Excellent ☐ Good ☐ Poor/Damaged:	Unit 1 Overall Condition: ☐ Excellent ☐ Good ☐ Fair ☐ Poor	Unit 1 Comments	

(continued on next page)

(continued)

Unit 2 Type: ☐ Studio ☐ 1BR ☐ 2BR ☐ Other:	Unit 2 Size	Unit 2 Kitchen: ☐ Excellent ☐ Good ☐ Poor/Damaged:	Unit 2 Kitchen Equipment: ☐ Refrigerator ☐ Stove ☐ Oven ☐ Microwave ☐ Other:	Unit 2 Bathroom: ☐ Excellent ☐ Good ☐ Poor/Damaged:
Unit 2 Floor Types: ☐ Wood ☐ Carpet ☐ Tile ☐ Other:	Unit 2 Floor Condition: ☐ Good ☐ Fair ☐ Damaged:	Unit 2 Wall/Ceiling Type: ☐ Paint ☐ Wallpaper ☐ Stucco ☐ Other:	Unit 2 Wall/Ceiling Cond.: ☐ Good ☐ Fair ☐ Damaged:	Unit 2 Lighting: ☐ Excellent ☐ Good ☐ Fair ☐ Poor
Unit 2 Living Room: ☐ Excellent ☐ Good ☐ Poor/Damaged:	Unit 2 Bedrooms: ☐ Excellent ☐ Good ☐ Poor/Damaged:	Unit 2 Overall Condition: ☐ Excellent ☐ Good ☐ Fair ☐ Poor	Unit 2 Comments	

Unit 3 Type: ☐ Studio ☐ 1BR ☐ 2BR ☐ Other:	Unit 3 Size	Unit 3 Kitchen: ☐ Excellent ☐ Good ☐ Poor/Damaged:	Unit 3 Kitchen Equipment: ☐ Refrigerator ☐ Stove ☐ Oven ☐ Microwave ☐ Other:	Unit 3 Bathroom: ☐ Excellent ☐ Good ☐ Poor/Damaged:
Unit 3 Floor Types: ☐ Wood ☐ Carpet ☐ Tile ☐ Other:	Unit 3 Floor Condition: ☐ Good ☐ Fair ☐ Damaged:	Unit 3 Wall/Ceiling Type: ☐ Paint ☐ Wallpaper ☐ Stucco ☐ Other:	Unit 3 Wall/Ceiling Cond.: ☐ Good ☐ Fair ☐ Damaged:	Unit 3 Lighting: ☐ Excellent ☐ Good ☐ Fair ☐ Poor
Unit 3 Living Room: ☐ Excellent ☐ Good ☐ Poor/Damaged:	Unit 3 Bedrooms: ☐ Excellent ☐ Good ☐ Poor/Damaged:	Unit 3 Overall Condition: ☐ Excellent ☐ Good ☐ Fair ☐ Poor	Unit 3 Comments	

Unit 4 Type: ☐ Studio ☐ 1BR ☐ 2BR ☐ Other:	Unit 4 Size	Unit 4 Kitchen: ☐ Excellent ☐ Good ☐ Poor/Damaged:	Unit 4 Kitchen Equipment: ☐ Refrigerator ☐ Stove ☐ Oven ☐ Microwave ☐ Other:	Unit 4 Bathroom: ☐ Excellent ☐ Good ☐ Poor/Damaged:
Unit 4 Floor Types: ☐ Wood ☐ Carpet ☐ Tile ☐ Other:	Unit 4 Floor Condition: ☐ Good ☐ Fair ☐ Damaged:	Unit 4 Wall/Ceiling Type: ☐ Paint ☐ Wallpaper ☐ Stucco ☐ Other:	Unit 4 Wall/Ceiling Cond.: ☐ Good ☐ Fair ☐ Damaged:	Unit 4 Lighting: ☐ Excellent ☐ Good ☐ Fair ☐ Poor
Unit 4 Living Room: ☐ Excellent ☐ Good ☐ Poor/Damaged:	Unit 4 Bedrooms: ☐ Excellent ☐ Good ☐ Poor/Damaged:	Unit 4 Overall Condition: ☐ Excellent ☐ Good ☐ Fair ☐ Poor	Unit 4 Comments	

Unit 5 Type: ☐ Studio ☐ 1BR ☐ 2BR ☐ Other:	Unit 5 Size	Unit 5 Kitchen: ☐ Excellent ☐ Good ☐ Poor/Damaged:	Unit 5 Kitchen Equipment: ☐ Refrigerator ☐ Stove ☐ Oven ☐ Microwave ☐ Other:	Unit 5 Bathroom: ☐ Excellent ☐ Good ☐ Poor/Damaged:
Unit 5 Floor Types: ☐ Wood ☐ Carpet ☐ Tile ☐ Other:	Unit 5 Floor Condition: ☐ Good ☐ Fair ☐ Damaged:	Unit 5 Wall/Ceiling Type: ☐ Paint ☐ Wallpaper ☐ Stucco ☐ Other:	Unit 5 Wall/Ceiling Cond.: ☐ Good ☐ Fair ☐ Damaged:	Unit 5 Lighting: ☐ Excellent ☐ Good ☐ Fair ☐ Poor
Unit 5 Living Room: ☐ Excellent ☐ Good ☐ Poor/Damaged:	Unit 5 Bedrooms: ☐ Excellent ☐ Good ☐ Poor/Damaged:	Unit 5 Overall Condition: ☐ Excellent ☐ Good ☐ Fair ☐ Poor	Unit 5 Comments	

Unit 6 Type: ☐ Studio ☐ 1BR ☐ 2BR ☐ Other:	Unit 6 Size	Unit 6 Kitchen: ☐ Excellent ☐ Good ☐ Poor/Damaged:	Unit 6 Kitchen Equipment: ☐ Refrigerator ☐ Stove ☐ Oven ☐ Microwave ☐ Other:	Unit 6 Bathroom: ☐ Excellent ☐ Good ☐ Poor/Damaged:
Unit 6 Floor Types: ☐ Wood ☐ Carpet ☐ Tile ☐ Other:	Unit 6 Floor Condition: ☐ Good ☐ Fair ☐ Damaged:	Unit 6 Wall/Ceiling Type: ☐ Paint ☐ Wallpaper ☐ Stucco ☐ Other:	Unit 6 Wall/Ceiling Cond.: ☐ Good ☐ Fair ☐ Damaged:	Unit 6 Lighting: ☐ Excellent ☐ Good ☐ Fair ☐ Poor
Unit 6 Living Room: ☐ Excellent ☐ Good ☐ Poor/Damaged:	Unit 6 Bedrooms: ☐ Excellent ☐ Good ☐ Poor/Damaged:	Unit 6 Overall Condition: ☐ Excellent ☐ Good ☐ Fair ☐ Poor	Unit 6 Comments	

MISCELLANEOUS CRITERIA

COMMENTS

Comments:

An investor should visit each property with a totally professional attitude, asking questions about the property's history, neighborhood, repair needs and seller motivation. Most importantly, the investor should make note of every aspect of the property. If more than one property is previewed, the investor will quickly find that details get confused. To assist in the initial visits, the following property inspection checklist will help. A camera would also be beneficial in taking photos of the property and its neighborhood.

Prioritize Preferences

As an investor compares inspected properties, it is necessary to continually prioritize preferences. If necessary, the real estate agent can arrange second and third visits to a property. Investors should drive by the top preferences at various times—evenings, mornings and weekends—to become aware of the property's characteristics at different times.

Buyer's remorse is common with many new investors who make large purchases, and real estate is obviously one of the largest purchases in a lifetime. However, buyer's remorse will not be as much of an issue if the investor takes due care during the shopping stage. The investor needs to remember that as the buyer, he or she is in control. If an investor can't make a decision about whether to buy or not, it just means that the investor doesn't have enough data or information on a property, and this particular transaction requires more research before the investor can come to a decision. Even in the worst case event that an investor passes up a good investment, experience shows that other opportunities will arise.

Negotiating Terms

When the investor finds a property that potentially would be a good investment, it is time to negotiate with the seller. The objective at this stage is to arrive at a fair contract that meets the goals of all parties. Unworthy actions on the part of an investor, such as trying to beat the seller down below a fair price at all costs, and even below the investor's own stated business objectives, usually are unsuccessful. They end up with the investor failing to achieve long term goals, not to mention the ill will generated by the conflict, and the seller's eventual perception of not wanting to do business with an investor who is unwilling to compromise. This "shoot-myself-in-the-foot" behavior should be avoided by the investor.

One tactic to remember, however, as an investor negotiates, is that an individual should never be afraid to say "no." An investor should never be afraid to lose a deal, thinking there will never be another one as profitable or desirable. Again, every transaction opportunity should be measured against the investor's business plan to validate the purchase. There will always be other opportunities for more investments. But it may be impossible to get out of a bad deal.

An investor's decisions and actions during this stage do become more important, while moving closer toward an obligation. But an investor is also moving toward what should be a profitable investment.

Steps to a Profitable Investment

- Due diligence
- Make a smart offer
- Buyer and seller negotiate price and terms
- Attorney review
- Professional inspection of the property
- Updated loan approval
- Obtain property insurance
- Prepare a budget and operations plan

Due Diligence

With residential properties, a buyer may only have a few days to conduct due diligence. Commercial properties provide a little more time and information. Regardless of the situation, it is important that an investor gather as much information as possible about the property. Due diligence investigations normally carry three goals.

- Calculating the value of the property

- Verifying the property's condition, income and expenses

- Confirming that it meets the investor's minimum requirements

A real estate agent can assist the investor in this stage by gathering information available both from city or county records as well as from the seller. Once an investor has all of the necessary facts, he or she will want to use those facts to conduct a feasibility study. The feasibility study analyzes the potential for profit and success. An accountant and a knowledgeable real estate agent are helpful assistants in the task of analyzing the property's finances to determine its projected income, expenses, capital requirements and profits.

Before making an offer and entering into negotiations with a seller, an investor should try to obtain information about the seller and the property that may be helpful during the negotiation. An important objective here should be to try to discover the seller's motivation. The simplest way is to just ask.

Making a Smart Offer

If due diligence gives the investor a green light, it is time to make an offer. What should the opening bid be? If the price matches the investor's objectives, the investor can accept it or start 5% to 10% lower—but not too much lower unless there is a compelling reason for doing so. Due diligence may have shown the investor that the property is overpriced and the opening bid should reflect the selling price of similar properties in the area. Before negotiations begin, the investor should already know what is needed to ensure profitability and success.

These are not clear-cut rules. Negotiating the price is more an art than a science. An investor must be aware of local economic conditions, especially whether the market is a buyer's market, which would allow the investor to bargain more aggressively, or a seller's market, in which the seller can be more demanding and there might be other offers to consider. A guiding principle should be to respect the seller. Again, the goal is to arrive at a fair and workable price.

The best negotiator is always the one who is willing to walk away from a bad deal. This assumes, of course, that the investor understands the difference between a good deal and a bad one. That is where a business plan, research and preparations are important.

Buyer and Seller Negotiate Price and Terms

If the seller believes that the investor is making a serious offer, a series of counter-offers will often follow. With luck, both buyer and seller will eventually arrive at a fair agreement. It is important to remember during this period, however, that price is not the only determinant of value. The terms of the purchase agreement can be just as important as the price. For example, an investor may be willing to give a little on price if the seller is willing to include some valuable concessions, such as paying the closing costs or making improvements.

Attorney Review

Before signing the contract, an investor may want to make sure that it has an attorney review clause. This provision normally gives a buyer a certain number of days to have an attorney review the contract. If a buyer's attorney finds something wrong or disagreeable, the attorney review clause allows the buyer to request changes or cancel the contract.

Professional Inspection of the Property

As soon as the contract has been signed by all parties, the investor should immediately arrange for a professional inspection of the property. With larger properties, the certified inspector should have an engineering background. The inspector will check the property's functional, structural and economic condition. If the inspector finds major problems, the investor can negotiate with the seller for concessions or—if the property no longer makes sense—a cancellation. Generally, the contract contains a clause allowing the buyer to have a certain number of days to approve the property inspection.

Updated Loan Approval

An investor should also inform the loan officer that he or she has signed a purchase contract, and should take steps to start a formal loan application. The lender will need to order an appraisal of the property and finalize the investor's mortgage loan commitment. A lender probably will ask for additional documents and most current information from the investor prior to the closing. An investor should be ready to satisfy these conditions immediately, as the loan cannot close and disburse without them.

Obtaining Property Insurance

Many mortgage lenders require a one-year prepaid insurance policy prior to the closing. Even if the transaction is all cash it is smart business to have insurance protection. The insurance agent should be able to provide coverage in less than an hour. Commercial properties, however, may require more time.

Preparing a Budget and Operations Plan

Before closing, the investor should prepare a budget and operations plan. The budget should rely on the due diligence and appraisal report for facts and assumptions as well as the investor's personal goals for the property. The operations plan is meant to give the investor the benefit of being prepared to be a new landlord or property owner. For example, the investor should have lease forms, notices and dedicated bank accounts ready.

Closing the Purchase and Taking Over

The final stage of the real estate purchase is the closing, or settlement. Depending on the state, this may be conducted at the offices of a title company, an attorney or an escrow holder. The closing is scheduled soon after the loan is fully approved and all documents and verifications have been collected by the closing agent.

Steps for a Successful Purchase

Prepare

- There are a great many tasks that the investor can do before the closing, which can ease the post-closing take-over. For example, if the investor plans to redecorate, rehab or improve the property in other ways, the property inspection results can be used to start planning the work.

Relax

- The stress of pre-closing requirements and the closing itself can be aggravating. Investors learn that they must accept this as a normal part of many closings, especially closings that involve creative financing. Successful investors learn to stay calm, as purchases occasionally fail to close on time or at all. This is part of the investment process, but an investor can learn from the mistakes and problems involved and avoid them on the next transaction.

Obtain Closing Instructions

- The closing agent will provide instructions on how to get to the closing and what to bring. If additional down payment and closing cost funds are required, the investor probably will be instructed to bring a cashier's check made out for the amount needed.

Close the Transaction

- The closing will last about one hour for a smooth transaction and much longer for more complicated ones. The investor should be prepared to sign numerous documents, including trust deed or mortgage and promissory note.

Take-Over

- The closing session ends with the investor receiving the keys to the new property, either from the closing agent, real estate agent or attorney. This is where earlier preparations, especially of the operations plan, will pay off. The investor will have much to do to ensure a smooth and profitable operation, and must not delay implementing the necessary changes. A take-over checklist is provided here.

Take-Over Checklist

Current Tenancy:

❑ Tenants informed of new ownership and rent payment information? .... ❑ Yes ❑ No

❑ Seller indicated _____ of _____ units were occupied. Verified?................ ❑ Yes ❑ No

❑ Current leases executed and in place? .... ❑ Yes ❑ No

❑ Are all rents current? .... ❑ Yes ❑ No

❑ List of all residents? .... ❑ Yes ❑ No

❑ Tenant home & work phone numbers? .... ❑ Yes ❑ No

❑ Security deposit amounts verified with lease? .... ❑ Yes ❑ No

❑ Security deposit amounts verified with tenants? .... ❑ Yes ❑ No

❑ Any pending legal actions involving tenants? .... ❑ Yes ❑ No

❑ All vacant units verified as really vacant? .... ❑ Yes ❑ No

❑ Are delinquent renters in possession of their units? .... ❑ Yes ❑ No

❑ Have all delinquent renters been served Termination Notices? .... ❑ Yes ❑ No

Services Requiring Continuation:

❑ Has electric company been notified of changes? .... ❑ Yes ❑ No

❑ Has electric company made final readings? .... ❑ Yes ❑ No

❑ Has gas company been notified of changes? .... ❑ Yes ❑ No

❑ Has gas company made final readings? .... ❑ Yes ❑ No

❑ Has water company been notified of changes? .... ❑ Yes ❑ No

❑ Has water company made final readings? .... ❑ Yes ❑ No

❑ Has scavenger company been notified of changes? .... ❑ Yes ❑ No

❑ Have you provided for ongoing janitorial services? .... ❑ Yes ❑ No

❑ Have you provided for ongoing maintenance services? .... ❑ Yes ❑ No

❑ Have you provided for ongoing landscape services? .... ❑ Yes ❑ No

Building Code Issues:

❑ Have the sellers provided any existing Notices of Violations? .... ❑ Yes ❑ No

❑ Are there any existing Notices of Violations? .... ❑ Yes ❑ No

❑ Does each unit have an operating smoke detector? .... ❑ Yes ❑ No

❑ Are carbon monoxide detectors in place? .... ❑ Yes ❑ No

❑ Are there proper locks on windows and doors? .... ❑ Yes ❑ No

❑ Are all windows and screens in good repair? .... ❑ Yes ❑ No

❑ Have you provided for ongoing janitorial services? .... ❑ Yes ❑ No

Emergency Procedures:

❑ Have you contracted with an answering service for after hours? .... ❑ Yes ❑ No

❑ Have current tenants been informed of any changes they must make?................ ❑ Yes ❑ No

(continued on next page)

(continued)

Take Over Checklist

❑ Have emergency point people been identified?...❑ Yes   ❑ No

❑ Do you have an emergency procedures plan?...❑ Yes   ❑ No

❑ Have emergency service providers been identified/contracted?.............................❑ Yes   ❑ No

Reports Provide by Seller/Agent:

Regulatory Agreements	❑ Received	❑ Missing	❑ N/A
Financial Reports	❑ Received	❑ Missing	❑ N/A
Inventory	❑ Received	❑ Missing	❑ N/A
Security Deposit Listing	❑ Received	❑ Missing	❑ N/A
Waiting Lists	❑ Received	❑ Missing	❑ N/A
Legal Actions	❑ Received	❑ Missing	❑ N/A
Current Billing	❑ Received	❑ Missing	❑ N/A
Personnel Records	❑ Received	❑ Missing	❑ N/A
Service Contracts in Place	❑ Received	❑ Missing	❑ N/A

Immediate Actions Needed:

❑ _____

❑ _____

❑ _____

❑ _____

❑ _____

❑ _____

❑ _____

❑ _____

❑ _____

❑ _____

Comments:

In an ideal world, detailed plans can be made and expected to happen like clockwork. That doesn't always happen. Many real estate transactions have fallen through at the last minute, or even during the closing itself. A common problem for many beginning investors is that they make firm commitments to events that must happen immediately after the scheduled closing.

For example, the closing is scheduled for Friday morning. The investor has already contracted for the laborers and remodeling supplies to arrive at the subject property on Friday afternoon—intending to save some money by saving a little time. Instead, the closing runs late and eventually fails to consummate. Because of those prior commitments, the investor is under even greater stress during the failed closing. As the lawyers or real estate agents try to reschedule the closing or salvage the deal, the investor must scramble to re-arrange those delivery commitments.

REAL ESTATE INVESTMENT ANALYSIS TOOLS

The specific measure of a property's profitability usually depends on who is doing the analysis. How does a buyer get beyond the marketing hype of the sellers or their agents? For lenders, the bottom line often focuses on the debt service ratio. With larger investors, the focus is normally on the anticipated return on investment (ROI) and the capitalization rate. A serious investor must understand the key financial and analysis terms involved with real estate investments to be successful in the long run.

Fortunately, the technical details and analysis terms are not difficult to understand for most people. These terms are not accidental concepts. They were developed as a way to measure a subject property's chances for success. Many beginning and novice real estate investors feel overwhelmed when these terms and figures are used, but in many ways the concepts are common sense.

Investment Concepts

- Operating expenses
- Carrying costs
- Net operating income
- Debt service ratio
- Return on investment
- Development market's cycle

Operating Expenses

As the name suggests, operating expenses include all regular expenses associated with the running of a property. They include trash collection, janitorial, maintenance and management services, as well as utilities, fees, service contracts, supplies, taxes, insurance and advertising. The underlying theme to operating expenses is that they are costs involved with the day-to-day operations of the investment.

It is also necessary for the beginning investor to understand the difference between operating expenses and those expenditures for the property that are not operating expenses. Just because money is spent on a property does not make that expenditure an operating expense. Understanding this difference could mean thousands of dollars in additional cash refunds from an investor's tax withholdings.

One misconception that new investors have is in thinking that operating expenses include mortgage payments and other debt servicing. Not all properties have a mortgage lien against them, and mortgages are actually part of the acquisition cost, not the operating cost. The following is a breakdown of typical costs which are considered operating expenses and others that are not.

OPERATING EXPENSES	NON-OPERATING EXPENSES
Maintenance and janitorial	Acquisition (closing) costs
Repair and decoration	Mortgages and debt servicing
Service contracts	Capital improvements
Supplies	Equipment and fixtures
Trash pickup	Marketing, selling costs
Management fees	
Accounting and administrative services	
Advertising and leasing services	
Insurance premiums	
Real estate and corporate taxes	
Government fees and licenses	
Utilities (paid by owner)	

As you can see, capital improvements are separated from operating expenses. Unlike repairs, which serve to maintain the property's current value, capital improvements are additional investments made to the property that will increase its value. For example, building additions, major renovations and installation of a security system are considered capital improvements, because they add to the value of the property. This distinction between repairs and capital improvements becomes very important when income taxes and capital gains come into play.

Accurate identification of operating expenses is important for real estate investors, primarily because the operating expenses are necessary to determine the net operating income. Investors who are investing in real estate for its cash flow and income profits need to examine operating expenses carefully.

Operating expenses are those costs that the investor can reasonably expect during the ownership of the property. A property's income stream and operating profits are improved in one of two ways: increasing revenue or lowering operating expenses. Experienced investors will often focus on the operating expenses—looking for potential reductions and savings—when analyzing a potential cash flow investment.

Another advantage with understanding the difference involves actual dollars and cents the investor can get through depreciation. The building (though not the land), fixtures and equipment can be depreciated. The process of calculating depreciation is discussed at the beginning of this chapter.

Maximizing Depreciation Deductions

Michele owns a four-plex that is basically breaking even, after paying her operating expenses, debt servicing and other out-of-pocket expenses. But she's not disheartened, because breaking even means that she won't have to pay any income taxes. What's more, while her property is appreciating in value, she also intends to benefit from her depreciation deduction.

Carrying Costs

Speculators and real estate investors who purchase property with the primary goal of reselling for profit must be especially concerned with the project's carrying costs. Carrying costs refer to the net amount of expenditures that investors must outlay before the property is resold and profits are realized. The carrying costs usually exclude the purchase price and deduct operating income.

Unfortunately, uninformed real estate investors often look at just the purchase and resell prices. On the surface, buying a property for $100,000 and reselling it for $150,000 would seem like a good investment. This transaction, however, would be a disastrous decision if the carrying costs came to $60,000.

Smart investors know that the purchase price is only part of the total expenses required by a real estate investment. Carrying costs include the operating expenses, as well as the acquisition costs, mortgage payments, capital improvements and selling costs.

For example, an investor may be interested in buying a seemingly undervalued house for $100,000 and resell it within six months for $120,000. That would seem like a reasonable investment for a $20,000 profit. But look again.

Purchase price		$100,000
Purchase closing costs	$4,000	
Clean-up and decoration	$3,000	
Mortgage interest payments (at 8%)	$3,600	
Real estate taxes	$1,000	
Hazard insurance	$300	
Utilities	$600	
Supplies	$300	
Resale broker commission	$6,000	
Resale closing costs	$2,500	
Total 6-month carrying costs		$21,300
Total Investment		$121,300
Resale price		$120,000
Net gain/loss		-$1,300

As you can see in this example, the investor will probably lose $1,300 in this investment. The net loss, moreover, does not take into account the investor's time or interest income lost by pulling cash out of savings to use as a down payment. This net loss also does not take into account possible capital gain taxes that the investor may incur, even with the operating loss.

Rule of Thumb for Quick Buy-Resale

The reason an investor would want a quick resale on a property rather than wait for time to build a profit is this: if the property is priced remarkably below market value and is in good enough condition for the fast turnaround with an attractive profit.

In most cases, however, an investor must resell a property for at least 11% more than the original purchase price just to break even. When the investor bought it, probably the typical total closing costs were about 3% of the purchase price. When the investor resells it, expected closing costs usually are about 1.5% to 2%. On top of that, the usual selling commission to real estate brokers will be 6%. This doesn't include the cost of the investor's time or the lost interest income from the money used to make the down payment for the purchase. This rule of thumb also assumes that the investor sells the property right away. Every day the investor waits to resell the property means additional costs.

Understanding carrying costs is often the difference between success and failure as a real estate investor, particularly for speculators. Actually, a smart investor may still be able to make the above project work by successfully eliminating some of the expenses and/or increasing income. For example, the investor may decide to rent out the garage for storage and the house to seasonal renters for additional income of $5,000 over six months, making the property more desirable to a prospective buyer and thus encourage a faster sale.

Net Operating Income

A common method to determine the value of income producing property is to use the projected net operating income as the basis to calculate the value. This approach estimates the present worth of future benefits from ownership of a property by looking at its capacity to continue producing an income.

The process of calculating a property's present worth on the basis of its capacity to continue producing an income stream is called *capitalization*. This process converts the future income stream into an indication of the property's present worth. The expected future income and expenses of a property are evaluated to determine its present value.

The investor, however, must determine how much and how reliable the income is, and how long the income stream will last. There are *five basic steps* to determine a property's present worth using the capitalization approach.

(1) *Calculate the annual gross income.*
   The gross income is the total annual income from the property (minus any vacancy or rental losses). That includes rental income plus any other income generated by the property such as laundry room income or parking fees. Loss of income because of a vacant unit is known as the *vacancy factor.* Current market rents are used to determine the loss from the vacancy factor. *Market rent* is the rent the property should bring in the open market, while *contract* rent is the actual, or contracted, rent being paid by the tenants.

(2) *Determine operating expenses.*

Expenses are generally classified as being either fixed or variable.

Fixed Expenses	Variable Expenses
•Property taxes	•Management
•Insurance	•Maintenance
	•Utilities

(3) *Calculate net operating income.*

The key to this method is in correctly determining the net operating income. Starting with the annual gross income, which includes all revenues generated by the property, including rent, laundry income, late fees and parking charges (less an annual vacancy factor or any rental losses), we would subtract the operating expenses to calculate the net operating income (NOI).

Calculating Net Operating Income (Annual Calculation)

Rental income	$24,000	
Laundry income	$4,000	
Penalties and late fees	$300	
Storage and parking	$2,700	
Interest income	$50	
Gross operating income		**$31,050**
Maintenance and repair	$2,500	
Supplies and janitorial	$1,800	
Scavenger	$1,400	
Utilities	$2,800	
Advertising and promotions	$500	
Administrative	$5,000	
Tax and licenses	$300	
Insurance	$700	
Operating expenses		**$15,000**
Net operating income (NOI)		**$16,050**

The NOI is the annual gross income minus the operating expenses, as we have seen. Again, the NOI does not include mortgage and other debt servicing payments in its calculation, nor does the NOI take into account capital improvements and acquisition costs. The operative term is "operating." The net operating income consists of the annual gross income less the operating expenses.

(4) *Select a capitalization rate (cap rate).*

The cap rate provides a handy tool for comparing different types of real estate investments. It allows the investor to make a sound choice between putting money in the purchase of a shopping mall or an office building, between a farm or a car wash. The cap rate is a simple calculation involving two elements: the purchase price (or value) and the net operating income (NOI). The cap rate is calculated by dividing the NOI by the property's price.

The capitalization rate is the rate of interest which is considered a reasonable return on an investment and is used in the process of determining value based on net income. It may also be described as the yield rate that is necessary to attract the money of the average investor to a particular kind of investment. In the case of property with improvements (as opposed to raw land), depreciation is a factor taken into consideration in the recapture of the initial investment. The capitalization rate provides for the return of invested capital plus a return on the investment. A capitalization rate is designed to reflect the recapture of the original investment over the economic life of the improvement (building) to give the investor an acceptable rate of return on the original investment and to provide for the return of the invested equity.

The rate is dependent upon the return a buyer will demand before investing money in the property and measures the risk involved. The greater the risk of recapturing the investment price (making a profit), the higher the cap rate and the lower the price. The lower the risk, the lower the cap rate and the higher the price of the property.

> **Cap Rate Example #1:**
>
> *An investor is considering the purchase of a piece of land in downtown Chicago. The land is being leased to a developer, on a 50-year lease, that generates $1.2 million in annual rent for*
>
> *(continued on next page)*

Cap Rate Example #1:   *(continued)*

the landowner. The developer has an office building on the land, and the building will revert to the landowner at the end of the lease. The only landowner expense is the real estate tax of about $200,000 per year, so the property has an NOI of $1 million. The current landowner wants to sell it for $20 million. That would mean a cap rate of 5%.

Projected NOI: $200,000

Purchase price: $1,000,000

$20,000,000 divided by $1,000,000 = $20,000 or 5%

Cap rate = 5%

For many investors, a 5% cap rate is too low. But the cap rate is primarily used for income-producing properties. So a low cap rate may be acceptable for investors who are speculating on future values. For example, this same $20 million property may be worth more than $100 million in 10 years. In that case, the low cap rate would be acceptable if the investor can handle the carrying costs.

Cap Rate Example #2:

An office building generates $200,000 per year when fully occupied. Its occupancy rate, however, is only 90%; and its operating expenses average $100,000 per year.

$200,000 × .90 = $180,000

$180,000 (gross income) – $100,000 (expenses) = $80,000

$80,000 (NOI)

If the seller wanted a final price of $1 million, that would mean an 8% cap rate.

$80,000 divided by $1,000,000 = .08 or 8% cap rate

Would $1,000,000 be a fair price? An informal rule of thumb for most real estate investors is that a property's fair price is one that produces an average 10% cap rate. In this case, an $800,000 price would produce a 10% cap rate. But the fair price all depends on the market. In some areas, a much lower cap rate is not only acceptable, it is the norm.

For most investors, their due diligence (inspection and investigation of the property) will involve a lot of time confirming the true cap rate. The following is a step-by-step guide to verifying a property's true capitalization rate.

(1) Confirm rental rates

(2) Confirm vacancy rate

(3) Confirm all other income sources

(4) Check cap rates in new listings and real estate advertising

(5) Calculate gross operating income (make sure to deduct vacancy rate)

(6) Confirm past operating expenses

(7) Investigate deferred maintenance expenses to be absorbed

(8) Calculate net operating income (NOI)

(9) Calculate capitalization rate

(5) *Divide the net income by the chosen capitalization rate to determine market value.*
    After calculating the annual gross income, determining operating expenses, calculating net operating income and selecting a capitalization rate, the investor divides the net income by the chosen cap rate to determine the present market value of the property in question.

Debt Service Ratio

The debt service ratio (DSR) is a lender's preferred measurement of a property's ability to pay its mortgage debts, not the borrower's ability to make the payments. Many investment property loans give the lender the right to step in and begin collecting the rent and other revenues if the borrower defaults on the loan. In some cases this right is available after default and a complete foreclosure is not required. So the DSR lets the lender gauge whether the property can support itself with decent management.

Two elements are required to calculate the property's DSR: its net operating income (NOI) and the projected loan payments. The DSR is basically the net operating income (NOI) divided by the projected loan payments (debt servicing).

Calculating DSR (Annual Calculation)

Gross operating income	$31,050
Operating expenses	$15,000
Net operating income (NOI)	$16,050
Projected loan payments	$13,000
Projected DSR (NOI divided by payments)	1.23%

Most lenders seek a minimum DSR of 1.2, which means that the net operating income should be large enough to cover the mortgage payments, plus have an additional 20% buffer. If the DSR is too low, the lender will lower the loan amount that it would be willing to lend. This would mean that the borrower will have to make up the difference, with a bigger down payment.

Most real estate investors do not really use the DSR, but they are all familiar with it, since many banks and commercial lenders depend on it. Note that lowering the loan amount is only one way to increase the DSR ratio. The other way is to increase the net operating income by either lowering the expenses or increasing the revenue.

For example, the current owner/seller may have set rents too low, which may explain why the DSR is also low. Fortunately, the appraisal report will provide a market survey of average rents in the area for similar units. Most lenders will allow the buyer to use these market rents to calculate the property's projected NOI, thus allowing the DSR to increase.

Return On Investment

The return on investment (ROI) is a calculation of the property's true earnings, with the emphasis on the meaning of "true." The ROI compares what the investor has put into the property and what that same investor has gotten out of it. The ROI tries to provide a big picture analysis of the property's profitability. For investors, the ROI describes how well or poorly they are investing their money.

The ROI can be used on both rental properties and speculative investments. Moreover, it can be used to compare all types of potential investments, not just real estate. The smart investor can use it to compare a stock purchase against a real estate investment. Would the investor be better off putting a $20,000 bonus in the company's stock plan or in the purchase of a ranch? For income-producing properties, the ROI is basically the net earnings divided by the capital investments made by the investor.

Calculating ROI (Annualized Calculation)

- Net operating income: $30,000
- Less (loan) debt servicing: $20,000
- Appreciation in property's value: $25,000
- Projected returns: $35,000
- Capital investment (down payment or other cash input) $400,000
- Projected ROI: 8.75%

As noted above, the capital investment in the ROI calculation is not the purchase price. The capital investment instead concerns the down payment, any portion of the purchase price or closing costs paid out of pocket by the investor, and additional cash input (from the investor) for other capital improvements.

Calculating ROI

David is considering the purchase of a $200,000 car wash business. He plans on making a down payment of $45,000 and is anticipating about $5,000 in closing costs, for a total investment of $50,000. He is told that it generates a net operating income of $5,000, for a base return on income (ROI) rate of 10% ($5,000 divided by $50,000).

However, David is planning to sell it in one year for an additional net profit of $10,000. As a total investment, this project would have an ROI of 25% ($15,000 divided by $50,000).

A 25% ROI is a very good prospect, particularly for a one-year investment. Compare that to a CD that at best would garner you 4.5% (2002) or a S&P-based mutual fund generating less than 10% return.

Unfortunately, not all real estate investments are so rosy. A decrepit property may require lots of additional capital improvements and outlays from the investor. The unprepared investor may be lucky to get out of the investment with a small loss. In such a case, that very safe 4.50% CD begins to look very attractive indeed.

Again, the return on investment describes the property's true earnings. But there are also different ways to measure ROI and subsets of ROI measurements, such as the internal rate of return or the equity dividend rate.

Another way to look at and use the ROI calculation is to consider how quickly an investor can get his or her money back. Here's a concept that all beginning real estate investors must quickly realize: there are risks in all investments, but the quicker you get your investment back, the lower your risk of losing any of it.

When considering a potential investment's ROI, an investor should never consider that ROI calculation in a vacuum. It must be compared with other, possibly safer, ROI investments, such as CDs and savings accounts. The ROI must also be adjusted for other factors, both tangible and intangible, that are often overlooked.

- *Liquidity:* How long will it take and how much will it cost an investor to liquidate the investment? Real estate is a non-liquid hard asset that often takes weeks, if not months, to sell. It can take less than 10 minutes to liquidate a CD. The ROI must be adjusted to account for the cost of selling, as well as the time involved.

- *Management:* How much is an investor's time worth? Certain investments require more time from the investor than other investments. Unfortunately, many investors fail to understand the value of their time. A CD may only be earning 5%, but the investor doesn't have to do any work. Real estate holdings may be generating 10%, but if an investor has to spend 20 hours a week on the property, it may mean losing money. Putting it another way, if an investor spent that 20 hours a week at a second job, earning a steady income, how much would the individual earn? If that hypothetical second job was considered an operating expense, how much would that drag down the overall ROI?

- *Risk:* What are the odds that the investor will lose money or get it back? Risk is an intangible element, but it is all too real for accountants, actuaries and investors. An investor has almost no risk at all with CDs, which accounts for the low rate. In comparison, junk bonds are very risky and so must promise higher returns. To investors who understand and can carry the risk, the pursuit of higher returns may be worthwhile. For others, it could be unacceptable.

> ## ROI Risk
>
> *Alison is considering a real estate investment. It has a base ROI of 16%; it's not great, on the surface. But then she begins to estimate adjustments to the ROI.*
>
> *(1)* **Comparison:** *Alison wants to compare this potential investment to a regular savings account, earning 4.75%.*
>
> *(2)* **Liquidity:** *The property is an older office building in a primarily residential neighborhood. It would be fairly difficult to liquidate quickly. Because her financial situation is rather tight, that could hurt. She subtracts 5% from the ROI.*
>
> *(3)* **Management:** *Because it is an older building, Alison will have to be more involved in its management. She calculates that her minimum five hours per week will decrease the ROI by another 4%.*
>
> *(4)* **Risk:** *This office building is somewhat risky, but has had a good track record of full occupancy. However, Alison is somewhat inexperienced and knows that she faces an acceptable learning curve as a property manager. She subtracts another 4% for her risk exposure.*
>
> *Alison's total adjustments come to about 13%. When subtracted from the property's ROI, her adjusted ROI comes down to 3%. In this case, the savings account is obviously a much better choice.*

But there may be other factors, such as tax deductions and special grants, that also affect the overall ROI. Experienced investors must look at properties over their entire investment period — from the purchase to the final resale, with everything in between.

Development Market's Cycle

Successful real estate investment and development requires good timing. Decades of modern study have uncovered a clear pattern or cycle that seems to govern most real estate markets, assuming they are exposed to normal market conditions.

Understanding this cycle will help an investor make better investment decisions. The duration, shape and severity of the different stages of the cycle will vary for each area and market, but industry professionals tend to recognize a four-part cycle that controls the supply of real estate.

- *Absorption:* Coming out of the down cycle, when construction has slowed or ceased, the market is able to absorb existing supply of real estate. As occupancy rates increase, prices may begin to follow.

- *New Construction:* Many developers may not be able to predict areas or periods of future high demand, but they usually know it when it finally arrives. The new construction cycle generates construction to meet rising or perceived demand.

- *Saturation:* This stage begins as soon as supply has clearly overshot demand. As such, vacancy rates begin to increase and prices may begin to plateau or actually decrease as it has become a buyer's market. This is obviously not a good time to start a project that will only add unneeded supply in the face of lackluster demand.

- *Down:* The line between saturation and down cycle stages is a blurred one, but investors know when they are in a down cycle stage. There is already too much supply to meet existing demand. High or increasing vacancy rates will force developers to slow or stop new developments.

Real estate investors, especially developers, must understand where their target area falls within this development cycle before they invest in existing or new supply. Even if demand is high, values can stagnate or still decline if the incoming supply is too great in relation to that demand.

The Development Cycle in Action

A city's downtown area is relatively stable with enough traffic to maintain a balance between demand for office space and the downtown area's supply; but there are still significant vacancies. The city's downtown sector is in the absorption stage.

Now the civic leaders initiate an aggressive growth strategy that lures many high-tech and cutting edge businesses into the downtown sector. Many such businesses start coming, and the supply of office buildings

(continued on next page)

> ### The Development Cycle in Action   *(continued)*
>
> *has to be increased to meet this new demand. Because of this increased demand, rental rates begin to increase as incoming businesses scramble to get the best or available properties. The downtown sector is now in the new construction stage.*
>
> *As the influx of new businesses and office tenants begins to level off, combined with the increased supply of newly constructed office building, there is now a renewed balance between demand and supply. The city's downtown sector is now in the market saturation stage.*
>
> *Construction of new office buildings begins to taper off, but not before these developers realize too late that they may have overbuilt. Meanwhile, many of these new businesses inevitably start to fail and the regional economy takes a downturn. The area's vacancy factor begins to increase dramatically, forcing rental rates to drop. The downtown sector is now in a down stage of the cycle.*

Investors must understand this cycle when seeking to buy investment property. The investor's objectives and tactics must be grounded in such understanding. If the investor is seeking an investment with strong rental income, the best deals are often found during the new construction and early market saturation stage.

Investors seeking appreciation profit can find potential investments in all four stages, but the thinking must adapt to each stage. Nevertheless, many speculative investors focus on areas that are in the absorption stage or late down markets—when there is strong potential for new development and construction. Smart investors will also enter during the new construction stage, if they can time their entry just right. Few investors will enter the late saturation stage, unless they spot an underperfoming property.

REAL ESTATE INVESTMENT TACTICS

What separates the one successful real estate investor from the nine or so other investors who lost money in real estate? Luck is often a factor. But for the serious, long-term investor, the main factor is knowledge of the different ways to make (and lose) money in any particular real estate project.

There are many ways to make money through real estate investing, and there are probably many more that have not yet been designed or uncovered. As mentioned at the start of this chapter, successful real estate investing depends on knowing how you plan to generate profits and avoid expenses.

This section introduces the most common, as well as some less common, profit-generating tactics available to real estate investors.

- Collateral
- Income stream
- Value appreciation
- Subdivision
- Development
- Options
- Master lease
- Tax shelters
- Tax free exchanges

Not all tactics are applicable to all properties. Some properties use several strategies at once to generate profits for the investor. The choice of tactics always depends on the subject property. The successful investor will be the one who can look at a piece of property and understand what its profit potential is and which tactics will unlock that potential.

There is one recommendation that fits all real estate investments: never fall in love with a property. Such properties will usually result in losses or severely depressed profits. Real estate investment requires objective decisions. Unfortunately, many novice investors become so infatuated with a specific piece of property that they completely lose objectivity. The best way to approach real estate investing is to start with a plan that works for each individual, then find a property that fits into that plan. An investor should avoid starting with the property, then trying to fit the plan to that property.

Collateral

A very common, but often overlooked, reason for investing in real estate is to build collateral for future investments. The value of real estate is widely recognized and accepted by the market. Lenders are more lenient and generous to borrowers with real estate holdings, because real estate is considered a highly useful collateral.

For many consumers, the chief purpose of their only real estate holding is to provide a home for their families. Our homes actually offer much more.

In fact, Americans who own real estate have a multitude of opportunities available to them that are not available to typical renters. The reason is that real estate provides the owner with a collateral instrument. Even if the property is highly mortgaged, it can still be used as collateral for more debt.

Many commercial and small business banks are often more willing to lend money to borderline enterprises, if the business owners agree to use their real estate properties as collateral for the loan.

Collateral Example:

Alice runs a cafe. Business is booming, and she needs to expand. Unfortunately, the bank has reservations about lending to Alice because her credit shows a few late payments, she has owned the café for only two years and the restaurant industry in general is always somewhat risky. The bank offers to provide the loan if Alice agrees to allow the bank to place a lien against her home. Alice is able to get her needed financing, by using her real estate as collateral.

Of course, if her business fails, the business loan will remain as a lien against her home until it is paid off. But if Alice didn't own property, she would have a more difficult time obtaining a business loan. A possible alternative: if Alice owned other property, she could elect to have the lien placed against those properties.

Real estate can still be used as collateral for a loan, even if it has no equity available. The value of real estate goes beyond its resale or appraised value. Consider that the property's income stream is also a valuable asset that is often included in the use of real estate as collateral. For example, Fred takes out a mortgage loan on a piece of farmland that he rents out to a local farmer; if he ever defaults, his mortgage allows the bank to start collecting the rental income to offset the unpaid loan payments.

Some Real Estate Investment Trusts (REITs) function in a similar manner. The trust is a security instrument sold to investors. The trust itself can be collateralized by the income generated by the properties underpinning the REIT.

Another use of this collateral tactic is to create a chain-reaction acquisition scheme.

Collateral Example:

Maria buys a duplex to live in for $100,000. She fixes it up and it appraises for $150,000; she then takes out an equity loan of $50,000 against the property's equity. She uses that $50,000 to pick up two more properties and does the same thing with them. After amassing 15 properties, she obtains a $500,000 credit line using her properties as collateral even though they already have mortgages on them. She then uses her credit line as down payments as she begins investing in larger apartment buildings and other commercial properties.

When property is being used for or considered as collateral, the investor's primary responsibility will be maintaining that collateral's value. This task obviously begins with basic maintenance. The property's value, however, is affected more by its locale and location. The investor must therefore stay attuned to developments in the neighborhood and market area. Crime prevention, street improvements, zoning, new developments and tax issues will all affect the property's value; and property investors must remain aware, if not involved, to make sure that their property values are not damaged.

Income Stream

Many people buy investment real estate to generate additional income for themselves. Success for such investors means positive cash flow, or profits, from the property's operation. That's easier said than done, for most consumers.

If an investor is interested in finding properties that can generate a solid income stream, the following four issues are critical to a successful venture.

- Understanding cash flow
- Improving cash flow
- Recognizing profit-generating properties
- Finding underperforming properties

Understanding Cash Flow

On a practical level, a property's rental income and other revenue must exceed its operating costs and debt servicing. Unfortunately, many novice investors fail to understand that there are two types of cash flow figures.

- *Pre-Tax Cash Flow:* The cash flow calculation before taxes due for the investment project are calculated.

- *After-Tax Profits:* The net profits from an investment after taxes have been deducted.

Many investors find it easy to ignore the tax implications of their investments, often because income taxes do not provide a billing statement like their operating expenses. But the bill will finally come, unless the investor takes steps to reduce the impact of income taxes.

Investors should focus more on the after-tax cash flow as the property's real profits. Depending on the precautions the investor takes, the after-tax profits can be close to or even improve pre-tax cash flow.

When analyzing the cash flow of a prospective or current purchase, real estate investors must examine the project's operating expenses, net operating income, rate of return and finally capitalization rate. Experienced investors have learned never to accept the seller's estimates at face value. Sellers always try to put the best spin on their properties' numbers in order to make the sale more attractive.

Investors should always insist on sufficient documentation, before making any final decisions.

- *Profit and Loss (P&L) Statement:* It is a common practice for sellers of apartment buildings and other commercial properties that are currently generating rental income to provide an annual profit and loss (P&L) statement for the property. Unfortunately, this usually does not apply to smaller two- to four-unit properties. Investors should request a previous year P&L, as well as a year-to-date P&L statement.

- *Rent Roll and Leases:* The income figures on the P&L statement should be supported by rent rolls and, preferably, lease agreements and deposit receipts. When no leases are available, some investors have their attorneys request all of the seller's tenants to sign *estoppel* statements, confirming their current rent status. Whenever possible, the buyer should try to ascertain the vacancy rates and history of the rental units.

• *Service Contracts:* Service contracts are standard elements for most building operation, especially for trash pick-up, elevators and some leasing services.

• *Utility Bills:* The seller should provide copies of utility bills for at least a 12-month period, on those utilities that the property owner (landlord) must cover. These utilities have to be factored into the operating expenses.

• *Appraisal Reports:* The investor's lender will order an appraisal report for the property, which will survey market averages for the property's area. The investor should ask the lender for a copy, so the investor can understand what the prevailing rates for the area are.

• *Professional Inspections:* The investor has the right, in most cases, to conduct a professional inspection of the property. An experienced inspector, with an engineering background, can point out deferred maintenance and potential expenses that the investor may eventually face.

Improving Cash Flow

A thorough verification of the property's income and expenses is important, because it points to the two ways that any investor can maintain or improve cash flow.

• *Lower Expenses:* Slashing costs, without affecting quality, is the quickest way to improving a property's cash flow. Economies of scale (i.e., bulk purchases) and negotiating with service providers are effective methods for immediate results.

• *Increase Income:* Somewhat more difficult, but just as important, for successful cash flow management is increasing the property's revenue. For most properties, increasing income will primarily revolve around increasing rent rates and lowering vacancies. Experienced investors, however, must also consider alternative income sources, such as laundry income, garage rental and storage spaces.

Improving cash flow generates another benefit that is often overlooked when the investor's primary focus is the income stream: appreciation. Increasing profits will typically increase value, because the value of most income-generating investments is based on their profits, or net operating income (NOI).

> ### Cash Flow Example #1:
>
> *Edna purchased a 10-unit apartment building with an annual NOI of $20,000 at a sales price of $200,000 (a 10% capitalization rate). Edna applied disciplined management to lower expenses and increase revenue, resulting in a higher NOI of $25,000. Because of her work, Edna can reasonably expect her property to be worth about $250,000, assuming that the market maintains a 10% cap rate.*

Sometimes the owner can increase the property's value, without improving its cash flow.

> ### Cash Flow Example #2:
>
> *For example, Farley owns a four-plex in Chicago's increasingly trendy Lakeview neighborhood, which he inherited from his mother. Farley barely maintains the rental units; consequently, his annual NOI has stayed at $15,000. He had it appraised 10 years ago (when he inherited it) for $150,000, with the same NOI. However, he is now fielding offers of $450,000 for his sorely-in-need-of-total-rehab property.*

Increased equity cannot be counted in the property's cash flow statement. Nevertheless, it is still there. When investors are primarily or only concentrating on the property's income stream, they often fail to consider the property's potential for value appreciation. A property may have a poor income stream and not seem worthy of purchase, but when appreciation rates in the area are considered, that same property may look like a gold mine.

The bottom line when considering income stream as a tactic is the bottom line. Investors who seek an income stream will need to be property managers, or hire and supervise a manager. Either way, that investor must keep an eye on the bottom line. Cash flow management will require the investor to always run all prospective expenses and investments through a cost-benefit analysis, unless those repairs or improvements are absolutely necessary: what will this expense cost and what benefit will it generate.

Investing for income stream is difficult, but still feasible, for small investors. Larger investors are more successful, because they can save money through economies of scale. The more rental units an investor owns and manages, the less each unit will (or should) cost on a per-unit basis.

This should not discourage novice investors, however, because even large investors start small. Disciplined management and thorough preparation can ensure better odds for success, regardless of the investor's resources and experience. Perhaps that is what investors should first ask themselves before undertaking this tactic: do they have the discipline needed to be successful entrepreneurs.

Recognizing Profit-Generating Properties

Here's a somewhat discouraging piece of news: few two- to four-unit residential properties listed for sale in America's urban centers generate enough rental income to cover their operating expenses and debt servicing. Worse still, most of those properties are in deteriorating and often undesirable areas. The situation is somewhat better with larger properties.

It seems that rental rates have not kept pace with increases in real estate prices. Still, there are opportunities to be found for those willing to search for them. The trick is to find those few properties that actually have a positive cash flow, after paying the mortgage. It comes down to the investor who must ultimately find the profitable investment, but only after becoming knowledgeable about the entire process from start to finish.

Learning how to recognize these properties is the bottom line of investing, after all is said and done. Also, after locating a property, the investor must be willing to trust his or her instincts and research and make the offer. The following are some due diligence tips to help the investor separate the good from the bad investment.

- *The 1% Rule:* A rule of thumb that some investors use is the 1% rule—to break even, the property's monthly income should be at least one percent (1%) of the sales price. This is useful when skimming through several potential properties. Be warned, however, that this is a rule of thumb that assumes average expenses, properties and markets.

• *Focus on the NOI:* As you become more serious about a specific property, you must begin to focus on its annual net operating income (NOI). You must concentrate your due diligence on verifying the property's true NOI—never take the seller's word for it.

• *Cap Rate:* The NOI should lead you to the capitalization rate: NOI divided by the price. If your goal is positive cash flow, you want a minimum cap rate of 10%. Single-digit cap rates should be avoided, unless you are looking at the value appreciation.

Finding Underperforming Properties

Assuming that the investor understands how to distinguish properties with profitable income streams, the next logical step is finding those properties. Technology and a dynamic real estate market makes this easier than one would think.

The following are several suggestions for uncovering underperfoming properties.

• *Low Rents:* Ignore metropolitan rent averages. Real estate investment is about location, location and location. For example, average rent for a two-bedroom in the city of Chicago may be $750; but some areas can easily demand $1,500, while some areas can't find tenants at $350. Search by areas—after researching average rent rates—and look for listings that have low rent rates and the potential for quick increases.

• *Below Median Price:* Interested in something that you can buy and sell right away? First target an area that has an active market, in which average marketing time is under 60 days. Then calculate the median price level in that target area for common property types (two-flats, single-family homes, etc.). Then concentrate on those properties whose asking price is below the median. If you find a good property in the bunch, there is a good chance that you can resell it at a price near or above the median, perhaps with a little cosmetic work.

• *Poor Management:* Some properties are underperforming because of poor management. A more dedicated, informed and organized investor can do wonders with such properties. Look for properties in promising areas that appear unkempt or ill-managed, and use that condition to your advantage.

- *Distress:* One way to increase the capitalization rate is to lower the sales price. Sellers in distress, foreclosure, bankruptcy or financial pressures are often willing to cut their asking price to drastic levels for a quick sale. However, an investor might need to be able to close right away.

- *Aggressive Advertising:* Usually, it is only the property sellers who advertise. This puts creative real estate investors in an advantageous position, as they don't have too many competitors. Use classified ads and flyers to get the word out that you are looking to buy property. Possible message: "Investor looking to buy; can close right away." The people replying to such a message probably will be in distress and would be willing to cooperate if the investor can close immediately. The investor, in turn, must be able to close immediately and will need a firm mortgage pre-approval.

- *Spreadsheet Listings:* The web and many Multiple Listing Services (MLS) now allow real estate agents to download all rental properties that meet your search criteria. These files can then be arranged in a spreadsheet to automatically calculate the NOI, mortgage payment and cap rate for each property. They can then be sorted based on the cap rate and neighborhood.

Value Appreciation

Many real estate investors are speculators betting that they will be able to resell their property for much more than their purchase (and carrying) cost. The great thing about this approach is that most speculators do almost nothing with the property. At best, they are land speculators trying to anticipate a potential development trend. At worst, they are poor investors, trying to squeeze every dime from a piece of property.

Other speculators are more pro-active in increasing the value of their property. Some land speculators may survey and subdivide the larger parcel, while others may go further and begin initial development with sewer access, water lines and roads. Such speculators are actually partaking in development.

All of these real estate investors share a common tactic of pursuing potential appreciation. In truth, history is very supportive of such speculators. Although some areas have experienced reduction of property value, these periods are usually the result of a preceding boom that went too far. These periods tend to be short. In the long run, the value of real estate has continued on a steady march upwards—for practically all properties. The value of all real estate has continued to increase over the centuries, especially in areas of increasing population density.

Note that there is a relatively finite supply of real estate, at least until we begin colonizing other planets on a major scale. As such, the price of real estate—and thus its value—is really controlled by demand.

Subdivision

Sometimes the whole is not greater than the sum of its parts. Real estate occasionally offers opportunities for the parts to be worth much more than the unified whole.

That is the theory behind the tactic of subdivision. The real estate investor acquires property, cuts it up and sells the pieces for much more than the original purchase price.

The most common examples of subdivision have occurred through much of modern history whenever raw land was subdivided into smaller plots to meet the needs of a growing town or city. It continues today. Investors purchase farm or open land and legally subdivide it into smaller parcels that are then sold to potential home builders. In such cases, subdividing normally entails the following steps.

- *Survey:* A property survey is conducted that provides for a graphic subdivision of the parcels. This survey will create a plat that establishes the boundary of each parcel, as the greater property is subdivided.

- *Easements:* The plat must be designed to provide adequate easements for all of the parcels. Easements must be provided for streets, utilities, sidewalks and other necessary access. Remember that basic property laws provide that no parcel of land be landlocked, so that the property owner must always have access to and egress from his or her parcel.

- *Legal Subdivision:* Establishing legally separated parcels involves having the subdivision plan approved and recorded by the local governing body. Subdivision and land development is now strictly controlled, as many areas have discovered too late the true cost of uncontrolled growth. Through their plat approval powers and impact fees cities ensure minimum sewer, curb and other regulatory requirements.

In most cases, the developer undertaking a residential subdivision will build the streets, sewers, main utility lines, curbs and other elements throughout the entire project. The individual parcel buyers/owners will be responsible for building and improving their parcels. Sometimes, such as in large rural subdivisions, the developer may only establish a dirt road to the parcel entrances.

A recently more prevalent example of subdivision in urban areas has been the condominium conversion, whereby an apartment complex is subdivided into individually owned units. Condominiums demonstrate the evolution of property laws by not so much subdividing the land—which essentially remains intact—but subdividing the project's air spaces.

Subdivision development can be highly profitable; the past few paragraphs have only provided a brief introduction.

Development

The big money in real estate investment is most often generated through development. It is also lost there. Development entails creating or evolving an existing piece of property to a real estate project with greater market value. This may involve subdividing or keeping the property in one piece and building on it.

Development may entail immediately selling the property upon completion or keeping it long-term for its income stream. There are many types of developers in the real estate market today.

- *Converters:* Some developers avoid massive from-the-ground-up construction projects and focus on changing the property's use or type. For example, converters may change a factory building into stylish offices or an apartment building into condominiums.

- *Fee Developers:* Many developers do not develop their own land; instead they are hired by the property owner to develop, market and/or manage the owner's real estate. For such developers, their risk exposure is much lower than if they were tackling their own project.

- *Land Developers:* Some developers prefer to focus on just the land preparation portion of a development project. Land developers will typically develop the land's infrastructure—such as sewers, streets and utilities—usually after subdividing the property. The prepared parcels are then sold to buyers who will be responsible for developing their separate parcels. For example, industrial land developers may subdivide 500-acres of land into 25-acre parcels with wide streets for semi-trucks and adequate sewers and utilities to meet the needs of manufacturers and industrial tenants.

- *Merchant Builders:* To minimize their risk exposure, many developers do not start or complete projects until they have a commitment from a buyer to purchase the completed development. Merchant builders typically develop properties for immediate resale after completion, usually with a firm commitment from the eventual buyer. For example, XYZ Home Builders are developing several parcels they own in a subdivision. Before they begin custom construction, however, the buyer must obtain a purchase loan commitment.

- *Renovators:* Similar to converters, renovators or rehabbers seek to upgrade, improve or modify a property's condition, with the goal of establishing higher value. The most widely recognized form of this approach are the rehabbers who buy cheap properties, fix them up and resell them for profit.

- *Speculative Developers:* Major developers willing to accept greater risk exposure will sometimes develop properties without any forward commitments from potential tenants or buyers. They are speculating that the market will have a demand for their real estate.

As you can surmise from the review of the different types of developers, there are different types of development projects. In a sense, practically all real estate investors wear the hat of developer. But beginning real estate investors should avoid major development projects, without strong outside support, as the risks are as tremendous as any potential rewards.

Purchase Options

The option instrument is a little known tool with powerful choices for real estate investors. Usually called an option to purchase, the option instrument gives the real estate investor the right to purchase a piece of property, usually for a set price, to take advantage of increases in appraised market value.

This ability to set the price for a long period of time is perhaps the primary benefit that options offer to beginning investors. Successful real estate investors can exploit the equity difference between the option's set price and the property's actual market value.

> *Option Example:*
>
> *Donna sees an undervalued property that the seller is considering selling, but has had no serious takers. Donna offers the seller $5,000 for a purchase option with a term of three years and a fixed price of $100,000. If Donna were to buy the property now, the best loan she could qualify for would be an 80% LTV loan—$80,000. After one year, Donna can still only get an $80,000 loan. But now she is able to appraise the property for its full market value of $140,000; and 80% of that appraised value is $112,000, more than enough to pay off the seller completely.*

Master Lease

Smart real estate investors do not have to own a property in order to profit from it. The master lease is a tactic anyone can use to obtain possession of a property and use it to their profit for a limited period.

> *Master Lease Example:*
>
> *Angie leases an entire office building from Bill for a monthly total of $2,000. Angie then markets and subleases the units within the building to individual tenants, grossing over $4,500 per month. The title to the office building will remain in Bill's name. However, the master lease gives Angie possession of the property and the right to manage and market its use.*

The master lease can and should be legally recorded, so that public notice is given to any prospective buyer of the property. Of course, the basic lease will not give Angie the right to sell or otherwise encumber the property. Some leases do contain an option to purchase, which would be an extra bonus for the buyer/lessee as explained in the preceding section.

Tax Shelters

Real estate no longer offers the tax shelters to institutional investors that it formerly did. Prior to the 1980s, institutional investors actively sought real estate that could provide a paper loss, which the investor could then use to offset income from other sources. Changes to the tax code have minimized or eliminated many such tax shelters, but tax advantages still remain with real estate investments.

Real estate investors can exploit tax advantages in three general areas.

• Operating losses

• Capital gain

• Depreciation

Operating Losses

Actively managing and operating a real estate investment is, for all practical and legal purposes, operating a business. As such, real estate investments that declare profit are taxed on that income; on the other hand, real estate investments that declare losses avoid taxes and can sometimes use those losses to offset income in other investments.

Current tax codes distinguish between passive and active income, as well as between passive and active losses. Losses from passive investments, such as most stocks, bonds and some real estate investments, can only be deducted against income from similar passive investments. They cannot be used to offset income from active endeavors, such as primary employment and personally owned and operated businesses.

This is not an issue for most beginning real estate investors, because their real estate investments are usually active income and losses. Such investors can use declared losses from their real estate investments to offset their taxable income.

Capital Gain

When investors sell their investment—whether stocks, bonds, a business or real estate—they must pay capital gain tax on the resale profit. However, there are methods for deferring these capital gain taxes.

All serious real estate investors should be aware of how capital gain may affect them. An old saying about investing is that building wealth is often not so much about how much you make, but how much you keep.

In most cases consumers only pay capital gain tax on investment properties. If a consumer is selling a property that qualifies as a primary residence (having lived in it for at least two years out of the past five years), he or she can qualify for a capital gain tax exemption. For sole owners, a capital gain exemption of up to $250,000 is allowed, with joint owners allowed exemptions of up to $500,000 on their primary residence. Recent tax changes have made this available to all homeowners once every two years.

Depreciation

For real estate investors, depreciation is perhaps one of the most important deductions to understand. Through the concept of depreciation, properties that earn a marginal profit can be made to look as if it were just breaking even or losing money. Moreover, even though a property may be appreciating in value, the investor can still deduct for the property's depreciation.

Beginners can best understand the concept of depreciation by considering a small business that has bought a new drilling machine for $10,000. This machine, according to the IRS, may have a useful life of five (5) years. As each year passes, the drilling machine will lose its value. For example, by the second year, it may only be worth $8,000. If the business is allowed to depreciate the cost of this machine over five years, that business can write off $2,000 per year on its tax returns.

Depreciation is not allowed on land. However, depreciation is allowed on improvements to the land, such as buildings and other developments. The amount of depreciation is governed by IRS-issued tables. Residential real estate properties are currently depreciated over 27.5 years, while commercial real estate is depreciated over 39 years—depending on when the real estate was purchased and placed into service.

Note that depreciation does not restrict appreciation. The strange thing about real estate is that the property's value will often continue to appreciate, even while the investor is deducting depreciation.

There is one minor drawback with taking depreciation. When an investor sells the property, he or she has to add the total dollar amount of depreciation taken, to the cost basis of the property, making the amount of the capital gain larger by the amount of the depreciation. But this is negligible for three reasons.

- *Time Value of Money:* The money that an investor gets today from depreciation deductions is worth much more than the "paper" money that he or she has to add back to the cost basis later.

- *Depreciation Tax Rate vs. Capital Gain Rate:* Remember that long-term capital gains are taxed at about 20%, currently. Meanwhile, depreciation deductions recapture funds in the investor's tax bracket. If you're in the 28% bracket, you're still coming out ahead by 8%.

•*Capital Gain Deferral:* Through a trade or exchange transaction, an investor can defer capital gains indefinitely into the future.

One way an investor can conservatively take advantage of the depreciation deduction is to take the profits from those deductions and put them into high-yield CDs or market funds. When the investor finally sells the property, the investor will discover that the capital gains hit on the added-back depreciation is more than offset by the income from the depreciation deduction funds.

Tax-Deferred Exchanges

Investors face capital gains taxes on their profits from the sale of real estate, and these capital gain taxes can be significant. However, investors have a way to defer paying any capital gains by selling their property through a trade. IRS tax codes only assess taxes on capital gains realized from a sale of property.

Through a 1031 exchange, investors can defer capital gains taxes if they trade their property—instead of selling it—for a like-kind property. The courts have taken a very lenient approach to the term "like-kind," so any type of real estate can be exchanged for any other type of real estate, as long as it is investment real estate. Cars can be traded for cars, and jewelry can be traded for jewelry.

With 1031 "Starker" exchanges, the seller/exchanger must identify the target property within 45 days of the sale of the current property. The exchanger can target up to three potential properties of any (unlimited) market value, subject to final decision. Moreover, the exchanger must receive title to that target property within 180 days of the sale of the original property. Note that sellers who are in the midst of the 180-day period should not file their tax returns—but instead ask for an extension—because tax laws shorten that 180-days.

Thank you to Rey Villar for his generous help in providing resource information for this chapter.

Dignity Mortgage Corp., Rey Villar, Jr., 1929 W. Foster, Chicago, IL 60640
Phone: (773) 769-5729
RVillar@DignityMortgage.com

CHAPTER QUIZ

1. All of the following are types return on investment in real estate except:

   a. cash flow
   b. return on taxes
   c. depreciation
   d. appreciation

2. Depreciation for tax purposes is based on:

   a. the calculated useful life of the property
   b. the actual life of the property
   c. the future market rent of a property
   d. the future contract rent of a property

3. Capital gains taxes are always due on the sale of all except:

   a. an apartment building
   b. a personal residence with certain exceptions
   c. land
   d. a commercial building

4. Operating expenses include:

   a. debt service
   b. capital improvements
   c. equipment and fixtures
   d. taxes

5. What may not be depreciated?

   a. land
   b. fixtures
   c. improvements
   d. equipment

6. Gross income is:

   a. the total annual income less vacancy or rental losses
   b. the total annual income less expenses
   c. the net income less debt service
   d. the net income less improvements

7. The net operating income may be calculated by:

   a. subtracting the debt service
      from the annual gross income
   b. subtracting operating expenses
      plus debt service from the annual
      gross income
   c. subtracting operating expenses
      from the annual gross income
   d. subtracting the vacancy loss from
      the annual gross income

8. What is one way to improve cash flow?

   a. increase expenses
   b. lower expenses
   c. refinance at a higher rate of interest
   d. get a partner

9. A condo conversion may be said to:

   a. subdivide a property's air space
   b. subdivide a property's total space
   c. subdivide a property's tax base
   d. subdivide a property's common area

10. When investors sell real property they must pay:

    a. installment taxes
    b. capital gain taxes
    c. real property taxes
    d. deferred gain taxes

ANSWERS

1. *c*
2. *a*
3. *b*
4. *d*
5. *a*
6. *a*
7. *c*
8. *b*
9. *a*
10. *b*

10

chapter ten

Choosing a Lender

INTRODUCTION

Imagine how a first-time home buyer feels upon finding the house of his or her dreams, only to be confronted with the overwhelming task of applying for, and obtaining, the necessary financing to purchase the property. Too often the mortgage loan professional the buyer has chosen uses puzzling terms such as FICO® score, debt-to-income ratio, loan-to-value ratio, servicing-disclosure statement or fair-lending notice. The dazed borrower hears a litany of costs that include such expenses as escrow fee, buy-down points, flood certification and tax stamps. It's no wonder borrowers suffer from anxiety and fear of the unknown when they apply for a loan.

The job of a mortgage loan professional is to help the customer complete a loan application and explain what documents or verifications, such as credit card numbers, evidence of employment, tax returns, or bank account references are needed. Many prospective borrowers have never been involved in the loan procedure before and require understanding and patience while they learn about the process of obtaining a loan. If the mortgage broker wants to build a clientele for future business, that broker will be helpful, fair and respectful toward the loan applicant.

A completed loan application is the starting point for the lending process or loan origination. There are, however, only so many consumers in need of a loan at any one time. Depending on the health of the national economy and the cost and availability of mortgage money, there may be many more lenders in need of a borrower, than the other way around. To attract customers, or borrowers, many mortgage brokers or lenders offer to meet with the borrower at the borrower's convenience. A basic feeling of trust should be developed between the borrower and mortgage loan professional, thus meeting in the borrower's home allows the borrower to relax and feel comfortable with the loan process. We all think our transaction is the most important thing happening and the smart loan professional will acknowledge that fact, giving customers the extra attention they deserve.

Another fairly recent convenience to a borrower is being able to make a loan application over the telephone. Because of the speed of computers and access to credit information, a lender can give a preliminary qualification to a borrower within minutes based on the borrower's income and credit score. The loan application itself generally takes no more than 10 minutes. The borrower then receives hard copies of required disclosures and instructions about what verifications and other documents are required to complete the application process by fax or mail.

HOW CONSUMERS CHOOSE A LENDER

There are many reasons why a prospective borrower would choose one lender over another. Each borrower has individual requirements, but there are some basic needs that must be met by a mortgage lender in order to attract customers.

The most common way for a mortgage lender to attract customers is by referral from a real estate sales agent. The majority of buyers do not have a relationship with a mortgage loan professional when they start looking for a property. An active real estate agent should work with one or two mortgage loan professionals who are always available, always reliable, always trustworthy—and who can offer a variety of loans, depending on the need of the buyer. A successful mortgage loan professional is one who is informed and can relate to customers in a friendly and professional manner. Ultimately, buyers will return to the real estate agent *and* mortgage loan professional who, working together, make the purchase of the desired property possible. A partnership between these two professionals is likely to benefit the real estate agent, the mortgage broker and the buyer.

Most buyers are interested in saving money on the purchase of their property. They can save money by paying less for the real estate and/or they can save it on the loan costs. There are several ways borrowers can save money related to their loans. One way is to shop around for a loan with few or no points, sometimes called the loan fee. The most critical charge to a borrower, however, is the interest rate. Lenders who offer low mortgage loan rates are likely to attract a large part of the market share of prospective borrowers.

It's one thing to offer low interest rates, and another to successfully fund a loan according to the promises made to the buyer. A lender's reputation in the business community is another of the standards that a prospective borrower will use in selecting a loan provider. Among other issues, inefficient loan agents, dubious business practices or lack of resources are all reasons for a prospective borrower to seek a lender with better references.

In a loan transaction everyone wants to be treated fairly and courteously. A cheerful, smiling loan agent encourages a borrower not only to return for another loan, but to refer friends as well because of the friendliness of the loan officer. A loan officer who is surly and uninterested in a borrower is indeed creating an unpleasant and unprofessional impression of his or her employer.

Another reason for choosing one lending institution over another is if the borrower has had a pleasant experience in the past with that lender. That would include everything from the product to the personnel with whom the borrower came into contact.

Many lending institutions and other mortgage loan professionals spend a large advertising dollar to attract borrowers. We all recognize names like Wells Fargo, Bank of America, Washington Mutual, Chase Manhattan, World Savings and others because we see them advertised on television, on billboards and through direct mailing pieces. A borrower may feel secure choosing from one of these familiar companies because of the duration and market strength of its mortgage loan business.

In today's mortgage loan marketplace, a lender has to offer a variety of what is called product. Thirty years ago, a borrower generally had a choice of a 30-year, fixed rate loan or no loan. As a result of market driven as well as court directed changes in the banking world during the 1980s, consumers have benefited by the creation of various new types of loans. The competitive lender will be one who offers the most loan products or types of loans.

Finally, convenience of application could be an issue with some borrowers. The lender who offers to come to the borrowers home or place of business or takes the application over the telephone is the one who will get the business in today's busy world.

HOW LOANS ARE ORIGINATED

Commonly, mortgage loans are offered directly to borrowers by a lender who completes the loan process directly in a retail loan operation. An alternate approach is when a third party, or loan broker, who will charge a fee to connect the borrower and the lender originates the loan in a wholesale approach to dealing with borrowers.

Retail Loan Origination

When consumers need to obtain a mortgage loan, they may think of their own bank or a bank close by their home. This bank will probably deal with them directly and perform all of the steps necessary during the origination process. This retail approach to loan origination is likely to be used by smaller banks or financial institutions with the larger lenders having more resources to offer loans in more diverse ways.

Another candidate for the retail approach to lending in the refinance market is the mortgage lender with enough assets to make real estate loans and keep the loans in its own portfolio instead of selling them on the secondary market. These lenders are likely to be among the largest lending institutions and only want the best quality loans in their portfolios. Best quality loans have the least risk of default because the borrowers have solid financial histories as well as perfect credit. Many times this type of retail lender will seek out preferred borrowers who have been selected for the offer based on information contained in a report made available by consumer reporting agencies such as Equifax Options, Experian Information Solutions and Trans Union Marketing. The desired borrower will be pre-approved because he or she meets the pre-determined criteria for creditworthiness.

Most borrowers, however, don't seek out their own mortgage lender and usually count on their real estate agents to recommend one. A real estate agent is the most likely source to connect borrowers and lenders, because generally the agent deals with buyers *before* the buyer becomes involved in the search for an attractive lender. Retail lenders know that a common path to their door is through the local real estate industry, and aggressively market their product to real estate agents with the hope that the agents will direct their clients to the most persistent lenders.

The lenders, however, have to earn the reward of increased market share they will get because of their connection with busy real estate agents. By being helpful, courteous, efficient, knowledgeable and—above all—competitive with their product, the retail lenders will be assured of the continuing business of real estate professionals who want to make their clients happy and repeat customers.

A retail mortgage lender will employ commissioned loan officers as well as loan representatives who confidently market the lender's mortgage loan products. While the loan officers may remain at the lending establishment, the loan representatives energetically solicit business by making a connection with real estate agents at local real estate offices.

A retail mortgage loan originator is normally paid a commission of 1% of the loan amount, payable upon funding of the loan. This is generally called the origination fee. If a lender uses a quota system to pay the loan professionals, sometimes a smaller commission per loan is paid until the required quota has been reached and then the commission is increased to a higher amount. Most lenders base payment to their loan professionals on some kind of a commission scale, but some pay a salary only.

A prospective borrower should expect the retail lender to complete the following tasks as part of the loan origination.

Loan Origination

A retail lender:

- Completes application with borrower
- Orders all employment, income and deposit verifications
- Orders appraisal
- Orders credit report
- Prepares loan for underwriting
- Underwrites the loan application
- Approves or rejects the loan application
- Closes and funds the approved loan portfolio or sells the loan

Wholesale Loan Origination

Since the mid-1980s, mortgage lending has not been the same. Dynamic changes have swept the industry, bringing desirable diversity in a conservative business that has usually been consumed with resisting change. The basics of mortgage lending have not changed, but a few powerful factors have played a part in contributing to the new face of mortgage lending.

Forces of Change in Mortgage Lending

- High volatility and instability of interest rates was a major force of change in the mortgage lending market. Fixed rates ranged from 9% in 1979 to 18% in 1982; below 7% in 1993; rising to 8% in the late 1990s; only to fall to the lowest rates in at least 20 years in the early 2000s.

- Tremendous swings in one-to-four family mortgage originations from year to year led to widespread insecurity in the mortgage loan market because even experts could not predict what trends would give lenders any kind of a healthy indication of future business.

- Unpredictable cycles of originations in different areas of the country prevented mortgage bankers from making long-term projections about where mortgage money was going to be needed.

- Increased competition between traditional and non traditional lenders forced both types of lenders to be more dynamic and competitive, resulting in a benefit for consumers.

- The appearance of technology in mortgage lending caused the process to become less expensive and more sophisticated. Computers provided the means for lenders to qualify borrowers in minutes and to research the borrowers' credit history over the telephone.

- Servicing loans became almost a sub-industry of the mortgage lending business. As the number of loans and the amounts of those loans grew, their servicing, or collecting payments and keeping track of due dates, payoffs, and other incidentals of each particular loan became very profitable.

Mortgage Originations: Total, Refinance, and Purchase 1990 to 2005

	Mortgage Originations (Bil.$)	Refinance Originations (Bil.$)	Purchase Originations (Bil.$)
1990	459	70	389
1995	640	145	494
1997	833	243	590
1998	1,656	862	795
1999	1,379	500	878
2000	1,139	234	905
2001	2,243	1,283	960
2002	2,854	1,757	1,097
2003	3,812	2,532	1,280
2004	2,773	1,463	1,309
2005	2,908	1,397	1,512

Source: Mortgage Bankers Association of America, Washington DC

These forces have caused mortgage lending to transform itself into an industry that is more responsive to consumers needs than it was 20 years ago. The practice of wholesale mortgage lending has grown out of borrowers' demand for a more efficient loan process and more variety in loan products. Sometimes called "third party-origination" or TPO, these loans are originated by mortgage loan correspondents and loan brokers who then sell them to acquiring wholesale mortgage lenders.

Mortgage Loan Professionals

When a mortgage lender acquires a processed loan from another loan professional who has originated the loan, the operation is called wholesale mortgage lending. The reason a lender would buy a loan or group of loans from the originating loan professional is that it is less expensive to buy the loans than to originate, process, underwrite and fund the loan. The originating lender from whom the loan has been purchased can be a mortgage loan broker or loan correspondent. The mortgage loan broker has probably only originated the loan and sold it, while the loan correspondent most likely has processed and funded the loan before selling it. In some cases, the loan broker completes the loan application with the borrower, and orders some of the verifications, such as employment, income, and bank account information. When the acquiring lender gets the loan package, the underwriting and funding may be completed at that time.

The loan processing and underwriting decision may be made by a loan correspondent, however, who may or may not fund the loan. If the acquiring lender funds the loan, the process is called table funding. The correspondent, in the course of table funding, closes a mortgage loan with funds belonging to the acquiring lender. The loan, upon closing, is then assigned to that lender who supplied the funds. Being known as a direct lender, then, gives the loan correspondent possible market advantage over other brokers.

The mortgage loan correspondent is particularly interested in having the underwriting decision on any loan sold to a wholesale lender done quickly. If the loan is declined, for some reason, the originating loan correspondent will need to renegotiate with the prospective borrower regarding any problems with the loan application.

There is a niche for everyone in the mortgage loan business. The loan professional who chooses to originate loans and sell them immediately to a wholesale lender requires a certain profit and is willing to take no risk for the larger profit that may come with processing and funding of loans. The loan correspondent typically will get an interest rate commitment on a loan from the wholesale lender before completing the origination process with the borrower.

An originating lender generally gets paid through an application fee paid by the prospective borrower, as well as an origination fee of usually 1 point, or 1% of the loan amount. Either the borrower or the acquiring lender pays the point.

After the loan has been transferred to the wholesale lender, and has been funded either before the transfer or by the wholesale lender, it will be held in the lender's portfolio or sold on the secondary loan market.

Why Wholesale Lending?

There are pluses and minuses to wholesale loan origination. The most important benefit to the wholesale lender is the large number of mortgage loans that may be provided by the loan broker and may be acquired more economically than if the lender originated the loans. Because the acquiring lender does not need to hire a large staff to process the loans, the profit margin is greater.

Another benefit to a wholesale lender is flexibility in the market. Money markets may change quickly and a wholesale lender can move swiftly to another attractive locale to do business without being concerned about personnel or even a physical location. If a market declines rapidly, a wholesale lender can stop purchasing loans in a profitless area of the country and start up in another location where the market is attractive.

Wholesale lenders are eager to acquire as many loans as rapidly as possible to add to their portfolios. Using the wholesale approach, the more loans a lender purchases, the larger the profits through the servicing revenue, which is the whole point of the business. After the loans are bought from the originating brokers they are sold at once into the secondary mortgage market, with the wholesale lender holding the servicing rights.

A loan is only as good as the originator and the issue of quality control can be a negative factor for a wholesale lender. The lender purchasing a loan has no control over the quality of the loans bought, since the loans may have been processed and underwitten by the mortgage loan originator with little care for the character of the loan. Loan wholesalers must try and deal only with well-established, respectable brokers who want repeat business and will work hard to earn the respect of the wholesale lender. Appraisals, important employment and credit verifications, as well as other critical information gathering must be held to the highest standards to avoid the serious problems that come with default on a loan.

CHAPTER QUIZ

1. The retail approach to loan origination is most likely to be used by:

    a. smaller banks
    b. large financial institutions
    c. Fannie Mae
    d. Ginnie Mae

2. A retail mortgage loan originator is normally paid a commission of _____ % of the loan amount, payable upon funding of the loan.

    a. 5%
    b. 4%
    c. 2%
    d. 1%

3. What was a major force of change in the mortgage lending market in the early 1980s?

    a. turnover in banking personnel
    b. economic prosperity
    c. stability of interest rates
    d. high volatility and instability of interest rates

4. Unpredictable cycles of originations in different areas of the country prevented mortgage bankers from:

    a. working nine to five
    b. charging points to originate loans
    c. making long term projections about where mortgage money was going to be needed
    d. raising interest rates

5. Who originates third-party-origination loans?

    a. consumer
    b. mortgage loan correspondents
    c. Fannie Mae
    d. HUD

6. When a mortgage lender acquires a processed loan from another loan professional who has originated the loan, the operation is called:

   a. retail mortgage lending
   b. consumer mortgage lending
   c. wholesale mortgage lending
   d. pass-through mortgage lending

7. After the loan has been transferred to the wholesale lender, and has been funded either before the transfer or by the wholesale lender:

   a. it will be held in the lender's portfolio or sold on the secondary loan market
   b. it must be held for 6 months by the wholesale lender before it can be sold
   c. it is processed by the wholesale lender
   d. it is reconveyed by the wholesale lender

8. How does an originating lender get paid?

   a. through an application fee paid by the prospective borrower, as well as an origination fee of usually 1 point, or 1 percent of the loan amount
   b. by the mortgage loan servicer
   c. only by the lender
   d. from regular loan payments made by the borrower

9. What is the most important benefit to the wholesale lender?

   a. building a personal relationship with the borrower
   b. the large number of mortgage loans that may be provided by the loan broker and may be acquired more economically than if the lender originated the loans
   c. being able to work in only a small section of the market
   d. being able to process and approve each new loan

10. A negative factor for a wholesale lender is:

    a. too many loans are sold to
       the wholesale dealer
    b. flexibility in the mortgage
       loan marketplace
    c. no money to be made in
       servicing loans
    d. quality of loans

ANSWERS

1. *a*
2. *d*
3. *d*
4. *c*
5. *b*
6. *c*
7. *a*
8. *a*
9. *b*
10. *d*

11

chapter eleven

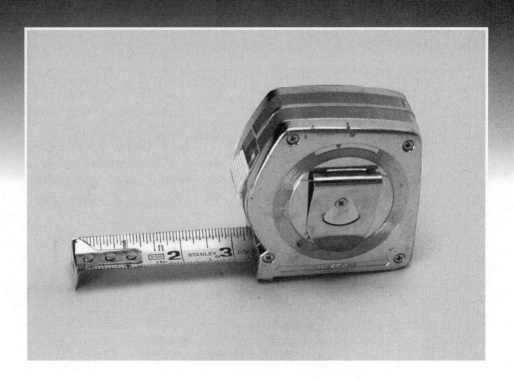

Appraisal

INTRODUCTION

Probably the most asked question in real estate is, "How much do you think it's worth?" Every day a client or customer will ask about the fair price or fair rental for a property, and a real estate agent must be prepared to answer knowledgeably after researching the property.

The prospective buyer or seller is not the only one interested in the value of the property, however. A mortgage lender will want to know the value of a property before applying loan-to-value ratios to determine the risk involved in making the loan. Information about the value of the property being used as security for a loan is just as important to the lender as personal information about the borrower's ability and desire to repay the loan. The next two chapters will go into detail about the subject of processing, underwriting and closing the loan.

Part of the processing procedure of the loan will include getting information from an appraiser about the value of the property being used as security for the loan. The appraisal may be done by an appraiser who works for the lender or a private fee appraiser who works as an independent contractor to several lenders.

This chapter will examine the appraisal process and the methods used to determine property values so that an appraiser can answer, when a real estate agent or mortgage lender asks the question, "How much do you think it's worth?"

DEFINITION OF APPRAISAL

An appraisal is an unbiased estimate or opinion of the property value on a given date. *Value* is the present worth of rights to future benefits that come from property ownership. An appraiser gives his or her opinion of value in a written statement called an appraisal report. It is the conclusion of the appraiser's research and analysis of all relevant data regarding the subject property.

Most of the time, an objective, third-party opinion is needed to determine the value of real property. The professional appraiser, because of training, experience and ethics, is responsible for giving clients an objective opinion of value, reached without bias. An appraiser has a serious responsibility to be correct in evaluating data and not allow other factors to influence evaluation of a property. The appraiser must remember to be a neutral party, responding only to the forces affecting value, and not to any other special interests who might want to influence his or her judgment.

There are several different reasons for determining the value of a particular property.

Reasons For An Appraisal

- Transfer of property ownership
- Financing and credit
- Taxation
- Condemnation
- Insurance

The estimate of value given for each of the above listed reasons may be different, depending on the reason for ordering the appraisal. The condemnation value is going to be different from the taxation value, the insurance value or the market value. An appraiser must know what those differences are and how to estimate the value of a property based on the purpose for which it is being used.

FAIR MARKET VALUE

Real estate includes both land and anything belonging to the land, as well as rights or interests in that land. The price a property would bring if freely offered on the open market, with both a willing buyer and a willing seller, is known as *fair market value*—or market value.

A property that is offered for sale as a result of default, foreclosure, bankruptcy, divorce, death or any other unusual circumstances cannot be said to be freely and willingly offered on the open market, and the sale price of such properties would not represent fair market value. An appraiser would take into account that there were special circumstances in those sales and would not use the price paid as a comparable measure of value. The following can be assumed of all fair market sales.

Fair Market Sales

- Buyer and seller are operating in their own interest.
- Buyer and seller are knowledgeable about the transaction and make careful decisions.
- The property is available for a reasonable time on the open market.
- The sale is for cash or trade, or is specifically financed.
- Normal financing, available to qualified borrowers, is used.

PRICE, COST AND VALUE

Market price is what a property *actually* sold for, where market value, or fair market value as it is sometimes called, is the price that it *should* have sold for.

Sometimes, *value* and *price* or *cost* are the same, but they aren't necessarily. Circumstances of one buyer and one seller may affect the sale of a specific property, giving it its own value, apart from some other similar parcel. The job of an appraiser is to determine the special factors of a sale and assign a value based on each individual transaction.

Price, Cost and Value

• Price is what is paid for something.

• Cost represents expenses in money, labor, material or sacrifices in acquiring or producing something. Cost is not an essential element of value.

• Value has to do with the present and future anticipated enjoyment, or profit of something.

The value of a parcel can be defined in many ways. There is utility value, or the usefulness of the property. This is the subjective value, or the value given for personal reasons. For example, a swimming pool might be important to one family, but of little value to another. Other amenities fall into this category as well. Six bedrooms would not be useful or have utility value to a couple with no children, nor would a home deep in the woods to a city worker.

Market value represents the amount in money for which a property can be sold in current market conditions at a given time. This is sometimes called the objective value, since it may be determined by actual data.

Four Elements of Value   There are only four elements of value, all of which must be considered in estimating the worth of a property. These are demand, utility, scarcity and transferability.

The Four Elements of Value

D emand: the desire to buy and the ability to pay

U tility: usefulness

S carcity: the fewer available, the more valuable

T ransferability: title must be marketable, unclouded

The appraiser must decide if there is a demand for a property, such as a high-rise residential building, or a low-cost housing project. Can it be used for the purpose it was intended, such as a family home, or residential complex? How many projects like this one are there in the area? The fewer there are, the more value the subject property has. Is the title clear and can the seller easily give ownership to a buyer? As you can see, all of these factors are important in assigning a value to a property. An appraiser must hold each one up to the property in question to arrive at a correct estimate of value.

FORCES INFLUENCING VALUE

The essence of life is change, and real estate is not excluded from that force. Value is created, maintained, modified and destroyed by the relationship of the following four forces.

Forces Influencing Value

Environmental and Physical Characteristics

- This includes quality of conveniences, availability of schools, shopping, public transportation, churches, similarity of land use. Environmental forces may be climate, soil, topography, oceans and mountains.

Social Ideals and Standards

- Population growth and decline, age, marriage, birth, divorce and death rates all combine to cause changes in social patterns.

Economic Influences

- Some economic forces that influence value are natural resources, industrial and commercial trends, employment trends, wage levels, availability of money and credit, interest rates, price levels, tax loads, regional and community economic base, new development, and rental and price patterns.

Political or Government Regulations

- Some political forces that can affect value are building codes, zoning laws, public health measures, fire regulations, rent controls, environmental legislation and community economic base.

OTHER FACTORS INFLUENCING VALUE

Directional growth: This is determined by how the area or city expands. Property in a growth area tends to increase in value.

Location: This may be the most important factor influencing value, as far as highest and best use.

Utility: The property's ability to be used for the purpose it was intended fulfills its utility. Building restrictions and zoning ordinances affect utility.

Size: The use of a property may be determined by the width and depth of the land.

Corner influence: Commercial properties benefit from more exposure, while residential parcels may lose privacy and incur higher maintenance costs from increased frontage.

Shape: Irregular-shaped lots are more difficult and expensive to develop.

Thoroughfare conditions: Width of streets, traffic congestion and condition of pavement affect the value of properties fronting on those streets.

Exposure: The south and west sides of business streets are usually preferred by shopkeepers, because customers will seek the shady side of the street, and window displays will not be damaged by the sun.

Business climate: The presence of shopping areas, offices and medical suites as well as financial, wholesale, industrial and other consumer-friendly businesses is important to establishing value.

Plottage or assemblage: By putting several smaller, less valuable parcels together under one ownership (through plottage or assemblage), rather than being owned by separate people, the value of the parcels will be increased.

Topography and soil: Construction costs will be affected by the terrain and soil condition.

Obsolescence: This may be caused by external or economic changes, and decreases usefulness of property or results in deterioration.

Building restrictions and zones: These may increase or depress values.

PRINCIPLES OF VALUATION

A real estate agent or a professional appraiser must know the following basic principles of valuation before assigning value to any property.

Principle of Conformity

When land uses are compatible and homes are similar in design and size, the maximum value is realized.

Principle of Change

Cities and neighborhoods are always changing, and individual homes within those neighborhoods reflect that change. An appraiser must be aware of trends that affect the value of real estate. Economic, environmental, government and social forces are always dynamic, causing changing values in real property.

Principle of Substitution

The basis of the appraisal process, this principle is the foundation of estimating the value of real property. Explained simply, value is set by the cost of getting an equally desirable substitute. An owner cannot expect to sell for more than someone would ordinarily pay for a similar property, under similar conditions.

Principle of Supply and Demand

Increasing supply or decreasing demand will reduce the price in the market. Reducing supply or increasing demand will raise the price in the market. The less there is of something, the higher the cost; the more there is, the lower the cost.

Principle of Highest and Best Use

This principle is based on the reasonable use of real property, at the time of the appraisal that is most likely to produce the greatest net return to the land and/or the building over a given period of time. Evaluating the highest and best use includes assessing buyers' reasons for buying, the existing use of the property, the permitted use, zoning, benefits of ownership, the market's behavior and community or environmental factors.

Principle of Progression

A lesser valued property will be worth more because of the presence of a greater valued property nearby.

Principle of Regression

A greater valued property will be worth less because of the presence of a lower valued property nearby.

Principle of Contribution

The worth of an improvement is what it adds to the entire property's market value, regardless of the actual cost of the improvement. A remodeled attic may not contribute its entire cost to the value of the property, but a new family room could increase the value of the house by more than the cost to build. This principle must be kept in mind by homeowners who want to change the character of their house in such a way that it no longer fits in the neighborhood. The cost of the improvement may not add to the value if the house is overbuilt for the area.

Principle of Anticipation

Probable future benefits to be derived from a property will increase the value. An appraiser estimates the present worth of future benefits when he or she assigns a value based on anticipated returns.

Principle of Competition

When considerable profits are being made, competition is created. When there is a profitable demand for homes, there will be competition among builders. The supply would then increase in relation to the demand, bringing lower selling prices and unprofitable competition, leading to more decline in supply.

Principle of Balance

When contrasting, opposing or interacting elements are in balance in a neighborhood or area, value is created. A careful mix of varying land use creates value also. Over-improvement or under-improvement will cause imbalance.

Principle of Three-Stage Life Cycle

All neighborhoods change. They start out as young, dynamic areas, and eventually disintegrate in the process of passing years. All property goes through three distinct stages.

Three Stages Of Property Change

(1) Development

(2) Maturity

(3) Old age

Growth and decline is normal in all areas, and many times it can be reversed just as it reaches the last stages. For example, when a lovely neighborhood grows to be old and worn out, young families may choose to move in and completely restore the process of change. They start the life cycle of the neighborhood all over again with development.

THE APPRAISAL PROCESS

At the end of an appraisal, an appraiser must be prepared to answer two questions: What is the highest and best use of the property, and what is this use worth?

Professional appraisers have developed an orderly systematic method— known as the appraisal process—to arrive at an estimate of value. Not every step is used on every property, but—whether you are an appraiser or a real estate agent—there is a check list to help you evaluate the worth of a property in a consistent orderly way.

The Appraisal Process is Made Up of Four Steps

(1) State the problem.

(2) Gather data (general and specific).

(3) Decide on the appraisal method to be used.

(4) Reconcile or correlate the data for final value estimate.

State the Problem

The appraiser must know why the appraisal is necessary. Is it for a sale, a mortgage loan or some other purpose? He or she must identify and describe the property to be evaluated, and indicate the purpose of the appraisal. Then the extent of ownership to be appraised must be identified.

Rights affect value because they set the limits within which the property may be used, and so the appraiser must know how the property is owned in order to determine the value of those rights. Is it a fee simple, are there restrictions on use, or possibly a life estate or co-ownership? The purpose of the appraisal will determine the types of information that will be gathered.

Purposes of an Appraisal

- Market value for a sale
- Value for mortgage loan purposes
- Value for insurance purposes
- Value for condemnation proceedings
- Value for inheritance purposes
- Value for Internal Revenue Service purposes
- Value for property tax purposes

Once the appraiser knows the purpose for the property evaluation, it is possible to move on to the next step.

Gather the Data
A general, preliminary survey of the neighborhood and the site must be made by the appraiser to determine the highest and best use of the property. The type of property will determine the kind of specific data that will be needed. An appraisal of a single-family residence will require information about similar owner-occupied properties, while a residential income (apartment) building will require data on income and expenses of similar properties. So first, general data is gathered, such as information on the region, the city and the neighborhood. Then specific data is gathered on the location, the particular lot and improvements.

Information Gathered for Appraisal

General Data
- Region
- City
- Neighborhood

Specific Data
- Location
- Lot
- Improvements (buildings)

Demand and purchasing power available will affect the value of a property. Data should be obtained on population trends, income level and employment opportunities.

Information Sources

- General data can be obtained from government publications, newspapers and magazines.
- Regional data (metropolitan areas such as the San Francisco Bay Area, Southern California or the Central Coast) can be gathered from monthly bank summaries, regional planning commissions and government agencies.

(continued on next page)

(continued)
Information Sources

- Community data (town or city) can be obtained from the Chamber of Commerce, City Planning Commission, city government agencies, banks and real estate board.
- Neighborhood data can be obtained from personal inspections, real estate agents or area builders. The appraiser notices the age and appearance of the neighborhood; any negative influences such as physical or social hazards (run-down buildings, evidence of criminal activity); evidence of future development; proximity to schools, business, recreation and transportation.

Market data must be collected and analyzed for sales and listing prices of property in the area. Sources for sales information are assessors' records and county recorders' offices, title insurance companies, other property owners in the area, the appraiser's own data base. Age of the buildings and other information regarding improvements can be gathered from the tax assessor's office, city building department or personal inspection of the improvements.

Site Analysis

Appraisers rely on available market information such as listings, offers, leases and sales reports as the foundation of their appraisal methods.

Even though the location of the neighborhood and city must be considered in any analysis of a specific site, or a plot of ground, the exact spot of the site itself is the most important factor in determining value. Since most sites are different sizes and in different locations, some are more desirable than others and should be evaluated separate from the improvements for highest and best use.

Location and Types of Lots

Cul-de-sac

- A cul-de-sac is sometimes known as a dead-end street. It is a street that has only one way in and the same way out. This may be desirable because of the privacy and quiet, but the lot may be oddly pie-shaped if it is on the turn-around section of the street.

(continued on next page)

Location and Types of Lots   *(continued)*

Corner lot
- A corner lot is found at the intersection of two streets. It may be desirable because of its accessibility, but may also be noisy and expensive to maintain because of the increased frontage.

Key lot
- A key lot, so named because it resembles a key fitting into a lock, is surrounded by the back yards of other lots. It is the least desirable because of the lack of privacy.

T-intersection lot
- A t-intersection lot is one that is fronted head-on by a street. The noise and glare from headlights may be detractors from this type of lot.

Interior lot
- An interior lot is one that is surrounded by other lots, with a frontage on the street. It is the most common type lot and may be desirable or not, depending on other factors.

Flag lot
- A flag lot looks like a flag on a pole. The pole represents the access to the site, which is usually located to the rear of another lot fronting a main street.

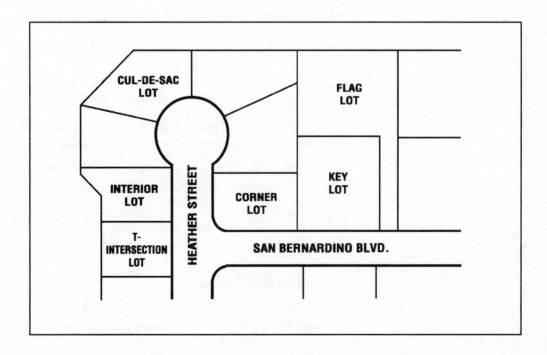

Appraiser Must Evaluate All Legal Data Connected With Site

- Legal description
- Taxes
- Zoning and general plan
- Restrictions and easements
- Determination of other interests in property

Physical Factors of Site for Appraiser to Consider

- Shape of the lot
- Topography and soil conditions
- Corner influence
- Relations of site to surroundings
- Availability of public utilities
- Encroachments
- Landscaping and subsurface land improvements

Buildings and Other Permanent Structures

When an appraiser considers *improvements*, it means looking at any buildings or other permanent structures, such as fences, swimming pools, saunas or built-in Jacuzzis. Real property is divided into land and improvements, as you recall from previous chapters, and each adds its own value to a site. We have discussed the desirable characteristics of land. Now let's look at the improvements—both on-site and off-site.

Improvements

- On-site improvements: structures permanently attached to the land, such as buildings, swimming pools and fences
- Off-site improvements: areas bordering site improved by the addition of street lights, sidewalks, greenbelts and curbs

Construction Basics

It is important for the appraiser to know a few basics of construction in order to evaluate a property. The following are common terms used in building.

1. *Anchor bolt*—Attaches mud sill to foundation; embedded in concrete foundation

2. *Bracing*—Diagonal board nailed across wall framing to prevent sway

3. *Building paper*—Waterproof paper used between sheathing and roof covering

4. *Closed sheathing*—Foundation for exterior siding; boards nailed to studding

5. *Crawlspace*—Area between floor and ground under the house

6. *Cripple*—Stud above or below a window opening or above a doorway

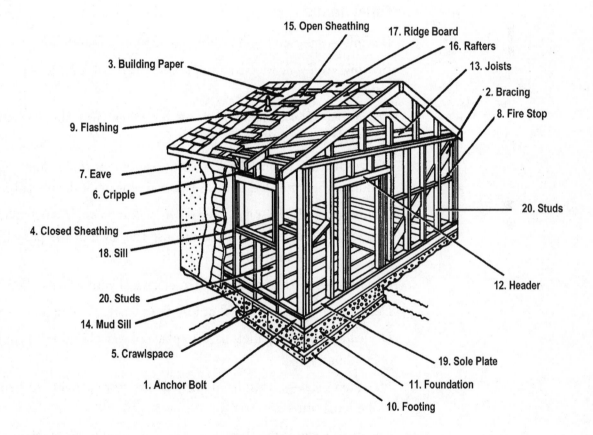

7. *Eaves*—Part of roof that hangs over the exterior walls

8. *Fire stop*—Boards nailed between studs to block the spread of fire in the walls

9. *Flashing*—Sheet metal that keeps the water out

10. *Footing*—Extended part of foundation

11. *Foundation*—Base of house; usually concrete

12. *Header*—The board over a doorway or window opening

13. *Joists*—Boards supporting floors or ceilings (A board supporting them is a girder.)

14. *Mud sill*—Redwood board that is fastened with bolts to the foundation

15. *Open sheathing*—Boards nailed to rafters to form foundation for roof

16. *Rafters*—Slanted boards that support the roof boards and shingles

17. *Ridge board*—Highest part of a frame building

18. *Sill*—Board along the bottom of window or door opening

19. *Sole plate*—Support for studs

20. *Studs*—Vertical 2"x 4" boards in the walls spaced 16" on center

Other Terms

Backfill—Soil used to fill in holes or support a foundation

Bearing wall—A wall that supports a vertical load as well as its own weight

Board foot (144 cubic inches)—A measurement of lumber equal to the volume of a board 12"x12"x1"

BTU (British Thermal Unit)—A measurement that calculates heat; the amount of heat needed to raise 1 pound of water 1 degree Fahrenheit

Compaction—Extra soil matted down or compressed, which may be added to a lot to fill in the low areas or raise the level of the parcel; also used where the soil is unstable

Conduit—A flexible pipe in which electrical wiring is installed

Deciduous—Certain trees that lose their leaves seasonally

Drywall—Gypsum panels used in place of wet plaster to finish the inside of buildings

Elevation sheet—Shows front and side exterior views of finished buildings in the blueprint stage

Energy Efficient Ratio (EER)—A measurement of the efficiency of energy; used to determine the effectiveness of appliances

Hoskold tables—A method used to value an annuity that is based on reinvesting capital immediately; used by appraiser to valuate income property

Insulation—Insulation's resistance to heat is measured by the R factor: When the R value is higher, the insulation is better

Inwood tables—Means by which an income stream can be converted into present value; used by appraisers to valuate income property

Kiosk—A free-standing information booth, such as a flower or newspaper stand

Minimum residential ceiling height—7.5 feet

Normal residential ceiling height—8 feet

Percolating water—Underground water not flowing in a specific channel

Percolation test—A test used by builders to determine the ability of the land to absorb and drain water

Potable—Water that is safe to drink

R-Value—Used to calculate the heat resistance of insulation; the higher the better

Setback—A certain distance a building must be set back from the street; usually determined by local building code

Shopping centers—Neighborhood shopping center (5,000-10,000 population required); Major shopping center or mall (50,000-100,000 population required)

Wainscoting—The bottom portion of a wall that is covered with wood siding; the top part is treated with another material

Water table—The natural level at which water will be found, either above or below the surface of the ground

Water pressure—Can be tested by turning on all faucets and flushing all toilets at the same time

Roof Types

Roof types are determined by the direction, steepness and number of roof planes. (See diagram for illustrations.)

Single Dormers

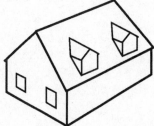

Gambrel

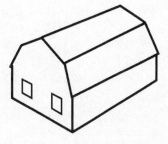

Mansard

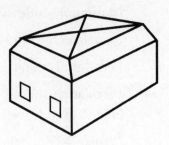

Pyramid

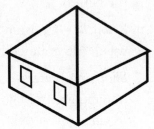

**Dust Pan
or Shed Dormer**

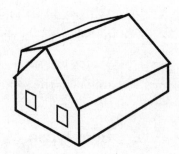

Gable

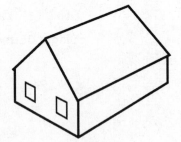

Flat

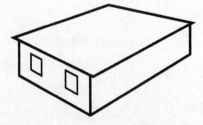

House Styles

Traditional House Styles used in building are interesting for their variety, and important for a real estate agent to know. (See diagram for illustrations.)

(1) Cape Cod

(2) Colonial

(3) Contemporary

(4) English Tudor

(5) Mediterranean

(6) Ranch

(7) Split Level

(8) Townhouse

(9) Victorian

Cape Cod

Colonial

Contemporary

English Tudor

Mediterranean

Ranch

Split Level

Townhouse

Victorian

THREE METHODS OF APPRAISING PROPERTY

There are three main approaches to valuation of real property.

Three Approaches to Appraising Property

Sales (or Market) Comparison Approach

- Recent sales and listings of similar properties in the area are evaluated to form an opinion of value.

Cost Approach

- This approach estimates the value of the land as if vacant, and adds that to the depreciated cost of new improvements to determine an estimate of value for the entire property.

Income Capitalization (or Income) Approach

- The potential net income of the property is considered and then capitalized into value.

Many times an appraiser will use all three methods to arrive at the market value of a property. In most appraisals, all three approaches will have something to add. Each method is used independently to reach an estimated value. Finally, by giving to each separate value a weight that is most compatible to the subject property, the appraiser will arrive at a value for the property. This process is called *reconciliation* or *correlation*.

Sales (or Market) Comparison Approach

This approach is the one most easily and commonly used by real estate agents. It is best for single family homes or condominiums and vacant lots because sales information is readily available and easily compared. Also, the process is relatively simple to learn and use. The market comparison approach uses the principle of substitution to compare similar properties.

As you recall, the principle of substitution says that a buyer will not pay more for a property than the cost of a similar one. The market comparison approach takes the current selling price of a similar property and adjusts it for any differences to arrive at the market value for the subject property.

The appraiser will collect data on comparable (called comps) properties that are as "like-kind" to the property in question as possible, in certain categories.

Like-Kind Comparison

• Neighborhood location

• Size (comparable number of bedrooms/bathrooms as well as square footage)

• Age

• Architectural style

• Financing terms

• General price range

The market comparison approach is based on the idea that property is worth what it will sell for when there is no extra stress, if reasonable time is given to find a buyer. Because of this, the appraiser will research comparable sales to discover any special circumstances influencing those sales. Only those similar properties—sold on the open market, with approval of the seller, offered for a reasonable length of time—will be used for comparables. Also, if possible, only those properties that have sold within the past 6 months are selected. If the comparables are older than that, they are considered less reliable.

Features in either the property or the transaction itself are elements that can cause appraisals to vary.

Elements Causing Estimates of Value to Vary

• Financing terms

• Time of sale

• Sale conditions (arm's length)

• Location

• Physical features

• Income (if any) from the property

Thus, a price is found for each comparable property that should reflect its present value in the current market where the subject property is being sold. Those properties not as comparable are excluded, and greater weight is given to the comparable sales most like the property being appraised.

By using judgment to reconcile the comparables, the appraiser arrives at the final estimate of value for the subject property, using the compatible comparables to arrive at that value.

Advantages of Sales Comparison Approach

- Most easily understood method of valuation and most commonly used by real estate agents
- Easily applied for the sale of single-family homes

Disadvantages of Sales Comparison Approach

- Finding enough recently sold similar properties to get comparable values
- Correctly adjusting amenities to make them comparable to the subject property
- Older sales unreliable with changing economic conditions
- Difficulty in confirming transaction details

The Procedure

(1) Find similar properties, select and verify data.

(2) Select appropriate elements of comparison, adjust sales price of each comparable. (Adjustment is always made to the comparable, not the subject property.)

(3) Adjust sales prices of comparables by *subtracting* the adjustment if the subject property is inferior to the comparable and by *adding* the adjustment if the subject property is superior.

(4) Use the sales comparison approach as the best for single-family homes or condominiums and vacant lots.

Cost Approach

The cost approach looks at the value of the appraised parcel as the combination of two elements: the value of the land as if vacant, and the cost to rebuild the appraised building as new on the date of valuation, less the accrued depreciation.

Formula for Determining Value Based on Cost Approach

Value of the land

+ Cost to build structure new

− Accrued depreciation
_____

Value of property

Using the principle of substitution, a person will not pay more for a substitute if he or she can get the subject property for less. In the cost approach, the substitute is the cost of reconstructing the present building new on vacant land. The cost approach tends to set the upper limit of value for a property; in other words, the most something would cost if it were built new.

The Procedure

(1) Estimate the value of the land as if it were vacant, using comparable land sales. (Principle of Substitution)

(2) Estimate the replacement or reproduction cost of the existing building as of the appraisal date.

(3) Estimate the amount of accrued depreciation to the improvements.

(4) Deduct the amount of the accrued depreciation from the replacement cost (new) to find the estimate of the depreciated value of the improvements.

(5) Add the estimated present depreciated value for the improvements to the value of the land. The result is an estimate of value for the subject property.

The cost approach is used most often for appraising new buildings and special-purpose or unique structures. Depreciation on a new building is relatively easy to determine, whereas the cost approach is impractical with older buildings because of the difficulty in estimating depreciation. The cost approach is also used with buildings where it is difficult to find comparables because they are unique or one-of-a-kind, such as a church, fire station or hospital.

Occasionally, the cost approach is the only one an appraiser can use. If there have been no recent sales (such as during recession or when interest rates are too high), there will be no comparables for the market comparison approach. If the subject is not an income-producing property, the income method (to be discussed next) cannot be used. So the cost method is a reliable way for an appraiser or real estate agent to determine the value of a property when all else fails.

Estimating the Cost of New Buildings

Square-foot method

The square-foot method is the most common, used by appraisers and real estate agents to estimate the cost of construction. The size of the building in question is compared, by square foot, to other buildings with the same area. The building being appraised is compared with the most comparable standard building and its cost per square foot is used for the subject property. This is the fastest way to estimate value using the cost method. Cost services, such as Marshall & Swift, are used extensively by appraisers to calculate the cost to build a property.

Cubic-foot method

This is a lot like the square-foot method, except that it takes height as well as area into consideration. The cubic contents of buildings are compared instead of just the square footage.

Quantity survey method

This method is a detailed estimate of all labor and materials used in the components of a building. Items such as overhead, insurance and contractor's profit are added to direct costs of building. This method is time consuming but very accurate.

Unit-in-place cost method

Cost of units in the building as installed is computed and applied to the structure cost. The total costs of walls in place, heating units and roof are figured on a square-foot basis, including labor, overhead and profit. This is the most detailed method of estimating value.

Depreciation

Depreciation means loss in value from any cause. It is usually measured by estimating the difference between the current cost to replace new and the estimated value of the property as of the date of appraisal.

The opposite of depreciation is *appreciation,* or an increase in value, usually as a result of inflation or some special supply and demand force relating to that specific property. Appreciation may balance the normal decrease of value due to depreciation.

All of the influences that reduce the value of a property below its cost new are included in the definition of depreciation.

Three Main Types of Depreciation

Physical Deterioration

- This type of depreciation can come from wear and tear, negligent care (sometimes called deferred maintenance), damage by dry rot or termites or severe changes in temperature. This may or may not be curable.

Functional Obsolescence

- Poor architectural design and style can contribute to functional obsolescence, as can lack of modern facilities, out-of-date equipment, changes in styles of construction or changes in utility demand. It may or may not be curable.

Economic Obsolescence

- This type of depreciation occurs because of forces outside the property. Changes in the social or economic make-up of the neighborhood, zoning changes, over-supply of homes, under-supply of buyers, recession or legislative restrictions can cause economic obsolescence. It is almost always incurable.

Depreciation for income tax purposes is book depreciation, or a mathematical calculation of steady depreciation or loss, from the owner's original purchase price (cost basis). This allows the owner to recover the cost of investment over the useful life of the building. It is mathematically accrued annually and taken as an income tax deduction from the owner's gross income.

Many times, this deduction makes gross income a negative amount on paper. The building seems to be losing value, giving the owner a "paper loss" that can be offset against other income. This "paper loss," or tax shelter, is why many people invest in income property.

Book value is the current value (for accounting purposes) of a property, calculated as the original cost, plus capital improvements, minus accumulated or accrued depreciation. Remember, this is used as an accounting method, not to be confused with actual depreciation of a building. Depreciation is allowed on buildings only, not on land. The depreciation, for accounting—or tax—purposes, is only a mathematical wasting away of the improvements.

Book Value

The *book value* of a property may be calculated by adding the depreciated value of the improvement (the building) to the assigned value of the land. It is important to remember that book value and book depreciation are used only to figure income tax, and are not particularly relevant to an appraiser.

> Original Cost
> + Improvements
> − Accrued Depreciation
> _____
> Book Value

The book depreciation calculated by an accountant is not the depreciation considered by the appraiser, as we have seen. The appraiser doesn't look at the owner's original cost to purchase, but uses the cost to build new on the date of the appraisal as the basis for evaluation, using the cost method. An appraiser subtracts the estimate of accrued *actual* (not book) depreciation on the building from the cost to build new.

As you recall, in using the cost method, the value of the land and the value of the building (improvements) are determined separately, then added together to calculate the value of the entire property. So, the appraiser figures the actual depreciation on the building and subtracts it from the cost to construct the building new. The next step is to add that amount to the value given the land (using the principle of substitution from other land sales) to estimate the value of the whole parcel. There are several ways to calculate accrued depreciation; however, for our purposes we will only discuss the straight-line (or age-life) method. It is the one most commonly used by real estate agents and appraisers because it is easy to calculate, is used by the Internal Revenue Service and is easily understood by the consumer.

Using the straight-line method to determine accrued depreciation, the appraiser assumes a building will decline in value the same amount each year, until nothing is left. For example, a property with an estimated effective age of 50 years would be said to depreciate at an equal rate of 2% per year (2% x 50 years equals 100% depreciation). In using this method of calculating accrued depreciation, the appraiser probably will not use the actual age of the building, rather the effective age, which is determined by its condition, not the number of years since it was built.

Actual age is the real age of a building. *Effective age* is not determined by the actual age of a building, but by its condition and usefulness. Economic life is the estimated period over which a building may be profitably used. For example, if the subject property was really 25 years old, but was as well maintained and would sell for as much as nearby 20-year-old properties, it would be said to have an effective age of 20 years.

Income Capitalization (or Income) Approach

The income approach estimates the present worth of future benefits from ownership of a property. The value of the property is based on its capacity to continue producing an income. This method is used to estimate the value of income-producing property (rentals), usually in combination with one or both of the other methods. The process of calculating a property's present worth on the basis of its capacity to continue producing an income stream is called *capitalization*. This approach is based mainly on the appraisal principles of comparison, substitution and anticipation.

Using the Income Approach

- The value of the property is based on its capacity to continue producing an income

Capitalization converts the future income stream into an indication of the property's present worth. The appraiser evaluates the expected future income and expenses of a property using the income approach to determine its present value.

**Formula Used by an Appraiser to Estimate
the Value of an Income Property**

•Net Income divided by the capitalization rate (cap rate)
equals the value of the property.

$$\frac{\text{Net Income}}{\text{Capitalization Rate}} = \text{Value of Property}$$

The appraiser must determine how much and how reliable the income is, and how long the income stream will last. There are *five basic steps* to do this.

(1) *Calculate the annual effective gross income.*

The effective gross income is the total annual income from the property minus any vacancy or rental losses. That includes rental income plus any other income generated by the property such as laundry room income or parking fees. Loss of income because of a vacant unit is known as the vacancy factor. Current market rents are used to determine the loss from the vacancy factor. Market rent is the rent the property should bring in the open market, while contract rent is the actual, or contracted, rent being paid by the tenants. The appraiser uses the market rent in his calculations.

Example:

Gross Scheduled Annual Income	$36,000
Annual Vacancy Factor/Rental Loss	−3,600
Effective Gross Income	$32,400

(2) *Determine operating expenses.*

Expenses are generally classified as being either fixed or variable.

Fixed Expenses Include:
•Property Taxes
•Insurance

Variable Expenses Include:
•Maintenance
•Management
•Utilities

(3) *Calculate net operating income.*

> **Example:**
>
> | | |
> |---|---|
> | Taxes | $1,920 |
> | Insurance | 480 |
> | Management | 2,400 |
> | Maintenance | 1,000 |
> | Utilities | 800 |
> | + Reserves (roof, paint, carpets, water heaters, etc.) | 800 |
> | Total Expenses | $7,400 |

(4) *Select a capitalization rate.*

The capitalization rate provides for the return of invested capital plus a return on the investment. The rate is dependent upon the return a buyer will demand before investing money in the property. The greater the risk of recapturing the investment price (making a profit), the higher the cap rate and the lower the price. The lower the risk, the lower the cap rate and the higher the price of the property.

> **About Cap Rates**
>
> - The greater the risk, the higher the cap rate and the lower the price.
> - The lower the risk, the lower the cap rate and the higher the price.

Choosing a capitalization rate is the hardest part for appraisers using the income approach. Generally, a real estate agent will need further study and practice to use this approach to valuation. Capitalization rates are determined by a market analysis of similar income properties and using the same capitalization rate as have those recent sales. The net income is divided by the sales price to determine the cap rate used in each sale. There are other methods of calculating a capitalization rate which may be learned through more study of appraisal.

(5) *Divide the net income by the chosen capitalization rate to determine market value.*

• Net Income divided by Capitalization Rate = Market Value

Example:

Net Operating Income = $25,000

Capitalization Rate = 8%

$$\frac{\$25,000}{.08} = \$312,500$$

Market Value = $312,500

Gross Rent Multiplier

The *gross rent multiplier* is used by real estate agents and appraisers to quickly convert gross rent into market value. It is used for income producing properties and is an easy way to get a rough estimate of the value of rental units.

Gross rent is income (which may be figured annually or monthly) received before any expenses are deducted. A gross rent multiplier, when multiplied by the total annual rents, will give a rough estimate of a property value that can then be compared with other like properties. Generally, gross multipliers will be somewhere between x5 and x10, depending on the market, the condition and the location of the property.

In other words, a property with a gross annual income of $36,000, when multiplied by the current gross multiplier of 10, will be valued roughly at $360,000. So when you hear property values described as 10 times gross, or 5 times gross, or 7 times gross, it means the value is shown by whatever multiplier is used, times the gross income. This is only a quick estimate of value, as you can see, and is not meant to take the place of a professional appraisal.

The reverse process can be used to calculate the gross multiplier, rather than the market value. The reason you might want to do that is to compare properties to see if they are priced right, or are above or below market value. If you know that most rental properties are selling for around 8 times the gross annual multiplier (8 times gross), simply divide the listed price by the gross income to arrive at the multiplier.

Listed Price = $360,000

Gross Annual Income = $36,000

$$\frac{\$36,0000}{\$36,000} = 10 \text{ (the Gross Multiplier is 10)}$$

The gross rent multipliers of several income properties may then be compared, using the market comparison method to estimate their value. A gross rent multiplier can be stated on either an annual or monthly basis.

RECONCILE OR CORRELATE

The final step in an appraisal, then, is to examine the values derived by the various approaches. *Reconciliation* or *correlation* of value occurs when the appraiser decides which of the values is the most appropriate for the subject property, and uses that figure to determine the final estimate for the property in question.

Appraisal Approaches

- Single-family homes: market comparison approach
- New or unusual buildings: cost approach
- Rental properties: income approach

THE APPRAISAL REPORT

Each written appraisal report must be prepared in one of these three formats: Self-Contained Appraisal Report; Summary Appraisal Report; or Restricted Use Appraisal Report.

Three Types of Appraisal Reports

• Self Contained Appraisal Report

• Summary Appraisal Report

• Restricted Use Appraisal Report

When the intended users of the report include parties other than the client, the report must be either a Self-Contained Appraisal Report or a Summary Appraisal Report. When the intended users do not include parties other than the client, the report can be a Restricted Use Appraisal Report. The difference among the options is in the content and level of information provided.

An appraiser must be careful in deciding which type of report to use. Appraisal standards set minimum requirements for the content and level of information in each type of report.

The Self-Contained Appraisal Report includes the indentity of the client and any intended users (by name or type), the intended use of the appraisal, the real estate involved, the real property interest appraised, the purpose of the appraisal, and dates of the appraisal and of the report. It also describes work used to develop the appraisal, the assumptions and limiting conditions, the information that was analyzed, the procedures followed, and the reasoning that supports the conclusions. The report states the current use of the real estate and the use reflected in the appraisal; the support for the appraiser's opinion of the highest and best use; and any departures from the standards. It includes a signed certification.

The Summary Appraisal Report covers the same categories as the Self-Contained Appraisal Report, but where the Self-Contained Appraisal Report includes descriptions, the Summary Appraisal Report contains summaries.

The Restricted Use Appraisal Report covers the came categories as the other two reports with several differences: only the client is named because there are no other users; the use of the report is limited to the client; and the report refers to the appraiser's work file as the source of necessary additional information about the appraisal.

Uniform Residential Appraisal Report   File

The purpose of this summary appraisal report is to provide the lender/client with an accurate, and adequately supported, opinion of the market value of the subject property.

SUBJECT

Property Address	City	State Zip Code
Borrower	Owner of Public Record	County

Legal Description
Assessor's Parcel #   Tax Year   R.E. Taxes $
Neighborhood Name   Map Reference   Census Tract
Occupant ☐ Owner ☐ Tenant ☐ Vacant   Special Assessments $ ☐ PUD HOA $ ☐ per year ☐ per month
Property Rights Appraised ☐ Fee Simple ☐ Leasehold ☐ Other (describe)
Assignment Type ☐ Purchase Transaction ☐ Refinance Transaction ☐ Other (describe)
Lender/Client   Address
Is the subject property currently offered for sale or has it been offered for sale in the twelve months prior to the effective date of this appraisal? ☐ Yes ☐ No
Report data source(s) used, offering price(s), and date(s).

CONTRACT

I ☐ did ☐ did not analyze the contract for sale for the subject purchase transaction. Explain the results of the analysis of the contract for sale or why the analysis was not performed.

Contract Price $ Date of Contract   Is the property seller the owner of public record? ☐ Yes ☐ No Data Source(s)
Is there any financial assistance (loan charges, sale concessions, gift or downpayment assistance, etc.) to be paid by any party on behalf of the borrower? ☐ Yes ☐ No
If Yes, report the total dollar amount and describe the items to be paid.

NEIGHBORHOOD

Note: Race and the racial composition of the neighborhood are not appraisal factors.

Neighborhood Characteristics	One-Unit Housing Trends	One-Unit Housing	Present Land Use %
Location ☐ Urban ☐ Suburban ☐ Rural	Property Values ☐ Increasing ☐ Stable ☐ Declining	PRICE AGE	One-Unit %
Built-Up ☐ Over 75% ☐ 25–75% ☐ Under 25%	Demand/Supply ☐ Shortage ☐ In Balance ☐ Over Supply	$ (000) (yrs)	2-4 Unit %
Growth ☐ Rapid ☐ Stable ☐ Slow	Marketing Time ☐ Under 3 mths ☐ 3–6 mths ☐ Over 6 mths	Low	Multi-Family %
Neighborhood Boundaries		High	Commercial %
		Pred.	Other %

Neighborhood Description

Market Conditions (including support for the above conclusions)

SITE

Dimensions   Area   Shape   View
Specific Zoning Classification   Zoning Description
Zoning Compliance ☐ Legal ☐ Legal Nonconforming (Grandfathered Use) ☐ No Zoning ☐ Illegal (describe)
Is the highest and best use of the subject property as improved (or as proposed per plans and specifications) the present use? ☐ Yes ☐ No If No, describe

Utilities	Public	Other (describe)		Public	Other (describe)	Off-site Improvements—Type	Public	Private
Electricity	☐	☐	Water	☐	☐	Street	☐	☐
Gas	☐	☐	Sanitary Sewer	☐	☐	Alley	☐	☐

FEMA Special Flood Hazard Area ☐ Yes ☐ No FEMA Flood Zone   FEMA Map #   FEMA Map Date
Are the utilities and off-site improvements typical for the market area? ☐ Yes ☐ No If No, describe
Are there any adverse site conditions or external factors (easements, encroachments, environmental conditions, land uses, etc.)? ☐ Yes ☐ No If Yes, describe

IMPROVEMENTS

General Description	Foundation	Exterior Description materials/condition	Interior materials/condition
Units ☐ One ☐ One with Accessory Unit	☐ Concrete Slab ☐ Crawl Space	Foundation Walls	Floors
# of Stories	☐ Full Basement ☐ Partial Basement	Exterior Walls	Walls
Type ☐ Det. ☐ Att. ☐ S-Det./End Unit	Basement Area sq. ft.	Roof Surface	Trim/Finish
☐ Existing ☐ Proposed ☐ Under Const.	Basement Finish %	Gutters & Downspouts	Bath Floor
Design (Style)	☐ Outside Entry/Exit ☐ Sump Pump	Window Type	Bath Wainscot
Year Built	Evidence of ☐ Infestation	Storm Sash/Insulated	Car Storage ☐ None
Effective Age (Yrs)	☐ Dampness ☐ Settlement	Screens	☐ Driveway # of Cars
Attic ☐ None	Heating ☐ FWA ☐ HWBB ☐ Radiant	Amenities ☐ Woodstove(s) #	Driveway Surface
☐ Drop Stair ☐ Stairs	☐ Other Fuel	☐ Fireplace(s) # ☐ Fence	☐ Garage # of Cars
☐ Floor ☐ Scuttle	Cooling ☐ Central Air Conditioning	☐ Patio/Deck ☐ Porch	☐ Carport # of Cars
☐ Finished ☐ Heated	☐ Individual ☐ Other	☐ Pool ☐ Other	☐ Att. ☐ Det. ☐ Built-in

Appliances ☐ Refrigerator ☐ Range/Oven ☐ Dishwasher ☐ Disposal ☐ Microwave ☐ Washer/Dryer ☐ Other (describe)
Finished area **above** grade contains: Rooms   Bedrooms   Bath(s)   Square Feet of Gross Living Area Above Grade
Additional features (special energy efficient items, etc.)

Describe the condition of the property (including needed repairs, deterioration, renovations, remodeling, etc.).

Are there any physical deficiencies or adverse conditions that affect the livability, soundness, or structural integrity of the property? ☐ Yes ☐ No If Yes, describe

Does the property generally conform to the neighborhood (functional utility, style, condition, use, construction, etc.)? ☐ Yes ☐ No If No, describe

(continued on next page)

Uniform Residential Appraisal Report

File #

| There are | comparable properties currently offered for sale in the subject neighborhood ranging in price from $ | to $ |
| There are | comparable sales in the subject neighborhood within the past twelve months ranging in sale price from $ | to $ |

FEATURE	SUBJECT	COMPARABLE SALE # 1	COMPARABLE SALE # 2	COMPARABLE SALE # 3
Address				
Proximity to Subject				
Sale Price	$	$	$	$
Sale Price/Gross Liv. Area	$ sq. ft.	$ sq. ft.	$ sq. ft.	$ sq. ft.
Data Source(s)				
Verification Source(s)				

VALUE ADJUSTMENTS	DESCRIPTION	DESCRIPTION	+(-) $ Adjustment	DESCRIPTION	+(-) $ Adjustment	DESCRIPTION	+(-) $ Adjustment
Sale or Financing Concessions							
Date of Sale/Time							
Location							
Leasehold/Fee Simple							
Site							
View							
Design (Style)							
Quality of Construction							
Actual Age							
Condition							
Above Grade	Total Bdrms. Baths	Total Bdrms. Baths		Total Bdrms. Baths		Total Bdrms. Baths	
Room Count							
Gross Living Area	sq. ft.	sq. ft.		sq. ft.		sq. ft.	
Basement & Finished Rooms Below Grade							
Functional Utility							
Heating/Cooling							
Energy Efficient Items							
Garage/Carport							
Porch/Patio/Deck							
Net Adjustment (Total)		☐ + ☐ -	$	☐ + ☐ -	$	☐ + ☐ -	$
Adjusted Sale Price of Comparables		Net Adj. % Gross Adj. %	$	Net Adj. % Gross Adj. %	$	Net Adj. % Gross Adj. %	$

I ☐ did ☐ did not research the sale or transfer history of the subject property and comparable sales. If not, explain

My research ☐ did ☐ did not reveal any prior sales or transfers of the subject property for the three years prior to the effective date of this appraisal.

Data source(s)

My research ☐ did ☐ did not reveal any prior sales or transfers of the comparable sales for the year prior to the date of sale of the comparable sale.

Data source(s)

Report the results of the research and analysis of the prior sale or transfer history of the subject property and comparable sales (report additional prior sales on page 3).

ITEM	SUBJECT	COMPARABLE SALE # 1	COMPARABLE SALE # 2	COMPARABLE SALE # 3
Date of Prior Sale/Transfer				
Price of Prior Sale/Transfer				
Data Source(s)				
Effective Date of Data Source(s)				

Analysis of prior sale or transfer history of the subject property and comparable sales

Summary of Sales Comparison Approach

Indicated Value by Sales Comparison Approach $

Indicated Value by: Sales Comparison Approach $ Cost Approach (if developed) $ Income Approach (if developed) $

This appraisal is made ☐ "as is", ☐ subject to completion per plans and specifications on the basis of a hypothetical condition that the improvements have been completed, ☐ subject to the following repairs or alterations on the basis of a hypothetical condition that the repairs or alterations have been completed, or ☐ subject to the following required inspection based on the extraordinary assumption that the condition or deficiency does not require alteration or repair:

Based on a complete visual inspection of the interior and exterior areas of the subject property, defined scope of work, statement of assumptions and limiting conditions, and appraiser's certification, my (our) opinion of the market value, as defined, of the real property that is the subject of this report is $, as of   , which is the date of inspection and the effective date of this appraisal.

Vertical labels: SALES COMPARISON APPROACH / RECONCILIATION

(continued on next page)

Uniform Residential Appraisal Report

File #

A D D I T I O N A L   C O M M E N T S

COST APPROACH TO VALUE (not required by Fannie Mae)

Provide adequate information for the lender/client to replicate the below cost figures and calculations.

Support for the opinion of site value (summary of comparable land sales or other methods for estimating site value)

C O S T   A P P R O A C H

ESTIMATED ☐ REPRODUCTION OR ☐ REPLACEMENT COST NEW	OPINION OF SITE VALUE .... = $
Source of cost data	Dwelling Sq. Ft. @ $ .... =$
Quality rating from cost service Effective date of cost data	Sq. Ft. @ $ .... =$
Comments on Cost Approach (gross living area calculations, depreciation, etc.)	
	Garage/Carport Sq. Ft. @ $ .... =$
	Total Estimate of Cost-New .... = $
	Less Physical	Functional	External
	Depreciation =$( )
	Depreciated Cost of Improvements..=$
	"As-is" Value of Site Improvements..=$
Estimated Remaining Economic Life (HUD and VA only) Years	Indicated Value By Cost Approach ....=$

INCOME APPROACH TO VALUE (not required by Fannie Mae)

I N C O M E

Estimated Monthly Market Rent $ X Gross Rent Multiplier   = $ Indicated Value by Income Approach

Summary of Income Approach (including support for market rent and GRM)

PROJECT INFORMATION FOR PUDs (if applicable)

P U D   I N F O R M A T I O N

Is the developer/builder in control of the Homeowners' Association (HOA)? ☐ Yes ☐ No   Unit type(s) ☐ Detached ☐ Attached

Provide the following information for PUDs ONLY if the developer/builder is in control of the HOA and the subject property is an attached dwelling unit.

Legal name of project

Total number of phases   Total number of units   Total number of units sold

Total number of units rented   Total number of units for sale   Data source(s)

Was the project created by the conversion of an existing building(s) into a PUD? ☐ Yes ☐ No   If Yes, date of conversion

Does the project contain any multi-dwelling units? ☐ Yes ☐ No   Data source(s)

Are the units, common elements, and recreation facilities complete? ☐ Yes ☐ No   If No, describe the status of completion.

Are the common elements leased to or by the Homeowners' Association? ☐ Yes ☐ No   If Yes, describe the rental terms and options.

Describe common elements and recreational facilities

APPRAISAL LICENSING STANDARDS

The Appraisal Foundation, a non-profit educational organization, was established in 1987 in response to the crisis in the savings and loan industry in the early 1980s. This crisis confirmed the importance of basing appraisals on established, recognized standards, free from outside pressures.

The Appraiser Qualifications Board was included in the Foundation structure to develop these standards. It created the Uniform Standards of Professional Appraisal Practice (USPAP) and established educational and experience requirements for the licensing of appraisers in all states. USPAP is recognized nationwide as the standard of professional appraisal practice, and all appraisers are required to abide by these standards.

Types of Appraisal Licenses

There are four levels of real estate appraiser licensing

- Trainee License
- Residential License
- Certified Residential License
- Certified General License

Each level requires a specific amount of education and experience, and each licensee must pass a state exam. Trainees must work under the supervision of a licensed appraiser. The type of structures that can be appraised are specified for each level. Continuing education is required to maintain the license. Visit http://www.appraisalfoundation.org for more information.

PROFESSIONAL APPRAISAL ORGANIZATIONS

The major objective of these organizations is to make sure the members of the appraisal profession are knowledgeable and conform to a code of ethics and standards of professional appraisal practice.

The main professional organization is the Appraisal Institute (AI). Members may hold the title of Member Appraisal Institute (MAI), or Senior Residential Appraiser (SRA).

CHAPTER QUIZ

1. The most appropriate use of the income approach is for:

    a. new residences
    b. old residences
    c. rental propery
    d. a church

2. The most thorough and complete appraisal report is:

    a. a short form report
    b. a long form report
    c. a narrative report
    d. an oral report

3. In estimating the value of land, what is the least important element?

    a. size
    b. sales price of comparable land
    c. cost to build on it
    d. price asked

4. Granite Elvis statues on the front of an apartment building are considered a type of:

    a. functional obsolescence
    b. social obsolescence
    c. economic obsolescence
    d. physical deterioration

5. The first thing to do in the appraisal process is:

    a. arrange the data
    b. make beginning appraisal plan
    c. define the appraisal problem
    d. separate the data

6. Which is the least desirable type of lot?

    a. flag lot
    b. corner lot
    c. key lot
    d. cul de sac lot

7. The term "highest and best use" means:

    a. highest net return
    b. greatest population density
    c. highest gross return
    d. highest elevation

8. Which of the following reflects the price paid?

    a. book value
    b. appraised value
    c. accrued value
    d. market value

9. All of the following are elements of value except:

    a. scarcity
    b. demand
    c. utility
    d. plottage

10. Which of the following is needed to use the capitalization approach?

    a. adjusted cost
    b. sales price
    c. net income
    d. gross income

ANSWERS

1. *c*
2. *c*
3. *d*
4. *a*
5. *c*
6. *c*
7. *a*
8. *a*
9. *d*
10. *c*

12

chapter
twelve

Processing the Loan

INTRODUCTION

From the time a hopeful borrower makes the decision to apply for a loan and submits an application, through the time the request is presented to an underwriter who will decide whether or not the package meets required loan standards, certain actions and procedures are necessary before the loan can be funded. The careful, thoughtful, lawful and professional processing of the loan is critical to the success of a mortgage lender as much as it is to the hopeful borrower.

Processing a loan is probably the most time consuming part of the loan procedure and the most important. All important information must be gathered and evaluated to determine whether a loan fits certain guidelines, along with risk analysis to prevent loss to investors. In this chapter we shall see how loan processing is critical to mortgage lending.

OVERVIEW OF THE LOAN PROCESS

In the "olden" days, when someone wanted a home loan they walked downtown to the neighborhood bank or savings and loan. If the bank had extra funds laying around and considered the consumer a good credit risk, it would lend him or her the money from its own funds.

It doesn't generally work like that anymore. Most of the money for home loans comes from three major institutions.

- Fannie Mae
  (FNMA—Federal National Mortgage Association)

- Freddie Mac
  (FHLMC—Federal Home Loan Mortgage Corporation)

- Ginnie Mae
  (GNMA—Government National Mortgage Association)

Today, a consumer talks to several lenders and applies for a loan from one of them. The mortgage lender does all the processing and verifications, and finally the consumer owns the house, with a home loan and mortgage payments to make. The new homeowner might be making payments to the company who originated the loan, or the loan might have been sold to another institution.

The company to which payments are made very rarely owns the loan. They are the *servicer* of the mortgage. They are called the servicer because they are simply *servicing* your loan for the institution that does own it.

What happens behind the scenes is that the loan got packaged into a *pool* with a lot of other loans and sold off to one of the three institutions listed above. The servicer of the loan gets a monthly fee from the investor for processing payments and taking care of your loan. This fee is usually only 3/8ths of a percent or so, but the amount adds up. There are companies that service over billions of dollars of home loans. Three-eighths of a percent on a billion dollars is a tidy amount.

In fact, mortgage servicing is where lenders make the real money. The entire system of originating mortgages, including wholesale lenders, mortgage brokers and mortgage bankers, is designed so that servicers get loans into their portfolio—hopefully at a break-even level—but often at a loss. Mortgage servicing is where they make their profit. Once a loan has been packaged into a pool and sold to Fannie Mae, Freddie Mac, Ginnie Mae or another investor, the lender uses the money from the sale of the loans to make more loans, then package those loans and sell them, so they can get more money to make more loans and so on. This is the cycle that allows institutions to lend consumers money.

THE PROCEDURE

First there is the application form, which asks, among other queries, for detailed information about the borrower, his or her employment record, information regarding and the address of the property desired. The lender will need documentation pertaining to the borrower's personal finances—earnings, monthly expenses and debts—to help gauge the borrower's willingness and ability to repay the mortgage.

Lenders also will examine the borrower's file at the credit bureau to learn if he or she pays bills on time. A lender may reject an application if the report shows that the borrower has a poor credit history. Thus, a borrower may want to make sure his or her credit file is accurate before applying for a mortgage loan. The borrower has a right to know what information is contained in the credit report and to have someone from the credit bureau explain what the report says.

To figure the mortgage payment, the lender will begin by asking for the loan amount. The maximum loan amount will be determined by the value of the property and the borrower's personal financial condition. To estimate the value of the property, the lender will ask a real estate appraiser to give an opinion about its value. The appraiser's opinion can be an important factor in determining whether the borrower qualifies for the size of mortgage he or she wants.

Lenders usually will lend the borrower up to a certain percentage of the appraised value of the property, such as 80 or 90% and will expect a down payment making up the difference. If the appraisal is below the asking price of the home, the down payment the borrower planned to make and the amount the lender is willing to lend may not be enough to cover the purchase price. In that case, the lender may suggest a larger down payment to make up the difference between the price of the house and its appraised value.

Debt-to-Income Ratios

To determine a consumer's maximum mortgage amount, lenders use guidelines called debt-to-income ratios. This is simply the percentage of a consumer's monthly gross income (before taxes) that is used to pay his or her monthly debts. Because there are two calculations, there is a "front" ratio and a "back" ratio and they are generally written in the following format: 33/38.

The front ratio is the percentage of the borrower's monthly gross income (before taxes) that is used to pay housing costs, including principal, interest, taxes, insurance, mortgage insurance (when applicable) and homeowners association fees (when applicable). The back ratio is the same thing, only it also includes the borrower's monthly consumer debt. Consumer debt can be car payments, credit card debt, installment loans, and similar related expenses. Auto or life insurance is not considered a debt.

A common guideline for debt-to-income ratios is 33/38. Borrowers' housing costs consume 33% of their monthly income. Add their monthly consumer debt to the housing costs, and it should take no more than 38% of their monthly income to meet those obligations.

The guidelines are just guidelines and they are flexible. If a borrower makes a small down payment, the guidelines are more rigid. If a borrower has marginal credit, the guidelines are more rigid. If a borrower makes a larger down payment or has sterling credit, the guidelines are less rigid. The guidelines also vary according to loan program. FHA guidelines state that a 29/41 qualifying ratio is acceptable. VA guidelines do not have a front ratio at all, but the guideline for the back ratio is 41.

> *Example:* If a borrower makes $5,000 a month, with 33/38 qualifying ratio guidelines, his or her maximum monthly housing cost should be around $1,650. Including his or her consumer debt, the monthly housing and credit expenditures should be around $1,900 as a maximum.

The borrower must be prepared to provide certain documentation about his or her income (W2s for prior years and year-to-date pay stubs), current debts (account number, outstanding balance, and creditor's address for each), and the purchase contract for the desired property.

If a loan application is turned down, federal law requires the lender to tell the borrower, in writing, the specific reasons for the denial. Factors that may affect the loan decision include the following.

Credit History

Is the lender doubtful—because of the borrower's level of debt or credit history—about the borrower's ability to make the monthly payment?

Appraisal

Is the size of the mortgage required too high, given the property's appraised value? If similar properties in the neighborhood have sold for considerably less than the property in question, the amount of the down payment will have to be increased or the agreed upon purchase price reduced.

LOAN APPLICATION PACKAGE

The loan application package commonly includes:

(1) The loan request—This is the actual application form containing the borrower's name, the amount and terms of the requested loan, the purpose of the loan and how and when it will be repaid.

(2) Borrower information—This helps the lender judge the borrower's ability and willingness to repay the loan.

- Purpose of the loan (sale, refinance).

- Type and duration of employment. If under 2 years of employment at the current site, the lender will require more information about past employment.

- Amounts of other income such as rents, annuities, royalties.

- How many dependents must be supported by the borrower and for how long?

- What are the borrower's living expenses? How much of gross income is available for loan payments, taxes and insurance? What are the borrower's other debt obligations and liabilities?

- What previous experience has the lender had with the borrower?

- What is the applicant's debt repayment record? What kind of credit and other references does the borrower have?

- Type, location, value, encumbrances and repayment obligations for other real property the applicant owns.

- Borrower's other assets such as bank and savings accounts, personal property.

(3) Property information—The property itself is the lender's only security for repayment of the loan if the borrower defaults. The lender's decision about whether or not to fund the loan depends on the value of the property just as much as the ability of the borrower to pay off the loan. Lenders will make a loan up to a certain percentage of the property value and therefore need to know what that value is. This part of the loan application package includes:

- Specific identification of the property, including legal description and common address (street address).

- Title information such as vesting, claims, encumbrances, liens, mortgages.

- Description of the land and type of improvements, including work done within the last 90 days that might be subject to Mechanics' Liens.

- Purchase price and terms such as date purchased, taxes, zoning, assessments. The lender will usually request a copy of the original offer to purchase if the sale is conditional on the funding of the loan.

- If the property is income producing (apartment or commercial buildings), the lender will want information about operating expenses and income for several years as well as how any negative cash flow will be paid.

- Present value, which might be different from the purchase price.

(4) Credit analysis—The lender will judge the ability and willingness of the borrower to repay the loan based on the following.

- An analysis of the information presented in the application and supporting documents.

- Information received by the lender in checking the credit of the prospective borrower.

- Verification of information presented in the application.

(5) Lender's actions—The decision to make the loan rests with a lender's loan committee or a single person whose job it is to approve loan applications based on the borrower's conformity with the lender's guidelines.

(6) Processing check list—The lender will use a check list of steps and documentation necessary to close the loan after approval is given.

STEPS INVOLVED IN GETTING A REAL ESTATE LOAN

Someone has to gather information about a prospective borrower from a loan application, analyze the financial and personal data that's been presented there in hopeful anticipation by the anxious homebuyer, and finally decide whether or not the applicant is a qualified candidate for the loan. After a decision has been made to fund the loan and approval given by the lender's underwriter, the paperwork must be processed and the loan closed.

> **Four Steps in Getting a Real Estate Loan**
>
> (1) Application
>
> (2) Processing
>
> (3) Underwriting (risk analysis)
>
> (4) Closing

Application

In the distant past, when everyone lived within the community where the bank was located and the banker knew everyone in town, all a consumer needed to do to borrow money to purchase real estate was ask the banker. The banker then approved the loan based on a life-long relationship with the borrower and/or the borrower's family. The loan was made and repayment promised with a handshake.

As the level of sophistication, distance and relationship changed between banker and borrower, so did the process for obtaining the loan. Lenders began requiring would-be borrowers to complete a written application, with a written promise to repay the loan.

At first these forms varied from lender to lender. Because there was no standardized form, approval requirements might be different as well. If lenders all asked different questions of potential borrowers, it was reasonable to believe that a borrower might be accepted by one lender and turned down by another, even though the borrower may or may not be qualified for the loan by anyone's standards.

Today, a standard form for residential mortgage loan applications is commonly used: the FHLMC/FNMA 1003 form (Uniform Residential Loan Application). The standardized form makes it possible for lenders to sell their loans on the secondary money market (FNMA, FHLMC, GNMA) because the approval requirements are consistent and conforming. The Departments of Housing and Urban Development (HUD) and Veterans Affairs (VA) also approved the form for use in processing FHA and VA loans in 1992. Nearly all portfolio lenders, or lenders who want to keep their mortgage loans within their own house, have adopted the Uniform Residential Loan Application to make sure the loans conform to the required standards of the secondary market, should they want to sell the loans at a future time.

With the same necessary information supplied by every borrower, the buyers of these loans can presume the borrowers and the loan security are consistently loan worthy and assess the risk based on their analysis of the standardized loan application.

Uniform Residential Loan Application (FHLMC/FNMA 1003)
The commonly used Uniform Residential Loan Application will request the following specific information from the borrower.

Uniform Residential Loan Application

- Type of mortgage and terms of loan
- Property information and purpose of loan
- Borrower information
- Employment verification
- Monthly income and combined housing expense information
- Assets and liabilities
- Details of transaction
- Declaration
- Acknowledgement and agreement
- Information for government monitoring purposes

Type of Mortgage and Terms of Loan: The first section of the loan application is a request for a specific type of mortgage loan by the prospective borrower, listing the amount and terms of the anticipated loan.

Property Information and Purpose of Loan: The second section of the application lists the address and legal description of the desired property, the purpose of the loan, how title will be held and the source of the down payment.

Borrower/Co-Borrower Information: Information about the buyer helps the lender decide whether or not the borrower has the ability and willingness to repay the loan. This section asks for name, social security number, marital status, number of dependents, and address/former addresses.

Employment Verification: Evidence that a borrower *can* pay back the loan is shown by his or her employment. This section asks for the name and address of the borrowers employer, the borrower's position and how long employed.

Monthly Income and Combined Housing Expense Information: This section will inform the lender about the borrower's current and proposed (if the loan gets funded) income and housing expense.

Assets and Liabilities: Assets include checking and savings accounts, stocks and bonds, life insurance, real estate owned, retirement funds, net worth of a business owned, automobiles owned and any other items of value. Liabilities are listed as credit card accounts, pledged assets, alimony or child support owed, job-related expenses and any other amounts that may be owed.

Details of Transaction: A detailed listing of the purchase price, the loan amount, as well as other costs of obtaining the loan are included in this section for the benefit of borrower and lender.

Declaration: This is a list of questions that must be answered by the borrower regarding judgments, bankruptcies, foreclosures, lawsuits or any other voluntary or involuntary legal obligations.

Acknowledgement and Agreement: This is a final declaration by the borrower regarding the statements and information made in the application as well as an acknowledgment of the borrower's awareness of his or her obligation regarding the loan. The borrower and co/borrower must sign and date this section.

Information for Government Monitoring Purposes: This section is optional and may or may not be completed by the borrower. It includes the disclosure that the lender is held liable for complying with state and federal fair housing laws as well as home mortgage disclosure laws.

Uniform Residential Loan Application

This application is designed to be completed by the applicant(s) with the Lender's assistance. Applicants should complete this form as "Borrower" or "Co-Borrower," as applicable. Co-Borrower information must also be provided (and the appropriate box checked) when ☐ the income or assets of a person other than the Borrower (including the Borrower's spouse) will be used as a basis for loan qualification or ☐ the income or assets of the Borrower's spouse or other person who has community property rights pursuant to state law will not be used as a basis for loan qualification, but his or her liabilities must be considered because the spouse or other person has community property rights pursuant to applicable law and Borrower resides in a community property state, the security property is located in a community property state, or the Borrower is relying on other property located in a community property state as a basis for repayment of the loan.

If this is an application for joint credit, Borrower and Co-Borrower each agree that we intend to apply for joint credit (sign below):

_____   _____
Borrower   Co-Borrower

I. TYPE OF MORTGAGE AND TERMS OF LOAN

Mortgage Applied for:	☐ VA ☐ FHA	☐ Conventional ☐ USDA/Rural Housing Service	☐ Other (explain):	Agency Case Number	Lender Case Number
Amount $	Interest Rate %	No. of Months	Amortization Type:	☐ Fixed Rate ☐ GPM	☐ Other (explain): ☐ ARM (type):

II. PROPERTY INFORMATION AND PURPOSE OF LOAN

Subject Property Address (street, city, state & ZIP)					No. of Units
Legal Description of Subject Property (attach description if necessary)					Year Built

Purpose of Loan	☐ Purchase ☐ Refinance	☐ Construction ☐ Construction-Permanent	☐ Other (explain):	Property will be: ☐ Primary Residence ☐ Secondary Residence ☐ Investment

Complete this line if construction or construction-permanent loan.

Year Lot Acquired	Original Cost $	Amount Existing Liens $	(a) Present Value of Lot $	(b) Cost of Improvements $	Total (a + b) $ 0.00

Complete this line if this is a refinance loan.

Year Acquired	Original Cost $	Amount Existing Liens $	Purpose of Refinance	Describe Improvements ☐ made ☐ to be made Cost: $

Title will be held in what Name(s)	Manner in which Title will be held	Estate will be held in: ☐ Fee Simple ☐ Leasehold (show expiration date)
Source of Down Payment, Settlement Charges, and/or Subordinate Financing (explain)		

III. BORROWER INFORMATION

Borrower	Co-Borrower
Borrower's Name (include Jr. or Sr. if applicable)	Co-Borrower's Name (include Jr. or Sr. if applicable)

Social Security Number	Home Phone (incl. area code)	DOB (mm/dd/yyyy)	Yrs. School	Social Security Number	Home Phone (incl. area code)	DOB (mm/dd/yyyy)	Yrs. School

☐ Married ☐ Unmarried (include ☐ Separated single, divorced, widowed)	Dependents (not listed by Co-Borrower) no. ages	☐ Married ☐ Unmarried (include ☐ Separated single, divorced, widowed)	Dependents (not listed by Borrower) no. ages
Present Address (street, city, state, ZIP) ☐ Own ☐ Rent ___ No. Yrs.		Present Address (street, city, state, ZIP) ☐ Own ☐ Rent ___ No. Yrs.	
Mailing Address, if different from Present Address		Mailing Address, if different from Present Address	

If residing at present address for less than two years, complete the following:

Former Address (street, city, state, ZIP) ☐ Own ☐ Rent ___ No. Yrs.	Former Address (street, city, state, ZIP) ☐ Own ☐ Rent ___ No. Yrs.

IV. EMPLOYMENT INFORMATION

Borrower		Co-Borrower	
Name & Address of Employer ☐ Self Employed	Yrs. on this job	Name & Address of Employer ☐ Self Employed	Yrs. on this job
	Yrs. employed in this line of work/profession		Yrs. employed in this line of work/profession
Position/Title/Type of Business	Business Phone (incl. area code)	Position/Title/Type of Business	Business Phone (incl. area code)

If employed in current position for less than two years or if currently employed in more than one position, complete the following:

Freddie Mac Form 65   7/05   Page 1 of 5   Fannie Mae Form 1003   7/05

(continued on next page)

(continued)

Borrower			IV. EMPLOYMENT INFORMATION (cont'd)		Co-Borrower	
Name & Address of Employer	☐ Self Employed	Dates (from – to)	Name & Address of Employer	☐ Self Employed	Dates (from – to)	
		Monthly Income $			Monthly Income $	
Position/Title/Type of Business		Business Phone (incl. area code)	Position/Title/Type of Business		Business Phone (incl. area code)	
Name & Address of Employer	☐ Self Employed	Dates (from – to)	Name & Address of Employer	☐ Self Employed	Dates (from – to)	
		Monthly Income $			Monthly Income $	
Position/Title/Type of Business		Business Phone (incl. area code)	Position/Title/Type of Business		Business Phone (incl. area code)	

V. MONTHLY INCOME AND COMBINED HOUSING EXPENSE INFORMATION

Gross Monthly Income	Borrower	Co-Borrower	Total	Combined Monthly Housing Expense	Present	Proposed
Base Empl. Income*	$	$	$ 0.00	Rent	$	
Overtime			0.00	First Mortgage (P&I)		$
Bonuses			0.00	Other Financing (P&I)		
Commissions			0.00	Hazard Insurance		
Dividends/Interest			0.00	Real Estate Taxes		
Net Rental Income			0.00	Mortgage Insurance		
Other (before completing, see the notice in "describe other income," below)			0.00	Homeowner Assn. Dues		
				Other:		
Total	$ 0.00	$ 0.00	$ 0.00	Total	$ 0.00	$ 0.00

*   Self Employed Borrower(s) may be required to provide additional documentation such as tax returns and financial statements.

Describe Other Income

Notice: Alimony, child support, or separate maintenance income need not be revealed if the Borrower (B) or Co-Borrower (C) does not choose to have it considered for repaying this loan.

B/C		Monthly Amount
		$

VI. ASSETS AND LIABILITIES

This Statement and any applicable supporting schedules may be completed jointly by both married and unmarried Co-Borrowers if their assets and liabilities are sufficiently joined so that the Statement can be meaningfully and fairly presented on a combined basis; otherwise, separate Statements and Schedules are required. If the Co-Borrower section was completed about a non-applicant spouse or other person, this Statement and supporting schedules must be completed about that spouse or other person also.

Completed ☐ Jointly ☐ Not Jointly

ASSETS Description	Cash or Market Value	Liabilities and Pledged Assets. List the creditor's name, address, and account number for all outstanding debts, including automobile loans, revolving charge accounts, real estate loans, alimony, child support, stock pledges, etc. Use continuation sheet, if necessary. Indicate by (*) those liabilities, which will be satisfied upon sale of real estate owned or upon refinancing of the subject property.		
Cash deposit toward purchase held by:	$			
List checking and savings accounts below		**LIABILITIES**	Monthly Payment & Months Left to Pay	Unpaid Balance
Name and address of Bank, S&L, or Credit Union		Name and address of Company	$ Payment/Months	$
Acct. no.	$	Acct. no.		
Name and address of Bank, S&L, or Credit Union		Name and address of Company	$ Payment/Months	$
Acct. no.	$	Acct. no.		
Name and address of Bank, S&L, or Credit Union		Name and address of Company	$ Payment/Months	$
Acct. no.	$	Acct. no.		

Freddie Mac Form 65   7/05   Page 2 of 5   Fannie Mae Form 1003   7/05

(continued on next page)

(continued)

VI. ASSETS AND LIABILITIES (cont'd)			
Name and address of Bank, S&L, or Credit Union	Name and address of Company	$ Payment/Months	$
Acct. no. $	Acct. no.		
Stocks & Bonds (Company name/ number & description) $	Name and address of Company	$ Payment/Months	$
	Acct. no.		
Life insurance net cash value $	Name and address of Company	$ Payment/Months	$
Face amount: $			
Subtotal Liquid Assets $ 0.00			
Real estate owned (enter market value from schedule of real estate owned) $			
Vested interest in retirement fund $			
Net worth of business(es) owned (attach financial statement) $	Acct. no.		
Automobiles owned (make and year) $	Alimony/Child Support/Separate Maintenance Payments Owed to:	$	
Other Assets (itemize) $	Job-Related Expense (child care, union dues, etc.) $		
	Total Monthly Payments	$	
Total Assets a. $ 0.00	Net Worth (a minus b) ▶ $ 0.00	Total Liabilities b. $ 0.00	

Schedule of Real Estate Owned (If additional properties are owned, use continuation sheet.)

Property Address (enter S if sold, PS if pending sale or R if rental being held for income) ▼	Type of Property	Present Market Value	Amount of Mortgages & Liens	Gross Rental Income	Mortgage Payments	Insurance, Maintenance, Taxes & Misc.	Net Rental Income
		$	$	$	$	$	$
Totals		$ 0.00	$ 0.00	$ 0.00	$ 0.00	$ 0.00	$

List any additional names under which credit has previously been received and indicate appropriate creditor name(s) and account number(s):

Alternate Name	Creditor Name	Account Number

VII. DETAILS OF TRANSACTION		VIII. DECLARATIONS				
a.	Purchase price	$	If you answer "Yes" to any questions a through i, please use continuation sheet for explanation.	**Borrower**		**Co-Borrower**
				Yes No		Yes No
b.	Alterations, improvements, repairs		a. Are there any outstanding judgments against you?	☐ ☐		☐ ☐
c.	Land (if acquired separately)		b. Have you been declared bankrupt within the past 7 years?	☐ ☐		☐ ☐
d.	Refinance (incl. debts to be paid off)		c. Have you had property foreclosed upon or given title or deed in lieu thereof in the last 7 years?	☐ ☐		☐ ☐
e.	Estimated prepaid items		d. Are you a party to a lawsuit?	☐ ☐		☐ ☐
f.	Estimated closing costs		e. Have you directly or indirectly been obligated on any loan which resulted in foreclosure, transfer of title in lieu of foreclosure, or judgment?	☐ ☐		☐ ☐
g.	PMI, MIP, Funding Fee		(This would include such loans as home mortgage loans, SBA loans, home improvement loans, educational loans, manufactured (mobile) home loans, any mortgage, financial obligation, bond, or loan guarantee. If "Yes," provide details, including date, name, and address of Lender, FHA or VA case number, if any, and reasons for the action.)			
h.	Discount (if Borrower will pay)					
i.	Total costs (add items a through h)	0.00				

Freddie Mac Form 65   7/05   Page 3 of 5   Fannie Mae Form 1003   7/05

(continued on next page)

(continued)

VII. DETAILS OF TRANSACTION		VIII. DECLARATIONS				

		If you answer "Yes" to any questions a through i, please use continuation sheet for explanation.	Borrower		Co-Borrower	
			Yes	No	Yes	No
j.	Subordinate financing	f. Are you presently delinquent or in default on any Federal debt or any other loan, mortgage, financial obligation, bond, or loan guarantee? If "Yes," give details as described in the preceding question.	☐	☐	☐	☐
k.	Borrower's closing costs paid by Seller	g. Are you obligated to pay alimony, child support, or separate maintenance?	☐	☐	☐	☐
l.	Other Credits (explain)	h. Is any part of the down payment borrowed?	☐	☐	☐	☐
m.	Loan amount (exclude PMI, MIP, Funding Fee financed)	i. Are you a co-maker or endorser on a note?	☐	☐	☐	☐
		j. Are you a U.S. citizen?	☐	☐	☐	☐
n.	PMI, MIP, Funding Fee financed	k. Are you a permanent resident alien?	☐	☐	☐	☐
		l. Do you intend to occupy the property as your primary residence? If "Yes," complete question m below.	☐	☐	☐	☐
o.	Loan amount (add m & n) 0.00	m. Have you had an ownership interest in a property in the last three years?	☐	☐	☐	☐
p.	Cash from/to Borrower (subtract j, k, l & o from i)	(1) What type of property did you own—principal residence (PR), second home (SH), or investment property (IP)?				
		(2) How did you hold title to the home—solely by yourself (S), jointly with your spouse (SP), or jointly with another person (O)?				

IX. ACKNOWLEDGEMENT AND AGREEMENT

Each of the undersigned specifically represents to Lender and to Lender's actual or potential agents, brokers, processors, attorneys, insurers, servicers, successors and assigns and agrees and acknowledges that: (1) the information provided in this application is true and correct as of the date set forth opposite my signature and that any intentional or negligent misrepresentation of this information contained in this application may result in civil liability, including monetary damages, to any person who may suffer any loss due to reliance upon any misrepresentation that I have made on this application, and/or in criminal penalties including, but not limited to, fine or imprisonment or both under the provisions of Title 18, United States Code, Sec. 1001, et seq.; (2) the loan requested pursuant to this application (the "Loan") will be secured by a mortgage or deed of trust on the property described in this application; (3) the property will not be used for any illegal or prohibited purpose or use; (4) all statements made in this application are made for the purpose of obtaining a residential mortgage loan; (5) the property will be occupied as indicated in this application; (6) the Lender, its servicers, successors or assigns may retain the original and/or an electronic record of this application, whether or not the Loan is approved; (7) the Lender and its agents, brokers, insurers, servicers, successors, and assigns may continuously rely on the information contained in the application, and I am obligated to amend and/or supplement the information provided in this application if any of the material facts that I have represented herein should change prior to closing of the Loan; (8) in the event that my payments on the Loan become delinquent, the Lender, its servicers, successors or assigns may, in addition to any other rights and remedies that it may have relating to such delinquency, report my name and account information to one or more consumer reporting agencies; (9) ownership of the Loan and/or administration of the Loan account may be transferred with such notice as may be required by law; (10) neither Lender nor its agents, brokers, insurers, servicers, successors or assigns has made any representation or warranty, express or implied, to me regarding the property or the condition or value of the property; and (11) my transmission of this application as an "electronic record" containing my "electronic signature," as those terms are defined in applicable federal and/or state laws (excluding audio and video recordings), or my facsimile transmission of this application containing a facsimile of my signature, shall be as effective, enforceable and valid as if a paper version of this application were delivered containing my original written signature.

Acknowledgement. Each of the undersigned hereby acknowledges that any owner of the Loan, its servicers, successors and assigns, may verify or reverify any information contained in this application or obtain any information or data relating to the Loan, for any legitimate business purpose through any source, including a source named in this application or a consumer reporting agency.

Borrower's Signature	Date	Co-Borrower's Signature	Date
X		X	

X. INFORMATION FOR GOVERNMENT MONITORING PURPOSES

The following information is requested by the Federal Government for certain types of loans related to a dwelling in order to monitor the lender's compliance with equal credit opportunity, fair housing and home mortgage disclosure laws. You are not required to furnish this information, but are encouraged to do so. The law provides that a lender may not discriminate either on the basis of this information, or on whether you choose to furnish it. If you furnish the information, please provide both ethnicity and race. For race, you may check more than one designation. If you do not furnish ethnicity, race, or sex, under Federal regulations, this lender is required to note the information on the basis of visual observation and surname if you have made this application in person. If you do not wish to furnish the information, please check the box below. (Lender must review the above material to assure that the disclosures satisfy all requirements to which the lender is subject under applicable state law for the particular type of loan applied for.)

BORROWER ☐ I do not wish to furnish this information	**CO-BORROWER** ☐ I do not wish to furnish this information
Ethnicity: ☐ Hispanic or Latino ☐ Not Hispanic or Latino	**Ethnicity:** ☐ Hispanic or Latino ☐ Not Hispanic or Latino
Race: ☐ American Indian or Alaska Native ☐ Asian ☐ Black or African American ☐ Native Hawaiian or Other Pacific Islander ☐ White	**Race:** ☐ American Indian or Alaska Native ☐ Asian ☐ Black or African American ☐ Native Hawaiian or Other Pacific Islander ☐ White
Sex: ☐ Female ☐ Male	**Sex:** ☐ Female ☐ Male

To be Completed by Interviewer This application was taken by: ☐ Face-to-face interview ☐ Mail ☐ Telephone ☐ Internet	Interviewer's Name (print or type)	Name and Address of Interviewer's Employer
	Interviewer's Signature Date	
	Interviewer's Phone Number (incl. area code)	

REQUIRED DISCLOSURES UPON APPLICATION FOR A LOAN (RESPA)

The *Real Estate Settlement Procedures Act (RESPA)* is a consumer protection statute, first passed in 1974. The purposes of RESPA are:

- To help consumers become better shoppers for settlement services

- To eliminate kickbacks and referral fees that unnecessarily increase the costs of certain settlement services

Special Information Booklet

Under RESPA, when borrowers apply for a mortgage loan, mortgage brokers and/or lenders must give the borrowers a *Special Information Booklet*, which contains consumer information regarding various real estate settlement services (required for purchase transactions only).

Part One of this booklet describes the settlement process and nature of charges and suggests questions borrowers might ask of lenders, attorneys and others to clarify what services they will provide for the charges quoted. It also contains information on borrower's rights and remedies available under RESPA, and alerts borrowers to unfair or illegal practices.

Part Two of the booklet is an item-by-item explanation of settlement services and costs, with sample forms and worksheets that will help the borrower in making cost comparisons.

Part I

- What Happens and When
- Shopping for Services
- Role of the Broker
- Negotiating a Sales Contract
- Selecting an Attorney
- Selecting a Lender
- Selecting a Settlement Agent
- Securing Title Services

(continued on next page)

Part I   *(continued)*

- Home Buyers' Right
- Special Information Booklet
- Good Faith Estimate
- Lender Designation of Settlement Service Providers
- Disclosure of Settlement Costs One Day Before Closing and Delivery
- Escrow Closing
- Truth in Lending
- Protection Against Unfair Practices
- Kickbacks
- Title Companies
- Fair Credit Reporting
- Equal Credit Opportunity
- The Right to File Complaints
- Home Buyer's Obligation (Repayment of Loan and Maintenance of Home)

Part II

- Specific Settlement Services
- HUD-1 Settlement Statement
- Settlement Costs Worksheet
- Comparing Lender Costs
- Calculating the Borrower's Transaction
- Reserve Accounts

Good Faith Estimate (GFE)

Borrowers must be given a *Good Faith Estimate* (GFE) of settlement costs within three days of submitting a loan application. This is only an estimate and the actual charges may differ. A Good Faith Estimate is a document that tells borrowers the approximate costs they will pay at or before settlement or closing, based on common practice in the locality.

An accurate CCU Good Faith Estimate of closing costs is essential for borrowers to make an informed decision. The purpose of the good faith estimate is exactly what it says—to provide the borrower with the information needed to shop for a loan effectively.

Mortgage Loan Disclosure Statement/Good Faith Estimate

Borrower's Name(s): _____

Real Property Collateral: The intended security for this proposed loan will be a Deed of Trust on (street address or legal description):

_____

This joint Mortgage Loan Disclosure Statement/Good Faith Estimate is being provided by:

_____

a real estate broker acting as a mortgage broker, pursuant to the Federal Real Estate Settlement Procedures Act (RESPA) and similar state law. In a transaction subject to RESPA, a lender will provide you with an additional Good Faith Estimate within three business days of the receipt of your loan application. You will also be informed of material changes before settlement/close of escrow. The name of the intended lender to whom your loan application will be delivered is:

☐ Unknown   ☐ _____ (Name of lender, if known)

GOOD FAITH ESTIMATE OF CLOSING COSTS

The information provided below reflects estimates of the charges you are likely to incur at the settlement of your loan. The fees, commissions, costs and expenses listed are estimates; the actual charges may be more or less. Your transaction may not involve a charge for every item listed and any additional items charged will be listed. The numbers listed beside the estimate generally correspond to the numbered lines contained in the HUD-1 Settlement Statement which you will receive at settlement if this transaction is subject to RESPA. The HUD-1 Settlement Statement contains the actual costs for the items paid at settlement. When this transaction is subject to RESPA, by signing page two of this form you are also acknowledging receipt of the HUD Guide to Settlement Costs.

HUD-1	ITEM	Paid to Others	Paid to Broker
800	**Items Payable in Connection with Loan**		
801	Lender's Loan Origination Fee	$ _____	$ _____
802	Lender's Loan Discount Fee	$ _____	$ _____
803	Appraisal Fee	$ _____	$ _____
804	Credit Report	$ _____	$ _____
805	Lender's Inspection Fee	$ _____	$ _____
808	Mortgage Broker Commission/Fee	$ _____	$ _____
809	Tax Service Fee	$ _____	$ _____
810	Processing Fee	$ _____	$ _____
811	Underwriting Fee	$ _____	$ _____
812	Wire Transfer Fee	$ _____	$ _____
		$ _____	$ _____
_____	_____	$ _____	$ _____
900	**Items Required by Lender to be Paid in Advance**		
901	Interest for _____ days at $ _____ per day	$ _____	$ _____
902	Mortgage Insurance Premiums	$ _____	$ _____
903	Hazard Insurance Premiums	$ _____	$ _____
904	County Property Taxes	$ _____	$ _____
905	VA Funding Fee	$ _____	$ _____
		$ _____	$ _____
_____	_____	$ _____	$ _____
1000	**Reserves Deposited with Lender**		
1001	Hazard Insurance: _____ mos at $ _____ /mo.	$ _____	$ _____
1002	Mortgage Insurance: _____ mos at $ _____ /mo.	$ _____	$ _____
1004	Co. Property Taxes: _____ mos at $ _____ /mo.	$ _____	$ _____
1008	Aggregate Escrow Adjustment	$ _____	$ _____
		$ _____	$ _____
_____	_____	$ _____	$ _____
1100	**Title Charges**		
1101	Settlement or Closing/Escrow Fee	$ _____	$ _____
1105	Document Preparation Fee	$ _____	$ _____
1106	Notary Fee	$ _____	$ _____
1108	Title Insurance	$ _____	$ _____
		$ _____	$ _____
_____	_____		
1200	**Government Recording and Transfer Charges**		
1201	Recording Fees	$ _____	$ _____
1202	City/County Tax/Stamps	$ _____	$ _____
		$ _____	$ _____
1300	**Additional Settlement Charges**		
1302	Pest Inspection	$ _____	$ _____
_____	_____	$ _____	$ _____
		$ _____	$ _____
		$ _____	$ _____

Subtotals of Initial Fees, Commissions, Costs and Expenses $ _____ $ _____

Total of Initial Fees, Commissions, Costs and Expenses $ _____

Compensation to Broker (Not Paid Out of Loan Proceeds):

Mortgage Broker Commission/Fee $ _____

Any Additional Compensation from Lender   ☐ No ☐ Yes $ _____ (if known)

(continued on next page)

(continued)

Additional Required Disclosures

I. Proposed Loan Amount: $ _____

    Initial Commissions, Fees, Costs and
    Expenses Summarized on Page 1: $ _____

    Payment of Other Obligations (List):
      Credit Life and/or Disability Insurance (see VI below) $ _____

    _____ $ _____

    _____ $ _____

Subtotal of All Deductions: $ _____

Estimated Cash at Closing ☐ **To You** ☐ **That you must pay** $ _____

II. Proposed Interest Rate: _____ %   ☐ Fixed Rate   ☐ Initial Variable Rate

III. Proposed Loan Term: _____   ☐ Years   ☐ Months

IV. Proposed Loan Payments: Payments of $ _____ will be made ☐ Monthly ☐ Quarterly ☐ Annually for _____ (number of months, quarters or years). If proposed loan is a variable interest rate loan, this payment will vary (see loan documents for details).

    The loan is subject to a balloon payment: ☐ No ☐ Yes. If Yes, the following paragraph applies and a final balloon payment of $ _____ will be due on _____ [estimated date (month/day/year)].

    Notice to Borrower: IF YOU DO NOT HAVE THE FUNDS TO PAY THE BALLOON PAYMENT WHEN IT COMES DUE, YOU MAY HAVE TO OBTAIN A NEW LOAN AGAINST YOUR PROPERTY TO MAKE THE BALLOON PAYMENT. IN THAT CASE, YOU MAY AGAIN HAVE TO PAY COMMISSIONS, FEES, AND EXPENSES FOR THE ARRANGING OF THE NEW LOAN. IN ADDITION, IF YOU ARE UNABLE TO MAKE THE MONTHLY PAYMENTS OR THE BALLOON PAYMENT, YOU MAY LOSE THE PROPERTY AND ALL OF YOUR EQUITY THROUGH FORECLOSURE. KEEP THIS IN MIND IN DECIDING UPON THE AMOUNT AND TERMS OF THIS LOAN.

V. Prepayments: The proposed loan has the following prepayment provisions.

    ☐ No prepayment penalty.

    ☐ Other (see loan documents for details).

    ☐ Any payment of principal in any calendar year in excess of 20% of the ☐ original balance ☐ unpaid balance will include a penalty not to exceed _____ months advance interest at the note rate, but not more than the interest that would be charged if the loan were paid to maturity (see loan documents for details).

VI. Credit Life and/or Disability Insurance: The purchase of credit life and/or disability insurance by a borrower is NOT required as a condition of making this proposed loan.

VII. Other Liens: Are there liens currently on this property for which the borrower is obligated? ☐ No ☐ Yes
If Yes, describe below:

Lienholder's Name	Amount Owing	Priority
_____	_____	_____
_____	_____	_____

Liens that will remain or are anticipated on this property after the proposed loan for which you are applying is made or arranged (including the proposed loan for which you are applying):

Lienholder's Name	Amount Owing	Priority
_____	_____	_____
_____	_____	_____

NOTICE TO BORROWER: Be sure that you state the amount of all liens as accurately as possible. If you contract with the broker to arrange this loan, but it cannot be arranged because you did not state these liens correctly, you may be liable to pay commissions, costs, fees, and expenses even though you do not obtain the loan.

Name of Broker	License #	Broker's Representative	License #

Broker's Address _____

Signature of Broker	Date	OR	Signature of Representative	Date

VIII. NOTICE TO BORROWER: THIS IS NOT A LOAN COMMITMENT. Do not sign this statement until you have read and understood all of the information in it. All parts of this form must be completed before you sign. Borrower hereby acknowledges the receipt of a copy of this statement.

Borrower	Date	Borrower	Date

Mortgage Servicing Disclosure Statement

A *Mortgage Servicing Disclosure Statement*, which discloses to the borrower whether the lender intends to service the loan or transfer it to another lender. It also provides information about complaint resolution.

FICTITIOUS CREDIT CORPORATION
LOAN SERVICING DISCLOSURE STATEMENT

NOTICE TO FIRST LIEN MORTGAGE LOAN APPLICANTS: THE RIGHT TO COLLECT YOUR MORTGAGE LOAN PAYMENTS MAY BE TRANSFERRED.   FEDERAL LAW GIVES YOU CERTAIN RELATED RIGHTS. IF YOUR LOAN IS MADE, SAVE THIS STATEMENT WITH YOUR LOAN DOCUMENTS.   SIGN THE ACKNOWLEDGMENT AT THE END OF THIS STATEMENT ONLY IF YOU UNDERSTAND ITS CONTENTS.

Because you are applying for a mortgage loan covered by the Real Estate Settlement Procedures Act (RESPA) (12 U.S.C. § 2601 et seq.) you have certain rights under federal law. This statement tells you what the chances are that the servicing for this loan may be transferred to a different loan servicer. "Servicing" refers to collecting your principal, interest and escrow account payments, if any. If your loan servicer changes, there are certain procedures that must be followed. This statement generally explains those procedures.

Transfer Practices and Requirements

If the servicing of your loan is assigned, sold or transferred to a new servicer, you must be given written notice of that transfer. The present loan servicer must send you notice in writing of the assignment, sale or transfer of the servicing not less than 15 days before the effective date of the transfer. The new loan servicer must also send you notice within 15 days after the effective date of the transfer. The present servicer and the new servicer may combine this information in one notice, so long as the notice is sent to you 15 days before the effective date of transfer. The 15-day period is not applicable if a notice of prospective transfer is provided to you at settlement. The law allows a delay in the time (not more than 30 days after a transfer) for servicers to notify you, upon the occurrence of certain business emergencies.

Notices must contain certain information. They must contain the effective date of the transfer of the servicing of your loan to the new servicer, the name, address and toll-free or collect-call telephone number of the new servicer, and toll-free or collect-call telephone numbers of a person or department for both your present servicer and your new servicer to answer your questions. During the 60-day period following the effective date of the transfer of the loan servicing, a loan payment received by your old servicer before its due date may not be treated by the new loan servicer as late, and a late fee may not be imposed on you.

Complaint Resolution

Section 6 of RESPA (12 U.S.C. § 2605) gives you certain consumer rights, *whether or not your loan servicing is transferred*. If you send a "qualified written request" to your servicer, your servicer must provide you with a written acknowledgment within 20 Business Days of receipt of your request. A "qualified written request" is a written correspondence, other than notice on a payment coupon or other payment medium supplied by the servicer, which includes your name and account number and the information regarding your request. Not later than 60 Business Days after receiving your request, your servicer must make any appropriate corrections to your account, or must provide you with a written clarification regarding any dispute. During this 60-Business Day period, your servicer may not provide information to a consumer reporting agency concerning any overdue payment related to such period or qualified written request.

(continued on next page)

(continued)

A Business Day is any day in which the offices of the business entity are open to the public for carrying on substantially all of its business functions.

Damages and Costs

Section 6 of RESPA also provides for damages and costs for individuals or classes of individuals in circumstances where servicers are shown to have violated the requirements of that section.

Servicing Transfer Estimates

1. The following is the best estimate of what will happen to the servicing of your mortgage loan.

    We assign, sell or transfer servicing of some of our loans while the loan is outstanding depending on the length of loan and other factors. For the program you have applied for, we expect to sell all of the mortgage servicing.

2. For all the first lien mortgage loans that we make in the next twelve month period, we estimate the percentage of such loans for which we will transfer servicing is:

    76% - 100%

    This is only the best estimate and it is not binding. Business conditions or other circumstances may affect future transferring decisions.

3. This is our record of transferring the servicing of the first mortgage loans made in the past.

    1997   0%
    1998   0%
    1999   0%

Acknowledgment of Mortgage Loan Applicant

I/We have read this disclosure form which was received with the application package and understand its contents, as evidenced by my/our signature(s) below. I/We understand that this acknowledgment is a required part of the mortgage application.

_____
Applicant's Signature

_____
Date

_____
Co-Applicant's Signature

_____
Date

Note: This document must be signed and dated by all applicants and returned with your completed application in the postage-paid envelope provided. Please retain a copy for your records.

If the borrowers don't get these documents at the time of application, the lender must mail them within three business days of receiving the loan application. If the lender turns down the loan within three days, however, then RESPA does not require the lender to provide these documents.

The RESPA statute does not provide an explicit penalty for the failure to provide the Special Information Booklet, Good Faith Estimate or Mortgage Servicing Statement. However, bank regulators may choose to impose penalties on lenders who fail to comply with federal law.

RESPA protects borrowers who apply for most residential mortgage loans used to finance the purchase of one- to four-family properties, such as a house, a condominium or cooperative apartment unit, a lot with a manufactured home, or a lot on which a house will be built or a manufactured home be placed immediately following settlement. RESPA does not apply to loans to refinance homes. RESPA is not designed to set the prices of settlement services. Instead, it provides borrowers with information to take the mystery out of the settlement process, so that borrowers can shop for settlement services and make informed decisions.

Under RESPA, Upon Loan Application, Borrowers Must Be Given:

- A Special Information Booklet
  (purchase loan only)

- A Good Faith Estimate

- A Mortgage Servicing Disclosure Statement

Affiliated Business Arrangement (AfBA) Disclosure

An *Affiliated Business Arrangement (AfBA) Disclosure* is required whenever a settlement service provider involved in a RESPA covered transaction refers the consumer to a provider with whom the referring party has an ownership or other beneficial interest.

AFFILIATED BUSINESS ARRANGEMENT
DISCLOSURE STATEMENT

To: _____   Property:_____

                                             _____

From: John Doe Properties of Northeast   Date:_____
        Florida, Inc.

In connection with the transfer of this property, you may need to obtain title insurance and closing services. We recommend XIX Title, LLC ("XIX"), located at 0000 Somewhere St. East, Suite 000, Good Town, FL 00000, telephone number (000) 555-0000. XIX provides efficient and professional services at competitive rates. Please note that the owner of John Doe Properties of Northeast Florida, Inc. ("John Doe Properties") has a beneficial interest in XIX. Because of this relationship, this referral may provide the owner of John Doe Properties a financial or other benefit.

Set forth below is the estimated charge or range of charges by XIX for services listed. You are NOT required to use XIX for title insurance. **THERE ARE FREQUENTLY OTHER SETTLEMENT SERVICE PROVIDERS AVAILABLE WITH SIMILAR SERVICES. YOU ARE FREE TO SHOP AROUND TO DETERMINE THAT YOU ARE RECEIVING THE BEST SERVICES AND THE BEST RATE FOR THESE SERVICES.**

<u>XIX Settlement Services</u>   <u>Charge or Range of Charges</u>

Title Examination Fee $175.00
Closing/Settlement Fee $175.00
Mortgage Closing Fee $100.00
Title Insurance Premiums   **As per State of Florida Promulgated Rates:**
                                            Based upon the purchase price or mortgage amount,
                                            whichever is greater.

	Per Thousand
From $0 to $100,000 of coverage written	$5.75
From $100,000 to $1 million, add	$5.00
<u>Over $1 million and up to $5 million, add</u>	$2.50
<u>Over $5 million and up to $10 million, add</u>	$2.25
Over $10 million, add	$2.00

Plus $25 per each required endorsement, except 10% of risk rate for Florida Form 9 or Navigational Servitude Endorsements.

ACKNOWLEDGEMENT

I/we have read this disclosure form, received a signed duplicate, and understand that John Doe Properties of Northeast Florida, Inc. is referring me/us to purchase the above-described settlement service and that its owner may receive a financial or other benefit as the result of these referrals.

_____   _____
                Date   Date

The referring party must give the AfBA disclosure to the consumer at or prior to the time of referral. The disclosure must describe the business arrangement that exists between the two providers and give the borrower an estimate of the second provider's charges.

Except in cases where a lender refers a borrower to an attorney, credit reporting agency or real estate appraiser to represent the lender's interest in the transaction, the referring party may not require the consumer to use the particular provider being referred.

Required Disclosures Upon Application for a Loan—Truth in Lending Act

The Truth in Lending Act (TILA), Title I of the Consumer Credit Protection Act (implemented by Regulation Z), is aimed at promoting the informed use of consumer credit by requiring disclosures about its terms and costs.

TILA requires lenders to make certain disclosures on loans subject to the Real Estate Settlement Procedures Act (RESPA) within three business days after their receipt of a written application. This early disclosure statement is partially based on the initial information provided by the consumer. A final disclosure statement is provided at the time of loan closing. The disclosure is required to be in a specific format and include the following information.

Truth in Lending Disclosure Requirements

- Name and address of creditor
- Amount financed
- Itemization of amount financed (optional, if Good Faith Estimate is provided)
- Finance charge
- Annual percentage rate (APR)
- Variable rate information
- Payment schedule
- Total of payments
- Demand feature
- Total sales price
- Prepayment policy
- Late payment policy
- Security interest
- Insurance requirements
- Certain security interest charges
- Contract reference
- Assumption policy
- Required deposit information

TRUTH-IN-LENDING DISCLOSURE STATEMENT

Creditor: Wonderful Bank of California, National Association   **Date of Transaction:** November 15, 20XX
Borrower(s) Name: and
Borrower(s) Address:

ANNUAL PERCENTAGE RATE	FINANCE CHARGE	AMOUNT FINANCED	TOTAL OF PAYMENTS
The cost of your credit as a yearly rate	The dollar amount the credit will cost you	The amount of credit provided to you or on your behalf	The amount you will have paid after you have made all payments as scheduled
6.25%	$424,605.55	$348,677.00	$773,282.55

YOUR PAYMENT SCHEDULE WILL BE:

Number of Payments	Amount of Payments	When Payments Are Due
1	$2,811.11	Monthly beginning 01/01/20XX
359	$2,146.16	Monthly beginning 02/01/20XX and continuing on the 1st of each month thereafter until 12/01/20XX

Home Improvement Construction Loan: [ ] If checked this provides for the payment of interest only during the construction period. Beginning _____, _____ you will make monthly payments of interest only during the construction period, followed by payments of principal and interest as scheduled above.

Variable Rate: [ ] If checked, this loan contains a variable rate feature. Disclosures about the variable rate feature have been provided to you earlier.

Security: You are giving a security interest in:
[ ] The goods or property being purchased;
[X] Real Estate;
[ ] Other (please specify type) _____

Security Interest Fees: $ _____

Late Charge: If a payment is late, you will be charged 4% of the payment.

Prepayment: If you pay your loan off early, you may have to pay a prepayment penalty.

Assumption: If this loan is made to purchase your principal dwelling, someone buying your house [ ] may, subject to conditions be allowed to assume the remainder of the mortgage or real property loan on the original terms.

See your contract documents for any additional information about nonpayment, default, any required repayment in full before the scheduled date, and assumption policy.

'e' means estimate

NOTICE TO THE BORROWER

YOU MAY BE REQUIRED TO PURCHASE PROPERTY INSURANCE AS A CONDITION OF RECEIVING THE LOAN. IF PROPERTY INSURANCE IS REQUIRED, YOU MAY SECURE INSURANCE FROM A COMPANY OR AGENT OF YOUR CHOOSING.

ACKNOWLEDGEMENT

By signing below, you acknowledge that you have received a completed copy of this Federal Truth-In-Lending Disclosure statement prior to the execution of any closing documents.

_____   November 15, 20XX   _____[SEAL]
Witness

                                               _____[SEAL]

                                               _____[SEAL]

_____   November 15, 20XX   _____[SEAL]
Witness

                                               _____[SEAL]

(continued on next page)

(continued)

ANSWERS TO FREQUENTLY ASKED
TRUTH-IN-LENDING QUESTIONS

Q.   What is a Truth-In-Lending Disclosure and why did I receive it?
A.   The Truth-In-Lending Disclosure (T-I-L) is designed to give you information about the costs of your loan so you may compare these costs with those of other loan programs. Federal law requires this disclosure statement.

ANNUAL PERCENTAGE RATE The cost of your credit as a yearly rate. A	FINANCE CHARGE The dollar amount the credit will cost you. B	Amount Financed The amount of credit provided to you or on your behalf. C	Total of Payments The amount you will have paid after you have made all payments as scheduled D

Q.   What is the Annual Percentage Rate? (Box "A" above)
A.   The Annual Percentage Rate (APR) is the cost of your credit expressed as a yearly rate. For many loans, the APR may be different than the loan interest rate. It is common for the APR to be higher than the interest rate because you may be paying "prepaid" Finance Charges at or before closing. Prepaid Finance Charges are Finance Charges, other than interest, that are paid outside of closing (POC), at closing, or are withheld from the loan proceeds. Examples of Prepaid Finance Charges include, but are not limited to, the origination fee, application fee, broker fee, and discount points.

Q.   What is the Finance Charge? (Box "B" above)
A.   The Finance Charge is the amount you will pay back to Wonderful Bank of California, National Association over the life of the loan in addition to the principal amount you borrowed. The Finance Charge includes such items as interest accruing on the outstanding principal balance plus any prepaid Finance Charge. The figure in block B is calculated based on the assumption that your loan will not be paid off early.

Q.   What is the Amount Financed? (Box "C" above)
A.   TIL requires a lender to disclose the Amount Financed as the loan amount minus any prepaid Finance Charges. Because of this requirement, if your loan has prepaid Finance Charges, the Amount Financed will be less than the actual loan amount. For example, if you applied for a $50,000 loan and have a $2,000 prepaid Finance Charge, the Note amount would be $50,000, the Amount Financed would be disclosed as $48,000.

Q.   What is the Total of Payments? (Box "D" above)
A.   This figure represents the total amount you should pay if you make the required payment for the entire term of the loan. This payment includes principal and interest. It does not however, include payments for real estate taxes, property insurance premiums, or any late charge that may be incurred. The total of payments block assumes the same number of days between each payment.

Q.   Does the schedule of payments shown represent the amounts I will pay each month?
A.   The monthly payments include principal and interest. The payments, as disclosed, do not include any escrow requirement for taxes or property insurance premiums, or any late charge that may be assessed.

If your loan is an Adjustable Rate Mortgage (ARM), payments are based on the "formula rate" (i.e., index plus margin). This disclosure is based on the current formula rate, and does not predict future changes in the payments due to an increase in your interest rate.

**If you have questions concerning your Truth-In-Lending Disclosure,
please contact your Loan Processor at (888) 555-5555.**

NOTE: These brief explanations are intended to assist you in understanding the Truth-In-Lending Disclosure Statement. They are not complete and do not include all possible situations. These explanations should not be considered legal advice.

Annual Percentage Rate (APR)

In comparing any type of loan, whether it be a fixed rate loan to a fixed rate loan, adjustable rate loan to adjustable rate loan or fixed rate loan to adjustable rate loan, there is one way that can be used to compare apples to apples and even apples to oranges.

Annual Percentage Rates (APRs) are designed to do just that. APRs are a way to calculate the annual cost of loans, taking into consideration loan origination fees (points) and the other costs associated with securing a loan. The additional costs include appraisal and credit report fees as well as processing and document fees.

One confusing aspect of APRs is that the APR on 15 year loans will carry a higher relative rate due to the fact that the points are amortized over the 15 year term rather than the 30 year term. When a Regulation Z disclosure (Reg Z, the mortgage companies disclosure of cost for the loan) is prepared for a buyer/borrower the prepaid interest is also included in the APR calculation. For our illustrations we will use only the points, appraisal, credit report, processing and document fees.

As a means of protecting consumers from companies who did not disclose the fees associated with a particularly low start rate on an adjustable rate loan or below market rate on a fixed rate loan, APRs give consumers a way to check the true cost of a loan.

One common situation that occurs when a borrower receives a Reg Z, and a copy of their note, is the column that indicates the amount financed is less than the loan amount the borrower is actually financing. It is here that many borrowers leap before they look and call to find out why they are only receiving a $146,925 loan when they applied for a $150,000 loan. It is here that APRs enter the picture.

Let's look at how APRs are calculated. For our illustration we will assume a 8.50% fixed rate interest. For a 30 year loan the monthly payments for a $150,000 loan are $1,153.37.

In order to calculate the APR for this loan we subtract $2,250.00 (1.50 points), $275.00 appraisal fee, $50.00 credit report fee, $500.00 processing, document and other fees ($150,000−$3,0750 = $146,925). The $146,925 is then used as the present value/loan amount to determine the true cost of this loan. By solving for the new interest rate for a $146,925 loan with the same payment of $1,153.37, the APR is calculated as 8.73%.

Processing

After the optimistic borrower submits the loan application to the mortgage lender, the application is assigned to a processor who will order an appraisal of the property and a credit report on the borrower. The processor will also send out the necessary verification letters to confirm the borrower's employment, income, bank accounts and other liquid assets, and any other claims made by the borrower that need to be verified.

The Loan Processor

- Orders the appraisal
- Orders the credit report
- Sends out employment, income, bank account verification

The processor then compares the information on the returned verifications with the borrower's loan application to make sure they are the same. If not, the borrower is asked to explain the differences.

Not surprisingly, the lender is particularly interested in how likely the borrower is to repay the loan. By looking at the credit report, the lender will see how the borrower has behaved in the past regarding repayment of debts. The report should show the borrower's credit patterns over the last 7 years and must be less than 90 days old. Credit information from two national credit agencies must be collected, and a search of public records is made for judgments, divorces, tax liens, foreclosures, bankruptcies or any other possibly damaging information that might indicate a credit risk. The credit report should include information on the borrower's employment and should reflect any credit inquiries made by any creditor within the last 90 days.

Because of increasing technological advances, lenders may automate some of the steps of the mortgage loan process. These advances have increased the speed and efficiency of lending decisions, and decreased the cost of the loan origination process.

One new technological advance being used by the mortgage lending industry is automated underwriting (AU). Using AU systems, lenders quickly evaluate a wide range of information including consumer credit history, property information and loan type to determine the probability of the borrower repaying the loan. Credit bureau scores are used in AU to indicate consumer credit history, thus are a primary factor in the evaluation of mortgage applications.

Processor's Final Checklist

❑ Residential Loan Application—FNMA/FHLMC form or other approved equivalent

- Typed copy preferred
- Completed in full including borrower's signature
- Occupancy status indicated
- Application matches verification documents

❑ Residential Mortgage Credit Report

- All supplements, including public records examination
- All open credit accounts listed on the loan application

❑ Additional credit documentation

- Direct verification included for any accounts not listed on the credit report
- Letter of explanation included for adverse items

❑ Verification of Income, Verification of Employment (VOE)

- VOE's covering the past 2 years' work history
- Overtime and bonuses verified (if needed to qualify)
- Year-to-date and last year's earnings sections completed
- If borrower has sizeable commission income, 2 years' signed tax returns included with schedules
- Employment gaps explained, self-employed documentation
- Two years' signed tax returns with schedules
- Current and past two years' financial and income statements
- Income analysis forms

❑ Verification of Deposit (VOD)

- Verified funds sufficient for closing
- Average balance for past 2 months listed—if not, last two monthly statements
- Source of funds: explanation of any significant changes in account balances or any recently opened accounts or gift letter if applicable
- Gift letter with verification of gift funds, if available
- Gift donor member of the borrower's immediate family
- Completed in full, including borrower's signature

❑ Residential Appraisal Report—FNMA/FHLMC form or other-approved equivalent

- Photos of subject property, street scene and comparables
- Review appraisal included (if available)
- All addendums and explanations

❑ Sales Contract and/or escrow instructions

- Document includes all addendums and is signed by all parties
- If earnest money is equal to 50% or more of the ultimate down payment, proof of payment included (canceled checks, deposit receipt, etc.)

❑ Additional documents that may be required

- Divorce decree/separation agreement (if applicable)
- Verification of child support/alimony if such income is being used to qualify or if borrower is obligated to pay support/alimony
- Signed construction cost breakdown (if applicable)
- Most recent 12-month payment history on previous mortgages
- Rental agreements or leases (if applicable)
- Any other clarifying documents
- Bankruptcy filing statement, schedule of debt, discharge and explanation (if applicable)

   Documents must not be over 120 days old unless the property is new construction—then documents may be up to 180 days old.

❑ Eligible alternative documentation

Verification of Employment alternatives

- Pay stub or salary voucher for the most recent 30-day period with year-to-date earnings indicated and
- IRS W-2 forms for the previous 2 years and
- Documented telephone verification

Verification of Deposit alternative

- The most recent 3 months' depository institution statements. Borrowers must, at a minimum, report the ending balance, and all transactions (deposits and withdrawals)

Verification of Mortgage Payment alternatives

- A credit report reference for the last 12 months, or
- A mortgage payment history for the last 12 months, or
- A copy of all canceled checks for the most recent 12-month period

FICO® Scores

Fair, Isaac & Company (FICO®) created the FICO® credit scoring system that is used by virtually all major mortgage lenders to evaluate the credit worthiness of applicants. Credit scores, also known as FICO® scores, are numbers that measure the risk of delinquency or default to a lender by a consumer seeking a mortgage loan. The higher the FICO® score, the more risk worthy the borrower appears. Lenders use credit scores to rank consumers and determine whether a consumer qualifies for a loan, how much and at what interest rate the loan will be. The use of credit scores to evaluate a borrower's willingness to repay a loan has increased significantly in recent years, even as the usefulness and sophistication of the scoring process has improved.

FICO® scores run from the 300s to above 900, and are generated through complex statistical models created by Fair, Isaac, based on computer analyses of millions of consumers' credit histories.

The mortgage loan industry uses credit scores as a significant factor in its decision-making process. Indeed, credit scores are commonly used in the mortgage lending business as an initial screen for potential borrowers and many times become the compelling basis for loan approval or not.

National credit scoring companies have sold over 10 billion credit scores to mortgage lenders who use the scores in the risk analysis process before approving borrowers for new mortgage loans. These credit scores are a determining factor in a majority of all consumer credit decisions in the United States.

A variety of credit-scoring methods are used to generate credit scores. The primary sources for credit scores used in mortgage-lending decisions are the three national Credit Reporting Agencies, which collectively store over 450 million files on individual consumers and process over 1 billion pieces of consumer-credit data each month.

Credit scores are based upon credit reports of consumers who have obtained credit in the past. These credit reports are statistically evaluated to identify characteristics that predict the likelihood of debt repayment. Each of these characteristics is then assigned a weight based on how well it predicts that likelihood. A credit report includes four categories of data that have been collected and reported to the credit bureaus.

- Personal information
- Credit information
- Public record information
- Inquiries

The three credit bureaus collect data independently and use the data to create a consumer credit report. Certain factors such as gender, income, race, religion, marital status and national origin may not be used to inform a credit score, according to the Equal Credit Opportunity Act (ECOA).

The Three Major Credit Reporting Agencies

- **Experian**
  P.O. Box 2104, Allen, TX 75013
  1-(800)-682-7654

- **TransUnion**
  P.O. Box 390, Springfield, PA 19064
  1-(800)-916-8800

- **Equifax**
  P.O. Box 105873, Atlanta, GA 30348
  1-(800)-685-1111

In the mortgage lending world, FICO® scores either make or break a borrower when it comes to obtaining a home mortgage or getting the best rate. FICO® scores are calculated by evaluating a borrower's credit history, or histories from all three credit reporting agencies and assigning a number that reflects the perceived risk of that particular consumer defaulting on a mortgage loan.

The better a consumer's credit history, the higher the FICO® score will be; the worse the credit history, the lower the score. In some instances, lack of credit will result in no score on a credit report, and will require a prospective borrower to provide alternative credit via rental or utility payment histories.

Listed below are the five main categories of information that FICO® scores evaluate and their weightings in importance.

> ### Weightings of Credit History Factors Used to Develop FICO® Scores
>
> - 35%—Payment histories on credit accounts. Credit cards, department store accounts, car loans.
> - 30%—Amounts owed to creditors. Total of what is owed on all accounts, whether borrower carries an unpaid balance on certain accounts like credit cards.
> - 15%—Length of time borrower has been a credit user. The longer the better, as long as payments were made in a timely manner.
> - 10%—Has borrower been getting new credit in recent months? The more credit acquired, the lower the score goes.
> - 10%—Types and mix of credit uses. The borrower gets a lower score if credit has been secured through finance companies or other credit lenders who might have a higher rate of default.

A FICO® score takes into consideration all these categories of information, not just one or two. No one piece of information or factor alone will determine the final score.

The importance of any factor depends on the overall information in the consumer's credit report. For some people, a given factor may be more important than for someone else with a different credit history. In addition, as the information in a credit report changes, so does the importance of any factor in determining the score. Thus, it's impossible to say exactly how important any single factor is in determining a score. What's important is the mix of information, which varies from person to person, and for any one person over time.

A FICO® score only looks at information in the consumer's credit report. However, lenders look at many things when making a credit decision including income, length of time at a present job and the kind of credit being requested.

A FICO® score considers both positive and negative information in a credit report. Late payments will lower the score, but having established or re-established a good track record of making payments on time will raise the score.

Perhaps the most important element of obtaining a good rate on a mortgage is a borrower's credit history. The following chart is a general guide to what is called "A-B-C-D" credit. These are typical of the requirements used by many lenders, but are not absolute grades—lenders typically have similar but somewhat different specifications.

FICO® Credit Scoring

A+ to A-
Considered the best credit rating. FICO® scores are generally 620 and up with no lates on mortgage and one 30-days late on revolving or installment credit. No bankruptcy within past 2–10 years. Maximum debt ratio is 36–40% while maximum loan-to-value ratio is 95–100%. This type credit will demand the best interest rate available.

B+ to B-
General good credit with FICO® scores from 581–619. Two or three 30-days late on mortgage and two to four 30-days late on revolvingor installment credit. Cannot have any 60-day lates. Must be 2 to 4 years since bankruptcy discharge. Maximum debt ratio averages 45–50% while maximum loan-to-value ratio is 90–95%. This type of credit will obtain rates 1–2% higher than current market rate.

C+ to C-
Fair credit with FICO® scores from 551–580. Three to four 30-days late on mortgage are allowed. Installment or revolving credit can have four to six 30-days late or two to four 60-days late. Must have 1–2 years since bankruptcy discharge. Maximum debt ratio runs around 55% with maximum loan-to-value ratio averaging 80–90%. This type of credit will generate rates 3–4% higher than current market.

D+ to D-
Overall poor credit history with FICO® scores from 550 and lower. Two to six 30-days late on mortgage or one to two 60-days late, with isolated 90-days late. Revolving and installment lates show poor payment record with pattern of late payments. Possible current bankruptcy or foreclosure allowed with all unpaid judgments to be paid with loan proceeds. Must have stable employment. Maximum debt ratio averages 60% with maximum top loan-to-value of 70–80%. This type of credit will result in high interest rates (12–14%), but borrower can always refinance after one year of on-time mortgage payments to bring rate down.

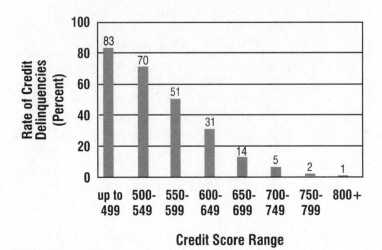

Delinquency* Rates by Credit Score

Source: Fair, Isaac and Company, Inc. (2008)

AARP Public Policy Institute

*Delinquencies are payments that are at least 90 days late on any credit accounts.

Sunnyvale National Bank
Building N82
1111 North Anywhere Avenue
Yourtown, CA 00000-0000

March 25, 20XX

Re: Application Number   000 0000000000

Dear Applicant:

Sunnyvale National Bank of California ("SUN-CA") is required by California law to provide you with the following notice.

Notice to Home Loan Applicant

In connection with your application for a home loan, SUN-CA must disclose to you the score that a credit bureau distributed to users and SUN-CA used in connection with your home loan, and the key factors affecting your **credit scores.**

The **credit score** is a computer generated summary calculated at the time of the request and based on information a credit bureau or SUN-CA has on file. The scores are based on data about your credit history and payment patterns. **Credit scores** are important because they are used to assist SUN-CA in determining whether you will obtain a loan. They may also be used to determine what interest rate you may be offered on the mortgage. **Credit scores** can change over time, depending on your conduct, how your credit history and payment patterns change, and how credit scoring technologies change.

Because the score is based on information in your credit history, it is very important that you review the credit-related information that is being furnished to make sure it is accurate. Credit records may vary from one company to another.

If you have questions about your **credit score** or the credit information that is furnished to you, contact the credit bureau at the address and telephone number provided with this notice, or contact SUN-CA, if SUN-CA developed or generated the **credit score**. The credit bureau plays no part in the decision to take any action on the loan application and is unable to provide you with specific reasons for the decision on a loan application.

Your Credit Score: 808 (Range of Possible Scores: 300 – 900)

Key Factors Affecting Your Score:
Length of time accounts have been established
Too many accounts opened in the last 12 months
Too many accounts with balances
Proportion of balances to credit limits is too high on revolving accts

Credit Bureau: Good Shield (888-555-5555), P.O. Box 000, Good, CA 00000

If you have any questions concerning the terms of the loan, contact me at (888) 555-5555, x000.

Sincerely,
JANE DOE
Sunnyvale National Bank of California

I have read this disclosure form, and understand its contents, as evidenced by my signature below. I understand that this acknowledgment is a required part of the mortgage loan application.

_____ Date

Keep in mind these are general guidelines. Some lenders place different grades based upon their own method of evaluation.

After collecting all the necessary information, the loan processor reviews the loan file to make sure all required documents are included before sending the file to an underwriter who will evaluate the risk involved in making the loan.

CHAPTER QUIZ

1. Most of the money for home loans comes from three major institutions. Which of the following is not included in the three?

   a. Fannie Mae (FNMA—Federal National Mortgage Association)
   b. Freddie Mac (FHLMC—Federal Home Loan Mortgage Corporation)
   c. Ginnie Mae (GNMA—Government National Mortgage Association)
   d. Federal Reserve System—the Fed

2. The company to which loan payments are made is referred to as the:

   a. servicer
   b. processor
   c. originator
   d. payee

3. To determine a consumer's maximum mortgage amount, lenders use guidelines called:

   a. income-to-value ratios
   b. upside-down ratios
   c. debt-to-income ratios
   d. borrower-lender ratios

4. Which of the following serves as the lender's only security for repayment of the loan if the borrower defaults?

    a. borrower's personal assets
    b. property
    c. borrower's promise to pay
    d. promissory note

5. The standard loan application form used by almost every lender is called:

    a. Uniform Residential Loan Application
    b. Federal Residential Loan Application
    c. HUD Residential Loan Application
    d. Borrower's Residential Loan Application

6. The loan processor does all of the following except:

    a. orders the appraisal
    b. orders the credit report
    c. sends out employment, income, bank account verification
    d. funds the loan

7. One new technological advance being used by the mortgage lending industry is:

    a. redlining
    b. automated underwriting (AU)
    c. automatic funding
    d. distance funding

8. FICO® scores are used for:

    a. evaluating appraisals
    b. using the date of application to determine who gets a loan
    c. updating loan servicing contracts
    d. evaluating the credit worthiness of loan applicants

9. What do the following have in common: Experian, TransUnion, Equifax?

    a. they are all mortgage lenders
    b. they are all title companies
    c. they are all credit bureaus
    d. they are all software programs

10. The most important element of obtaining a good interest rate on a mortgage is:

    a. borrower's credit history
    b. mortgage market history
    c. current rates
    d. secondary mortgage market guidelines

ANSWERS

1. *d*
2. *a*
3. *c*
4. *b*
5. *a*
6. *d*
7. *b*
8. *d*
9. *c*
10. *a*

Underwriting and Closing the Loan

INTRODUCTION

All the paperwork has been collected by the loan processor and the loan package is complete. It is now the job of the underwriter to use the information in the loan package to determine, according to conforming guidelines, whether the loan will be funded. The purpose of sending a completed loan package to an underwriter is to accomplish the desired result of funding a loan that conforms to the standards of the secondary mortgage market and is an acceptable risk for the investor. This analyzing of the information relating to risk and making a decision about funding the loan is the only step left for the loan process to be concluded.

RISK ANALYSIS

The practice of analyzing the degree of risk involved in a mortgage loan is known as *underwriting*. Basically, the underwriter determines whether the borrower has the ability and willingness to repay the debt and whether the property being pledged as collateral is adequate security for the debt. The process also involves the evaluation of both the property and the borrower to determine whether or not the loan package conforms to the guidelines for selling on the secondary mortgage market or to some other permanent investor directly.

In any case, the loan must be attractive to an investor as far as the risk of default, as well as being profitable. If any part of the loan process is lacking, such as poor processing or underwriting, the mortgage lender might find it difficult to sell the loan. Also, if the borrower defaults on a carelessly underwritten loan, the loss to the mortgage lender could be considerable. For example, if the appraisal was too high and the borrower defaulted, the lender could end up with a loss when the property does not sell, at the foreclosure sale, for the amount needed to repay the loan and other costs of the default.

UNDERWRITING GUIDELINES

If lenders expect to sell their loans on the secondary market, they must follow the standards set by Fannie Mae and Freddie Mac in analyzing the important information necessary to approve a borrower and still protect the assets of the lender or some future owner of the loan.

Upon receiving the loan package, the underwriter begins the process of evaluating the risk factor of certain elements at the heart of the application.

Categories for Risk Analysis

- Loan-to-value ratios
- Loan amount
- Down payment
- Income ratios
- Employment
- Credit history
- Appraisal

Loan-to-Value Ratios

The *loan-to-value ratio (LTV)* is the relationship between the amount borrowed and the value of the property. For example, if the property in question is valued at $100,000 and the loan amount requested is $80,000, the loan-to-value ratio would be 80%. The difference between the amount borrowed and the value is made up by the down payment from the borrower. The down payment is the equity the borrower has in the property.

Loan Amount

Evaluating the loan-to-value ratio (LTV) is probably the most important aspect of the underwriting process. The greater the down payment from the borrower, which would lower the LTV ratio, the less risk it is to the lender. The risk involved to the mortgage lender would be the risk of the borrower's default, the property going into foreclosure and selling for less than the loan amount. The lender would find itself either getting the property back at the foreclosure sale or getting a deficient amount at the sale, neither of which is desirable from the point of view of a good investment. So the underwriter makes certain the LTV falls within the guidelines for that particular loan.

Down Payment

Most lenders require some kind of down payment to show that a borrower does have a monetary, or equitable, interest in the property. The thinking is that the borrower will protect his or her interest to a greater degree if there is some personal money invested in the purchase. The down payment has been verified during loan processing by checking the bank account of the borrower to make sure the money is there. The VOD (Verification of Deposit) will establish the existence and history of funds to be used for a down payment as well as determining how long the funds have been in the account. The reason for that is to make sure the applicant has not borrowed it recently from a friend or relative, and therefore does not actually have any personal money invested in the purchase.

Income Ratios

A lender is concerned about whether or not the borrower can repay the loan. The underwriter will use income ratios to determine the risk of default because of lack of ability to make the payments in a timely manner. Using the long history of mortgage lending as a guideline for making mortgage loans with a low risk of default, the mortgage debt ratio (or front-end ratio) is determined by calculating the percentage of monthly income necessary to meet the monthly housing expense.

The percentage of income that can be used for housing debt varies depending on what kind of loan is being made, whether it is conventional, FHA or VA. Assuming the loan is conventional (not government sponsored or private party), the following monthly housing expenses (or monthly share of annual expenses) are added together.

**Housing Expenses Used to Determine
Housing Debt to Income Ratio**

- Principal
- Interest
- Hazard insurance
- Property taxes
- Mortgage insurance premiums
- Homeowners' association dues
- Ground rents if any
- Second mortgage payment if applicable

The total of the monthly housing expense should not be more than 28% of the gross monthly income of the borrower. In some cases the lender will allow a higher ratio if the borrower has strong credit and no long-term debts.

Most borrowers have monthly payments other than housing to repay. Other expenses might include credit cards, alimony or child support, student loan repayment, car payment or any number of installment type expenses. These expenses, when added to the housing debt, become known as back-end debt or total debt service. Ratios for back-end debt are calculated separately from the front-end ratio of housing expense to gross monthly income.

Commonly, lenders will use the guideline that the total of all debt should not be more than 36% of the borrower's gross monthly income. Certain other factors might be used to determine a higher debt-to-income ratio if the borrower can show:

- a larger down payment than normal
- a large amount of cash in savings
- an extra solid credit rating
- a large net worth
- a great potential for high future earnings

Employment

An underwriter will seek out the VOE (Verification of Employment) in the processed file to determine how the loan will be repaid by the borrower. The following factors are of concern to the underwriter.

- Salary/wages are consistent with the application
- Probability of continued employment with the same employer
- Overtime/bonus income is likely to continue
- Dates of employment are consistent with the application
- Employer has signed the VOE
- At least 2 years employment with current employer (if not, a VOE from the former employer is requested)

Credit History

A mortgage lender is concerned not only about whether a borrower *can* repay the loan, but whether he or she *will* repay the loan. An underwriter will review the Residential Mortgage Credit Report to see whether the borrower has a credit history of meeting payments according to contract terms, in a timely manner. If the credit report shows a positive borrowing history, the underwriter will use that as an encouraging sign of a worthy borrower.

Appraisal

After reviewing the loan-to-value ratios, loan amount, down payment, income ratios, employment, and credit history in the loan package, the underwriter must determine the adequacy of the security for the loan. Since the mortgage loan will be secured by the property, the value of the property must be determined to validate the loan-to-value ratio. The valuation is determined by the appraisal.

The underwriter wants to make sure that the lender is protected from loss through default and foreclosure by establishing the value of the property upon which the loan-to-value ratio is applied. For example, if the lender's loan-to-value ratio for making the loan is 80%, the loan cannot exceed more than 80% of the value of the property.

> *Example:*
>
> $100,000   Value of Property
> × 0.80   Loan-to-Value Ratio
> $80,000   Loan Amount

If the property goes into foreclosure, the lender can feel reasonably safe as far as risk of loss goes because of the 20% percent cushion between the loan amount and the value of the property. Lenders do make loans with higher ratios, with more risk involved for them. In that case, the comfort zone of the 20% percent cushion is smaller, with a greater risk of loss. The cost for 80, 90 or even 100% percent loans goes up according to the perceived risk to the lender. Interest rates and points are all increased to protect the lender in case of default, and the buyer is normally required to purchase mortgage insurance.

FEDERAL AND STATE DISCLOSURES AND NOTICE OF RIGHTS

Lenders who make mortgage loans and brokers who arrange mortgage loans must comply with various federal and state disclosure laws and regulations. Underwriters must be aware of these laws and act in accordance with them.

Settlement, or closing as it is called in some states, is the formal process by which ownership of real property passes from seller to buyer. It is the end of the home buying process, the time when title to the property is transferred from the seller to the buyer.

Certain disclosures that protect consumers from unfair lending practices are required at different times during a loan transaction.

In the previous chapter, we discussed disclosures required when the borrower applies for the loan: the Special Information Booklet (not necessary for refinances); the Good Faith Estimate; the Mortgage Servicing Disclosure Statement; and Truth-in-Lending Disclosure Statement.

Disclosures at Settlement/Closing

The *HUD-1 Settlement Statement* is a standard form that clearly shows all charges imposed on borrowers and sellers in connection with the settlement. RESPA allows the borrower to request to see the HUD-1 Settlement Statement one day before the actual settlement. The settlement agent must then provide the borrowers with a completed HUD-1 Settlement Statement based on information known to the agent at that time.

The HUD-1 Settlement Statement shows the actual settlement costs of the loan transaction. Separate forms may be prepared for the borrower and the seller. Where it is not the practice that the borrower and the seller both attend the settlement, the HUD-1 should be mailed or delivered as soon as practicable after settlement.

The Initial Escrow Statement itemizes the estimated taxes, insurance premiums and other charges anticipated to be paid from the Escrow Account

A. **Settlement Statement**   U.S. Department of Housing
and Urban Development   OMB Approval No. 2502-0265

B. Type of Loan

1. ☐ FHA 2. ☐ FmHA 3. ☐ Conv. Unins.	6. File Number:	7. Loan Number:	8. Mortgage Insurance Case Number:
4. ☐ VA 5. ☐ Conv. Ins.			

C. Note: This form is furnished to give you a statement of actual settlement costs. Amounts paid to and by the settlement agent are shown. Items marked "(p.o.c.)" were paid outside the closing; they are shown here for informational purposes and are not included in the totals.

D. Name & Address of Borrower:	E. Name & Address of Seller:	F. Name & Address of Lender:

G. Property Location:	H. Settlement Agent:	
	Place of Settlement:	I. Settlement Date:

J. Summary of Borrower's Transaction		**K. Summary of Seller's Transaction**	
100. Gross Amount Due From Borrower		**400. Gross Amount Due To Seller**	
101. Contract sales price		401. Contract sales price	
102. Personal property		402. Personal property	
103. Settlement charges to borrower (line 1400)		403.	
104.		404.	
105.		405.	
Adjustments for items paid by seller in advance		**Adjustments for items paid by seller in advance**	
106. City/town taxes to		406. City/town taxes to	
107. County taxes to		407. County taxes to	
108. Assessments to		408. Assessments to	
109.		409.	
110.		410.	
111.		411.	
112.		412.	
120. Gross Amount Due From Borrower		**420. Gross Amount Due To Seller**	
200. Amounts Paid By Or In Behalf Of Borrower		**500. Reductions In Amount Due To Seller**	
201. Deposit or earnest money		501. Excess deposit (see instructions)	
202. Principal amount of new loan(s)		502. Settlement charges to seller (line 1400)	
203. Existing loan(s) taken subject to		503. Existing loan(s) taken subject to	
204.		504. Payoff of first mortgage loan	
205.		505. Payoff of second mortgage loan	
206.		506.	
207.		507.	
208.		508.	
209.		509.	
Adjustments for items unpaid by seller		**Adjustments for items unpaid by seller**	
210. City/town taxes to		510. City/town taxes to	
211. County taxes to		511. County taxes to	
212. Assessments to		512. Assessments to	
213.		513.	
214.		514.	
215.		515.	
216.		516.	
217.		517.	
218.		518.	
219.		519.	
220. Total Paid By/For Borrower		**520. Total Reduction Amount Due Seller**	
300. Cash At Settlement From/To Borrower		**600. Cash At Settlement To/From Seller**	
301. Gross Amount due from borrower (line 120)		601. Gross amount due to seller (line 420)	
302. Less amounts paid by/for borrower (line 220)	( )	602. Less reductions in amt. due seller (line 520)	( )
303. Cash ☐ From ☐ To Borrower		**603. Cash ☐ To ☐ From Seller**	

Section 5 of the Real Estate Settlement Procedures Act (RESPA) requires the following: • HUD must develop a Special Information Booklet to help persons borrowing money to finance the purchase of residential real estate to better understand the nature and costs of real estate settlement services; • Each lender must provide the booklet to all applicants from whom it receives or for whom it prepares a written application to borrow money to finance the purchase of residential real estate; • Lenders must prepare and distribute with the Booklet a Good Faith Estimate of the settlement costs that the borrower is likely to incur in connection with the settlement. These disclosures are manadatory.

Section 4(a) of RESPA mandates that HUD develop and prescribe this standard form to be used at the time of loan settlement to provide full disclosure of all charges imposed upon the borrower and seller. These are third party disclosures that are designed to provide the borrower with pertinent information during the settlement process in order to be a better shopper.

The Public Reporting Burden for this collection of information is estimated to average one hour per response, including the time for reviewing instructions, searching existing data sources, gathering and maintaining the data needed, and completing and reviewing the collection of information.

This agency may not collect this information, and you are not required to complete this form, unless it displays a currently valid OMB control number.

The information requested does not lend itself to confidentiality.

(continued on next page)

L. Settlement Charges

		Paid From Borrowers Funds at Settlement	Paid From Seller's Funds at Settlement
700. Total Sales/Broker's Commission based on price $ @ % =			
Division of Commission (line 700) as follows:			
701. $ to			
702. $ to			
703. Commission paid at Settlement			
704.			
800. Items Payable In Connection With Loan			
801. Loan Origination Fee %			
802. Loan Discount %			
803. Appraisal Fee to			
804. Credit Report to			
805. Lender's Inspection Fee			
806. Mortgage Insurance Application Fee to			
807. Assumption Fee			
808.			
809.			
810.			
811.			
900. Items Required By Lender To Be Paid In Advance			
901. Interest from to @$ /day			
902. Mortgage Insurance Premium for months to			
903. Hazard Insurance Premium for years to			
904. years to			
905.			
1000. Reserves Deposited With Lender			
1001. Hazard insurance months@$ per month			
1002. Mortgage insurance months@$ per month			
1003. City property taxes months@$ per month			
1004. County property taxes months@$ per month			
1005. Annual assessments months@$ per month			
1006. months@$ per month			
1007. months@$ per month			
1008. months@$ per month			
1100. Title Charges			
1101. Settlement or closing fee to			
1102. Abstract or title search to			
1103. Title examination to			
1104. Title insurance binder to			
1105. Document preparation to			
1106. Notary fees to			
1107. Attorney's fees to			
(includes above items numbers:)			
1108. Title insurance to			
(includes above items numbers:)			
1109. Lender's coverage $			
1110. Owner's coverage $			
1111.			
1112.			
1113.			
1200. Government Recording and Transfer Charges			
1201. Recording fees: Deed $; Mortgage $; Releases $			
1202. City/county tax/stamps: Deed $; Mortgage $			
1203. State tax/stamps: Deed $; Mortgage $			
1204.			
1205.			
1300. Additional Settlement Charges			
1301. Survey to			
1302. Pest inspection to			
1303.			
1304.			
1305.			
1400. Total Settlement Charges (enter on lines 103, Section J and 502, Section K)			

during the first 12 months of the loan. It lists the Escrow payment amount and any required cushion. Although the statement is usually given at settlement, the lender has 45 days from settlement to deliver it.

Disclosures after Settlement

Loan servicers must deliver to borrowers an Annual Escrow Statement once a year. The annual Escrow account statement summarizes all escrow account deposits and payments during the servicer's 12 month computation year. It also notifies the borrower of any shortages or surpluses in the account and advises the borrower about the course of action being taken.

A Servicing Transfer Statement is required if the loan servicer sells or assigns the servicing rights to a borrower's loan to another loan servicer. Generally, the loan servicer must notify the borrower 15 days before the effective date of the loan transfer. As long the borrower makes a timely payment to the old servicer within 60 days of the loan transfer, the borrower cannot be penalized. The notice must include the name and address of the new servicer, toll-free telephone numbers, and the date the new servicer will begin accepting payments.

HUD created the following table illustrating the disclosures that may be relevant to the simplification and consolidation process.

Timing of Disclosure	TILA (Truth-in-Lending Act)	Real Estate Settlement Procedures Act (RESPA)
At or before referral	None	Affiliated Business Arrangement Disclosure
At or before application	(1) Home Equity Line of Credit (HELOC) booklet and disclosures; (2) Adjustable rate booklet and disclosures	None
Within 3 days of application	TILA Disclosure Statement (including APR and finance charge)	(1) Special Information Booklet (2) Good Faith Estimate; (3) Required Provider Information; (4) Initial Transfer of Servicing Disclosure
3 days prior to closing	(1) Section 32 disclosures (an annual adjustment of the dollar amount that triggers additional disclosures under the Truth in Lending Act for mortgage loans that bear rates or fees above a certain amount (2) Reverse Mortgage disclosures	None
1 day prior to closing	None	Right to inspect HUD-1 or HUD-1A
At closing	(1) TILA Disclosure Statement; (2) Rescission notice	(1) HUD-1 or HUD-1A; (2) Initial Escrow Account Statement (within 45 days after closing)

CLOSING

After all information needed to make a decision about approving the loan has been received, processed and analyzed, and the security for the loan has been verified as sufficient, the decision must be made to accept or reject the loan application. That could be done by a loan officer whose job it is to decide which loans to fund, or by a loan committee. In any case, once approved, the loan goes to the final stage of the mortgage loan process, the loan closing, where necessary documents are prepared and executed.

The borrower receives the package of closing documents, some of which must be signed before a notary. The note and trust deed must be signed as well as various disclosures. When all documents have been executed by the borrower, the trust deed will be recorded and the loan funded.

CHAPTER QUIZ

1. The practice of analyzing the degree of risk involved in a mortgage loan is known as:

    a. loan processing
    b. loan approval
    c. loan steering
    d. loan underwriting

2. The process of _____ involves the evaluation of both the property and the borrower.

    a. loan application
    b. warehousing
    c. redlining
    d. loan underwriting

3. Upon receiving the loan package, the underwriter begins the process of:

    a. evaluating the risk factor of certain elements of the application
    b. closing the loan
    c. gathering information about the borrower
    d. gathering information about the property

4. The loan-to-value ratio (LTV) is the relationship between the:

    a. borrower's income and the value of the property
    b. amount borrowed and the value of the property
    c. lender's liability and borrower's risk
    d. loan and the future value of the property

5. The greater the borrower's _____, which would lower the LTV ratio, the less risk the loan is to the lender.

    a. income
    b. down payment
    c. mortgage insurance
    d. collateral

6. The underwriter will use _____ to determine the risk of default because of lack of a buyer's ability to make the payments in a timely manner.

    a. risk ratios
    b. liability ratios
    c. income ratios
    d. loan-to-value ratios

7. Mortgage debt ratio (or front-end ratio) for a loan is determined by:

    a. calculating the percentage of monthly income necessary to meet the monthly housing expense
    b. calculating the percentage of monthly income necessary to meet total household expenses
    c. calculating the percentage of monthly income necessary to meet future, projected household expenses

d. calculating the percentage of monthly income necessary to meet the monthly housing expense less any long-term debt

8. Monthly payments other than housing are known as:

   a. long-term debt
   b. back-end debt
   c. front-end debt
   d. forebearance debt

9. What determines how the loan will be repaid by the borrower?

   a. bank account
   b. employment
   c. credit history
   d. personal verifications

10. The value of the property is determined by the:

    a. opinion of the borrower
    b. opinion of the lender
    c. appraisal
    d. underwriter

ANSWERS

1. *d*
2. *d*
3. *a*
4. *b*
5. *b*
6. *c*
7. *a*
8. *b*
9. *b*
10. *c*

Loan Servicing

INTRODUCTION

Loan servicing is the performance of obligations and tasks that are necessary to the good health of a loan during its life, both from the point of view of the lender and the borrower, as well as producing a profit for the servicer. The servicer is required to perform day-to-day management of individual loans, as well as the entire servicing portfolio, making sure the interests of both the mortgagor and investor are protected.

A function required for all mortgage loans, servicing may be performed by the lender who originated the loan or it may be sold to another lender or investor who will do the servicing. When a consumer applies for a home mortgage, he or she may think that the lender, or loan originator, will service the loan until it is paid off or the property is sold. This is not always true. In today's market, mortgage servicing rights often are bought and sold.

Commonly, mortgage lenders who are only involved in the origination of the loans, such as mortgage brokers, transfer the servicing of their loans to other mortgage lenders or investors. Because the service contract is something of value, the transferring broker might get a fee, called a servicing release fee or premium, from the investor to whom the contract is sold.

In 1990, the National Affordable Housing Act was passed to protect borrowers from abuses that were occurring during the loan servicing period, or life of the loan.

WHAT ARE THE RESPONSIBILITIES OF A MORTGAGE SERVICER?

The mortgage servicer collects monthly payments and handles the escrow account if one has been set up. An escrow account is a fund that the lender establishes in order to pay property taxes and hazard insurance as they become due on the property during the year. In this way, the lender uses the escrow account to guard its investment in the property.

When the escrow account is first established, the mortgage servicer must give the borrower a statement disclosing the estimated taxes, insurance premiums and other charges that are anticipated over the next 12 months, and the expected totals of those payments.

The mortgage servicer also is required to give the borrower an annual statement that details the activity of the escrow account. This statement shows the account balance and reflects payments for property taxes and homeowners insurance.

WHAT DOES THE HOUSING ACT REQUIRE LENDERS OR SERVICERS TO DO?

To protect consumers, the National Affordable Housing Act requires lenders or servicers to do the following.

Provide a Disclosure Statement

The disclosure statement says whether the lender intends to sell the mortgage servicing immediately, whether the mortgage servicing can be sold at any time during the life of the loan, and the percentage of loans the lender has sold previously. During 1992, lenders had to disclose the percentage of loans for which the servicing was sold in 1990 and 1991. Beginning in 1993, lenders had to report figures for the previous 3 years.

The percentages should be noted in the ranges 0–25%, 26–50%, 51–75%, and 76–100%. The lender also must provide information about servicing procedures, transfer practices and complaint resolution.

If a borrower has a face-to-face interview with a lender, he or she must receive the disclosure statement at the time of the loan application. If the borrower applies for a loan by mail, the lender has 3 business days to send the disclosure statement after receiving the application. If the borrower does not return a signed disclosure statement, the lender cannot fund the mortgage.

Give Proper Notification When the Loan Servicing is Going to Be Sold

If the current servicer plans to sell the loan servicing, the borrower must be notified at least 15 days before the effective date of the transfer unless he or she received a written transfer notice at settlement. The effective date is when the first mortgage payment is due at the new servicer's address. Under certain circumstances, the current servicer has up to 30 days after the effective date of the transfer to send notification.

These circumstances include:

- The lender terminating the contract because the borrower has defaulted on the loan.
- The servicer filing for bankruptcy.
- The Federal Deposit Insurance Corporation or the Resolution Trust Corporation beginning proceedings to take over the servicer's operations.

If the loan servicing is going to be sold, the borrower should receive two notices—one from the current servicer and one from the new mortgage servicer. The new servicer must notify the borrower not more than 15 days after the transfer has occurred.

The notices must include the following information.

- The name and address of the new servicer.
- The date the current servicer will stop accepting mortgage payments, and the date the new servicer will begin accepting them.
- Free or collect-call telephone numbers for both the current servicer and the new servicer that a borrower can call for information about the transfer of service.

- Information that tells whether a borrower can continue any option insurance, such as mortgage life or disability insurance, and what action, if any, a borrower must take to maintain coverage. A borrower also must be told whether the insurance terms will change.

- A statement that the transfer will not affect any terms or conditions of the mortgage documents, except the terms that are directly related to the servicing of the loan. For example, if under the contract, a borrower specifically was allowed to pay property taxes and insurance premiums on his or her own, the new servicer cannot demand that the borrower establish an escrow account. However, if the contract was neutral on this issue or merely limited the actions of the old lender, the new servicer may be able to require such an account.

Grant a Grace Period During the Transfer of the Loan Servicing

After the transfer, there is a 60-day grace period. During this time a borrower cannot be charged a late fee for mistakenly sending a mortgage payment to the old mortgage servicer instead of the new one. In addition, the fact that the new servicer may have received the borrower's payment late cannot be reported to a credit bureau.

Respond Promptly to Written Inquiries

If a borrower believes there is an improperly charged penalty or late fee, or there are other problems with the servicing of the loan, the borrower should contact the servicer in writing. The account number must be included and the borrower must explain why he or she believes the account is incorrect.

Within 20 business days of receiving the borrower's inquiry, the servicer must send a written response acknowledging the inquiry. Within 60 business days, the servicers must either correct the account or determine if it is accurate.

The servicer must send the borrower a written notice of what action it took and why.

The borrower should not subtract any disputed amount from the mortgage payment. Many mortgage servicers will refuse to accept what they consider to be partial payments. They may return the check and charge a late fee, or declare the mortgage is in default and start foreclosure proceedings.

VALIDATION OF DEBT LETTER

John and Jan Doe
0000 Any Street
Yourtown, California 00000

February 3, 20xx

RE: Loan Number 0000000000

Dear Mr. and Mrs. Doe,

This letter is to inform you that your account with Wonderful Home Equity Bank formerly Anyone's Home Equity Bank, has been placed with Equity Servicing Corporation (EQSC) for servicing.   EQSC is responsible for providing monthly remittance processing as well as the collection of any amount in default.

Your financing agreement provides:

◆   Your full monthly payment is due each month on the due date.
◆   You are in default if you fail to make each payment in full as it becomes due.
◆   You may incur extra expenses if you fail to make timely payments.

With respect to your account with Wonderful Home Equity Bank we are providing the following information:

◆   Name of creditor: Wonderful Home Equity Bank, California, N.A., formerly Anyone's Home Equity Bank, California
◆   Time and place of the creation of the debt: 11/15/20xx, YOURTOWN, CALIFORNIA
◆   The merchandise, services or other things of value underlying the debt: Senior Lien
◆   The date when the account was turned over to EQSC: 20021126

If you have any questions, please contact EQSC Customer Service by calling 1-888-555-5555.   Our business hours are Monday through Friday, 5:30 AM – 5:30 PM, Pacific Time.

Sincerely,

Equity Servicing Corporation

Equity Servicing Corporation is a debt collector.   EQSC is attempting to collect a debt and any information obtained will be used for that purpose.

WHAT CAN A BORROWER DO IF THERE IS A COMPLAINT?

If a borrower believes the servicer has not responded appropriately to a valid written inquiry, the borrower should contact the local or state consumer protection office. A borrower also should contact the Department of Housing and Urban Development (HUD) to file a complaint under the National Affordable Housing Act. Find your local HUD field office by visiting http://www.hud.gov/localoffices.cfm.

A borrower also can send a complaint to the Federal Trade Commission (FTC). Although the FTC generally does not intervene in individual cases, the information a borrower provides may show a pattern of possible violations of laws that are enforced by the Commission. File a complaint with the FTC by visiting http://www.ftc.gov/ftc/cmplanding.shtm.

The borrower also may want to contact an attorney to be advised on legal rights. Under the National Affordable Housing Act, consumers can initiate class action suits and obtain actual damages, plus additional damages, for a pattern or practice of noncompliance. In successful actions, consumers also may obtain court costs and attorneys' fees.

WHAT CAN A BORROWER DO ABOUT PROBLEMS WITH A LOAN SERVICER?

There are a variety of licenses or authorities under which a mortgage company can service a home loan, including a real estate broker license issued by the Department of Real Estate. Regardless of the license or authority under which a company is operating, there are several things that a borrower can do in order to resolve a loan servicing problem.

Most loan servicers have an 800 customer service number. Consumers should call their servicer and explain the problem. They should be sure to have the loan number and pertinent documents in hand before calling. The call should be documented by writing down the name of the person to whom the borrower spoke, the date and time of the call and what was promised. If the customer service representative is unable to immediately resolve the problem, the borrower should be sure to ask for some sort of follow-up action, and when to expect a call-back or a time frame in which the problem will be resolved. After speaking with a customer service representative, or if the borrower is unable to successfully contact the servicer by telephone, a letter should be sent to the servicer, at the address for correspondence indicated on the monthly loan statement or documents.

Section 6 of the Real Estate Settlement Procedures Act (RESPA), which is enforced by the federal Department of Housing and Urban Development (HUD), requires a servicer to acknowledge such a written request to resolve a problem within 20 business days and to attempt to resolve the problem within 60 business days. If the correspondence is not acknowledged or the problem is not resolved within those time frames, the borrower may file a complaint with HUD at *http://www.hud.gov* or contact HUD's Enforcement Center at (202) 708-2350. The borrower may be able to file a civil lawsuit against the servicer. A sample letter to the loan servicer may also be found at their website at: *http://www.hud.gov/offices/hsg/sfh/res/reslettr.cfm*.

WHAT DOES TRANSFER OF SERVICING MEAN?

When a borrower takes out a mortgage with a mortgage company or a bank, there is always a possibility that the lender will sell or transfer the servicing of the loan to another institution. Servicing means the collection of payments and management of operational procedures related to mortgages. When servicing is sold, it means that another lender will be taking the payments, handling the escrow accounts, paying the insurance and taxes and answering the questions. This may happen right after the borrower closes the loan or several years later.

The practice of selling or transferring the servicing of a loan is legal and is very common in the mortgage industry. When the servicing is sold, it is usually packaged in a bundle with other loans. Some mortgage companies only originate loans and sell or transfer the servicing immediately. It is more cost-effective for these companies to do this because servicing is not a part of their business. It is not uncommon to get a mortgage from a neighborhood lender and have it transferred to an institution in another state. It is also possible for a mortgage servicing to be transferred more than once during the life of a loan.

Whether or not a borrower's servicing is sold has nothing to do with the quality of the loan or the payment history. It has, in fact, nothing whatever to do with the borrower personally.

How Does Transfer of Service Affect a Loan?

The company that holds a loan makes the decision to transfer servicing to another institution. The company does not have to ask the borrower's permission to transfer the servicing, but it does have to inform the borrower of the transfer.

The transfer of servicing should not affect the borrower or the mortgage adversely. The original terms and conditions of the mortgage will stay the same. The interest rate and duration of the loan will not change on fixed rate loans. The payment should stay the same or on the same schedule except in cases where changes in taxes or insurance requirements increase or decrease the escrow amount.

If the borrower has an adjustable rate mortgage (ARM), the original conditions of the mortgage contract stay in effect and the rate will change according to the adjustment periods (i.e. every 6 months, annually, every 3 years, etc). This information is contained in the contract, but the borrower may verify the information with the new servicer. If the original lender agreed to let the borrower refinance to a fixed-rate mortgage within a certain timeframe, the borrower should ask whether this agreement would be honored by the new lender.

When Will the Borrower Be Notified?

When the lender decides to transfer servicing, the borrower should receive a goodbye letter at least 5 to 15 days before the date the next payment is due. The letter should state who the new servicing company will be, where it is located, the name and phone number of a contact person or department, and where and when the borrower should send the next payment. The borrower should also receive a welcome letter from the new servicer that outlines the same information. Both letters should give the name of the new institution, a contact, phone number (toll-free if available), the new servicer's address, and instructions for making the next payment.

An Important Consumer Safeguard

It is very important that the borrower receive both letters. If the borrower receives only a letter from the new servicer, he or she should be sure to call the original servicer to verify that the loan actually has been transferred. It is extremely important that the borrower keep the servicer informed of his or her current mailing address, so that all relevant correspondence will be received.

Where Does the Borrower Pay the Next Payment?

If the borrower has received both letters or has verified the transfer of the mortgage with the old servicer, he or she should be sure to send all payments from that point on to the new servicer. If the payment is sent to the old servicer, the borrower runs the risk of the payment not reaching the correct lender in time, paying a late charge or having the payment get lost. It is the borrower's responsibility to send the payment to the new servicer once informed of the transfer.

The welcome letter from the new servicer will often inform the borrower of new payment coupons to come. But if the payment is due before the coupons arrive, the borrower should write the loan number on the check and send it to the address provided in the welcome letter. If the borrower has coupons from the previous servicer, one may be included with this payment.

The borrower will want to read the welcome letter carefully for payment instructions. The payment date will not change, since it is determined in the original mortgage documents. If the mortgage is paid through electronic funds transfer or automatic draft each month, the borrower will need to cancel that arrangement and fill out new forms for the payment to be sent to the servicer. Since this often takes time, the borrower may need to send a check for a payment until the electronic funds transfer is changed over. This is something that the borrower will need to do. The new servicer cannot take the payment from the borrower's savings or checking account without his or her signature.

If a borrower accidentally sends the payment to the old servicer, the company will usually forward the first payment to the new servicer, but this will not continue after the first month. By not sending the payment to the correct office, the borrower risks the payment being lost. There are some cases where the old servicer no longer exists due to a merger or take over. In that case, the payment may be returned by the postal service after several weeks, which may cause a late charge to be assessed to the borrower's account.

What Happens to the Borrower's Escrow Account?

It is the borrower's former servicer's responsibility to inform the insurance company and the borrower's tax authority of the change in servicer. If an escrow account is interest-bearing, all interest due should be credited to the account by the old servicer before the transfer takes place. The former servicer is responsible for handling these items prior to the transfer.

Some time after the loan servicing is transferred the new lender will make an analysis of the escrow. During the analysis, the lender reviews the escrow amount and determines if it is adequate to cover the fees for the insurance, taxes and any other premiums paid through escrow. If the amount is found to be insufficient, the lender may ask the borrower to increase the regular monthly payment. If it is the new servicer's policy to review escrow accounts as soon as the servicing is transferred, the payment may change immediately and the borrower should receive an explanation regarding any changes.

What About Insurance Policies and Taxes?

If the borrower receives a notice that either the insurance or taxes are due, he or she should call the new servicer to make sure the company has on file the information that funds have been escrowed for the premium. If the new company has not received a copy of that bill, it will probably direct the borrower to send in the bill for payment. If the borrower has a question after the transfer has taken place, he or she should contact the new servicer, even if the old servicer was the one that collected the funds for the insurance or tax payment.

Some mortgage companies offer to escrow life or disability insurance (that which would pay off the mortgage in case of death, or make payments in case disability). In these policies, the lender who originally made the loan is named as the beneficiary. If a borrower has these policies, the old servicer should inform the borrower of what effect the transfer of servicing will have on this insurance coverage and what action may be needed to maintain coverage.

On flood and hazard insurance, it is the responsibility of the old servicer to provide the insurance agent or company with a notice of transfer. The beneficiary may be able to be transferred from one company to the other, but it is wise for the borrower to make sure this occurs to be certain that, in case of a claim, the check is written and sent to the appropriate servicer.

Who Sends the Borrower the End of the Year Tax Statement?

The borrower should find out which lender will be reporting the interest paid for income tax purposes. Sometimes, both lenders will report on the time that they had the loan. Quite often, the new lender will compile the information and send the borrower one tax statement at the end of the year that covers the entire year. The borrower should find out about this at the time of the transfer to know if there will be one statement or two at the end of the year.

CONSUMER CHECKLIST

- A borrower should always keep the servicer informed of any changes in his or her address and phone number. This information should be provided in writing and forwarded to the address indicated in the welcome letter. This address is usually different from the one where payments are sent.

- When loan servicing is transferred, the borrower should receive both a goodbye letter and a welcome letter. If not, the borrower should call the former servicer to verify the transfer.

- When the borrower receives the letters, he or she should make note of the new servicer's name, address, phone number, contact name and payment information.

- When making the payments after the servicing has been transferred, the borrower should follow the instructions in the welcome letter.

- The borrower should make sure that insurance companies (homeowners, flood/hazard, life/disability) and tax authority have been notified of the transfer.

- The borrower should find out which company will be reporting on interest paid for income tax purposes.

- The borrower should ask questions at the time of the transfer. If there is a problem, it is easier to handle it as soon as it arises. If the borrower has questions after the transfer is completed, he or she should contact the new servicer.

CHAPTER QUIZ

1. Who is required to perform day-to-day management of individual loans, as well as the entire servicing portfolio, making sure the interests of both the mortgagor and investor are protected?

    a. loan processor
    b. loan servicer
    c. loan originator
    d. loan officer

2. What is an escrow account?

   a. an account established to provide money to the borrower to make loan payments
   b. an account established to provide interest payments to the lender
   c. a fund established to pay any foreclosure costs
   d. a fund that the lender establishes in order to pay property taxes and hazard insurance as they become due on the property during the year

3. What law was passed, in 1990, to protect borrowers from abuses that were occurring during the loan servicing period, or life of a loan?

   a. Real Estate Settlement Procedures Act (RESPA)
   b. Truth-in-Lending Act (Regulation Z)
   c. National Affordable Housing Act
   d. Financial Institutions Reform, Recovery and Enforcement Act (FIRREA)

4. If a borrower has a face-to-face interview with a lender, he or she must receive the disclosure statement:

   a. at the time of the loan application
   b. within 3 days
   c. within 1 week
   d. when the loan funds

5. If the current servicer plans to sell the loan servicing, the borrower must be notified at least _____ before the effective date of the transfer unless he or she received a written transfer notice at settlement.

   a. 15 days
   b. 30 days
   c. 45 days
   d. 60 days

6. Which of the following is not included in the disclosure of transfer of loan servicing that is sent to the borrower?

   a. whether the lender intends to sell the mortgage servicing immediately
   b. whether the mortgage servicing can be sold at any time during the life of the loan

    c. the percentage of loans the lender
       has sold previously

    d. the new interest rate

7. After the transfer of the servicing contract, there is a 60-day grace period during which:

    a. the loan can be cancelled

    b. the loan can be called due and payable

    c. the borrower cannot be charged a late fee for sending the payment to the wrong servicer

    d. the borrower must contact the new servicer and renew the servicing contract

8. If a borrower believes he or she has been improperly charged a penalty or late fee, or there are other problems with the servicing of the loan, the borrower should:

    a. contact the servicer in writing

    b. subtract the amount of the mistake from the next payment

    c. make the regular payment and ignore the mistake

    d. stop making payments until the loan servicer makes contact

9. Section 6 of the Real Estate Settlement Procedures Act (RESPA), which is enforced by the federal Department of Housing and Urban Development (HUD), requires a servicer to acknowledge a written request to resolve a problem within:

    a. 10 business days

    b. 20 business days

    c. 30 business days

    d. 40 business days

10. On flood and hazard insurance, whose responsibility is it to provide the insurance agent or company with a notice of transfer?

    a. the new servicer

    b. the old servicer

    c. the borrower

    d. the original lender

ANSWERS

1. *b*
2. *d*
3. *c*
4. *a*
5. *a*
6. *d*
7. *c*
8. *a*
9. *b*
10. *b*

15

chapter fifteen

Consumer Protection

INTRODUCTION

The Consumer Credit Protection Act of 1968—which launched Truth in Lending disclosures—was landmark legislation. For the first time, creditors had to state the cost of borrowing in a common language so that the consumer could figure out what the charges are, compare costs, and shop for the best credit deal.

Since 1968, credit protections have multiplied rapidly. The concepts of "fair" and "equal" credit have been written into laws that prohibit unfair discrimination in credit transactions, require that consumers be told the reason when credit is denied, let borrowers find out about their credit records, and set up a way for consumers to settle billing disputes.

Each law was meant to reduce the problems and confusion about consumer credit, which—as it became more widely used in our economy—also grew more complex. Together, these laws set a standard for how individuals are to be treated in their financial dealings.

WHAT CREDITORS LOOK FOR

Creditors look for an ability to repay debt and a willingness to do so—and sometimes for a little extra security to protect their loans. They speak of the *Three Cs of credit*: capacity, character and collateral.

> ## The Three Cs of Credit
>
> (1) Capacity
> (2) Character
> (3) Collateral

Capacity: Can the borrower repay the debt? Creditors ask for employment information: the borrower's occupation, how long he or she has worked there, and for what earnings. They also want to know what the borrower's expenses are: how many dependents there are, whether the borrower pays alimony or child support, and the amount of any other obligations.

Character: Will the borrower repay the debt? Creditors will look at the borrower's credit history: the amount of money owed, the frequency of borrowing, the timeliness of paying bills, and a pattern of living within one's means. Creditors also look for signs of stability: how long the borrower has lived at the present address, whether he or she owns or rents the home, and the length of present employment.

Collateral: Is the creditor fully protected if the borrower fails to repay? Creditors want to know what the borrower may have that could be used to back up or secure a loan, and any other resources the borrower has for repaying debt other than income, such as savings, investments or property.

Creditors use different combinations of these facts to reach their decisions. Some set unusually high standards; others simply do not make certain kinds of loans. Creditors also use different rating systems. Some rely strictly on their own instinct and experience. Others use a "credit-scoring" or statistical system to predict whether the borrower is a good credit risk. They assign a certain number of points to each of the various characteristics that have proved to be reliable signs that a borrower will repay. Then they rate the borrower on this scale.

Different creditors may reach different conclusions based on the same set of facts. One may find the applicant an acceptable risk, whereas another may deny the loan.

Information the Creditor Can't Use

The Equal Credit Opportunity Act does not guarantee that an applicant will get credit. The borrower must still pass the creditor's tests of creditworthiness. But the creditor must apply these tests fairly and impartially. The act bars discrimination based on age, gender, marital status, race, color, religion and national origin. The act also bars discrimination because the applicant receives public income, such as veteran's benefits, welfare or social security, or because he or she exercises rights under federal credit laws, such as filing a billing error notice with a creditor. This protection means that a creditor may not use any of these grounds as a reason to:

- Discourage a consumer from applying for a loan

- Refuse a consumer a loan if qualified

- Lend a consumer money on terms different from those granted another person with similar income, expenses, credit history and collateral

- Close an existing account because of age, gender, marital status, race, color, religion, national origin, receipt of public income or because a consumer exercises one's rights under federal credit laws

Although creditors may not discriminate on the basis of national origin, they may consider a borrower's immigration status when making a loan decision.

Special Rules

Rules for creditworthiness have changed dramatically over the past 35 years, and consumers can hardly be blamed for their ignorance regarding their rights when borrowing money. Consumer protection has become a complex matter, with myriad laws to defend everyone's right to equal protection under those laws.

Age

In the past, many older persons have complained about being denied credit because they were over a certain age. Or when they retired, they often found their credit suddenly cut off or reduced. So the law is very specific about how a person's age may be used in credit decisions.

A creditor may ask borrowers their age, but if they are old enough to sign a binding contract (usually 18 or 21 years old depending on state law), a creditor may not:

- Turn down a borrower, offer a borrower less credit, or less favorable credit terms because of his or her age

- Ignore a borrower's retirement income in evaluating the application

- Close a borrower's credit account or require a borrower to reapply for it because he or she has reached a certain age or retired

- Deny a borrower credit or close a borrower's account because credit life insurance or other credit-related insurance is not available to a person of a certain age

Creditors may "score" a borrower's age in a credit-scoring system, but if a borrower is 62 or older he or she must be given at least as many points for age as any person under 62.

Because individuals' financial situations can change at different ages, the law lets creditors consider certain information related to age, such as how long until a borrower will retire or how long a borrower's income will continue. An older applicant might not qualify for a large loan with a very low down payment and a long term, but might qualify for a smaller loan with a larger down payment and a shorter term. Remember that although declining income may be a handicap if a borrower is older, he or she can usually offer a solid credit history to his/her or their advantage. The creditor has to consider all the facts and apply the usual standards of credit worthiness to every borrower's particular situation.

Public Assistance

A borrower may not be denied credit just because of receiving social security or public assistance, such as Temporary Assistance to Needy Families (TANF). But as is the case with age, certain information on this source of income could clearly affect creditworthiness. A creditor may consider such things as how old a borrower's dependents are (because a borrower may lose benefits when he or she reaches a certain age) or whether a borrower will continue to meet the eligibility requirements for receiving benefits.

This information helps the creditor determine the likelihood that a borrower's public-assistance income will continue.

Housing Loans

The Equal Credit Opportunity Act covers a borrower's application for a mortgage or home-improvement loan. The act bars discrimination because of characteristics such as a borrower's race, color, gender or because of the race or national origin of the people in the neighborhood where a borrower lives or wants to buy a home. Creditors may not use any appraisal of the value of the property that considers the race of the people in the neighborhood.

Also, a borrower is entitled to receive a copy of an appraisal report that he or she paid for in connection with an application for credit, provided the borrower makes a written request for the report.

Gender Discrimination

Both men and women are protected from discrimination based on gender or marital status. But many of the law's provisions were designed to stop particular abuses that generally made it difficult for women to get credit. For example, denying credit or offering less favorable credit terms based on the misperception that single women ignore their debts when they marry, or that a woman's income "doesn't count" because she'll stop work to have and raise children, is unlawful in credit transactions.

The general rule is that a borrower may not be denied credit because she is a woman or because she is married, single, widowed, divorced or separated. Here are some important protections.

Gender and Marital Status: Usually, creditors may not ask a borrower's gender on an application form (one exception is on a loan to buy or build a home). A borrower does not have to use Miss, Mrs., or Ms. with her name on a credit application. But in some cases, a creditor may ask whether she is married, unmarried or separated (unmarried includes single, divorced and widowed).

Childbearing Plans: Creditors may not ask about a woman's birth-control practices or plans to have children, and they may not assume anything about those plans.

Income and Alimony: The creditor must count all of a woman's income, even income from part-time employment. Child support and alimony payments are a source of income for many women. A woman doesn't have to disclose these kinds of income, but if she does, creditors must count them.

Telephones: Creditors may not consider whether a woman has a telephone listing in her name because this factor would discriminate against many married women. (However, you may be asked if there's a telephone in your home.)

A creditor may consider whether income is steady and reliable, so a woman must be prepared to show that she can count on uninterrupted income, particularly if the source is alimony payments or part-time wages.

Her Own Account: Many married women once were turned down for credit in their own name. Or a husband had to cosign an account—that is, agree to pay if the wife didn't—even when a wife made sufficient income to easily repay the loan. Single women couldn't get loans because they were thought to be less reliable than other applicants. Women now have the right to their own credit, based on their own credit records and earnings. Their own credit means separate accounts or loans in their own names, not joint accounts with their husbands or duplicate cards on husbands' accounts. Here are the rules.

- Creditors may not refuse to open an account because of gender or marital status.

- A woman can choose to use her first name and maiden name (Mary Smith), her first name and husband's last name (Mary Jones), or a combined last name (Mary Smith-Jones).

- If she is creditworthy, a creditor may not ask her husband to cosign her account, with certain exceptions when property rights are involved.

- Creditors may not ask for information about a woman's husband or ex-husband when she applies for her own credit based on her own income unless that income is alimony, child support, or separate maintenance payments from a spouse or former spouse.

This last rule, of course, does not apply if a woman's husband is going to use the account or be responsible for paying the debts on the account or if a woman lives in a community property state. (Community property states are Arizona, California, Idaho, Louisiana, Nevada, New Mexico, Texas, Washington and Wisconsin.)

Change in Marital Status: Married women have sometimes faced severe hardships when cut off from credit after their husbands died. Single women have had accounts closed when they married, and married women have had accounts closed after a divorce. The law says that creditors may not make a woman reapply for credit because she marries or becomes widowed or divorced. Nor may they close a woman's account or change the terms of her account on these grounds. There must be some sign that her creditworthiness has changed. For example, creditors may ask a woman to reapply if she relied on her ex-husband's income to get credit in the first place.

Setting up her own account protects a woman by establishing her own history of how she handles debt. She can rely on this record if her financial situation changes or if she becomes widowed or divorced. When a woman plans to get married and will take her husband's surname, she should write to her creditors and tell them she wants to keep a separate account.

Application Denied

Remember, a borrower's gender or race may not be used to discourage the individual from applying for a loan. And creditors may not hold up or otherwise delay an application on those grounds. Under the Equal Credit Opportunity Act, a borrower must be notified within 30 days after making an application whether the loan has been approved or not. If credit is denied, this notice must be in writing, and it must explain the specific reasons that a borrower was denied credit, or tell the borrower of the right to ask for an explanation. A borrower has the same rights if an active account is closed.

If consumers are denied credit, they should find out why. They may have to ask the creditors for this explanation. It may be that the creditor thinks the borrower has requested more money than can be repaid from current income. It may be that a borrower has not worked or lived long enough in the community. A consumer can discuss terms with the creditor and ways to improve creditworthiness.

Building a Good Record

On a borrower's first attempt to get credit, it may mean facing a common frustration: sometimes it seems a borrower already has to have credit to get credit. Some creditors will look only at a borrower's salary and job and the other financial information on the application. But most also want to know about a borrower's track record in handling credit, namely how reliably the person has repaid past debts. They turn to the records kept by credit bureaus or credit-reporting agencies, whose business is to collect, store and report information about borrowers that is routinely supplied by many lenders. These records include the amount of credit a borrower has received and how faithfully it was repaid.

Here are several ways a borrower can begin to build a good credit history.

- Open a checking account or a savings account or both. These do not begin a borrower's credit file but may be checked as evidence that he or she has money and knows how to manage it. Cancelled checks can be used to show that a borrower pays utilities or rent bills regularly, a sign of reliability.

- Apply for a department store credit card. Repaying credit card bills on time is a plus in credit histories.

- Ask whether funds may be deposited with a financial institution to serve as collateral for a credit card; some institutions will issue a credit card with a credit limit usually no greater than the amount on deposit.

- If a borrower is new in town, write for a summary of any credit record kept by a credit bureau in the former town.

- If a borrower doesn't qualify on the basis of his or her own credit standing, ask to have someone cosign the application.

- If a borrower is turned down, find out why and try to resolve any misunderstandings.

Maintaining Complete and Accurate Credit Records

Mistakes on a borrower's credit record can cloud future credit. A consumer's credit rating is so important, the individual should be sure that credit bureau records are complete and accurate. The Fair Credit Reporting Act says that a borrower must be told what's in the credit file and have any errors corrected.

Negative Information

If a lender refuses a borrower credit because of unfavorable information in his or her credit report, a borrower has a right to get the name and address of the agency that keeps the report. Then, a borrower may either request information from the credit bureau by mail or in person. The borrower may not get an exact copy of the file, but will learn what's in the report. The law also says that the credit bureau must help a borrower interpret the data in the report, because the raw data may take experience to analyze. If a borrower is questioning a credit refusal made within the past 60 days, the bureau cannot charge a fee for explaining the report.

If a borrower notifies the bureau about an error, generally the bureau must investigate and resolve the dispute within 30 days after receiving the notice. The bureau will contact the creditor who supplied the data and remove any information that is incomplete or inaccurate from the credit file. If a borrower disagrees with the findings, he or she can file a short statement (100 words) in the record, giving the borrower's side of the story. Future reports to creditors must include this statement or a summary of it.

Old Information

Sometimes credit information is too old to give a good picture of a borrower's financial reputation. There is a limit on how long certain information may be kept in the file.

- Bankruptcies must not be reported after 10 years. However, information about any bankruptcies at any time may be reported if a borrower applies for life insurance with a face value over $150,000, for a job paying $75,000 or more, or for credit with a principal amount of $150,000 or more.

- Suits and judgments paid, tax liens, and most other kinds of unfavorable information must not be reported after 7 years.

A borrower's credit record may not be given to anyone who does not have a legitimate business need for it. Stores to which a borrower is applying for credit may examine the record; curious neighbors may not. Prospective employers may examine a borrower's record with his or her permission.

Filing a Complaint with Federal Enforcement Agencies

If a borrower has a complaint about a bank or other financial institution, the Federal Reserve System may be able to help. The Federal Reserve System investigates consumer complaints received against state-chartered banks that are members of the system. Complaints about these types of banks will be investigated by one of the 12 Federal Reserve Banks around the country. The Federal Reserve will refer complaints about other institutions to the appropriate federal regulatory agency and let the consumer know where the complaint has been referred. Or a consumer may write directly to the appropriate federal agency by referring to the listing later in this chapter. Many of these agencies do not handle individual complaints; however, they will use information about a consumer's credit experiences to help enforce the credit laws.

When writing to the Federal Reserve, a consumer should submit the complaint—and it should be in writing—to the Division of Consumer and Community Affairs, Board of Governors of the Federal Reserve System, Washington, DC 20551. Be sure to provide the complete name and address of the bank, a brief description of the complaint, and any documentation that may help to investigate the complaint. Do not send original documents, send only copies; and remember to sign and date the letter. The Federal Reserve will acknowledge the complaint within 15 business days, letting the consumer know whether a Federal Reserve Bank will investigate the complaint or whether the complaint will be forwarded to another federal agency for attention.

For complaints investigated by the Federal Reserve (those involving state-chartered member banks), the Reserve Bank will analyze the bank's response to the complaint to ensure that the consumer's concerns have been addressed, and will send the consumer a letter about the findings. If the investigation reveals that a Federal Reserve regulation has been violated, the Reserve Bank will inform the consumer of the violation and the corrective action the bank has been directed to take.

Although the Federal Reserve investigates all complaints about the banks it regulates, it does not have the authority to resolve all types of problems, such as contractual or factual disputes or disagreements about bank policies or procedures. In many instances, however, if a consumer files a complaint, a bank may voluntarily work with the consumer to resolve the situation. If the matter is not resolved, the Federal Reserve will advise the consumer whether he or she should consider legal counsel to resolve the complaint.

FEDERAL CONSUMER PROTECTION LAWS

The sweeping influence of the federal government in housing issues has provided a healthy background for the inspiring story of the persistent growth of private ownership of real property in the United States. Because laws requiring fair and equal treatment of all consumers have been passed, more people are able to buy their own homes now than in any time in history.

Equal Credit Opportunity Act (ECOA)

Credit is used by millions of consumers to finance an education or a house, remodel a home or get a small business loan.

The Equal Credit Opportunity Act (ECOA) ensures that all consumers are given an equal chance to obtain credit. This doesn't mean all consumers who apply for credit get it. As discussed earlier, factors such as income, expenses, debt and credit history are considerations for creditworthiness.

The law protects a borrower when dealing with any creditor who regularly extends credit, including banks, small loan and finance companies, retail and department stores, credit card companies and credit unions. Anyone involved in granting credit, such as real estate brokers who arrange financing, is covered by the law. Businesses applying for credit also are protected by the law.

Under ECOA, When a Borrower Applies For Credit, A Creditor May Not:

- Discourage the borrower from applying because of sexual orientation or gender, marital status, age, race, national origin, or because borrower receives public assistance income.

- Ask the borrower to reveal sex, race, national origin or religion. A creditor may ask a borrower to voluntarily disclose this information (except for religion) if applying for a real estate loan. This information helps federal agencies enforce anti-discrimination laws. A borrower may be asked about his or her residence or immigration status.

- Ask if the borrower is widowed or divorced. When permitted to ask marital status, a creditor may only use the terms married, unmarried or separated.

- Ask about the borrower's marital status if he or she is applying for a separate, unsecured account. A creditor may ask you to provide this information if you live in community property states, such as Arizona, California, Idaho, Louisiana, Nevada, New Mexico, Texas, Washington and Wisconsin. A creditor in any state may ask for this information if the borrower is applying for a joint account or one secured by property.

• Request information about the borrower's spouse, except when a spouse is applying with the borrower; a spouse will be allowed to use the account; the borrower is relying on a spouse's income or on alimony or child support income from a former spouse; or if the borrower resides in a community property state.

• Inquire about the borrower's plans for having or raising children.

• Ask if the borrower receives alimony, child support, or separate maintenance payments, *unless* he or she is first told there is no need to provide this information if not relying on these payments to get credit. A creditor may ask if the borrower has to pay alimony, child support or separate maintenance payments.

Under ECOA, When Deciding To Give a Borrower Credit, A Creditor May Not:

• Consider the borrower's sex, marital status, race, national origin or religion.

• Consider whether the borrower has a telephone listing in his or her name. A creditor *may* consider whether the borrower has a phone.

• Consider the race of people in the neighborhood where the borrower wants to buy, refinance or improve a house with borrowed money.

• Consider the borrower's age, unless:

   • The borrower is too young to sign contracts, generally younger than 18 years of age;

   • The borrower is 62 or older, and the creditor will favor the applicant because of age;

   • It's used to determine the meaning of other factors important to creditworthiness. For example, a creditor could use the borrower's age to determine if income might drop because of retirement.

• It's used in a valid scoring system that favors applicants age 62 and older. A credit-scoring system assigns points to answers provided to credit application questions. For example, length of employment might be scored differently depending on the person's age.

Under ECOA, When Evaluating a Borrower's Income, A Creditor May Not:

• Refuse to consider public assistance income the same way as other income.

• Discount income because of the borrower's sex or marital status. For example, a creditor cannot count a man's salary at 100 percent and a woman's at 75 percent. A creditor may not assume a woman of childbearing age will stop working to raise children.

• Discount or refuse to consider income because it comes from part-time employment or pension, annuity or retirement benefits programs.

• Refuse to consider regular alimony, child support or separate maintenance payments. A creditor may ask the borrower to prove receiving this income consistently.

Under ECOA, A Borrower Also Has The Right To:

• Have credit in one's own birth name (Mary Smith), own first name and spouse's last name (Mary Jones), or own first name and a combined last name (Mary Smith-Jones).

• Get credit without a cosigner, if the borrower meets the creditor's standards.

• Have a cosigner other than a borrower's husband or wife, if one is necessary.

• Keep his or her own accounts after a name change, marital status change, reaching a certain age, or retiring, unless the creditor has evidence that the borrower is not willing or able to pay.

- Know whether the borrower's application was accepted or rejected within 30 days of filing a complete application.

- Know why an application was rejected. The creditor must give the borrower a notice that tells either the specific reasons for the rejection or the borrower's right to learn the reasons within 60 days.

- Get acceptable reasons for rejection. Acceptable reasons include: "Your income was low," or "You haven't been employed long enough." Unacceptable reasons are: "You didn't meet our minimum standards," or "You didn't receive enough points on our credit-scoring system." Indefinite and vague reasons are illegal, so ask the creditor to be specific.

- Find out why the borrower was offered less favorable terms than he or she applied for—unless the borrower accepts the terms. Examples of less favorable terms include higher finance charges or less money than you requested.

- Find out why the borrower's account was closed or why the terms of the account were made less favorable unless the account was inactive or delinquent.

Remedy for Discrimination

If consumers can prove that creditors have discriminated against them for any reason prohibited by this act, they may sue—but as an individual—for actual damages plus punitive damages; that is—damages of up to $10,000 for the fact that the law has been violated. In a successful lawsuit, the court will award the consumer court costs and a reasonable amount for attorney's fees. Class action suits are also permitted.

If a consumer suspects discrimination, he or she should:

- Complain to the creditor. Make it known the consumer is aware of the law. The creditor may find an error or reverse the decision.

- Check with the state Attorney General to see if the creditor violated state equal credit opportunity laws. The state may decide to prosecute the creditor.

- Bring a case in federal district court. If the borrower wins, he or she can recover damages, including punitive damages. The borrower also can obtain compensation for attorney's fees and court costs.

- Join with other borrowers and file a class action suit. A borrower may recover punitive damages for the group of up to $500,000 or 1% of the creditor's net worth, whichever is less.

- Report violations to the appropriate government agency. If a borrower is denied credit, the creditor must supply the name and address of the agency to contact. While some of these agencies don't resolve individual complaints, the information provided helps them decide which companies to investigate. A list of agencies follows.

If a retail store, department store, small loan and finance company, mortgage company, oil company, public utility, state credit union, government lending program, or travel and expense credit card company is involved, contact:

> Consumer Response Center
> Federal Trade Commission
> Washington, DC 20580

The FTC cannot intervene in individual disputes, but the information provided may indicate a pattern of possible law violations that require action by the Commission.

If the complaint concerns a nationally-chartered bank (National or N.A. will be part of the name), write to:

> Comptroller of the Currency
> Compliance Management
> Mail Stop 7-5
> Washington, DC 20219

If the complaint concerns a state-chartered bank that is insured by the Federal Deposit Insurance Corporation but is not a member of the Federal Reserve System, write to:

> Federal Deposit Insurance Corporation
> Consumer Affairs Division
> Washington, DC 20429

If the complaint concerns a federally-chartered or federally-insured savings and loan association, write to:

> Office of Thrift Supervision
> Consumer Affairs Program
> Washington, DC 20552

If the complaint concerns a federally-chartered credit union, write to:

> National Credit Union Administration
> Consumer Affairs Division
> Washington, DC 20456

Complaints against all kinds of creditors can be referred to:

> Department of Justice
> Civil Rights Division
> Washington, DC 20530

Equal Credit Opportunity Act—Regulation B

Regulation B was issued by the Board of Governors of the Federal Reserve System to implement the provisions of the Equal Credit Opportunity Act (ECOA). The law was enacted in 1974 to make it unlawful for creditors to discriminate in any aspect of a credit transaction on the basis of sex or marital status. In 1976, through amendments to the Act, it became unlawful to also discriminate on the basis of race, color, religion, national origin, age, receipt of public assistance and the good faith exercise of rights under the Consumer Credit Protection Act.

The primary purpose of the ECOA is to prevent discrimination in the granting of credit by requiring banks and other creditors to make extensions of credit equally available to all creditworthy applicants with fairness, impartiality and without discrimination on any prohibited basis. The regulation applies to consumer and other types of credit transactions.

Real Estate Settlement Procedures Act (RESPA)

This law protects consumers from abuses during the residential real estate purchase and loan process and enables them to be better informed shoppers by requiring disclosure of costs of settlement services.

The federal Real Estate Settlement Procedures Act applies to all federally related mortgage loans used to purchase or refinance real property improved with one-to-four units, provided the property includes the principal residence of the borrower. These include most purchase loans, assumptions, refinances, property improvement loans, and equity lines of credit. HUD's Office of Consumer and Regulatory Affairs, Interstate Land Sales/RESPA Division is responsible for enforcing RESPA.

The U.S. Department of Housing and Urban Development's (HUD) Federal Housing Administration (FHA) administers several regulatory programs to ensure equity and efficiency in the sale of housing. The Real Estate Settlement Procedures Act (RESPA) applies to almost all mortgage loans and lenders, not just FHA-insured mortgages.

RESPA's Purposes

• To help consumers get fair settlement services by requiring that key service costs be disclosed in advance.

(continued on next page)

RESPA's Purposes   *(continued)*

• To protect consumers by eliminating kickbacks and referral fees that would unnecessarily increase the costs of settlement services.

• To further protect consumers by prohibiting certain practices that increase the cost of settlement services

RESPA requires that borrowers receive disclosures at various times. Some disclosures spell out the costs associated with the settlement, outline lender servicing and escrow account practices, and describe business relationships between settlement service providers.

RESPA protects consumers by mandating a series of disclosures that prevent unethical practices by mortgage lenders and that provide consumers with the information to choose the real estate settlement services most suited to their needs. The disclosures must take place at various times throughout the settlement process.

Disclosures at the Time of Loan Application

When a potential homebuyer applies for a mortgage loan, the lender must give the buyer:

• A Special Information Booklet, which contains consumer information on various real estate settlement services.

• A Good Faith Estimate of settlement costs, which lists the charges the buyer is likely to pay at settlement and states whether the lender requires the buyer to use a particular settlement service.

• A Mortgage Servicing Disclosure Statement, which tells the buyer whether the lender intends to keep the loan or to transfer it to another lender for servicing, and also gives information about how the buyer can resolve complaints. RESPA does not specify penalties for lenders that fail to provide these three items, but bank regulators can impose penalties on lenders.

If the borrowers don't get these documents at the time of application, the lender must mail them within 3 business days of receiving the loan application.

If the lender turns down the loan within 3 days, however, then RESPA does not require the lender to provide these documents.

The RESPA statute does not provide an explicit penalty for the failure to provide the Special Information Booklet, Good Faith Estimate or Mortgage Servicing Statement. However, bank regulators may choose to impose penalties on lenders who fail to comply with federal law.

Disclosures Before Settlement (Closing) Occurs

- An Affiliated Business Arrangement Disclosure is required whenever a settlement service refers a buyer to a firm with which the service has any kind of business connection, such as common ownership. The service usually cannot require the buyer to use a connected firm.

- A preliminary copy of a HUD-1 Settlement Statement is required if the borrower requests it 24 hours before closing. This form gives estimates of all settlement charges that will need to be paid, both by buyer and seller.

Disclosures at Settlement

- The HUD-1 Settlement Statement is required to show the actual charges at settlement.

- An Initial Escrow Statement is required at closing or within 45 days of closing. This itemizes the estimated taxes, insurance premiums, and other charges that will need to be paid from the escrow account during the first year of the loan.

Disclosures After Settlement

- An Annual Escrow Loan Statement must be delivered by the servicer to the borrower. This statement summarizes all escrow account deposits and payments during the past year. It also notifies the borrower of any shortages or surpluses in the account and tells the borrower how these can be paid or refunded.

- A Servicing Transfer Statement is required if the servicer transfers the servicing rights for a loan to another servicer.

Along with these disclosures, RESPA protects consumers by prohibiting several other practices.

- Kickbacks, fee-splitting, and unearned fees: Anyone is prohibited from giving or accepting a fee, kickback, or anything of value in exchange for referrals of settlement service business involving a federally related mortgage loan, which covers almost every loan made for residential property. RESPA also prohibits fee-splitting and receiving unearned fees for services not actually performed. Violations of these RESPA provisions can be punished with criminal and civil penalties.

- Seller-required title insurance: A seller is prohibited from requiring a homebuyer to use a particular title insurance company. A buyer can sue a seller who violates this provision.

- Limits on escrow accounts: A limit is set on the amount that a lender may require a borrower to put into an escrow account to pay taxes, hazard insurance and other property charges. RESPA does not require lenders to impose an escrow account on borrowers, but some government loan programs or lenders may require an escrow account. During the course of the loan, RESPA prohibits a lender from charging excessive amounts for the escrow account. Also, each year the lender must notify the borrower of any escrow account shortage and return any excess of $50 or more.

Persons who believe a settlement service provider has violated RESPA in an area in which the Department has enforcement authority may wish to file a complaint. The complaint should outline the violation and identify the violators by name, address and phone number. Complainants should also provide their own name and phone number for follow-up questions from HUD. Requests for confidentiality will be honored. Complaints should be sent to:

Director, Interstate Land Sales/RESPA Division
Office of Consumer and Regulatory Affairs
U.S. Department of Housing and Urban Development
Room 9146
451 7th Street, SW,
Washington, DC 20410

Truth in Lending Act— Regulation Z

The Truth in Lending Act (TILA), Title I of the Consumer Credit Protection Act, is aimed at promoting the informed use of consumer credit by requiring disclosures about its terms and costs. The Truth in Lending Act requires disclosure of the "finance charge" and the "annual percentage rate"—and certain other costs and terms of credit—so that a consumer can compare the prices of credit from different sources. It also limits liability on lost or stolen credit cards. In general, this regulation applies to each individual or business that offers or extends credit when the credit is offered or extended to consumers; the credit is subject to a finance charge or is payable by a written agreement in more than four installments; the credit is primarily for personal, family or household purposes; and the loan balance equals or exceeds $25,000.00 or is secured by an interest in real property or a dwelling.

TILA is intended to enable the customer to compare the cost of a cash versus credit transaction and the difference in the cost of credit among different lenders. The regulation also requires a maximum interest rate to be stated in variable rate contracts secured by the borrower's dwelling, imposes limitations on home equity plans that are subject to the requirements of certain sections of the act and requires a maximum interest that may apply during the term of a mortgage loan. TILA also establishes disclosure standards for advertisements that refer to certain credit terms.

The federal Truth in Lending Act was originally enacted by Congress in 1968 as a part of the Consumer Protection Act. The law is designed to protect consumers in credit transactions by requiring clear disclosure of key terms of the lending arrangement and all costs. The law was simplified and reformed as a part the Depository Institutions Deregulations and Monetary Control Act of 1980. The Truth in Lending Act is important for small businesses involved in consumer credit transactions or consumer leasing.

Regulations

The law has been implemented by the Federal Reserve Board through two key regulations.

Regulation Z explains how to comply with the consumer credit parts of the law. This law applies to each individual or business that offers or extends consumer credit if four conditions are met.

(1) The credit is offered to consumers.

(2) Credit is offered on a regular basis.

(3) The credit is subject to a finance charge (i.e. interest) or must be paid in more than four installments according to a written agreement.

(4) The credit is primarily for personal, family or household purposes.

If credit is extended to business, commercial or agricultural purposes, Regulation Z does not apply.

Regulation M includes all the rules for consumer leasing transactions. This law applies to contracts in the form of a bailment or lease where the use of personal property is primarily for private, family or household purposes. The lease period must exceed 4 months, and the total contractual obligations must not exceed $25,000, regardless of whether the lessee has the option to purchase the property at the end of the lease term.

Home Mortgages

One of the biggest lending transactions any individual is likely to enter is borrowing to purchase a home. These transactions have become more complicated in recent years. Historically, someone trying to buy a home had very few options. Often, only a traditional 30-year loan was available. Now, loans of various duration and interest rate variations are available to every home buyer. The Federal Reserve Board and the Federal Home Loan Bank Board have published a book entitled *Consumer Handbook on Adjustable Rate Mortgages* to help consumers understand the purpose and uses of adjustable rate mortgage loans. Regulation Z requires that creditors offering adjustable rate mortgage loans make this booklet, or a similar one, available to consumers.

Disclosure

Disclosure is generally required before credit is extended. In certain cases, it must also be made in periodic billing statements. Regulation M includes similar rules for disclosing terms when leasing personal property for personal, family or household purposes, if the obligations total less than $25,000.

In general, disclosure is required before any *closed end credit transaction* is completed. There is an exception where credit is extended over the telephone or by the mails. In those cases, a disclosure may be made after the fact. Disclosure is also required before the first transaction under an *open end account*, and again at the time the periodic billing statement is sent.

The term closed end credit transaction is defined by exclusion. That is, it includes any credit arrangement (either a consumer loan or credit sale) that does not fall within the definition of an open end credit transaction. Open end credit includes credit arrangements like revolving credit cards, where the borrower (that is the credit card holder) is not required to pay off the principal amount by any particular point in time. Rather, the borrower is simply charged interest periodically and is usually required only to make some minimum payment.

The term credit sale means a sale in which the seller is the creditor. That is, the amount of the purchase price is financed by the seller. This includes any consumer lease, unless the lease is terminable without penalty at any time by the consumer, or when:

- The consumer agrees to pay an amount substantially equal to, or more than, the total value of the property or services involved.

- The consumer has the opportunity to purchase the property for at least nominal consideration.

Under Regulation Z, disclosure must be made of the following important credit terms.

Finance charge: This is perhaps the most important disclosure made. This is the amount charged to the consumer for the credit.

Annual percentage rate: This is the measure of the cost of the credit which must be disclosed on a yearly basis. The method for calculating this rate is determined by the underlying transaction.

Amount financed: This is the amount that is being borrowed in a consumer loan transaction, or the amount of the sale price in a credit sale.

Total of payments: This includes the total amount of the periodic payments by the borrower/buyer.

Total sales price: This is the total cost of the purchase on credit, including the down payment and periodic payments.

Evidence of compliance with the Truth-in-Lending requirements must be retained for at least 2 years after the date of disclosure. Disclosures must be clear and conspicuous and must appear on a document that the consumer may keep.

Home Ownership and Equity Protection Act of 1994 (HOEPA)

The Home Ownership and Equity Protection Act of 1994 (HOEPA) deals with high-rate, high-fee mortgage loans that are a refinance or home equity installment loan.

The law addresses certain deceptive and unfair practices in home equity lending. It amends the Truth in Lending Act (TILA) and establishes requirements for certain loans with high rates and/or high fees. The rules for these loans are contained in Section 32 of Regulation Z, which implements the TILA, so the loans also are called "Section 32 Mortgages." Here's what loans are covered, the law's disclosure requirements, prohibited features, and actions a borrower can take against a lender who is violating the law.

What Loans Are Covered?   A loan is covered by the law if it meets the following tests.

- For a first-lien loan (the original mortgage on the property) the annual percentage rate (APR) exceeds by more than eight percentage points the rates on Treasury securities of comparable maturity;

- For a second-lien loan (a second mortgage) the APR exceeds by more than 10 percentage points the rates in treasury securities of comparable maturity; or

- The total fees and points payable by the consumer at or before closing exceed the larger of $488 or 8 percent of the total loan amount. (The $488 figure is for 2003. This amount is adjusted annually by the Federal Reserve Board, based on changes in the Consumer Price Index.) Credit insurance premiums for insurance written in connection with the credit transaction are counted as fees.

The rules primarily affect refinancing and home equity installment loans that also meet the definition of a high-rate or high-fee loan. The rules do not cover loans to buy or build a home, reverse mortgages or home equity lines of credit (similar to revolving credit accounts).

What Disclosures Are Required?   If a loan meets the above tests, a borrower must receive several disclosures at least three business days before the loan is finalized.

The lender must give the borrower a written notice stating that the loan need not be completed, even though he or she has signed the loan application and received the required disclosures. The borrower has three business days to decide whether to sign the loan agreement after receiving the special Section 32 disclosures.

The notice must warn the borrower that, because the lender will have a mortgage on that home, the borrower could lose the residence and any money put into it, if failing to make payments.

The lender must disclose the APR, the regular payment amount (including any balloon payment where the law permits balloon payments, discussed below), and the loan amount (plus where the amount borrowed includes credit insurance premiums, that fact must be stated). For variable rate loans, the lender must disclose that the rate and monthly payment may increase and state the amount of the maximum monthly payment.

These disclosures are in addition to the other TILA disclosures that the borrower must receive no later than the closing of the loan.

What Practices Are Prohibited?   The following features are banned from high-rate, high-fee loans.

- All balloon payments—where the regular payments do not fully pay off the principal balance and a lump sum payment of more than twice the amount of the regular payments is required—for loans with less than 5-year terms. There is an exception for bridge or swing loans of less than 1 year used by consumers to buy or build a home. In that situation, balloon payments are not prohibited.

• Negative amortization, which involves smaller monthly payments that do not fully pay off the loan and that cause an increase in the total principal debt.

• Default interest rates higher than pre-default rates.

• Rebates of interest upon default calculated by any method less favorable than the actuarial method.

• A repayment schedule that consolidates more than two periodic payments that are to be paid in advance from the proceeds of the loan.

• Most prepayment penalties, including refunds of unearned interest calculated by any method less favorable than the actuarial method. The exception is if:

  • The lender verifies that the total monthly debt (including the mortgage) is 50% or less of the borrower's monthly gross income;

  • The borrower gets the money to prepay the loan from a source other than the lender or an affiliate lender; and

  • The lender exercises the penalty clause during the first 5 years following execution of the mortgage.

• A due-on-demand clause. The exceptions are if:

  • There is fraud or material misrepresentation by the consumer in connection with the loan;

  • The consumer fails to meet the repayment terms of the agreement; or

  • There is any action by the consumer that adversely affects the creditor's security.

Creditors Also May Not:

- Make loans based on the collateral value of the secured property without regard to the borrower's ability to repay the loan. In addition, proceeds for home improvement loans must be disbursed either directly to the borrower, jointly to the borrower and the home improvement contractor or, in some instances, to the escrow agent.

- Refinance a HOEPA loan into another HOEPA loan within the first 12 months of origination, unless the new loan is in the borrower's best interest. The prohibition also applies to assignees holding or servicing the loan.

- Wrongfully document a closed-end, high-cost loan as an open-end loan. For example, a high-cost mortgage may not be structured as a home equity line of credit if there is no reasonable expectation that repeat transactions will occur.

How Are Compliance Violations Handled?   A borrower may have the right to sue a lender for violations of these new requirements. In a successful suit, the borrower may be able to recover statutory and actual damages, court costs and attorney's fees. In addition, a violation of the high-rate, high-fee requirements of the TILA may enable the borrower to rescind (or cancel) the loan for up to 3 years.

Other Features of the Truth in Lending Act

The Truth in Lending Act has other important features. If credit terms are advertised, the law requires disclosure of key lending terms. Also, the law entitles the consumer the right to rescind certain credit transactions within a short period, such as home equity loans.

To assist creditors, sellers and lessors, the Federal Reserve Board has provided a series of model disclosure forms and clauses for Regulation Z and Regulation M. Copies of these regulations and model forms may be found at most public libraries and law school libraries. Regulation Z is in the Code of Federal Regulations at 12 C. F. R. Part 226. Regulation M is also in the Code of Federal Regulations at 12 C. F. R. Part 213. (The librarian can use these citations to locate these regulations.)

The penalties for failure to comply with the Truth in Lending Act can be substantial. A creditor who violates the disclosure requirements may be sued for twice the amount of the finance charge. In the case of a consumer lease, the amount is 25% of the total of the monthly payments under the lease, with a minimum of $100 and a maximum of $1,000. Costs and attorney's fees may also be awarded to the consumer. A lawsuit must be begun by the consumer within a year of the violation. However, if a creditor sues more than a year after their violation date, violations of the Truth in Lending Act can be asserted as a defense.

Truth in Lending (Regulation Z)

The following questions and answers illustrate some aspects of the regulations covering advertising under Regulation Z of the Truth in Lending Law. Advertising includes newspaper and electronic media advertisements, as well as signs, handouts, brochures, etc.

(1) **May I advertise the interest rate only?**

No.

(2) **May I advertise the annual percentage rate (without disclosure of other terms)?**

Yes. (But if the rate varies, that fact must be disclosed.)

(3) **May I use the initials APR in the place of the term "annual percentage rate" in my advertising?**

No, you must use the term "annual percentage rate."

(4) **Without disclosing other terms, may I advertise, say "$10,000.00 down"?**

No, you must disclose the annual percentage rate and other terms.

(5) **Without disclosing other terms, may I advertise "no closing costs"?**

Yes.

(6) **Without disclosing other terms, may I advertise "small down payment"?**

Yes.

(continued on next page)

Truth in Lending (Regulation Z)   *(continued)*

(7) Without disclosing other terms, may I advertise "liberal rates"?

Yes.

(8) Without disclosing other terms, may I advertise "terms"?

Yes.

(9) Must I ever disclose in any residential real state advertisement the deferred payment price or the total of loan payments?

No.

(10) If I advertise only the sales price or loan amount and the annual percentage rate, must my advertisement include any other terms?

No, but remember, if you advertise rate, you must express it as annual percentage rate. (And if it is a variable rate loan, you must say so.)

(11) What are the general rules governing advertisement of terms?

If you advertise any one of the following:

a. The percentage or the amount of down payment;

b. The amount of any installment payment;

c. The dollar amount of the finance charge; OR

d. The number of installments or the period of repayment;

THEN you must include ALL of the following:

e. The amount or percentage of down payment;

f. The number, amount and periods of payments;

g. The amount of the finance charge expressed as an annual percentage rate.

(12) May I advertise a "$350.00 monthly payment"?

Yes, but you then must advertise the additional disclosure requirements listed in Answer 11.

(continued on next page)

Truth in Lending (Regulation Z)   *(continued)*

(13) May I advertise "assume 9% mortgage" or "11.9% financing"?

Yes, but you then must advertise the additional disclosure requirements listed in Answer 11.

(14) Can I use MLS sheets as credit advertising?

No.

Violations

The number of violations appears to be increasing, The penalties for violations are minimal. Moreover, many builders and lenders apparently do not understand the rules. It remains to be seen whether the Federal Trade Commission or the Federal Reserve Board will commence an enforcement program.

Real Estate Brokers Not Credit Arrangers

Regulation Z, promulgated by the Federal Reserve Board under the Truth in Lending Act, classifies mortgage lenders as "arrangers of credit." Thus, lenders must fill out settlement disclosure statements at all real estate closings. But what about real estate brokers? Are they "credit arrangers" when they close a contract sale, or an assumption sale, or some other seller financed sale? Must they fill out Truth in Lending disclosure statements? The answer is, real estate brokers have been generally exempt from this burden from the outset of Regulation Z.

However, as special financing has become so common, the Federal Reserve Board began to look again at real estate brokers. Finally, the Board tentatively announced an amendment to Regulation Z that would have redefined "credit arranger" to include brokers on seller financed sales. Because of protests, the Fed held up the amendment until Congress reviewed the question.

Congress finally settled the issue in favor of real estate brokers. The Depository Institutions Deregulation Act of 1982 prevents the Fed from assigning arranger of credit status to real estate brokers in seller financed transactions.

This means that brokers will remain generally exempt from the "credit arranger" rules of Regulation Z as before.

Of course, it does not mean that just because a broker has a real estate license, he or she is now automatically exempt from Regulation Z. If that broker has customarily financed sales and lent mortgage funds, he or she has been an arranger of credit the same as any other mortgage lender and must continue to comply, as before, with Regulation Z, just as in the past. The new act simply keeps Regulation Z from being extended to real estate brokers who have heretofore been exempt.

Rights to Financial Privacy Act

The Right to Financial Privacy Act provides that customers of financial institutions have a right to expect that their financial activities will have a reasonable amount of privacy from federal government scrutiny. The act establishes specific procedures and exemptions concerning the release of the financial records of customers and imposes limitations on and requirements of financial institutions prior to the release of such information to the federal government.

Expedited Funds Availability Act

The Expedited Funds Availability Act requires all banks, savings and loan associations, savings banks and credit unions to make funds deposited into checking, share draft and NOW accounts available according to specified time schedules and to disclose their funds availability policies to their customers. The law does not require an institution to delay the customer's use of deposited funds but instead limits how long any delay may last. The regulation also establishes rules designed to speed the return of unpaid checks.

Fair Debt Collection Practices Act

The Fair Debt Collection Practices Act is designed to eliminate abusive, deceptive and unfair debt collection practices. It applies to third-party debt collectors or those who use a name other than their own in collecting consumer debts. Very few commercial banks, savings banks, savings and loan associations, or credit unions are covered by this act, since they usually collect only their own debts. Complaints concerning debt collection practices generally should be filed with the Federal Trade Commission.

The Federal Trade Commission Act

The Federal Trade Commission Act requires federal financial regulatory agencies to maintain a consumer affairs division to assist in resolving consumer complaints against institutions they supervise. This assistance is given to help get necessary information to consumers about problems they are having in order to address complaints concerning acts or practices which may be unfair or deceptive.

Home Equity Loan Consumer Protection Act

The Home Equity Loan Consumer Protection Act requires lenders to disclose terms, rates and conditions (APRs, miscellaneous charges, payment terms, and information about variable rate features) for home equity lines of credit with the applications and before the first transaction under the home equity plan. If the disclosed terms change, the consumer can refuse to open the plan and is entitled to a refund of fees paid in connection with the application. The act also limits the circumstances under which creditors may terminate or change the terms of a home equity plan after it is opened.

Home Mortgage Disclosure Act (HMDA)

The Home Mortgage Disclosure Act (HMDA) requires certain lending institutions to report annually on their originations and acquisitions of home purchase and home improvement loans as well as applications for such loans. The type of loan, location of the property, race or national origin, sex and income of the applicant or borrower is reported. Institutions are required to make information regarding their lending available to the public and must post a notice of availability in their public lobby. Disclosure statements are also available at central depositories in metropolitan areas. This information can help the public determine how well institutions are serving the housing credit needs of their neighborhoods and communities.

Home Mortgage Disclosure Act Aggregation Project

Using loan data collected from each covered institution, the Federal Financial Institutions Examination Council (FFIEC) prepares disclosure statements and various reports for individual institutions in each metropolitan statistical area (MSA), showing lending patterns by location, age of housing stock, income level, sex and racial characteristics. The disclosure statements and reports are made available to the public at central depositories located in each MSA. Requests for the list of central depositories should be forwarded to the FFIEC.

Federal Financial Institutions Examination Council
2100 Pennsylvania Ave, NW
Suite 200
Washington, DC 20037

The Council is a formal interagency body empowered to prescribe uniform principles, standards, and report forms for the federal examination of financial institutions by the Board of Governors of the Federal Reserve System (FRB), the Federal Deposit Insurance Corporation (FDIC), the National

Credit Union Administration (NCUA), the Office of the Comptroller of the Currency (OCC), and the Office of Thrift Supervision (OTS) and to make recommendations to promote uniformity in the supervision of financial institutions.

National Flood Insurance Act

National Flood Insurance is available to any property holder whose local community participates in the national program by adopting and enforcing flood plain management. Federally regulated lenders are required to compel borrowers to purchase flood insurance in certain designated areas. Lenders also must disclose to borrowers whether their structure is located in a flood hazard area.

Credit Practices Rule

The Credit Practices Rule prohibits lenders from using certain remedies, such as confessions of judgment; wage assignments; and nonpossessory, nonpurchase money, security interests in household goods. The rule also prohibits lenders from misrepresenting a cosigner's liability and requires that lenders provide cosigners with a notice explaining their credit obligation as a cosigner. It also prohibits the pyramiding of late charges.

Electronic Fund Transfer Act

The Electronic Fund Transfer Act provides consumer protection for all transactions using a debit card or electronic means to debit or credit an account. It also limits a consumer's liability for unauthorized electronic fund transfers.

The Interstate Land Sales Full Disclosure Act

The Interstate Land Sales Full Disclosure Act protects consumers from fraud and abuse in the sale or lease of land. It requires land developers to provide each purchaser with a disclosure document called a Property Report. The Property Report contains relevant information about the subdivision and must be delivered to each purchaser before the signing of the contract. The act and regulations require also that certain provisions be included in the contract for sale to protect consumers from fraud and abuse in the sale or lease of land.

Fair Credit Reporting Act (FCRA)

One of the most important laws protecting consumer's identity and credit information is the Fair Credit Reporting Act. Designed to promote the accuracy, fairness and privacy of the information collected and maintained by credit reporting agencies, the FCRA gives consumers specific rights.

The Fair Credit Reporting Act establishes procedures for correcting mistakes on a person's credit record and requires that a consumer's record only be provided for legitimate business needs. It also requires that the record be kept confidential. A credit record may be retained 7 years for judgments, liens, suits, and other adverse information except for bankruptcies, which may be retained 10 years. If a consumer has been denied credit, a cost-free credit report may be requested within 30 days of denial.

A consumer may sue any credit-reporting agency or creditor for breaking the rules about who may see his or her credit records or for not correcting errors in a credit file. Again, a consumer is entitled to actual damages, plus punitive damages that the court may allow if the violation is proved to have been intentional. In any successful lawsuit, a consumer will also be awarded court costs and attorney's fees. A person who obtains a credit report without proper authorization or an employee of a credit-reporting agency who gives a credit report to unauthorized persons may be fined up to $5,000 or imprisoned for 1 year or both.

Consumers must be told if personal credit information is used against them. If a consumer is denied credit, employment or insurance because of information in the credit report, the denying party must alert the consumer and provide the name, address and phone number of the credit reporting agency used to support the denial.

A consumer has access to his or her file. Upon request, a credit reporting agency must give a consumer the information in the file and a list of everyone who has requested it within a certain time period. There is no charge if the consumer has been denied credit, employment or insurance because of items in the file (if a request is made within 60 days). In addition, a consumer is entitled to one free report every 12 months if unemployed or on welfare, or if there is proof that a report is inaccurate.

A consumer can dispute inaccurate information. A credit reporting agency must investigate items that a consumer reports as inaccurate. The consumer will receive a full copy of the investigation report. If the dispute is not settled to his or her satisfaction, the consumer may add a statement to the report.

Inaccurate information must be corrected or deleted. Credit reporting agencies are required to remove or correct inaccurate or unverified information. They are not required to remove accurate data unless it is outdated.

Access to a consumer's file is limited. Only people and institutions with needs recognized by the FCRA may legally gain access to a file. This normally includes creditors, government agencies, insurers, employers, landlords and some businesses.

A consumer can remove his or her name from credit reporting agency lists used for unsolicited credit and insurance offers. Unsolicited offers must include a toll-free phone number where the consumer can call to be removed from credit reporting agency lists.

The Community Reinvestment Act

The Community Reinvestment Act (CRA) is intended to encourage depository institutions to help meet the credit needs of the communities in which they operate, including low- and moderate-income neighborhoods. It was enacted by the Congress in 1977 and is implemented by Regulation BB.

Evaluation of CRA Performance

The CRA requires that each depository institution's record in helping meet the credit needs of its entire community be evaluated periodically. That record is taken into account in considering an institution's application for deposit facilities.

Neither the CRA nor its implementing regulation gives specific criteria for rating the performance of depository institutions. Rather, the law indicates that the evaluation process should accommodate an institution's individual circumstances. Nor does the law require institutions to make high-risk loans that jeopardize their safety. To the contrary, the law makes it clear that an institution's CRA activities should be undertaken in a safe and sound manner.

THE FAIR HOUSING LAWS

Over the past 140 years, as home ownership has become a reality for many Americans, the process has not always been fair to everyone. There is no area where the country has experienced more growing pains than in the area of discrimination and prejudice.

Over the years, however, laws have been created to make the housing market equitable, leveling the playing field for all Americans. Many of these laws have been aimed at discriminatory practices in the sale, financing and rental of houses. Since discrimination on the basis of race, creed, gender or national origin is not in the public interest, not to mention morally wrong, the federal government has taken an active role in the prohibition of discriminatory housing practices.

1866 Civil Rights Act

This federal law prohibits discrimination based on race in all property transactions. However, it was basically ignored until 1968.

U.S. Supreme Court Case of *Jones vs. Mayer* of 1968

Jones vs. Mayer prohibits discrimination based on race by upholding the 1866 Civil Rights Act and the 13th Amendment to the U.S. Constitution prohibiting slavery.

Civil Rights Act of 1968 and 1988 Amendments

In leasing or selling residential property, the Civil Rights Act of 1968 expands the definition of discrimination to include not only race, but national origin, color and religion. The Fair Housing Amendments Act of 1988 (effective March 12, 1989) further broadens the definition to include age, sex and handicapped status. Under these laws, real estate offices are required to display fair housing posters. Any complaints must be filed with HUD.

Fair Housing Act

The Fair Housing Amendments Act of 1988 and Title VIII of the Civil Rights Act of 1968, taken together, constitute the Fair Housing Act. Specifically, the Fair Housing Act provides protection against the following discriminatory housing practices if they are based on race, sex, religion, color, handicap, familial status or national origin.

- Refusing to rent housing

- Refusing to sell housing

- Treating applicants differently for housing

- Treating residents differently in connection with terms and conditions

- Advertising a discriminatory housing preference or limitation

- Providing false information about the availability of housing

- Harassing, coercing or intimidating people from enjoying or exercising their rights under the act

- *Blockbusting* for profit; persuading an owner to sell or rent housing by saying people of a particular race, religion, etc. are moving into the neighborhood

- Imposing different loan terms for purchasing, constructing, improving, repairing or maintaining a residence

• Denying use of or participation in real estate services, such as brokers' organizations or multiple listing services

Significant Recent Changes in the Fair Housing Act of 1988

In addition to expanding the number of protected classes and creating new enforcement procedures, the 1988 amendments to the Fair Housing Act also created an exemption to the provisions barring discrimination on the basis of familial status for those housing developments that qualified as housing for persons age 55 or older.

The Housing for Older Persons Act of 1995 (HOPA)

This law makes several changes to the 55 and older exemption. First, it eliminates the requirement that 55 and older housing have *significant facilities and services* designed for the elderly. Second, HOPA establishes a *good faith reliance* immunity from damages for persons who in good faith believe that the 55 and older exemption applies to a particular property, if they do not actually know that the property is ineligible for the exemption and if the property has formally stated in writing that it qualifies for the exemption.

HOPA retains the requirement that housing must have one person who is 55 years of age or older living in at least 80% of its occupied units. It also still requires that housing publish and follow policies and procedures that demonstrate an intent to be housing for persons 55 and older (rather than housing for adults or for singles, for example).

An exempt property will not violate the Fair Housing Act if it excludes families with children, but it does not have to do so. Of course, the property must meet the act's requirements that at least 80% of its occupied units have at least one occupant who is 55 or older, and that it publish and follow policies and procedures which demonstrate an intent to be housing for persons 55 and older.

HUD has prepared proposed regulations as required by Congress and they were published for public comment on January 14, 1997. Once final regulations have officially been adopted, HUD will remove regulations outdated as a result of the changed law.

Changes were made to enhance law enforcement including amendments to criminal penalties in section 901 of the Civil Rights Act of 1968 for violations of the Fair Housing Act in Title VIII.

Changes were made to provide incentives for self- testing by lenders for discrimination under the Fair Housing Act and the Equal Credit Opportunity Act.

Fair Housing Assistance Program

The purpose of the Fair Housing Assistance Program (FHAP) is to strengthen nationwide fair housing efforts by helping individual state and local governments administer laws of their own that are consistent with the Federal Fair Housing Act.

HUD awards FHAP grants to state and local government agencies who have entered into cooperative agreements with HUD and whose housing discrimination laws are substantially equivalent to the federal fair housing laws. This process allows the state or local government to investigate Fair Housing Act complaints in its jurisdiction.

Eligible grantees are state and local enforcement agencies administering statutes that HUD has found to be similar to the federal statute. The Fair Housing Act does not prescribe in any detail the methods to be employed by HUD in reimbursing local enforcement agencies.

Funding is provided to assist state and local authorities in carrying out activities related to the administration and enforcement of their fair housing laws and ordinances. Such activities include complaint processing, training, implementation of data and information systems, and other special projects specifically designed to enhance the agency's administration and enforcement of its fair housing law or ordinance.

Fair Housing Initiatives Program

The Fair Housing Initiatives program (FHIP) was established by the Housing and Community Development Act of 1987 (HCD Act of 1987) and was amended by the HCD Act of 1992. FHIP provides funding to public and private entities formulating or carrying out programs to prevent or eliminate discriminatory housing practices.

Through four distinct categories of funding, FHIP supports projects and activities designed to enhance compliance with the act and substantially equivalent state and local laws prohibiting housing discrimination. These activities include programs of enforcement, voluntary compliance, and education and outreach. The program provides a coordinated approach to:

(1) Further the purposes of the Fair Housing Act;

(2) Guarantee the rights of all Americans to seek housing in an open market free of discrimination; and

(3) Inform the American citizenry of its rights and obligations under the Fair Housing Act.

Enforcement of the Fair Housing Act

HUD has had a lead role in the administering the Fair Housing Act since its adoption in 1968. The 1988 amendments, however, have greatly increased the Department's enforcement role. First, the newly protected classes have proven significant sources of new complaints. Second, HUD's expanded enforcement role took the Department beyond investigation and conciliation into the mandatory enforcement area.

The Fair Housing Act gives HUD the authority to hold administrative hearings unless one of the parties elects to have the case heard in U.S. District Court and to issue subpoenas. The Administrative Law Judge in these proceedings can issue an order for relief, including actual damages, injunctive or other equitable relief and penalties.

Complaints filed with HUD are investigated by the Office of Fair Housing and Equal Opportunity (FHEO). If the complaint is not successfully conciliated then FHEO determines whether reasonable cause exists to believe that a discriminatory housing practice has occurred. Where reasonable cause is found, the parties to the complaint are notified by HUD's issuance of a Determination, as well as a Charge of Discrimination, and a hearing is scheduled before a HUD administrative law judge. Either party— complainant or respondent—may cause the HUD-scheduled administrative proceeding to be terminated by electing instead to have the matter litigated in federal court.

Whenever a party has so elected, the Department of Justice takes over HUD's role as counsel seeking resolution of the charge on behalf of aggrieved persons, and the matter proceeds as a civil action. Either form of action is subject to review in the U.S. Court of Appeals.

The penalties range from up to $10,000 for a first violation, to up to $50,000 for the third violation and those thereafter. The penalties are paid to the federal government. The damage payments go to the proven victims.

The act adds criminal penalties of a $100,000 maximum fine and imprisonment as sanctions against people who willfully fail to give information and evidence or who willfully give false information in a fair housing investigation or proceeding.

Age Discrimination Act of 1975

The Age Discrimination Act of 1975 prohibits discrimination on the basis of age in programs and activities receiving federal financial assistance. The act, which applies to all ages, permits the use of certain age distinctions and factors other than age that meet the act's requirements. The Age Discrimination Act is enforced by the Civil Rights Center.

The Age Discrimination in Employment Act of 1967 (ADEA)

The Age Discrimination in Employment Act of 1967 (ADEA) protects certain applicants and employees 40 years of age and older from discrimination on the basis of age in hiring, promotion, discharge, compensation, or terms, conditions or privileges of employment. The ADEA is enforced by the Equal Employment Opportunity Commission (EEOC).

Title II of The Americans with Disabilities Act of 1990 (ADA)

Title II of the ADA prohibits discrimination against persons with disabilities in all services, programs and activities made available by state and local governments. The Department of Justice (DOJ) has coordination authority for the ADA.

The DOJ regulations cover all state and local governments and extend the prohibition of discrimination in federally-assisted programs established by Section 504 of the Rehabilitation Act of 1973 to all activities of state and local governments, including those that do not receive federal financial assistance.

HUD is the designated agency for all programs, services and regulatory activities relating to state and local public housing, and housing assistance and referrals. In addition, HUD has jurisdiction over a state or local government activity when HUD has jurisdiction under Section 504 of the Rehabilitation Act of 1973.

The Architectural Barriers Act of 1968

The Architectural Barriers Act (ABA) requires buildings and facilities that are constructed by or on behalf of or leased by the United States, or buildings financed, in whole or in part, by a grant or loan made by the United States to be accessible to persons with mobility impairments. The Architectural and Transportation Barriers Board (ATBCB) has coordination authority for the ABA.

STATE LAWS

Many state laws also provide rights and remedies in consumer financial transactions. Unless a state law conflicts with a particular federal law, the state law usually will apply. Some states have usury laws, which establish maximum rates of interest that creditors can charge for loans or credit sales. The maximum interest rates vary from state to state and depend upon the type of credit transaction involved.

Complaint Filing Process

If the consumer has a complaint against a financial institution, the first step is to contact an officer of the institution and attempt to resolve the complaint directly. Financial institutions value their customers and most will be helpful. If the consumer is unable to resolve the complaint directly, the financial institution's regulatory agency may be contacted for assistance.

The agency will usually acknowledge receipt of a complaint letter within a few days. If the letter is referred to another agency, the consumer will be advised of this fact. When the appropriate agency investigates the complaint the financial institution may be given a copy of the complaint letter.

The complaint should be submitted in writing and should include the following.

- Complainant's name, address, telephone number;

- The institution's name and address;

- Type of account involved in the complaint—checking, savings, or loan—and account numbers, if applicable;

- Description of the complaint, including specific dates and the institution's actions (copies of pertinent information or correspondence are also helpful);

- Date of contact and the names of individuals contacted at the institution with their responses;

- Complainant's signature and the date the complaint is submitted to the regulatory agency.

The regulatory agencies will be able to help resolve the complaint if the financial institution has violated a banking law or regulation. They may not be able to help where the consumer is not satisfied with an institution's policy or practices, even though no law or regulation was violated. Additionally, the regulatory agencies do not resolve factual or most contractual disputes.

The following information will help in determining which agency to contact.

National Bank

The word *National* appears in the bank's name, or the initials N.A. appear after the bank's name. Agency to Contact: Comptroller of the Currency

State-Chartered Bank, Member of the Federal Reserve System

Two signs will be prominently displayed on the door of the bank or in the lobby. One will say "Member, Federal Reserve System." The other will indicate deposits are insured by the Federal Deposit Insurance Corporation and/or "Deposits Federally Insured to $100,000—Backed by the Full Faith and Credit of the United States Government." The word *National* does not appear in the name; the initials N.A. do not appear after the name. Agency to Contact: Federal Reserve Board for federal laws; State Banking Department for state laws.

State Non-Member Bank or State-Chartered Savings Bank, Federally Insured

A sign will be prominently displayed at each teller station that indicates deposits are insured by the Federal Deposit Insurance Corporation and/or "Deposits Federally Insured to $100,000—Backed by the Full Faith and Credit of the United States Government." There will not be a sign saying "Member, Federal Reserve System." The word *National* or the initials N.A. will not appear in the name. Agency to Contact: Federal Deposit Insurance Corporation for federal laws; State Banking Department for state laws.

Federal Savings and Loan Association or Federal Savings Association, Federally Insured

Generally, the word *Federal* appears in the name of the savings and loan association or its name includes initials such as *FA* which indicate its status as a federal savings and loan association. A sign will be prominently displayed at each teller station that says "Deposits Federally Insured to $100,000—Backed by the Full Faith and Credit of the United States Government." Agency to Contact: Office of Thrift Supervision.

Federal Savings Bank, Federally Insured

Generally, the word "Federal" appears in the name of the savings bank or its name includes the initials such as "FSB" which indicate its status as a federal savings bank. A sign will be prominently displayed at each teller station that says "Deposits Insured to $100,000—Backed by the Full Faith and Credit of the United States Government." Agency to Contact: Office of Thrift Supervision.

State-Chartered Federally Insured Savings Institution

There will be a sign prominently displayed at each teller station that says "Deposits Federally Insured to $100,000—Backed by the Full Faith and Credit of the United States Government." Agency to Contact: Office of Thrift Supervision.

State Chartered Banks or Savings Institutions without Federal Deposit Insurance

Institution has none of the above described characteristics. Agency to Contact: State Banking Department for state laws; Federal Trade Commission for federal laws.

Federally Chartered Credit Union

The term "Federal Credit Union" appears in the name of the credit union. Agency to Contact: National Credit Union Administration

State-Chartered, Federally Insured Credit Union

A sign will be displayed by stations or windows where deposits are accepted indicating that deposits are insured by NCUA. The term "Federal Credit Union" does not appear in the name. Agency to Contact: State Agency that regulates credit unions or Federal Trade Commission.

State-Chartered Credit Unions without Federal Insurance

The term "Federal Credit Union" does not appear in the name. Agency to Contact: State Agency that regulates credit unions or Federal Trade Commission.

Other

Institutions have none of the characteristics described. Agency to Contact: Appropriate State Agency for state laws; Federal Trade Commission for federal laws.

Complaints

Complaints should be mailed to the appropriate agency with copies of all relevant documents. Original documents or currency should not be sent. Websites for the federal agencies are:

> Board of Governors of the Federal Reserve System
> Consumer Information
> http://www.federalreserve.gov/consumerinfo
>
>
> Federal Deposit Insurance Corporation
> Consumer Protection
> http://www.fdic.gov/consumers
>
>
> Office of Thrift Supervision
> Consumer & Community
> http://www.ots.treas.gov/
>
>
> National Credit Union Administration
> http://www.ncua.gov/
>
>
> Office of the Comptroller of the Currency
> Consumer Complaints and Assistance
> http://www.occ.treas.gov/customer.htm
>
>
> Federal Trade Commission
> Bureau of Consumer Protection
> http://www.ftc.gov/bcp

CONSUMER PAMPHLETS AVAILABLE

- Consumer Handbook of Adjustable Rate Mortgages

- A Consumer's Guide to Mortgage Closing Costs

- A Consumer's Guide to Mortgage Lock-Ins

- A Consumer's Guide to Mortgage Refinancings

- A Guide to Business Credit for Women, Minorities, and Small Businesses

- Home Mortgages: Understanding the Process and Your Right to Fair Lending

- A Guide to Federal Reserve Regulations

- How To File a Consumer Credit Complaint

- Making Deposits: When Will Your Money Be Available?

- When Your Home is on the Line: What You Should Know About Home Equity Lines of Credit

Copies of these handbooks and other consumer pamphlets are available upon request from:

Publications Services
Division of Support Services
Board of Governors of the Federal Reserve System
Washington, D.C. 20551

CHAPTER QUIZ

1. What was the landmark legislation which launched Truth in Lending disclosures in 1968?

    a. The Consumer Credit Protection Act
    b. Real Estate Settlement Procedures Act (RESPA)
    c. Equal Credit Opportunity Act (ECOA)
    d. Community Reinvestment Act

2. Which of the following is not one of the three C's of credit?

    a. capacity
    b. character
    c. collateral
    d. cash

3. Under the Equal Credit Opportunity Act, a borrower must be notified within _____ after his or her application has been completed, whether the loan has been approved or not.

    a. 20 days
    b. 30 days
    c. 40 days
    d. 50 days

4. _____ ensures that all consumers are given an equal chance to obtain credit.

    a. RESPA
    b. The Equal Credit Opportunity Act (ECOA)
    c. Truth in Lending Act
    d. Rights to Financial Privacy Act

5. _____ establishes procedures for correcting mistakes on a person's credit record and requires that a consumer's record only be provided for legitimate business needs.

    a. Rights to Financial Privacy Act
    b. The Fair Trade Commission Act
    c. The Fair Credit Reporting Act
    d. Home Equity Loan Consumer Protection Act

6. _____ requires federal agencies to encourage depository financial institutions to help meet the credit needs of their communities, including low- and moderate-income neighborhoods.

    a. Electronic Funds Transfer Act
    b. Home Mortgage Disclosure Act
    c. The Community Reinvestment Act
    d. National Flood Insurance Act

7. When was the first civil rights legislation enacted?

    a. 1866
    b. 1966
    c. 1964
    d. 1988

8. _____ prohibits discrimination based on race by upholding the 1866 Civil Rights Act and the 13th Amendment to the U.S. Constitution prohibiting slavery.

    a. Ragin vs. *New York Times*
    b. Jones vs. Mayer
    c. Easton vs. Strassburger
    d. Span vs. the Avenel Corporation

9. _____ has had a lead role in the administering the Fair Housing Act since its adoption in 1968.

    a. HUD
    b. VA
    c. the FED
    d. FDIC

10. Under the Fair Housing Act, penalties range from up to _____ for a first violation.

    a. $2,000
    b. $5,000
    c. $10,000
    d. $20,000

ANSWERS

1. *a*
2. *d*
3. *b*
4. *b*
5. *c*
6. *c*
7. *a*
8. *b*
9. *a*
10. *c*

GLOSSARY
Real Estate Finance

acceleration clause

A clause in a loan document describing certain events that would cause the entire loan to be due. Possible events include sale of the property, or failure to repay the debt.

actual age

The chronological, real age of a building. It is the opposite of its effective age, which is determined by the building's conditions and utility.

adjustable rate mortgage (ARM)

A loan whose interest rate is periodically adjusted to more closely coincide with current interest rates. The adjustment amounts and times are agreed upon when the loan is created.

air rights

Property rights that extend to an indefinite distance upward from the land.

alienation clause

A clause in a contract giving the lender certain rights in the event of the sale or transfer of a mortgaged property.

all-inclusive trust deed (AITD)

A method of financing in which a new junior loan is created that includes both the unpaid principal balance of the first loan and whatever new sums are loaned by the lender. This method is commonly used when a seller acts as the lender in the sale of his or her own property. Interest is charged on the overall total of the AITD, invariably at a higher rate than that charged on the included trust deeds. Also called a wrap-around mortgage.

allodial system

Our modern system of free and full land ownership by individuals, as opposed to the feudal system in which land ownership was vested in the king and represented only the right to use the land.

amortized

The reduction of a debt through regular payments of both interest and principal.

anchor bolt

Attaches the mud sill to the foundation; embedded in concrete foundation of a building.

affiliated business arrangement

An Affiliated Business Arrangement Disclosure is required whenever a settlement service refers a buyer to a firm with which the service has any kind of business connection, such as common ownership. The service usually cannot require the buyer to use a connected firm.

annual percentage rate (APR)

The cost of a mortgage stated as a yearly rate; includes such items as interest, mortgage insurance and loan origination fee (points). Use of the APR permits a standard expression of credit costs, which facilitates easy comparison of lenders.

appreciation

An increase in value as a result of economic or other related changes. The increase may be temporary or permanent.

appurtenance

Any right, privilege or improvement that belongs to and transfers with property. Common appurtenances include rights-of-way, easements, water rights and property improvements.

assume

A term used in real estate transactions where the buyer may take over, or assume, responsibility for a pre-existing mortgage.

assumption clause

A clause in loan contracts that allows a buyer to take over the existing loan from the seller and become liable for repayment of the loan.

backfill

Material, usually earth, used to refill an excavated area. In home construction, backfill is used to fill in around foundation walls, to fill voids, or to compact loose soil.

balloon payment

A final loan payment that is substantially larger than the other payments and repays the debt in full.

bare legal title

Refers to the title held by a trustee to a trust deed.

base line and meridian

Refers to imaginary lines that intersect to become the start point in the U.S. Government Survey Section and Township method of land description. The meridian is a north-south line; the base line east-west.

bearing wall

A wall supporting a floor or the roof of a building. In condominiums all bearing walls are common walls, shared by two or more units.

bill of sale

A written agreement used to transfer ownership in personal property.

blanket loan

A loan secured by several properties. It is often used to secure construction financing.

blockbusting

The illegal practice of causing panic selling by telling people that values in a neighborhood will decline because of a specific event, such as the purchase of homes by minorities.

board foot

A measurement of lumber equal to 12 inches by 12 inches by 1 inch, or 144 cubic inches.

Board of Governors (BOG)

Created by the Federal Reserve Board, the BOG regulates the banking system and supervises certain types of financial institutions, overseeing a network of 12 Federal Reserve Banks (FRBs) and 25 branches that make up the Federal Reserve System.

bracing

Framing lumber nailed at an angle in order to provide rigidity.

British thermal unit (BTU)

A measurement that calculates heat; the amount of heat needed to raise one pound of water 1 degree Fahrenheit.

bundle of rights

The various interests or rights an owner has in a property. These rights include the right to own, possess, use, enjoy, borrow against and dispose of real property.

capacity

Legitimate legal status to enter into a contract (mentally competent and of legal age), one of the legal essentials of a valid contract.

capitalization

The process of calculating a property's present worth on the basis of its capacity to continue producing an income stream. This process converts the future income stream into an indication of the property's present worth. The expected future income and expenses of a property are evaluated to determine its present value.

chattel real

A personal property interest in real property, such as a lease. The lease itself is personal property, but it allows the holder to occupy real property.

closed end credit transaction

The term closed end credit transaction is defined by exclusion. That is, it includes any credit arrangement (either a consumer loan or credit sale) that does not fall within the definition of an open end credit transaction. Open end credit includes credit arrangements like revolving credit cards, where the borrower (that is the credit card holder) is not required to pay off the principal amount by any particular point in time.

closed sheathing

The foundation for exterior siding in a building; boards nailed to studding.

collateral

Something of value given as security for a debt.

community property

Property that is held jointly by a husband and wife. In some states, all property acquired by a married couple is presumed to be community property, unless otherwise stated in a written agreement. Community property includes all earned income and assets purchased with community property money.

community property with the right of survivorship

A type of vesting used in some states by spouses to describe a method of taking title that combines the benefits of community property and joint tenancy.

compaction

Extra soil matted down or compressed, which may be added to a lot to fill in the low areas or raise the level of the parcel; also used where the soil is unstable.

condition precedent

A condition that requires something to occur before a transaction becomes absolute and enforceable. For example, a sale may have a condition precedent requiring the buyer to obtain financing.

condition subsequent

A condition which, if it occurs at some point in the future, can cause a property to revert to the grantor. For example, a condition subsequent in a grant deed may require the buyer to use the property only as a private residence. If they later use it for a business, it reverts to the original owner.

conduit

Plastic or metal tubing that houses electrical wiring. Also a means of transmitting or distributing something.

constructive notice

Knowledge of a fact that is a matter of public record. The law presumes that everyone has knowledge of that fact. The opposite of actual notice.

contract of sale

A contract to purchase real property in which the seller agrees to defer all or part of the purchase price for a specified period of time.

corner influence

The affect on property value that a corner lot location produces. The value may be greater or less than inside lots, depending on the perceived benefits of being located on a corner.

cost

The amount paid for goods or services.

crawl space

The space between the first floor and the ground surface, often found in houses with no basement or the space between the ceiling of the top floor and the roof, often taking the place of an attic.

cripple

The stud above or below a window opening or above a doorway.

cubic-foot method

The cost of reproduction calculated by multiplying the number of cubic feet of a property by the construction cost per cubic foot.

debtor

One who owes debt; a borrower.

deciduous

Certain types of trees that lose their leaves seasonally.

deed of reconveyance

A document used to transfer legal title from the trustee back to the borrower (trustor) after a debt secured by a deed of trust has been paid to the lender (beneficiary). Also called a release deed.

default

Failure to pay a contractual debt. Also a failure to appear in court.

deficiency judgment

A judgment against a borrower for the balance of a debt owed when the security for the loan is not sufficient to pay the debt.

deregulation

A process by which financial institutions that were legally restrained in their lending activities are allowed to compete freely for profits in the marketplace.

discharge of the loan

Cancellation or termination of a loan contract. Some of the common grounds in which the obligations of a contract may be discharged are: mutual cancellation; rescission; performance or nonperformance; accord and satisfaction; illegality; and in certain circumstances, to the extent a court will not enforce the contract, by the statute of limitations, the statute of frauds, and the Bankruptcy Act. There is no discharge in the event of a breach of contract, but there are remedies to the non-breaching party.

discount rates

The interest rate charged by the Federal Reserve Bank to its member banks for loans. Changes in this rate have a significant impact on the real estate market. Also the percentage of discount charged by a bank for purchasing loans or commercial paper in advance of the date of maturity.

disintermediation

The process of a depositor removing funds from savings.

doctrine of correlative user

A property owner may take only a reasonable share of underground waters for his or her beneficial use.

drywall

Gypsum panels used in place of wet plaster to finish the inside of buildings.

due-on-sale clause

A provision in a mortgage that states that the balance of the loan is due if the property is subsequently sold.

eaves

The lower section of the roof that forms an overhang composed of a fascia, soffit and soffit molding.

effective age

The age of a building based on its physical condition; not necessarily the same as its chronological age.

egress

Exit from a property using an easement.

elevation sheet

Drawings that provide views of the front and sides of a building as it will appear when completed.

emblements

Annual crops produced for sale commercially; considered personal property.

energy efficient ratio (EER)

A measurement of the efficiency of energy; used to determine the effectiveness of appliances.

equitable right of redemption

The right of a debtor, before a foreclosure sale or in some cases, after the sale, to reclaim property that had been given up due to mortgage default. Also known as the right of redemption.

equitable title

The right to obtain absolute ownership to property when legal title is held in another's name. A buyer may sue in equity for performance if a seller refuses to transfer the property once a contract of sale is signed. The buyer has a right to demand that title be conveyed upon payment of the purchase. The right is transferable by deed, assignment, subcontract or mortgage, and passed to the vendee's heirs upon death.

equity of redemption

The right of a debtor, before a foreclosure sale, to reclaim property that had been given up due to mortgage default. Also known as the right of redemption.

estate

A right or interest in property, and the degree, quantity, nature and extent to which a person has that right or interest.

estates in fee

The most complete form of ownership of real property. It is of indefinite duration and may be inherited and transferred. Also known as an estate of inheritance.

execute

To perform or complete; to sign.

exposure

Where and/or how a property is situated in terms of compass direction or its accessibility to air, light or facilities. For example, many properties are offered as having a southern exposure or a high degree of exposure to sunlight. Many commercial tenants prefer the south and west sides of business streets because the pedestrian traffic seeks the shady side of the street in warm weather. In addition, merchandise displayed in store windows on this side of the street is less prone to damage by the sun. In marketing terms, a property must be exposed for sale in the open market. A property's exposure to the market includes how it is displayed, exhibited and/or allowed to be seen by qualified buyers.

fair market value

The price a property would bring if freely offered on the open market with both a willing buyer and a willing seller.

Federal National Mortgage Association (FNMA)

Popularly known as "Fannie Mae," an active participant in the secondary mortgage market. Fannie Mae was established as a federal agency in 1938 for the purpose of purchasing FHA loans from loan originators in order to provide some liquidity for government-insured loans in a Depression-wracked economy when few lending institutions would undertake this type of loan. In 1944, Veterans Administration (VA) loans were added to Fannie Mae's purchase program, allowing Fannie Mae to become a major source of funds for mortgage companies that offered FHA and VA loans. A private corporation.

fee simple defeasible estate

An ownership estate limited by restrictions and conditions. If the agreement is breached, the title may be returned to the seller or his or her heirs. Also known as fee simple qualified.

fee simple estate

The greatest interest one can have in real property. It is unqualified, indefinite in duration, freely transferable and inheritable. An unconditional, unlimited estate of inheritance that represents the greatest estate and most extensive interest in land that can be enjoyed; of perpetual duration.

fee simple qualified

An estate of ownership limited by restrictions and conditions. If the agreement is breached, the title may be returned to the seller or his or her heirs. Also known as fee simple defeasible.

financial intermediaries

An organization that obtains funds through deposits and then lends those funds to earn a return. Examples include saving banks, commercial banks, credit unions and mutual saving banks.

Federal Housing Administration (FHA)

A federal agency established in 1934 that encourages improvements in housing standards and conditions, provides an adequate home-financing system, and exerts a stabilizing influence on the mortgage market.

financing statement

A document showing the financial status, net worth, credits and debits of a person or company.

fire stop

A wooden block built between the wall studs or joists of a structure, with covered walls, which closes off the passage of air to limit the spread of fire.

fiscal year

The financial year that starts on July 1 and runs through June 30 of the following year; used for real property tax purposes.

fixture

Any personal property attached to land on a permanent or semi-permanent basis. It becomes real property through attachment.

flashing

Waterproof sheets of plastic or corrosion-resistant metal, installed along with exterior finishing materials for the prevention of water leakage in such places as the intersection of a wall and roof or the valley of a roof.

footing

The base or bottom of a foundation pier, wall or column; usually wider than the upper portion of the foundation. The footing transfers the structural loan to the ground.

foreclose

The legal process by which a borrower in default under a mortgage is deprived of his or her interest in the mortgaged property. This usually involves a forced sale of the property at public auction with the proceeds of the sale being applied to the mortgage debt.

foreclosure with power of sale

A forced sale when property is sold to satisfy a debt secured by a trust deed or mortgage where the security instrument allows the property to be sold at auction by a trustee or mortgagee.

freehold estate

Ownership rights and interests in real property that continue for an indefinite period of time. May be passed on to the owner's heirs after death. Also called fee estate.

fully amortized note

A note that is fully repaid at maturity through periodic reduction of the principal.

good faith estimate

When a potential homebuyer applies for a mortgage loan, the lender must give the buyer a good faith estimate of settlement costs, which lists the charges the buyer is likely to pay at settlement and states whether the lender requires the buyer to use a particular settlement service.

graduated payment mortgage

A loan in which the monthly payment graduates by a certain percentage each year for a specific number of years, then levels off for the remaining term of the loan.

header

The board over a doorway or window opening.

holder

The party to whom a promissory note is payable.

home equity line of credit (HELOC)

A home equity line of credit is a form of revolving credit in which a borrower's home serves as collateral. By using the equity in their home, borrowers may qualify for a sizable amount of credit, available for use when and how they please, at an interest rate that is relatively low. Furthermore, under the Tax Law—depending on each borrower's specific situation—he or she may be allowed to deduct the interest because the debt is secured by the person's home.

Hoskold Tables

An English mining engineer who originated the use of the "Hoskold" method of valuing coal mines, timberland and other types of real estate with depleting assets.

HUD-1 Settlement Statement

As a disclosure before settlement (closing) occurs, a preliminary copy of a HUD-1 Settlement Statement is required if the borrower requests it 24 hours before closing. This form gives estimates of all settlement charges that will need to be paid, both by buyer and seller.

hypothecation

To pledge property as security for a debt without actually giving up possession or title.

improvements

Structures, usually private, constructed on a property to facilitate its use and increase value.

income approach

The method by which the value of an income-producing property is estimated. The expected income from the property, over its remaining economic life, is capitalized.

insulation

Materials such as fiberglass, rock wool and urethane foam which are used to slow heat loss and electrical wiring. Insulation is placed in the wall, ceilings or floors of a structure.

interest

In real estate finance, the cost of borrowing money. Also, a right to or share of something; ownership that is incomplete or limited.

intermediate theory

Some states follow the intermediate theory that says a mortgage is a lien unless the borrower defaults. The title then is automatically transferred to the lender. In any case, the borrower enjoys possession of the property during the full term of the mortgage—no matter who is seen to hold title.

intermediation

The process of transferring capital from those who invest funds to those who wish to borrow.

Inwood Tables

A set of interest tables widely used by appraisers, before the popularity of calculators and computers, in computing the present value of an annuity for a number of years at various interest rates. Among their many uses, the tables enable an appraiser to estimate the value of a leasehold interest when the income stream (cash flow) is constant. The principle underlying the system is that a series of equal annual payments to be made in the future is not an annuity's present worth. The annuity is worth only the amount that, if deposited today at a fixed rate of interest compounded annually, would provide for the withdrawal at the end of the year of an amount equal to one annual payment.

joint tenancy

Equal ownership of real estate by two or more people, each of whom has an undivided interest and the right of survivorship. Thus, the death of one joint tenant does not destroy the tenancy; the remaining joint tenants acquire the deceased person's interest.

joists

A horizontal parallel beam directly supporting the boards of a floor or the laths of a ceiling.

judgment

The final legal decision of a judge in a court of law regarding the legal rights of parties in a dispute.

junior lien

An encumbrance second in priority to a previously recorded lien or to a lien to which the encumbrance has been subordinated.

judicial foreclosure

Foreclosure by court action.

junior trust deed

Any trust that is recorded after a first trust deed, and whose priority is less than the first.

kiosk

A small structure, usually constructed with one or more sides open, often used as a newsstand or small vending operation. The business occupying the kiosk often pays rent on a high percentage lease basis.

lease

An agreement to possess and use real property, for a finite period of time, in exchange for rent.

leasehold estate

An estate held by a tenant or renter.

less-than-freehold estate

A leasehold estate, considered to exist for a definite period of time or successive periods of time until termination.

leverage

The utilization of borrowed funds to increase purchasing power, or using a smaller, borrowed investment to generate a larger rate of return.

lien

A form of encumbrance that holds property as security for the payment of a debt.

life estates

An estate that is limited in duration to the life of its owner or the life of some other chosen person.

loan-to-value ratio (LTV)

The ratio of the amount borrowed to the appraised value or sales price of a parcel of real property; generally expressed as a percentage.

location

A particular surface on earth that is defined by legal description.

maker

The borrower who executed a promissory note and becomes primarily liable for payment to the lender.

margin

In an adjustable-rate loan, the amount added to the index rate that represents the lender's cost of doing business (includes costs, profits, and risk of loss of the loan). Generally the margin stays constant during the life of the loan.

metes and bounds

A method of land description in which the dimensions of the property are measured by distance and direction. Landmarks along specific boundaries are used as reference to measure the distances.

minimum residential ceiling height
> 7.5 feet.

monetary policy
> Monetary policy is carried out by the Federal Reserve System's actions to influence the availability and cost of money and credit, as a means of helping to promote national economic goals. Monetary policy is made by the Federal Open Market Committee, which consists of the Board of Governors of the Federal Reserve System and the Reserve Bank presidents.

mortgage banker
> A banker who originates new mortgage loans, and services and sells existing loans in the secondary mortgage market.

mortgage broker
> A banker who has access to many lenders and can locate and negotiate the best rates, terms and conditions for borrowers, thereby earning a commission.

Mortgage Servicing Disclosure Statement
> When a potential homebuyer applies for a mortgage loan, the lender must give the buyer a Mortgage Servicing Disclosure Statement, which tells the buyer whether the lender intends to keep the loan or to transfer it to another lender for servicing, and also gives information about how the buyer can resolve complaints. RESPA does not specify penalties for lenders that fail to provide these three items, but bank regulators can impose penalties on lenders. Must be given to a borrower at the time of the loan application.

mortgage
> The use of property as security for the payment of a debt; also the document used to establish a mortgage lien.

mortgagee
> The lender under a mortgage.

mortgagor
> A borrower who pledges property through a mortgage to secure a loan.

mud sill
> The lowest horizontal component of a structure, such as a foundation timber placed directly on the ground or foundation.

negative amortization
> Negative amortization occurs when the monthly payments on a loan are insufficient to pay the interest accruing on the principal balance. The unpaid interest is added to the remaining principal due.

negotiable instrument
> Any written instrument that may be transferred by endorsement or delivery.

net operating income (NOI)

The annual gross income of an investment, which includes all revenues generated by the property, including rent, laundry income, late fees and parking charges (less an annual vacancy factor or any rental losses), less operating expenses to calculate the net operating income (NOI).

non-amortizing loan

A loan with no payments; principal and interest due at the end of the term.

non-judicial foreclosure

The power to foreclose on a property without court approval. Also called a strict foreclosure or forfeiture.

normal residential ceiling height

8 feet.

novation

The substitution of a new obligation for an old one; substitution of new parties to an existing obligation, as where the parties to an agreement accept a new debtor in place of an old one.

obsolescence

A cause of depreciation in a property. Obsolescence may be external, such as zoning changes, or functional, such as a structural defect.

notice of default

A notice to a defaulting party that there has been non-payment of the debt.

open-market operations

The process where the Fed buys and sells government securities to influence the amount of available credit. When the Fed buys securities, more money is available in the banks to lend. When the Fed sells securities, the opposite is true. The open-market operations process is the most flexible and widely used technique for expanding or slowing the economy.

open sheathing

Boards nailed to rafters to form foundation for the roof.

open-end loan

A loan that is expandable by increments up to a certain amount. The total amount is secured by the same mortgage.

"or more" clause

A clause in a promissory note that allows a borrower to pay it off early with no penalty.

package loan

A loan on real property that can be secured by land, structure, fixtures or other personal property.

partially amortized installment note
A promissory note with a repayment schedule that is not sufficient to pay off the loan over its term. At maturity, the remaining principal balance is due in full.

pass-through securities
The proceeds from the sale of securities in the secondary market that are passed on to the securities buyer.

percolating water
Underground water not flowing in a specific channel.

percolation test
A test performed by a hydraulic engineer to determine the ability of soil to absorb water. This information is crucial to determining the amount of development an area can sustain.

pledge account
The transfer of property to a lender to be held as security for repayment of a debt.

plottage
The increase in value when two or more contiguous properties are joined together and made available as a single unit.

possession
Possessing or occupying property, whether actually or constructively. Actual possession is physically occupying the land; constructive possession is legally possessing title to a property.

potable
Water that is fit to drink according to water standards established by the Public Health Service.

power of sale
A clause in a trust deed or mortgage that gives the mortgage holder the right to sell the property in the event of default by the borrower.

prepayment clause
A clause in a trust deed that allows a lender to collect a certain percentage of a loan as a penalty for an early payoff.

price
The amount of money, or other consideration, paid for specific goods or services.

promissory note
A written promise or order to pay at a future specified time; evidence of a debt.

quantity survey method
A method of estimating building costs by calculating the cost of all of the physical components of the construction, adding those costs, plus the cost of the labor to assemble them, and insurance, taxes, etc. Also called "price take-off" method.

R-Value
Used to calculate the heat resistance of insulation; the higher the better.

rafters
Any of the beams that slope from the ridge of a roof to the eaves and serve as support for the roof.

Real Estate Investment Trust (REIT)
Investors who individually possess a small amount of capital pool their resources to buy real estate.

reconvey
The act of transferring title of property back to the original owner. In the case of a deed of trust, the borrower conveys title to a third-party trustee as security for the debt. When the debt is paid off, the property is reconveyed to the owner.

redemption
The legal right of a borrower to make good on a defaulted loan within a statutory period of time and thus regain the property.

reinstate
To bring current and restore.

remedy
Selection from several alternative courses of action to cure a breach of contract.

request for notice
A request for notice to be sent to any parties interested in a trust deed, informing them of a default.

reserve requirements
The amount of money and liquid assets the Federal Reserve requires member banks to set aside as a safety measure. The amount is usually a percentage of deposits.

reverse annuity mortgage
A loan that enables elderly homeowners to borrow against the equity in their homes by receiving monthly payments from a lender to help meet living costs.

ridge board
The highest horizontal member of a roof, running along the ridge, and meeting the rafters at right angles.

right of appropriation
The act of the government to divert water for public use.

rollover mortgage
A loan that allows the rewriting of a new loan at the termination of a prior loan.

satisfaction
Full payment of a debt.

securitizing

The pooling of traditional bank assets, loans, mortgages or other non-tradeable financial transactions, and converting them into tradeable securities.

security instrument

An instrument of finance, such as a mortgage or trust deed, used as security for a loan.

setback

A zoning restriction that specified the required distance between a house or building and the lot line.

shared appreciation mortgage

A mortgage in which the lender and borrower agree to share a certain percentage of the increase in market value of the property.

sheriff's deed

A deed given to a buyer when property is sold through court action in order to satisfy a judgment for money or foreclosure of a mortgage.

shopping centers

A modern classification of retail stores, characterized by off-street parking and clusters of stores, subject to a uniform development plan and usually with careful analysis given to the proper merchant mix.

sill

The lowest horizontal member of the house frame, which rests on top of the foundation wall and forms a base for the studs. The term can also refer to the lowest horizontal member in the frame for a window or door.

sole plate

Support for studs in a building.

Special Information Booklet

When a potential homebuyer applies for a mortgage loan, the lender must give the buyer a Special Information Booklet, which contains consumer information on various real estate settlement services.

square-foot method

A method for calculating the reproduction cost of a building by multiplying the number of square feet by the square-root cost of a recently built comparable structure.

statute of limitations

A statute limiting the period of time during which legal action may be taken on a certain issue. The statute attempts to protect against outdated claims where truth and justice may be difficult to determine.

statute

A law.

statutory foreclosure

The process of terminating a debtor's right to a property as a result of default on a mortgage or other lien. It typically involves the forced sale of the property at public auction, and the proceeds are used to repay the debt.

strict foreclosure

A foreclosure proceeding in which the debtor has a limited amount of time, once appropriate notice has been given, to repay the debt before their equitable and statutory redemption rights are waived and full legal title to the property is granted to the lender. This type of foreclosure is rarely used in contemporary markets.

studs

In wall framing, the vertical members to which horizontal pieces are attached. Studs are placed 16 to 24 inches apart and serve as the main support for the roof and/or the second floor.

"subject to" clause

A clause in escrow documents which states that the buyer will take over payments on an existing loan, but assumes no personal liability for the loan.

subordination clause

A clause in a contract in which the holder of a trust deed permits a subsequent loan to take priority.

swing loan or bridge loan

A short-term loan that allows a buyer to purchase property before selling another property, and receiving the money from the sale. Also called a bridge loan or gap loan.

tenancy in common

Ownership of property by two or more persons, each of whom has an undivided interest, without the right of survivorship. Upon the death of one of the tenants, that ownership share is inherited by the heirs or beneficiaries named in the decedent's will.

tenancy in partnership

Ownership by two or more persons who form a partnership for business purposes. Each partner has an equal right of possession. Upon the death of one of the partners, that partner's interest transfers to the remaining partner(s).

tenancy in the entirety

A special joint tenancy by a husband and wife in which they hold title together. In the event of one spouse's death, the surviving spouse becomes the owner of the entire property.

Real Estate Settlement Procedures Act (RESPA)

A federal law enacted in 1974 and later revised, that ensures that the buyer and seller in a real estate transaction have knowledge of all settlement costs when the purchase of one-to-four family residential dwelling is financed by a federally related mortgage loan.

title

Evidence of the ownership of land, publicly recorded in the county where the property is located.

title theory

The practice in some states of keeping the title to a mortgaged property with the lender until the loan is fully repaid. The borrower holds equitable title, or the right to use and possess the property.

trade fixtures

An article of personal property affixed to leased property by the tenant as a necessary part of business; it may be removed by the tenant upon termination of the lease. Depending on several factors, fixtures may become real property.

trust deed

A written document legally conveying property to a trustee. It is used as security for the payment of a debt. Deeds of trust are similar to mortgages. However, in a deed of trust there are three parties to the instrument: the borrower, the trustee, and the lender (beneficiary). Also called a deed of trust.

trustee's deed

A deed given to a buyer of real property at a trustee's sale.

underwriting

The process of determining a borrower's financial strength, so that the loan amount and terms can be established. Also, the practice of buying stocks or bonds, and then selling them to investors for a profit.

unit-in-place cost method

A method of calculating the reproduction cost of a building. The construction cost per square foot of each component part of the building (including material, labor, overhead and builder's profit) is multiplied by the square footage of the component part.

value

The significance placed on goods or services, current or future.

vendee

The buyer under a contract of sale.

Veterans Administration (VA)

The federal agency that provides benefits including VA loans to qualified veterans. The loan is guaranteed by the Veterans Administration and requires a low or no down payment from the borrower.

wainscoting

Wood paneling or tiles that cover an interior wall from the floor halfway to the ceiling; the remaining portion is painted or wallpapered.

warehousing

The process of assembling a number of mortgage loans into one package and holding them for a period of time prior to selling them to an investor. They are held while awaiting a lower discount.

water pressure

Can be tested by turning on all faucets and flushing all toilets at the same time.

water table

The level of water saturation in the ground. Also, the structure that protrudes from a house and deflects rainwater.

INDEX
Real Estate Finance

A

abstract of title, 68

acceleration clauses, 89

accountants, 243

ACH (automated clearing house), 188

acknowledgment, 46

acreage, figuring, 38–39

ADA (Americans with Disabilities Act), 442

addresses

    Comptroller of the Currency, 417

    consumer information pamphlets, 447

    credit reporting agencies, 369

    Federal Deposit Insurance Corporation, 418, 446

    Federal Reserve System, 411–12

    Federal Reserve System, Board of Governors, 446

    Federal Trade Commission, 394, 417, 446

    Housing and Urban Development, 394, 395

    National Credit Union Administration, 418, 446

    Office of the Comptroller of the Currency, 446

    Office of Thrift Supervision, 418, 446

    Publications Services, 447

    RESPA, consumer complaints to, 423

    see also web site addresses

adjustable rate mortgages (ARMs), 81–84

    caps and, 82–83

    indexes of, 82, 83–84

    margins and, 81–82

    Regulation Z requirements and, 424

advertising, 280

    mortgage loan industry and, 292

Affiliated Business Arrangement (AfBA) disclosure, 351–69, 421

after-tax profits, 275

age

    of building, 327–28

    discrimination on basis of, 405–6, 414–15, 439–40, 442

Age Discrimination Act, 442

age-life depreciation, 327–28

agents

    vs. brokers, 240

    buyer's brokers, 240

    closing agents, 199, 243

    insurance agents, 242

    listing agents, 241

    real estate agents, 291

    as resource during real estate investment, 240–42

agreement of sale, 106–7

air space rights, 28

AITDs (All-Inclusive Trust Deeds), 101–3

Aldrich-Vreeland Act, 180–81

alienation clauses, 88, 89

alimony, 407–8, 414, 415

All-Inclusive Trust Deeds (AITDs), 101–3

allodial system, 45

Americans with Disabilities Act (ADA), 442

Annual Escrow Statement, 385

annual gross income, calculating, 261

annual percentage rate (APR), 364, 426

anticipation, principle of, 309

appraisals, 242–43

    appraisal report, 367

    appraisers, 199, 337

    cost approach, 323–28

    data collection during, 311–12

    defined, 303–4

    depreciation and, 325–27

    fair market value and, 304

    form for reports, 334–35

    improvements and, 314–20

    income capitalization approach, 328–31

    vs. inspection, 242

    investment and, 276

    loan application process and, 344

    methods of, 321–32

    process of, 310–20

    professional appraisal organizations, 337

    purpose of, 310–11

    racial discrimination and, 407

    reconciliation or correlation and, 321, 332

    reports, types of, 332–35

    sales (or market) comparison approach, 321–23

    site analysis, 312–14

    substitution principle, 321

    underwriting and, 381–82

appreciation, 280–81, 286

    inflation and, 177

    investment real estate and, 229

APR (annual percentage rate), 364, 426

Architectural Barriers Act, 442

architectural styles, 319–20

ARMs. *See* adjustable rate mortgages (ARMs)

assets *vs.* liabilities of Americans, 19–20

assignment of rents clause in trust deed, 121

assumed loans, 87–88, 89

assumption clauses, 89

attachments and judgments, 60

attorneys and legal assistance, 238–49, 252–53, 394

AU (automated underwriting), 365

automated clearing house (ACH), 188

automated underwriting (AU), 365

B

"back" ratios, 343

balance, principle of, 309

balloon payment loans, 95, 427–28

Banking Act (1935), 183

bankruptcy, homestead exemption and, 65

banks

    banker's banks, 184–85, 444

    commercial banks, 153

    Federal Reserve System banks, 444

    free banks, 180

    legislation regarding, 180–81, 183

    mutual savings banks, 153, 165

    National Banking Act, 180

    "national" banks, 417, 444

    savings banks, 153, 163, 444, 445

    state-chartered banks, 418, 444

    see also Federal Reserve Bank System (the Fed)

bare legal title, 111–12

base lines, 39

basic security instrument, trust deeds as, 122

beneficiaries, 111, 122–23

bills of sale, 28

blanket loans, 100

Board of Governors (BOG), 185, 411–12

book value, 327–28

boots, 228

bridge loans, 100

brokers

    as "credit arrangers," 432–33

    mortgage brokers, 168–69

    mortgage loan brokers, 297

    real estate agents *vs.* real estate brokers, 240

    real estate brokers, 240, 432–33

budget and operations plan for investment properties, 253

buildings

    appraisal considerations for, 314–20

    common construction terms defined, 314–17

    house styles, 319–20

    roof types, 317–18

bundle of rights, 24–25

buyer's brokers, 240

buyer's remorse, 250

C

California Veteran Loans (Cal-Vet), 213–16

Cal-Vet (California Veteran Loans), 213–16

capital gains, 285

    capital gain deferral, 287

    and investment, 227

    rate, 286

capital improvements, 258

capitalization, 261

capitalization rates (cap rate), 257, 263–65, 279

    income capitalization appraisals and, 330

caps and adjustable rate mortgages (ARMs), 82–83

carrying costs, 259–60, 261

cash flow, 274–78

CCIM (Certified Commercial Investment Member of the Commercial Investment Institute) designation, 240

CC&Rs (Covenants, Conditions and Restrictions), 63

Certificate of Eligibility for VA home loans, 210

Certificate of Reasonable Value, 211

certificates of sale, 143

chattel real, 27

checks, chart of checking transactions, 189

children, 414

Civil Rights Acts, 438

closing, 199, 243, 254–57, 386

    disclosures required at, 382–85

    Good Faith Estimate (GFE) and closing costs, 354–59, 420

    legal assistance during, 239

closing agents, 199, 243

coinsurance, 207

collateral, 74, 111, 272–74, 404

commingling of property, 51–52

commissions, maximum allowable, 201

community property, 51–56, 409, 413

Community Reinvestment Act (CRA), 14, 437

competition, principle of, 309

Competitive Equality Banking Act, 15

complaints

    complaint procedures for credit consumers, 411–12

    state laws and consumer complaints, 443–47

    see also Specific agencies or lending institutions

concurrent ownership, 48–56

conditional sales contract, 106–7

condition precedent, 26, 63

condition subsequent, 63

conformity, principle of, 308

Consolidated Farmers Home Administration, 12

construction, common terms defined, 314–17

constructive notice, 47

Consumer Credit Protection Act, 13

Consumer Handbook on Adjustable Rate Mortgages, 424

consumer information pamphlets, 447

Consumer Protection Act, 11

contracts of sale, 106–7, 216

contribution, principle of, 308–9

converters, 282

conveyance, of title / trust deed, 123

corner lots, 307

correlation, 321, 332

costs

as appraisal approach, 323–28

estimating the cost of new buildings, 325

of property, 304–5

Covenants, Conditions and Restrictions (CC&Rs), 63

CRA (Community Reinvestment Act), 14, 437

credit

analysis of, 345

borrower's rights, 415–16

brokers as "credit arrangers," 432–33

capacity, 404

character, 404

collateral, 404

complaint procedures for consumers, 411–12

Consumer Credit Protection Act, 403

credit history and creditworthiness, 7, 293, 344, 381

Credit Practices Rule, 435

credit reporting agencies and reports, 199, 245, 342,
365–66, 369

denial, notification of, 409

discrimination in provision of, 405–9

Equal Credit Opportunity Act (ECOA), 405, 407, 409,
413–19

errors and/or out-of-date information, 410–11

federal legislation regarding, 13–14

FICO scores, 245, 368–74

gender and creditworthiness, 407–9

home equity line of credit, 96–99

improving your credit history, 409–10

inaccurate or out-of-date information in reports, 436

marital status and creditworthiness, 407, 409

record keeping, 410

reports, 410–11

see also Truth in Lending Act (TILA)

creditors, 110

Credit Practices Rule, 435

credit reporting agencies and reports, 199, 245, 342, 365–66, 369

credit unions, 153, 165

complaint procedures regarding, 418, 445

top 100 listed, 166–67

cubic-foot cost estimation, 325

cul-de-sacs, 312

D

dead gages, 3–4

death, property division in absence of a will, 52–53

debt collection practices, 433

debtors, 110

debt service ratio (DSR), 265–66

debt-to-income ratios, 343

declared homesteads, 64–67

deeds

foreclosure sales and, 143

priorities in recording and, 47–48

trustee's deed, 127

see also trust deeds

deeds of trust. *See* trust deeds

default

historical systems, 4–5

of mortgages, 136

partial payments and, 392

remedies for, 124, 136

trust deeds and, 112, 124

see also foreclosure; insurance

defeasance clause in mortgages, 135

deficiency judgments, 88

mortgages, 140

trust deeds, 124

Deficit Reduction Act, 15

delinquencies, credit scores and, 372

demand for housing, 10–11, 308

Department of Justice, 418

depository institutions, 152

Depository Institutions Deregulation and Monetary
Control Act, 14, 155

depreciation, 259, 286

appraisals and, 325–27

book depreciation, 326

calculation of, 226–27

obsolescence and, 326

physical deterioration as, 326

straight-line (age-life) depreciation, 327–28

deregulation, 155, 174, 175

development market's cycle, 269–71, 282–83

disabilities, 442

discharge of loan, 112

disclosures

Affiliated Business Arrangement (AfBA) disclosure,
351–69, 421

at closing/settlement, 382–85

escrow statements, 421–22

finance charges, 425

Good Faith Estimate (GFE), 354–59, 420

Home Mortgage Disclosure Act (HMDA), 14, 434

Home Ownership and Equity Protection Act (HOEPA)
requirements, 427–29

Homeowners Protection Act (HPA) and, 219–20

Interstate Land Sales Full Disclosure Act, 12

lending patterns, 434–35

loan servicing disclosure requirements, 390–91

Mortgage Loan Broker's Statement, 201

prior to closing, 421

Real Estate Settlement Procedures Act (RESPA)
requirements, 13, 253–359, 420–22

Regulation Z, Truth in Lending requirements, 423–26, 429

Seller Financing Disclosure Statement, 92–94

timing of, 385, 421–22

disclosures *(continued)*
  Truth in Lending Act, 100, 361–63
discount interest rates, 178
discrimination, 12
  age discrimination, 439, 442
  credit and, 405–9
  disabilities and, 442
  Equal Credit Opportunity Act (ECOA), 14, 407, 413–19
  Fair Housing Act, 12
  Fair Housing Laws, 437–41
  Fair Lending Practice Regulations, 14
  gender, 407–9
  marital status, 407, 409
  racial discrimination, 405, 407, 438
  remedies for, 416–19
disintermediation, 8, 154, 174
distress sales, 280
doctrine of correlative user, 29
documents
  closing documents, 243
  recording, 46–48
  required for financing real estate investments, 236, 253
  required for loan application, 253, 342, 344–45
  see also forms
down payments, 379
due diligence, 251–52
due-on-demand clauses, 428
due-on-sale clauses, 88
due-on-sale loans, 14–15

E

easements, 29, 60–62, 281
  creation of, 61–62
  easements in gross, 61
  termination of, 62
ECOA (Equal Credit Opportunity Act), 14, 407, 409, 413–19
economic system of the United States, 176
effective age *vs.* actual age of buildings, 328
egress rights, 60
Electronic Funds Transfer Act, 435
Emergency Home Finance Act, 13
employment
  rates and the real estate market, 18–19
  in real estate industry, 177
  Verification of Employment (VOE), 366, 367, 380–81
encroachments, 63–64
encumbrances
  chart illustrating, 57
  defined and described, 56–57
  easements, 60–63
  encroachments, 63–64
  liens (money encumbrances), 57–60
  money encumbrances (liens), 57–60
  non-money encumbrances, 60–64

restrictions, 63
  right of encumber, 25
English mortgage lending, 3–5
enjoyment, right of, 25
environmental characteristics and value of property, 306
environmental impact statements, 13
Equal Credit Opportunity Act (ECOA), 14, 407, 409, 413–19
  Regulation B, 419
equitable interest in property, 51
equitable right of redemption (equity of redemption), 4–5
equity
  vs. cash flow, 277
  Home Equity Loan Consumer Protection Act, 434
  of redemption for mortgages, 140
escrow accounts, 90–91, 92, 100, 169, 200, 215
  annual reports of activity, 390
  disclosure requirements, 421–22
  limits on, 422
  transfer of services and, 397–98
estates in real property
  condition precedent, 26
  condition subsequent, 26
  estates in fee, 25–26
  freehold estates, 25–27
  leasehold estates, 27
  less-than-freehold estates, 27
  life estates, 26–27
estoppel statements, 275
Expedited Funds Availability Act, 433
extended policy of title insurance, 69–70

F

Fair Credit Reporting Act (FCRA), 13, 435–37
Fair Debt Collection Practices Act, 433
Fair Housing Act, 12
Fair Housing Assistance Program (FHAP), 440
Fair Housing Initiatives Program (FHIP), 440
Fair Housing Laws, 437–41
Fair Lending Practice Regulations, 14
fair market value, 304
Fannie Mae (Federal National Mortgage Association FNMA), 12, 193–94, 195, 196, 199, 341
the Fed. *See* Federal Reserve Bank System (the Fed)
Federal Deposit Insurance Corporation (FDIC), 161, 162, 182
  address of, 418, 446
  federal legislation regarding, 15
Federal Farm Loan Act, 11
Federal Financial Institutions Examination Council (FFIEC), 434–35
Federal Home Loan Bank Act, 11, 157, 161, 162
Federal Home Loan Bank (FHLB), 9, 11, 14
  Federal Home Loan Bank Act, 11, 157, 161, 162
Federal Home Loan Mortgage Corporation (FHLMC or Freddie Mac), 195, 197–99, 341
Federal Homestead Act (1862), 67–68

Federal Housing Administration (FHA), 9, 193, 194, 196, 208–9

Federal National Mortgage Association (FNMA or Fannie Mae), 12, 193–94, 195, 196, 199, 341

Federal Open Market Committee (FOMC), 185, 186

federal programs and agencies, 9–10

federal regulation, value of property and, 306

Federal Reserve Act, 11, 181

Federal Reserve Banks (FRBs), 184–85

Federal Reserve Bank System (the Fed)

  address for consumer complaints, 446

  automated clearing house (ACH) and, 188

  bank regulation and supervision responsibilities, 186–87

  Board of Governors, 185, 186–87

  consumer credit complaints and, 411–12

  consumer protection, 187, 446

  financial services provided by, 187–90

  history of, 179–84

  interest rates set by, 178–79

  map of districts, 185

  monetary policy and, 178

  open market operations, 178

  organization and structure of, 188

  requirements (amount of money in circulation), 178

  responsibilities of, 178

  structure of, 184–87

  transfer of money and, 187–90

  Treasury's fiscal policy and, 183

Federal Reserve Board, Truth in Lending and, 13

Federal Savings and Loan Insurance Corporation (FSLIC), 9–10, 15, 17, 155, 157, 161

Federal Trade Commission, 394, 417, 433, 446

Federal Trade Commission Act, 433

fee developers, 282

fee estates, 25–27

fee simple defeasible estates, 26

fee simple estates, 25–26

fee simple qualified estates, 26

fee-splitting, 422

feudalism, 45

FFIEC (Federal Financial Institutions Examination Council), 434–35

FHLB (Federal Home Loan Bank), 9, 11, 14

FHLMC/FNMA 1003 form (Uniform Residential Loan Application), 345–52

FICO® (credit) scores, 245, 368–74

Financial Institutions Reform, Recovery and Enforcement Act (FIRREA), 15, 17, 161–63

financial instruments

  clauses in, 89–90

  contract of sale, 106–7

  see also loans; mortgages; trust deeds

financial intermediaries, 151–52

financing

  choosing a lender, 290–99

  credit scores and inquiries regarding, 245

  debt service ratio (DSR), 265–66

  federal regulation of, 11–15 (*see also* Truth in Lending Act (TILA))

  financial preparation for investment in real estate, 235–36

  loan officers as resources, 241–42

  table funding, 297

  see also interest rates; loans; mortgage lenders; mortgages

fixed-rate loans, 80

fixtures

  defined and described, 30–31

  legal tests of determinations, 31–32

  trade fixtures, 32

flag lots, 313

Flood Disaster Protection Act, 13

forebearance, 9

foreclosure

  bare legal title and, 112

  deficiency judgments, 140

  during Great Depression, 8–9

  judicial foreclosures, 124, 141, 142–47

  junior lienholders and, 147–48

  methods state-by-state list of, 145–46

  moratoria on, 8–9

  mortgages and, 140–48

  nonjudicial foreclosures, 141–42

  partial payments and, 392

  in Roman Empire, 3

  state by state listing, 143

  strict foreclosures, 141

  trust deeds and, 124, 125–33

  trustee's sale (trust deeds), 126–33

forms

  1003 form, 345–52

  Affiliated Business Arrangement (AfBA) disclosure statement, 360

  for appraisal reports, 334–35

  contract of sale, 106

  Deed of Trust, 113–20

  Good Faith Estimate (GFE), 355–58

  Homestead Declaration, 67

  HUD-1 Settlement Statement, 383–84

  mortgage, 137–39

  Notice of Default, 128

  promissory note, 76–78

  reconveyance of trust deeds, 125

  Request for Notice, 128

  Seller Financing Disclosure Statement, 93–94

  Truth-in-Lending Disclosure Statement, 362–63, 429

  Uniform Residential Loan Application (FHLMC/FNMA 1003 form), 349–52

for-sale-by-owner (FSBO) properties, 246

Freddie Mac (Federal Home Loan Mortgage Corporation FHLMC), 195, 197–99, 341

freehold estates, 25–27

"front" ratios, 343

full coverage mortgage insurance, 207

G

gages, "live" and "dead," 3–4
Garn-St. Germain Depository Institutions Act, 14–15, 159
German mortgage lending, 3
Ginnie Mae (Government National Mortgage Association
      GNMA), 13, 194, 196–97, 199, 341
Good Faith Estimate (GFE), 354–59, 420
Government National Mortgage Association (GNMA or Ginnie
      Mae), 13, 194, 196–97, 199, 341
grace period during transfer of loan servicing, 392
graduated payment mortgages (GPMs), 104–5
Great Depression, 182–83
      impact on real estate markets and practices, 8–10
      savings and loans and, 157
gross rent multiplier, 331–32
guarantee of title, 68

H

hard money loans, 95
hazard insurance, 200
HELOC (home equity line of credit), 96–99
      costs of, 98–99
      repayment of, 99
      vs. second mortgages, 99
highest and best use, principle of, 308
HMDA (Home Mortgage Disclosure Act), 14, 15
HOEPA (Home Ownership and Equity Protection Act),
      426–29
HOLA (Home Owners Loan Act), 9, 11–12, 157
holders in due course, 85–87
holders of notes, 75
home equity line of credit (HELOC), 96–99
      costs of, 98–99
      repayment of, 99
      vs. second mortgages, 99
Home Equity Loan Consumer Protection Act, 434
home equity loans, 95–96
Home Mortgage Disclosure Act Aggregation Project, 434
Home Mortgage Disclosure Act (HMDA), 14, 15
Home Ownership and Equity Protection Act (HOEPA),
      426–29
Home Owners Loan Act (HOLA), 9, 11–12, 157
Homeowners Protection Act (HPA), 217–20, 219–20
homestead exemptions and declared homesteads, 64–67
housing, demand for, 10–11, 308
Housing Act, 12
Housing and Community Development Act, 15
      Amendments, 14
Housing and Urban Development (HUD), 208
      Fair Housing Act, enforcement of, 441–42
      Housing and Urban Development Act, 12, 13
      HUD-1 Settlement Statement, 382–85, 421
      loan service complaints and, 394
Housing for Older Persons Act (HOPA), 439–40
HPA (Homeowners Protection Act), 217–20

HUD. *See* Housing and Urban Development (HUD)
HUD-1 Settlement Statement, 382–85, 421
Humboldt Base Line and Meridian, 33
hybrid notes, 84–85
hypothecation, 74

I

income capitalization appraisals, 328–31
income flow, 176
income ratios, 379–80
indexes, for adjustable rate mortgages (ARMs), 82, 83–84
inflation, 184
      appreciation and, 177
ingress rights, 60
initial public offerings (IPOs), 17
inspections and inspectors, 242, 246–50
      checklist for investor inspections, 247–48
      investment and professional inspections, 276
      professional inspections, 253
installment sales, 106–7, 227–28
institutional lenders, Great Depression and, 8
insurance
      agents, 242
      California Veteran Loans (Cal-Vet), 213–16
      coinsurance, 207
      Federal Housing Administration and, 208–9
      Federal Savings and Loan Insurance Corporation (FSLIC)
            and, 9–10, 15, 17, 155, 157, 161
      flood insurance, 435
      full coverage mortgage insurance, 207
      government insurance, 208–16
      hazard insurance, 200
      insurance companies as mortgage lenders, 165
      mortgage default insurance, 206–7
      National Flood Insurance Act, 435
      partial coverage mortgage insurance, 207
      private mortgage insurance (PMI), 200, 207, 217–20
      self-insurance, 207
      title insurance, 68–70, 422
      transfer of service and, 398
      types of mortgage insurance, 206–7
      Veterans Administration (VA), 208, 210–13
interest
      amortization and, 80–81
      financing statement and, 202–3
      security interest, 86–87, 110, 202
      see also interest rates
Interest Rate Adjustment Act, 12
interest rates
      annual percentage rate (APR), 364, 426
      California Veteran Loans (Cal-Vet), 214
      chart of, 80
      Federal Reserve Bank System and, 16–17, 178–79
      HOEPA and, 428
      impacts on real estate financing, 158–59

inflation, 184
Interest Rate Adjustment Act, 12
loan selection and, 292
locked in, 214
mortgage lending and, 295
usury and usury ceilings, 4, 14
interim caps, 82–83
interior lots, 313
intermediate theory in mortgages, 135
Interstate Land Sales Full Disclosure Act, 12, 435
investment companies, 169–71
investment in real estate
accountants, 243
analysis tools for, 257–71
annual gross income, calculating, 261
appraisals, 242
appreciation and, 229
attorneys and legal assistance, 238–49
budget and operations plan, 253
business plans for, 236–37, 244
buyer's brokers, 240
buyer's remorse, 250
capital gains and, 227, 285
capital improvements, 258
capitalization, 261
capitalization rates (cap rate), 257, 263–65
carrying costs, 259–60, 261
cash flow, 225, 274–78
checklist for investment, 229–30
closing agents, 199, 243
collateral built through, 272–74
defined, 223
depreciation, calculation of, 226–27
development market's cycle, 269–71
development projects, 282–83
due diligence, 251–52
as entrepreneurship or business, 231, 233–38, 268
financing, 235–36, 244–46
for-sale-by-owner (FSBO) properties, 246
goals of, 231–33
as income source, 274–78
inspection of properties, 242, 246–50
installment sales, 227–28
insurance agents, 242
legal assistance in process, 252–53
listing agents, 241
loan officers as resources, 241–42
loan pre-approval, 244–46
master leases as investment, 284
negotiating terms, 250–53
net operating income, 261–65, 279
offers for property, 252–53
1% rule, 278
operating expenses, 258–59, 262
operating losses, 285
personal investment questionnaire, 232–33
preparation and planning for, 231–38
process of, 230–57
property as non-liquid asset, 224, 268, 269
purchase options (option to purchase), 282–83
quick buy-resale, 260
real estate agents and, 240–41
Real Estate Investment Trusts (REITs), 273
reasons for, 224–25
resources for, 238–43
return on investment (ROI), 225–30, 257, 266–69
risks of, 224, 268–69
selecting properties for, 244–46, 250, 278–80
speculation and, 280–81
stages of process, 230–31
subdivision and development, 281–82
tactics for successful investment, 271–72
take-over checklist, 255–56
tax-deferred exchanges (1031 "Starker" exchanges), 228–29, 287
tax issues, 225–29, 259, 275, 284–85, 287, 326
time as part of investment, 268

J

joint tenancy, 49–50, 52
judgments and attachments, 60
judicial foreclosures
of mortgages, 141, 142–47
trust deeds, 124, 132–33
junior liens
foreclosure sales and, 147–48
priority of payment for mortgages, 144, 147
trustee's sales and, 126, 132
junior trust deeds, outside financing and, 90–91

K

key lots, 313
kickbacks, 422

L

land descriptions, 32–41
metes and bounds, 40–41
recorded lot, block and tract system, 40
section and township surveys, 32–39
land developers, 282–83
land sales contracts, 106–7, 216
leases, 27
annual gross income calculation and rents, 261
gross rent multiplier, 331–32
master lease, 284
rent averages and location, 279
rent rolls and leases, 275
legal assistance, 238–49
investment in real estate and, 252–53

legal assistance *(continued)*
  remedies for loan servicing infractions, 394
legislation, federal
  impacting mortgage lending, 11–15
  see also Specific legislation by name
lending
  choosing a lender, 290–99
  early lending practices, 2–9
  usury and interest charges, 4
  see also loans; mortgages
less-than-freehold estates, 27
leverage, 75
liability ratios, 19–20
licenses *vs.* easements in gross, 61
licensing and certifications
  CCIM (Certified Commercial Investment Member of the
      Commercial Investment Institute) designation, 240
  loan negotiation and, 200–201
liens
  judgments and attachments, 60
  junior liens, 126, 132, 147–48
  lis pendens, 60
  mechanic's liens, 58–60
  special assessments, 60
  specific *vs.* general, 57
  tax liens, 60
  trust deeds, 121
  trustee's sale and, 132
  types of, 57
  see also mortgages; trust deeds
lien theory in mortgages, 135
lifetime caps, 83
like-kind properties, 321–22
  exchange of, 228–29
liquidity, real estate as non-liquid asset, 224, 268, 269
lis pendens, 60
listing agents, 241
listings, obtaining, 246
"live" gages, 3
loan officers, 241–42
loans
  amount of, 379
  application for, 291, 293, 342, 344–53
  assumption of, 87–88, 89
  balloon payment loans, 95
  blanket loans, 100
  California Veteran Loans (Cal-Vet), 213–16
  choosing a lender, 290–99
  collateral for, 74
  commissions, maximum allowable, 201
  costs of, 292
  debt-to-income ratios, 343
  direct lenders, 297
  discharge of, 112
  documents required for application, 253, 344–45

down payments, 379
FHLMC/FNMA 1003 form (Uniform Residential Loan
      Application), 345–52
fixed-rates loans, 80
hard money loans, 95
home equity loans, 95–96
hypothecation and, 74
income ratios, 379–80
lending patterns, statistical information regarding, 434
leverage, 75
limits for conforming Fannie Mae and Freddie Mac loans, 195
loan-to-value ratios, 379
Mortgage Loan Disclosure Statement, 201
open-end loans, 100
origination of, 293–99
package loans, 100
pre-approval for, 244–46, 293
processing of, 365–68
processor's final checklist, 366–68
as products, 292
promissory notes, 74, 75–78
purchase money loans, 90–91, 95
reverse annuity loans, 209
secondary loans, 90
security agreements, 202
service of (*See* loan servicing)
"subject to" sales and, 99
swing (bridge) loans, 100
third-party origination (TPO) loans, 297
underwriting, 340, 377–82
unsecured loans, 103
Verification of Deposit (VOD), 366, 367
Verification of Employment (VOE), 366, 367, 380–81
wrap around loans, 101
see also mortgage lenders
loan servicing, 341–42
  complaint procedures, 394–95
  consumer checklist, 398–99
  defined, 389–90
  escrow accounts and, 397
  grace period during transfer of, 392
  insurance and, 398
  legislation regarding, 390–93
  Mortgage Servicing Disclosure Statement, 420
  notification of sale of, 391–93
  notification of transfer of service, 396
  responsibilities of mortgage servicer, 390
  taxes and, 398
  transfer of service, 392, 395–98
loan-to-value ratios, 7, 379
locating property. *See* property identification
location and value, 307, 312–14
lots
  appraisal and site analysis, 307, 312–14
  types of, described, 312–13

M

makers of notes, 75, 85–86

margins, 81–82

marital status, 413

market comparison appraisals, 321–23

market price, 304–5

market rent, 261

market value, 304

measures, land measurement units, 39

mechanic's liens, 58–60

median price, 279

merchant builders, 283

meridians, 39

metes and bounds land description, 40–41

mineral rights, 28

mixed capitalistic economic system, 176

monetary policy, 178

mortgage, payments, calculation of, 342

mortgage-backed securities, 191

mortgage bankers, 168–69

mortgage brokers, 168–69

mortgagees, 134, 136

    satisfaction of, 140

mortgage lenders

    commercial banks, 153

    deregulation and, 175

    as financial intermediaries, 174

    institutional lenders, 151–52

    insurance companies, 165

    investment companies, 169–71

    mortgage bankers, 168–69

    mortgage brokers, 168–69

    mutual savings banks, 153, 165

    non-financial institutions, 171

    non-institutional lenders, 151–52, 165, 168–71

    private individuals, 171

    Real Estate Investment Trusts (REITs), 169–71

    savings banks, 163, 444, 445

    Savings & Loans, 153, 154–63

    see also credit unions; savings and loan associations; thrifts

Mortgage Loan Broker's Statement, 201

mortgage related security (MRS), 191

mortgages

    adjustable rate mortgages (ARMs), 81–84, 176

    brokers, 297

    characteristics described, 136, 140

    choosing a lender, 290–99

    defeasance clause, 135

    deficiency judgments, 140

    defined, 134

    federal insurance of, 9–10, 15, 17, 155, 157, 161

    Federal National Mortgage Association (FNMA or Fannie Mae), 193–94, 195, 196, 199, 341

    financing process and, 74

    foreclosure and, 140–48

    forms, sample of, 137–39

    gages in early lending practice, 3

    Government National Mortgage Association (GNMA or Ginnie Mae), 194, 196–97, 199, 341

    graduated payment mortgages (GPMs), 104–5

    history of lending in the U.S., 5–9

    hybrid mortgages, 84–85

    insurance of (*See* insurance)

    judicial foreclosures, 141, 142–47

    laws impacting mortgage lending, 11–15

    loan-to-value ratios, 7

    mortgage market, 190–200

    nonjudicial foreclosures, 141–42

    origination statistics (1990-2003), 296

    origin of term "mortgage," 3–4

    parties involved, 134, 136

    pledged savings account mortgages, 104

    primary mortgage market, 190–91, 199

    priority of payment of, 144, 147

    real estate brokers and sales associates, 199

    reinstatement of, 136

    remedies for default, 136

    reverse annuity mortgages (RAM), 105, 209

    right of redemption, 140

    rollover mortgages, 105

    secondary mortgages and secondary mortgage market, 13, 191–99

    securitizing of, 197

    servicing of, 341–42

    shared appreciation mortgages, 105

    statute of limitations, 136

    title, theories of, 135–36

    title companies and, 199

    vs. trust deeds, 110–11, 134, 140

    variable rate mortgages (VRMs), 175

    see also mortgage lenders

Mortgage Servicing Disclosure Statement, RESPA requirement, 420

mortgagors, 134, 136

Mt. Diablo Base Line and Meridian, 33

multiple listing services, spreadsheet listings, 280

mutual savings banks, 153, 165

N

National Affordable Housing Act, 390–93

National Association of REALTORS® (NAR), 160

National Banking Act, 180

National Credit Union Administration (NCUA), 418, 435

    address for consumer complaints, 446

National Credit Union Association Board (NCUAB), 165

National Credit Union Share Insurance Fund, 165

National Environmental Policy Act, 13

National Flood Insurance Act, 435

National Housing Act, 12, 196

National Mortgage Association of Washington, 12

NCUAB (National Credit Union Association Board), 165

NCUA (National Credit Union Administration), 418, 435, 446

negative amortization, 428

negotiable instruments, 79

negotiating terms, 250–53

neighborhoods

 appraisals and racial demographics, 407

 survey during appraisal process, 311

 three-stage life cycle of, 309

net operating income (NOI), 261–65, 279

net worth, 5–10, 176

NOI (net operating income), 261–65, 279

nonamortizing loans, 6

nonjudicial foreclosures

 of mortgages, 141–42

 see also trustee's sale (nonjudicial foreclosure)

notes, 74, 75–78

 adjustable notes, 81–84

 defenses allowed against parties, 86

 holders in due course, 85–87

 hybrid notes, 84–85

 as negotiable instruments, 85

 trust deeds and, 86–87

 see also loans

notice of sale, 130

notice of trustee's sale, 126

notices of non-responsibility, 58

novation, 88

O

obsolescence and depreciation, 326

OCC (Office of the Comptroller of the Currency), 435, 446

offers for property, 252

Office of the Comptroller of the Currency (OCC), 435, 446

Office of Thrift Supervision (OTS), 15, 154, 435

 address of, 418, 446

 web site address of, 161

Omnibus Reconciliation Act, 14

1% rule, 278

open-end loans, 100

operating expenses, 262

operating losses, 285

option to purchase, 282–83

origination of loans

 retail loan origination, 293–94

 wholesale loan origination, 295–99

"or more" clauses, 90

OTS. *See* Office of Thrift Supervision (OTS)

ownership

 allodial system, 45

 community property, 51–56

 concurrent ownership, 48–56

 concurrent ownership, state-by-state list, 56

 feudalism and land ownership, 45

 joint tenancy, 49–50, 52

 partition actions, 51

 of real property, 48–56

 rights of, 24–25

 separate ownership (ownership in severalty), 48

 tenancy by the entirety, 53

 tenancy in common, 50–51, 54–56

 tenancy in partnership, 53–56

 see also titles

P

package loans, 100

partial coverage mortgage insurance, 207

partition actions, 51

partnership interest (tenancy in partnership), 53–56

pass-through securities, 196

payment caps, 83

payments

 balloon payments, 427–28

 electronic funds transfer, 397

 negative amortization, 428

 partial payments, 392

 transfer of service and, 396–97

payments services, the Fed and, 188

penalties for prepayment, 89–90, 428

personal property, 27–28, 202–3

physical characteristics and value of property, 306

pledge accounts, 104

pledged savings account mortgages, 104

possession, as constructive notice, 47

possession, right of, 25

power of sale, 124

 clause in trust deeds, 112, 121

 foreclosure of, 141

pre-approval for loans, 244–46

prepayment clauses and penalties, 89–90, 428

pre-qualification for loans, 244–46

pre-tax cash flow, 275

price

 disclosure of, 426

 market price, 304–5

 median price, 279

 negotiation of, 250–53

privacy, 52, 433

private mortgage insurance (PMI), 200, 207

 benefits of, 217

 cancellation or termination of, 218–19

 disclosures required, 219–20

 Homeowner's Protection Act (HPA) and, 217–20

 increase in property value and, 220

 requirements for, 217, 218

processor's final checklist, 366–68

professional organizations

 for appraisers, 337

 National Association of REALTORS® (NAR), 160

profit and loss (P&L) statements, 275

progression, principle of, 308

promissory notes, 74, 75–78, 110
  example of, 76–78
  fully amortized notes, 79–80
  as negotiable instruments, 79
  partially amortized notes, 81
  straight notes, 81
property identification, 32–41
property rights, bundle of rights, 24–25
property values, economic depression and, 8
public assistance, discrimination on basis of, 406–7
Publications Services, 447
public notice requirements, 47
purchase money loans, 90–91, 95
purchase options (option to purchase), 282–83

Q

quantity survey cost estimation, 325
quick buy-resale, 260–61

R

racial discrimination, 405, 407, 438
range lines, 34, 35, 39
real estate industry, roles in U.S. economy, 176–77
Real Estate Investment Trusts (REITs), 151, 169–71, 273
Real Estate Owned (REO) property, 142–43
Real Estate Settlement, loan servicing complaints and, 395
Real Estate Settlement Procedures Act (RESPA), 13, 15,
    253–359
  complaints, address for consumer complaints, 423
  consumer protection and, 419–26
  disclosure requirements, 253–359, 420
  disclosures required by, 420–22
  escrow accounts and, 422
  fee-splitting and, 422
  Good Faith Estimate, 354–59, 420
  kickbacks and, 422
  Special Information Booklet, 353–54, 359, 420
  title insurance and, 422
  unearned fees and, 422
real property
  appurtenances, 29–30
  defined, 28
  emblements, 29
  encumbrances on, 56–64
  fixtures, 30–32
  as investment (*See* investment in real estate)
  land, 28–29
  loan law and, 200–202
  as non-liquid asset, 224, 268, 269
  ownership of, 48–56
  vs. personal property, 27–28
  Real Estate Owned (REO) property, 142–43
  things "immovable by law," 30
reconciliation, 321, 332

Reconstruction Finance Act, 11
Reconstruction Finance Corporation (RFC), 9, 11
reconveyance, 112, 124–25
recorded lot, block and tract system, 40
recording of documents
  constructive notice, 47
  priority of deeds, 47–48
  public notice requirements, 47
recording titles documents, state recording acts, 46–48
redemption
  for mortgages, 140
  of trust deeds, 124
referee's deed in foreclosure, 143
regression, principle of, 308
Regulation B, Equal Credit Opportunity Act, 419
Regulation M, 424, 429
Regulation Z, 13, 423–26, 429–32
rehabbers, 283
reinstatement, of trust deeds, 124
REITs (Real Estate Investment Trusts), 151, 169–71, 273
remedies
  loan servicing infractions, 394
  for mortgage default, 136
renovators, 283
renting. *See* leases
residential lending, 7
  demand increase post W.W.II, 10
Resolution Trust Corporation (RTC), 161, 162
RESPA. *See* Real Estate Settlement Procedures Act (RESPA)
restricted use appraisal reports, 333
restrictions, 63
return on investment (ROI), 225–30, 257, 266–69
Revenue Act (1962), 158
reverse mortgages, 105, 209
RFC (Reconstruction Finance Corporation), 9, 11
rights
  of appropriation and water for public use, 29
  land as real property and, 28–29
  of privacy, 52, 433
  of redemption for mortgages, 140
  of survivorship, 52
Rights to Financial Privacy Act, 433
riparian rights, 29
risk
  creditworthiness and, 7
  investment and, 268–69
  title insurance and, 69–70
  see also underwriters and underwriting
rollover mortgages (ROMs), 105
Roman mortgage lending, 3
roof types, 317–18

S

sales comparison appraisals, 321–23
SAMs (shared appreciation mortgages), 105

San Bernadino Base Line and Meridian, 33

satisfaction of mortgages, 140

savings and loan associations, 153, 154–63

    complaint procedures, 418, 444–45

    Depository Institution's Deregulation and Monetary
        Control Act, 155

    failure of, 17

    federal regulation of, 154

    Federal Savings and Loan Insurance Corporation (FSLIC)
        and, 9–10, 15, 17, 155, 157, 161

    history of, 156–63

    Homeowners Loan Act and, 11–12

    profile of state-chartered, 164

    tax laws and, 154, 156

Savings Association Insurance Fund (SAIF), 161, 162

savings banks, 153, 163

secondary loans, 90

second mortgages, 13, 191–99

    vs. home equity line of credit (HELOC), 99

Section 203-B (FHA), 209

Section 245 GPM (FHA), 209

section and township surveys, U. S. Government, 33–39

sections, 37–38, 39

securitizing of mortgages, 197

security agreements, 202

security instruments, 110

security interest, 87, 110

self-contained appraisal reports, 333

self-insurance, 207

seller financing, 91–94

    Seller Financing Disclosure Statement, 92–94

separate ownership (ownership in severalty), 48

separate property, 51

service contracts, 276

Servicemen's Readjustment Act, 10, 12

settlement. *See* closing

shared appreciation mortgages (SAMs), 105

sheriff's deeds, 143

size, property value and, 307

social ideals and standards value of property, 306

special assessments, 60

Special Information Booklet, RESPA requirement, 353–54, 359,
    420

speculation, 283

square-foot cost estimation, 325

standard policy of title insurance, 68–70

"Starker" exchanges, 228–39, 287

state laws

    complaint procedures and, 443–47

    foreclosure options state by state, 143

    homestead exemption and, 64–65

    trust deeds , state by state list, 122

statute of limitations, mortgages and, 136

statute of limitations and trust deeds, 124

stock market, 1929 collapse, 156–57

stock rights in water, 29

straight-line depreciation, 327–28

subdivision, 281–82

"subject to" clauses, 89

"subject to" sales, 99

subordination clauses, 89

substitution, principle of, 308, 321

summary appraisal reports, 333

supply and demand, principle of, 308

survivorship, 52

swing loans, 100

T

table funding, 297

take-over checklist, 255–56

TANF (Temporary Assistance to Needy Families), 406–7

taxes and tax laws

    capital gains and, 227, 258

    deductions, 158

    depreciation deductions, 259, 286–87, 326

    end-of-year tax statements, 398

    federal regulation regarding, 14, 15

    installment sales, 227–28

    investment in real estate and, 225–29, 259, 284–85, 286

    savings and loan associations and, 154, 156, 157–58

    tax-deferred exchanges (1031 "Starker" exchanges),
        228–29, 287

    Tax Reform Acts, 15, 158, 160

    transfer of service and, 398

tax liens, 60

Tax Reform Acts, 15, 158, 160

telephones, creditworthiness and, 408, 414

Temporary Assistance to Needy Families (TANF), 406–7

tenancy by the entirety, 53

tenancy in common, 50–51, 54–56

tenancy in partnership, 53–56

third-party origination (TPO) loans, 297

three-stage life cycle, principle of, 309

thrifts

    mutual savings banks, 153, 165

    Office of Thrift Supervision and, 15, 154, 161, 418, 446

    savings banks, 153, 163, 444, 445

    see also credit unions; savings and loan associations

TILA. *See* Truth in Lending Act (TILA)

time value of money, 286

t-intersection lots, 313

Title I. *See* Truth in Lending Act (TILA)

titles

    abstract of title, 68

    bare legal titles, 111–12

    equitable titles, 107, 122

    guarantee of title, 68

    history of land titles, 44–45

    insurance, 68–70

    marketability of, 68

    mortgages and, 135–36

recording of documents, 46

title companies and the mortgage market, 199

title insurance, 422

trust deeds and, 111–12, 122, 123–24

see also encumbrances

title theory in mortgages, 135

Title VI. *See* Fair Credit Reporting Act (FCRA)

township lines, 34, 35, 39

townships, 34–35, 39

TPO (third-party origination) loans, 297

trade fixtures, 32

transfer, right of, 25

trust deeds, 110

All-Inclusive Trust Deeds (AITDs), 101–3

assignment of rents clause, 121

bare legal title and, 111–12

benefits of, 133

deficiency judgments and, 124

example of deed of trust, 113–20

execution of, 111

foreclosure and, 124, 125–33

judicial foreclosures, 124, 132–33

junior trust deeds, 90–103

as liens, 121

loans and, 74

maximum commissions, 201

vs. mortgages, 110–11, 134, 140

notes and, 86–87

parties involved in, 111, 122–23

power of sale, 121, 124

reconveyance of, 124–25

redemption of, 124

reinstatement of, 124

statute of limitations and, 124

statutory time frame and, 121

titles and, 111–12, 122, 123–24

trustee's sale (non-judicial foreclosure), 126–33

trustees, 111, 122–23

trustee's sale (nonjudicial foreclosure), 126–33

junior liens and, 132

notice of, 126

notice of default, 126–29

notice of sale, 130

public auction, 130–31

request for notice, 127, 129

statutory reinstatements period, 126

trustors, 111, 122–23

Truth in Lending Act (TILA), 13, 100, 361–63

Home Ownership and Equity Protection Act and, 426

penalties for noncompliance and, 429–30, 432

Regulation M, 424, 429

Regulation Z, 13, 423–26, 429–32

underwriters and underwriting, 340, 365, 377–82

undivided interest, 50

unearned fees, 422

Uniform Residential Loan Application (FHLMC/FNMA 1003 form), 345–52

United States, 5–10

Fiscal Policy and Treasury, 18–184

history of mortgage lending in, 5–10

national economy of, 176–77

net-worth of Americans, 5–10

unit-in-place cost estimation, 325

unsecured loans, 103

use, right of, 25

usury, 4

utility bills, 276

vacancy factor, 261

value of property

four elements of, 305

influences on, 306–7

market value appraisals, 242–43

principles of valuation, 308–9

variations in estimates of, 322

see also appraisals

variable rate mortgages (VRMs), 175

vendees, 107

vendors, 107

Verification of Deposit (VOD), 366, 367

Verification of Employment (VOE), 366, 367, 380–81

Veterans Administration (VA), 208, 210–13

guaranteed loans, 194, 196

VOD (Verification of Deposit), 366, 367

VOE (Verification of Employment), 366, 367, 380–81

VRMs (variable rate mortgages), 175

water rights, 29

web site addresses

Housing and Urban Development, 395

Office of Thrift Supervision, 161

professional appraisal organizations, 337

wrap around loans, 101

U

V

W